FAYED

THE UNAUTHORIZED BIOGRAPHY

Blind Eye to Murder – the Pledge Betrayed

Klaus Barbie: Butcher of Lyons

The Paperclip Conspiracy

Maxwell: The Outsider

The Red Web

Tiny Rowland: The Rebel Tycoon

Heroes of World War II

The Perfect English Spy: Sir Dick White

Maxwell: The Final Verdict

Blood Money: The Swiss, the Nazis and the Looted Billions

TOM BOWER

FAYED

THE UNAUTHORIZED BIOGRAPHY

MACMILLAN

First published 1998 by Macmillan

an imprint of Macmillan Publishers Ltd
25 Eccleston Place, London SW1W 9NF
and Basingstoke

Associated companies throughout the world

ISBN 0 333 74554 X

5 7 9 8 6 4

A CIP catalogue record for this book is available from
the British Library.

Typeset by SetSystems Ltd, Saffron Walden, Essex
Printed and bound in Great Britain by
Mackays of Chatham plc, Chatham, Kent

To Horace Oram

and Professor J.A.G. Griffith

Contents

CONTENTS

List of Illustrations

The author and publishers wish to record their thanks to the owners and copyright holders of the illustrations used in this book for permission to reproduce them.

Sources and photograph credits are set out in brackets after each illustration.

LIST OF ILLUSTRATIONS

Preface

THE POLAROID PHOTOGRAPHS betrayed the entrapment. Polaroids are a trademark of Mohamed Fayed.

Mark Malloy, a thirtysomething chauffeur, formerly employed by Mohamed Fayed, offered the four Polaroids. The colour photographs showed a pile of three anonymous books. Sitting on a hard chair, his back to the door, Malloy had invited me to a drab hotel room on an unusually warm evening in south London on 22 February 1998 to tell a strange story. 'She took the books while he was away,' explained Malloy. 'From a cupboard in his study.' He was describing a theft by Karen McKenzie, his wife and Fayed's trusted housekeeper. The books' contents, he suggested, were explosive. 'They got the names of all his women with their photos. Then he's scribbled his comments next to each woman.' The sensitive record of Mohamed Fayed's sexual conquests was available for a steep price. '£40,000,' quoted Malloy. On the bed lay a colour photograph of Fayed, dressed in a tuxedo, standing between two women. 'Fayed called them, "The Madames",' said Malloy. 'And there are six others like that. All for £40,000.' Unknown to me I was being videoed by a concealed camera.

Near by in the same room sat Tony Evans, the intermediary. Evans, one of Fayed's former bodyguards, with ten years in the Parachute Regiment, seemed surprised by the price. He was even more surprised that Fayed's comments were, according to Malloy, written in Arabic. 'He can't write English,' explained the chauffeur. 'Don't be stupid,' scoffed Evans. 'Course he can.'

Since Malloy could not read Arabic, it seemed strange that he had understood Fayed's comments about the women's sexual performance. That inconsistency also occurred to the eaves-droppers.

Malloy's portable trilled. The chauffeur grunted. From a neighbouring room, the security chief issued instructions. After mild haggling, the price collapsed. Malloy was willing to consider just £1,000 for what was later called, 'dynamite'. His wife, he suggested, was too afraid to keep the books in the attic of their house. Their disposal was imperative. Why, after twelve years' faithful service, Karen McKenzie should seek to betray Fayed was unexplained. But the second telephone call on Malloy's portable confirmed the Polaroid plot. One thousand pounds was sufficient. The parting was amicable. My suspicions were not revealed.

Three weeks later, Evans telephoned. 'Let's meet in the hotel's car park,' he suggested. 'You can have the books and photographs for £1,000. In cash. We deal in the car. Nowhere else.'

'It's a set-up,' he was told wearily. 'If I come, four policemen will be waiting in a car to arrest me for buying stolen property.' Evans said nothing. 'He tried it with *Vanity Fair*,' Evans was told, about an attempted entrapment of the magazine's lawyer in the midst of a bitter legal struggle. 'He also tried it with an *Evening Standard* journalist. Entrapment is part of his armoury.' The telephone conversation was terminated.

The following morning, Monday, 16 March 1998, Royston Webb, Mohamed Fayed's trusted lawyer, telephoned.

'You know, Royston,' I said jovially, 'Mohamed should be careful. His staff are stealing his private papers and offering them for £40,000.'

'Are they stealing or are you asking them to steal?' asked Webb in his customary friendly manner.

'So you know about it?' I asked.

'Oh, yes,' replied Webb, confirming the failed entrapment. The conversation ended amicably.

One hour later, Webb called again. 'Mohamed's upset. He said that we used to be good friends. You even travelled on his helicopter to Paris. We've been friendly to you. Why have you changed?' There was nothing further to be said. Indisputably, after six years, my attitude towards Fayed had changed in the early summer of 1997.

We had first met in winter 1991. In the wake of Robert Maxwell's death, a publisher had finally agreed to commission a biography of Tiny Rowland. An obvious source of information was Mohamed Fayed. His information, given without strings or pressure, confirmed the accounts provided by many eyewitnesses about Rowland's chicanery and the partiality of the inspectors appointed by the Department of Trade and Industry to investigate Fayed's purchase of the House of Fraser.

Over the following years, I met Fayed occasionally, especially after his revelations in 1994 of paying Conservative MPs 'cash for questions'. In 1996, Michael Cole, his spokesman and someone I had known for twenty years at BBC Television, asked whether I would be willing to write Fayed's authorized biography. I declined. During August 1997, as Dodi Fayed's romance with Princess Diana dominated the newspapers, I met Fayed in his office as I continued to gather information about sleaze and the Conservative government. The putative book had become a biography of Fayed. As always, our meeting was jovial.

On Wednesday, 3 September 1997, three days after the crash killing Princess Diana and Dodi Fayed, Mohamed Fayed invited me to fly on his helicopter to Paris with John Macnamara, his security chief, Douglas Marvin, his Washington lawyer, and Professor Peter Vanezis, a Scottish pathologist. At Fayed's request, Vanezis would attempt to conduct an autopsy on Henri Paul, the driver of the Mercedes in which Dodi and

Diana had been travelling. It was a unique occasion to hear first hand whether Paul was drunk and, more importantly, interview all the Ritz employees who witnessed the last hours before the fatal crash. The result was a newspaper article and a surprising insight into Mohamed Fayed's world.

In October, as Fayed's public behaviour caused increasing consternation, Michael Cole invited me to Fayed's office as 'the first journalist he has met since the tragedy'. Once again, Fayed offered me help with this biography.

'I can give you some interesting documents,' he said as Cole sat near by.

Once again I declined, explaining that I was writing my own book. 'But I certainly want to talk to you when I'm further down the road,' I added.

'Fine,' concluded Fayed. 'I know you'll be fair.'

Thanks to Fayed, I was able to meet people whom he had employed after his arrival in Britain in the mid-1960s and I enjoyed three more long conversations with Royston Webb. But, just before Christmas 1997, Michael Cole told me that my request to meet Fayed was rejected. Two months later, the Fayed organization sought to entrap me. Inquiries also revealed that someone had surreptitiously obtained from British Telecom the records of all my telephone calls. The Fayed organization would angrily deny any responsibility, while alleging that some interviewees had complained of harassment. The accusatory letters from Fayed's lawyers to me and then to the publishers confirmed that our relationship was fractured. Nevertheless, I have not allowed his attitude to influence this biography.

Being hated equally by Tiny Rowland and Mohamed Fayed is an achievement of sorts. Their similarities fuelled their extraordinary vendetta and, extraordinarily, both used one similar ploy in their many protests to my lawyers before publication of their respective biographies.

In 1991, Rowland's lawyers protested to my publishers that the unauthorized biography would contain references to his

'homosexual practices' and 'bestiality'. In 1998, Fayed's lawyers complained that this biography would refer to their client's
'paedophilia'. Needless to say I never had any intention of
writing about any such matters. Amusingly, both suffered
similar anxieties. This book's description of Tiny Rowland and
his activities, it should be noted, was not, with a solitary
exception, amended on account of his death.

Like all powerful and rich men, Fayed loathes any challenge
or erosion of his total control. For a man determined to
influence British politics, the author of an unauthorized biography is an enemy. The objective truth is offensive to fantasists,
and Fayed would prefer the public to accept the image proffered at huge expense by his publicists. To his good fortune,
several newspaper editors, journalists and television producers
have been willing to accept or at least uncritically publish his
version of events which have altered the course of Britain's
history. To suggest that they will be persuaded by this book to
review their prejudices would ignore past experience, but the
reader should be aware that well over one hundred people,
eyewitnesses to Mohamed Fayed's life, have generously and
bravely provided information for this book. Uniformly, they
were motivated by one interest: that Mohamed Fayed's attempt
to foist his unique interpretation of history upon the world
should be properly understood.

For reasons explained in the source notes, I will not individually thank any of those who provided information. Needless
to say, I am immeasurably grateful for their time, assistance
and courage.

This book could also not have been written without the
help of many journalists who provided research, information
and advice.

In England, I was particularly grateful to Oliver Figg as
my full-time researcher. I also received generous help from
Martyn Gregory, Jo Jeffrey, Frances Hardy, Francis Wheen,
Nigel Rosser, Kate Adie, John Plender, Mark Hosenball, Sylvie
Deroche, Charles Masters, Kate Porter of the *Surrey Mirror*,

and David Love. In Paris, I was helped by Susan Bell; in America by Robert Fink; in Dubai by Linda Mahoney; in Finland by Rita Tyonola and Leena Järsta; and in Germany by Peter Bild.

At Macmillan, I was helped by William Armstrong, Mari Evans, Liz Davis and Kendall Duesbury. My editor, Peter James, was as ever magnificent. The picture research was efficiently conducted by Anne-Marie Ehrlich, and the thorough proof reading by John English. The legal chores were undertaken by David Hooper of Biddle. Michael Shaw of Curtis Brown was the friend and rock foundation on which this book could be written and completed. As always, my enduring gratitude is to my family, who suffer everything with good humour.

1

The Blonde

'MEOW, MEOW.'

The brown head emerged from the white Egyptian-cotton sheets.

'Come to me, pussycat,' sighed the blonde, stroking the fifty-two-year-old man.

'Meow.'

'Nice pussycat,' cooed the beautiful young model.

The Arab snuggled his head between the woman's breasts. 'Meow,' he whispered into her chest. Curling himself around the woman's long body, he delighted in being treated like a kitten. Thankfully, the blonde agreed to play mother cat. Perhaps one day she might even give him a saucer of milk. In gratitude, she was invited to stay in his London flat and occasionally he threw in some presents. Always some cash – usually £200 – and some clothes, and once he had paid £10,000 to furnish her house in northern England. He loved provincial English girls. Naive and star-struck, even the most stunning beauties were seduced by the allure of Arab wealth.

Minutes later, 'Michael from Saudi Arabia' was aroused. After just seconds, he grunted: the sex act was completed. Rising from the bed, the bachelor dressed himself. Always garish-coloured shirts, white starched collars and glowing yellow ties – such bad taste, but probably the only brightness about the man. 'Must go, Clara,' he muttered. 'You stay.' Opening a door leading out into the common parts of the apartment block at 60 Park Lane in Mayfair, 'Michael' disappeared, just minutes after his arrival.

'Wham, bam, thank you, Ma'am.' There was never an orgasm with 'Michael'. Some would complain that he was a selfish, Walter Mitty character, since he even denied his Egyptian nationality. So different from the blonde's former lover, the famous – and real – Saudi, Adnan Khashoggi. Everything was infinitely better in Adnan's world. For three years, the fashion model had gloried as one of Khashoggi's 'pleasure wives', flying in his private jets between the best hotels in Los Angeles, Las Vegas, Monte Carlo, Paris, Marbella and the *Nabila*, his amazing yacht. Life was an endless party. Every day Khashoggi spent millions of dollars to keep his friends and women happy: couture clothes, Cartier jewellery, champagne and unstinting pampering by maids and masseurs.

Adnan, the marathon man, had class, while everything about 'Michael' was G-Plan, which was precisely what the blonde was lying on – a boring G-Plan bed, surrounded by dull furniture familiar to guests of a Holiday Inn. Her presence was a convenience to both herself and her sugar-daddy, although in the second year of their relationship his repeated invitations to 'bring some of your model friends' bred suspicion. 'They can live here in the flat,' he offered. She had prevaricated. So unlike Adnan. Girls flocked to his camp. But she knew better than to mention Adnan's name to 'Michael'. Theirs was a relationship, as she had been warned by Dodi Fayed, that was marked by poison.

Dodi Fayed was the natural son of 'Michael' and was loved like a son by Adnan Khashoggi, his uncle. In 1982, after three years of partying with Adnan around the world, the blonde model had been eating dinner in Dodi's ostentatious flat at 60 Park Lane. It had been thanks to Dodi that she had met Adnan Khashoggi, and it was now thanks to Dodi again that she met his father Mohamed Fayed, alias 'Michael'. Occupying the penthouse on the top floor of Number 60, Fayed knew that his son was entertaining some glamorous young guests on the second floor. Unexpectedly, he ambled into his son's dining room. Amiable and charming, Mohamed Fayed had talked briefly with Dodi's blonde friend before slipping his card into her eager hand. 'Call me some time,' he said with a wink.

Thanks to Dodi, a relationship had started, founded on long conversations. The two compared notes about their hard lives, but in his strictly compartmentalized and secret world Mohamed Fayed revealed little about himself. Perhaps there was not much to discover since, compared to Khashoggi, he led a poor, unexciting life akin to a surburban slippers-and-pipe resident. Arabs, however, were known to be generous, and even famous models were grateful for undemanding relationships. From the flat, discreetly equipped with its own entrance into South Street, adjacent to Park Lane, the model could slip out at night and party at Tramp and Annabel's, London's peerless night clubs.

Tramp was Dodi Fayed's favourite. The Mecca for the 'fast crowd' and 'beautiful people' from the world of music, films, entertainment and the media, the club also attracted a mix of wealthy foreigners seeking glamour and young women. Among the young girls attracted to that hectic world was Louise Dyrbusz, a twenty-one-year-old prostitute working under the name Louise Michaels. Grouped with three other girls whom Michaels styled 'The Flying Squad', the prostitute particularly targeted rich Arabs who bought her jewellery, the best designer clothes, international travel and even a flat in Draycott Gardens, Knightsbridge. Serving Saudi princes, Iranian millionaires and Lebanese middlemen, she was nevertheless particularly struck by Dodi. On 8 August 1980, she had spent the evening with Mohamed Fayed's son at the night club and thereafter appeared regularly at 60 Park Lane. Strangely, Michaels was also meeting Ali Fayed, Dodi's uncle and his father's youngest brother, at the Connaught Hotel. In her diary, she recorded her fee for Ali as £200, half the price she charged a Saudi prince but the same as her fee for a son of Adnan Khashoggi, whom she visited at the Ritz in Paris. Her relationship with Dodi and Ali continued for some years, even extending to an exchange of Christmas cards with Ali. 'If you come to London,' wrote Ali in block letters, 'pse give me a call to catch up with what's happening.' Thoughtfully, Ali included his private telephone number.

Michaels's success was measured by her bank balance, which showed deposits in excess of £150,000. Surrounded by fashion models, actresses and hookers, Dodi Fayed was renowned as an unexceptional, gentle, generous playboy who introduced women to his father and uncle. It was a somewhat unusual lifestyle, in which bonding was furthered by shared sexual partners. Mohamed Fayed – unmarried and ambitious – relished the opportunities in London, but unlike most other aspiring Arabs he rarely appeared in clubs and restaurants. An inhibited, even a tortured soul, he disdained public scrutiny while fulfilling an obsession with obliterating his past. Secrecy was his protection.

Blurring fact and fiction about his life had, so far, caused little problem for Fayed in London. Anxious to satisfy Arab tradition, he had contrived his Big Lie to help sustain his mirage of dignity. In fact, he aroused so little interest that few cared about the fantasies he had spun about his past. In his closeted world, shared only with his two brothers and his son, Fayed shone as the patriarch who could speak with humorous charm and paraded his ego as a consummate showman. Like most Egyptians, who are not commonly associated with bravery, preserving his dignity meant never losing. If owed £1,000, he would risk £100,000 to recover the debt aggressively. His public displays of fearlessness disguised fear and even timidity. Insecure and discontented, he was afraid of rejection. Yet his cavalier use and misuse of people created enemies of those whose approval he sought. Some would whisper that Fayed was an Egyptian in denial since he never returned to his home. His reason was simple: there was no reason to return. There was no house, no tradition and no meaningful family – only embarrassments which he wanted to forget. In the early 1980s, the itinerant Arab was searching as much for an identity as for his fortune.

Darting around London in his chauffeur-driven Mercedes, Fayed was a ferocious personality fired by animal passion. Nervously eating pistachio nuts and dropping the shells on the floor, his hand would occasionally reach into the well by the gear lever for a Fox's Glacier Mint. He would bite into the sweet, spitting half into the wrapping paper and letting it likewise fall to the floor: he had long become accustomed to the English Misics – the Arabic for his donkeys – tending to his needs. No longer regarded as Wily Oriental Gentlemen, Arabs were fêted in London as astute businessmen. Yet Fayed was ashamed of his personal heritage. Oblivious to the praise heaped in Western societies on self-made tycoons, he depended for his self-confidence on a crudely manufactured autobiography. Convinced of the rightness of his own judgement, he was motivated by instinct rather than educated reason; he was a gambler who eagerly borrowed as much as possible to finance his ambitions, which others politely called 'visions'. To emulate Adnan Khashoggi, he spent more than he could afford, and what he could afford, compared to other players, was not very much. To gild the façade, he occasionally spoke of investing tens of millions, but always cautiously withdrew his pledges at the last moment. Yet there was style in his manner.

On his return once to Park Lane, he presented the blonde model with a diamond pendant for her birthday. Although far from the ostentatious style of Khashoggi, it seemed a generous gesture. Six months later, after the affair was over, the blonde submitted the diamond for valuation. 'Worthless,' she was told. Fayed had presented his mistress with a fake. Comically, she would discover that other girls around London had been presented with identical 'diamonds' by Fayed. 'The bastard had bought a batch at discount,' they chortled.

Fake diamonds, fake orgasms and a fake pasha: twelve years later, Fayed would also contrive a fake scandal, parading his virtue as a corrupter of politicians, in a vain bid to restore his reputation.

2

Fantasies and Fortune

HIS BIRTH IN 1929 was inauspicious, best buried and forgotten. Egypt, a byword in Europe for ineptitude and squalor, was an unfashionable birthplace for those harbouring financial and social ambitions. Although, compared to their untamed, tribal neighbours, educated Egyptians were admired in the Arab world, the inhabitants of the desert kingdom were castigated in Europe as corrupt and idle. Indisputably, the descendants of the great Pharaoh civilization, blessed by the Nile's irrigation of the rich cotton fields, had lost their way over the previous 3,500 years. The exception was Alexandria, the country's Mediterranean playground west of Suez. Here rich Egyptians, particularly Egyptian Jews, gloried in luxury, mixing with French, Greek, Italian, British and Lebanese businessmen along the town's idyllic waterfront. Cotton traders, shipbrokers, financiers and savvy middlemen inhabited splendid villas, ate in excellent restaurants, bathed on sandy beaches and earned fortunes in this exotic city linking Arabia and Europe. Loftily observing both the impoverished and the affluent were the British administrators and a substantial British military garrison. Egypt, and especially the Suez Canal, was the linchpin of the great British empire. Britain's vast interests in Palestine, Iraq, Iran, India, Saudia Arabia, the Persian Gulf, the Far East and across Africa came together in Egypt and the Canal. With their immaculately uniformed soldiers and sailors only too evident, the British dominated the country, evoking a mixture of deference and disdain. They helped develop an unintrusive bureaucracy. Employed among the ranks of this administrative class was the father of Mohamed Fayed.

Aly Aly Fayed was a school inspector whose most notable achievement was a modest degree of self-improvement. Born in Al-Rahmania, a nondescript village between Alexandria and Cairo, close to a tributary of the Nile Delta, Aly Aly qualified in 1917 as a teacher. Soon after, he married Hanem Kotb Hassan, the daughter of a neighbour. After teaching Arabic for a short period in the dusty village, Aly Aly found promotion at the Bousery Primary School in Alexandria. The newly weds rented a small flat at 53 El Shorbagy Lane, one of the dark, narrow, uneven and grimy roads in the El-Gomrok quarter close to Alexandria's busy port. Two daughters were born before Hanem gave birth in the family home to her first son. Mohamed Abdel Moneim Fayed was born on 27 January 1929. Two other sons followed, Salah in 1931 and Ali in 1933. By then, Aly Aly had been promoted to school inspector, an undemanding position but one providing a secure income.

Mohamed Fayed's childhood was neither happy nor blessed by innocence. Shortly after Ali's birth, Hanem died and many of Mohamed's subsequent traits and idiosyncrasies arose from the trauma of a motherless life dominated by a disciplinarian father. Aly Aly remarried and moved in November 1939 to a second-floor flat at 5 Ibn Wakia Street, in the same rundown area. By now ten years old, Mohamed Fayed violently resented his stepmother and detested his father. Weak, unambitious and dressed in a traditional nightdress-style dish-dash, he was ashamed of the polite, petty bureaucrat. 'He was useless,' the brash Egyptian would say years later. Rebelling against his father's uninspiring life, Fayed commanded the loyalty and support of his two younger brothers as he constructed a future from which the unforgivable sin of weakness would be brutally excluded.

Rebelling against their father, all three sons despised formal education and preferred to play football on the beach, occasionally with British soldiers. Enrolled at the Old Secondary

School for Boys in Alexandria, Fayed was a reluctant, argumentative pupil even among the not notably zealous children of the town's working class and his feckless attitude towards learning influenced his brothers. Fearful of his restless son's aggression, Aly Aly even asked a neighbour, Ibrahim Arabi Abou Hammad, who was one of Mohamed's fellow pupils, to report whenever his son caused trouble. Without money, status or a secure home life, the three brothers lacked any hope of further education or social advancement during an increasingly turbulent era.

As the British army retreated in the early 1940s towards Cairo, Egyptians speculated about the possibility of Erwin Rommel's Afrika Korps entering Alexandria and capturing the Canal. The image of the invincible British, tarnished by the fall of Tobruk, was only partially restored by final victory in 1945, the year that Mohamed Fayed left school. One of many uneducated adolescents roaming Alexandria, Fayed still felt a simple, emotional respect for the British that bore no relation to the reality of declining British influence and nationalistic fervour among Egyptians. Oblivious to the developing anti-British undercurrent, he stood out from his contemporaries by espousing ambitious fantasies about sharing the wealth and power of Alexandria's rich expatriates.

Imbued with some charm and a sense of humour, the teenager was driven by a passionate dream to escape from the drudgery and friction of his home. In formal terms, his possibilities were starkly limited. Selling, dealing and trading were instinctive to the citizens of Alexandria, but a lowly Egyptian deprived of any contacts among either the country's mercantile class or its foreign community would find it almost impossible to join the merchants. Since Fayed's horizons had never been raised by his father, his aspirations, for all his self-motivation, were limited to working in shops. In 1948 he was seen by Ibrahim Hammad, his former schoolfriend, selling bottles of Coca-Cola in the streets, and two years later, aged twenty-one, he was knocking on doors selling Singer sewing machines, which earned him a mere £E10 per month.

Fayed's salvation in 1952 was Tousson El Barrawi, a friend whose father manufactured tarbushes, the red fez hats popular in monarchist Egypt. Barrawi and a seventeen-year-old friend of his, Adnan Khashoggi, who lived in the apartment above him, had decided to start a business and sought an employee. Fayed's introduction to Khashoggi, a schoolboy from Saudia Arabia, was to change his life.

Adnan Khashoggi's Turkish forefathers had arrived in Saudi Arabia centuries before. In that remote, primitive Bedouin kingdom, Adnan's father was an exceptional figure. After educating himself to become one of Saudi Arabia's few doctors, Mohamed Khashoggi, an amusing, enterprising *bon vivant*, had been appointed the king's personal physician, entrusted by the ruling family with numerous privileges. In sharp contrast to Fayed's family, Dr Khashoggi had created an atmosphere of love and respect among his six children and, like all rich Arabs keen to provided a good education for his offspring, dispatched Adnan and his younger brothers and sisters to Victoria College in Alexandria, the elite institution based upon British traditions.

On the eve of graduating in 1952 and before enrolling at Stanford College in California, Adnan Khashoggi was planning his first business venture. Egyptian doctors hired to work in Saudi Arabia would be offered a service furnishing their new homes and surgeries with equipment shipped from Egypt, a potentially lucrative activity, since Saudi Arabia, slowly increasing its oil income, relied entirely on imports and foreigners to break loose from the Stone Age. Khashoggi's new business, established in collaboration with his cousin Anas Yassin, required an employee in Jeddah to oversee the importation and delivery of the furniture. Their ambition had brought Mohamed Fayed, in September 1952, to sit in the living room of Khashoggi's Alexandria apartment.

Excited by his good fortune in being invited into a wealthy home, the Egyptian understood precisely what was needed. Although six years older – age difference is a sensitive issue in Arab culture – Fayed used his humour, charm and unobstrusive servility to win the Bedouin's trust. Undistracted by his visitor's vulgar language, the Saudi was struck by the supplicant's dark, secret eyes. The result was a meeting of minds. In deference to his age, Fayed was offered a contract at £E100 per month and 10 per cent of the new company's profits. To overcome the complication of obtaining a Saudi work permit, it was agreed that Fayed would be employed by Khashoggi's father, recently promoted as Saudi Arabia's secretary general of public health. Fayed was to divide his time between the Health Ministry in Jeddah and the new business, the Al Nasr Trading and Industrial Corporation. Accepting employment from the younger Bedouin hurt Fayed's pride, but the humiliation was well concealed. The door had opened, offering him an escape from his vile world.

Ingratiating himself with Dr Khashoggi, Fayed proved to be polite, efficient, trustworthy and entertaining. To the secretary general's delight, his house guest regarded all problems as surmountable. Always willing to type letters, he was evolving into a businessman with an instinct for salesmanship. Defeat, he wrote to his son Adnan in California, was inconceivable to their employee. Within one year, Fayed had established himself as a star businessman, spotting and realizing every opportunity as he negotiated profitable contracts not only for the imported furniture and medical equipment, but also for Belrock, a Khashoggi company extracting gypsum in the desert. The rewards turned out to be greater than he had expected. By the end of the year he had accumulated $300,000 profits in the business, the equivalent today of $3 million. If Adnan Khashoggi had reason to be grateful, Fayed was ecstatic.

Angular, thin, with a small beard and often wearing sunglasses, Fayed had developed into a shrewd entertainer. In any social gathering among the dour, reserved Saudis, the witty

Egyptian's performance was warmly welcomed; to them he seemed dignified and sophisticated. Bereft of any inherited social qualities, Fayed had developed a theatrical shield to resolve the unnoticed inner conflict between the development of an imposing personality and his fear of exposure as the raw son of a school inspector. Unnoticed, he was quietly modelling himself on the Khashoggis, father and sons. Copying other people – adopting their mannerisms and even their biography – became the pattern of Fayed's self-education and self-improvement. His particular idiosyncracy, which provoked much amusement, was his strange habit of squeezing lemon juice on to his hands, especially after greeting people, on to his plate before food was served, and even on to his cutlery. 'He puts lemon on everything,' laughed Dr Khashoggi. 'He ruins all his food with it. Lemon over everything.' The young Egyptian, the doctor whispered, was a hypochondriac obsessed by potions.

*

DURING THAT FIRST YEAR, on the occasional trips back to Alexandria, Fayed had met, in the Khashoggi family's flat and also in Jeddah, sixteen-year-old Samira Khashoggi, Adnan's younger sister. Still attending Alexandria's Scottish School for Girls, the strong-willed, talented and attractive girl would in later years write eight love novels (three of which were adapted for feature films), establish *El Shakir*, a magazine which is still published in Beirut, and create Saudi Arabia's first women's club. Barely recalling his mother and hostile to his stepmother, Fayed was smitten for the first time by a woman who, by his reckoning, was a natural partner. Both were sharp, ambitious and lacking in intellect. Both would become masters of manufacturing an image for themselves.

At the beginning of 1954, Fayed won Samira's affections – the first man she had loved. Succumbing to her headstrong demands, the secretary general approved their marriage. Fayed, the Khashoggi family agreed, was deeply in love with Samira and should be accepted as a member of the family. Hearing the news in California, Adnan Khashoggi threw aside his unease about mixing business and family and returned to Alexandria for the wedding.

Three hundred guests were invited after the ceremony in Dr Khashoggi's Alexandria apartment on 16 July 1954 to the reception at the San Stefano Hotel. Preceeded by drummers and a belly dancer, and followed by Samira's sisters and cousins holding her long wedding train, the couple walked smiling into the reception amid cheers and laughter. As Fayed cast exhilarated glances around the lively throng, he acknowledged that his sudden elevation and unexpected stardom had expunged the irksome inheritance of his father, thankfully invisible somewhere in the hall. It was noticeable that most of the guests were the bride's family and friends. The only prominent Fayed was the elder of Mohamed's sisters, married to a talented Koranic sign writer, and his two brothers. As he sat with his bride on splendid thrones surrounded by flowers and guests, feasting on excellent food while a second belly dancer introduced a cabaret of singers and entertainers, it suited Mohamed to forget his past.

After the celebrations, Mohamed and Samira moved into an apartment rented by Fayed in Alexandria. While Samira completed her last year at school, Mohamed, whose marriage certificate recorded the twenty-five-year-old as a merchant, plotted his entry into Alexandria's wealthy society. Confident of his own abilities and ambitious to build his own business as a trader, he looked to Adnan Khashoggi as his best, indeed only, source of finance. For the young student, Fayed had proved to be a talented businessman who understood not only how to seduce potential customers but also how to overcome all the inevitable problems to close a deal. Generosity to his new family was a natural gesture and Adnan agreed not only to advance £100,000 to Fayed to be repaid in twenty instalments but also to help Ali Fayed. The quiet and uneducated twenty-year-old, totally obedient to his elder brother, was recruited by Khashoggi as his secretary in California to care for his business affairs while he attended lectures. As a formality, Ali was enrolled in nearby San Mateo College to study economics, but in reality he either worked for Khashoggi or spent time partying with his employer and Khashoggi's cousins.

Flush with money, Fayed established himself as a forwarding agent in Alexandria and travelled for the first time to Europe, a continent emerging from wartime austerity and crowded with traders and middlemen profiting from reconstruction. Visiting France, Italy and Switzerland, he witnessed the efficiency, luxury and civility of Europe and convinced himself that wealth begot wealth and that image could be more important than substance. Intoxicated by the atmosphere and impatient to realize his childhood fantasies of wealth, Fayed avoided presenting himself as the poor boy from the smelly streets of El-Gomrok, the former door-to-door salesman of Singer sewing machines, and instead introduced himself as a member of Alexandria's wealthy business community. Resolutely he believed that a new image could change reality, that life would be not only easier but more fun. With a theatrical flourish and ignoring the expense, he re-presented himself in Geneva wearing immaculately cut suits, occupying a room at the five-star Hôtel du Rhône and hiring a chauffeured Rolls-Royce to drive around the sedate town to establish his credentials among bankers, lawyers, shippers and merchants. The image reinforced his self-deceiving conviction that his good fortune was owed only to his talent rather than to his luck in meeting the Khashoggis. Circumstances did not require him to admit that he was a loner, fearful that people might turn against him if the truth was revealed. Spending money, he calculated, would tip the balance towards success.

On one return trip to the Middle East, the transformation of his image and even of his personality to match his reinvented background was especially noticeable. At a Khashoggi family wedding in Beirut, he posed for the photographers, surrounded by the Khashoggi clan. Although stern-faced and impassive behind expensive sunglasses, he evidently relished being the life and soul of the party. He was also celebrating the birth on 15 April 1955 of his first son, Emad, or Dodi. The proud father and mother portrayed in photographs suggested a happy family. The reality was different.

Politically, Egypt was in turmoil. In 1952, a group of revolutionary army officers had overthrown the obese and corrupt King Farouk. Two years later, General Gamal Abdel Nasser, a passionate nationalist, had ousted his former collaborators and assumed absolute power. The Fayeds and Khashoggis mourned the passing of the monarchy and feared Nasser's revolutionary zeal. Those fears intensified after Nasser nationalized the Suez Canal on 26 July 1956. Proclaiming his unique brand of Arab socialism and bolstered by an alliance with the Soviet Union, Nasser blocked the waterway in defiance of the Anglo–French–Israeli invasion and, after the foreign armies withdrew, threatened the foreign merchants in Alexandria, in particular the Jews, that their property would be confiscated and the owners expelled.

The revoluton coincided with a crisis between Fayed and Samira. During one of Mohamed's brief return visits to Alexandria, Samira sensed that her husband had been unfaithful. His expensive lifestyle in Europe and visits to night clubs, she suspected, had culminated in an affair. Challenged about his infidelity, Fayed confessed, a spontaneous reaction which he naively anticipated would be forgiven. To his surprise, Samira exploded in rage. Forgiveness, she screamed tearfully, was impossible: there could be no reconciliation. The marriage was finished. Stunned, Fayed sought Adnan Khashoggi's help. Weeping, he begged his brother-in-law to mediate, but the attempt failed. Samira's love had turned to hate. She demanded a divorce and Fayed's expulsion from the marital flat. Under Egyptian law, however, he could order his wife to remain confined indefinitely in her home. To avoid that fate, Samira fled the country – and the truth soon emerged. Secretly, Samira had always loved Anas Yassin, the cousin and business partner of Adnan Khashoggi. Fayed's confession of infidelity had merely confirmed her true feelings.

It was a bitter cure for honesty. Convinced that the Khashoggis had connived at his humiliation, Fayed fell into a deep depression. Embarrassed and deserted, he was above all devastated by the rejection. He had lost the woman whom he deeply loved and, overnight, he had ceased to be accepted within the intimate embrace of the Khashoggi family. His self-confidence was demolished. Overwhelmed by emotion and incapable of rational introspection, Fayed developed a furious sense of inferiority. He was shut out by the very people whose attention, respect and love he craved. His antidote, while swearing in silent anger against the Khashoggis, was to seek acceptance, fame and fortune from others. Obliterating his past became an obsession – not only his childhood years but also his relationship with the treacherous Saudis. Henceforth, he would win his independence by lying.

Under the initial agreement terminating his partnership with Khashoggi, Fayed accepted 50,000 Saudi riyals and a promise of 2 per cent in any future profits of Belrock, the mining company. But the initial agreement became entangled by arguments over the future of the Al Nasr trading company. Believing that he was entitled to a considerable share of the proceeds despite being a mere employee, Fayed had used his authority secretly to withdraw £100,000 from the company's bank account. A man's duty, he had shown, was to himself. 'He's rebelled against those who helped him smell money,' Khashoggi scoffed as the first spot of decay surfaced on the fruit.

By the terms of the divorce negotiated by the lawyer Mohamed Sabi, Fayed had in accordance with Egyptian law been granted custody of their young son. Dodi was entrusted to Salah Fayed, then aged twenty-five, and his new Italian wife, Adriana Funaro, under strict orders that he was to be isolated from Samira. Totally obedient to his elder brother's orders, Salah accepted the responsibility, not least because Mohamed was setting up a business to support the three brothers. Salah's new home, to be shared with Mohamed and Dodi, reflected their aspirations.

Hidden behind high walls, the sixteen-room colonial house surounded by five acres of garden at 15 Khaled Pasha Street in Alexandria was a classic bargain available to Egyptians in the wake of Nasser's revolution. Abandoned by its expelled British owner and boasting a huge kitchen, a children's wing and large staircases rising from the extensive reception area to the bedrooms, the house reflected its previous occupant's enormous wealth. Fayed and his brothers assumed that glamour for a pittance in rent. Dodi was to be brought up by reluctant relatives under the impression that his family had inherited a fortune.

Casting around for a business to substantiate the myth, Fayed alighted upon shipping. The blockade of the Suez Canal had propelled world shipping rates to unprecedented levels. As industrialists bid frantically to secure boats to transport their products, the Greek magnates, Onassis, Niarchos and their ilk, ranked among the world's richest tycoons. Fayed's talent was to spot an opportunity and instinctively dive into the gap and, thanks to the Khashoggis' tutorship and money, he understood how he could capitalize on Nasser's expropriation and profit from the misfortune of others. All over Alexandria, foreign businessmen fearing Nasser's threats of expropriation sought either to sell their assets or to form partnerships with Egyptians to protect themselves from socialism. The relationships with businessmen and bankers which Fayed had cultivated in Switzerland, he hoped, would be invaluable.

Among Nasser's victims was Leon Carasso, an elderly Alexandrian Jew and owner of a shipping agency. Carasso wanted to sell his agency and move to New York. To overcome Nasser's ban on transferring money out of Egypt, he sought a buyer who would deposit the purchase money in a European bank. His candidate was Fayed. Naturally, the price Fayed offered for the agency was considerably lower than its value before Nasser's threats of expropriation, but he promised to pay an agreed sum into a Swiss bank account. In return, Carasso undertook to manage the agency for two years, teach Fayed the business and introduce him to his clients in Europe. With the deal struck, Fayed created the Middle East Navigation Company to take over Carasso's business. Half the shares in the £500 company were held in trust for Dodi and the remainder were divided equally between Salah and Ali. The company's office at 2 Tousson Street in Alexandria was shared with Tousson El Barrawi, the friend who had introduced Fayed to Khashoggi.

Among the new businesses which Fayed attracted was the agency of Bozo Dabinovic, an ambitious Yugoslav shipbroker and kindred spirit, whom he had met in Geneva. Convinced by Fayed's Rolls-Royce and expensive lifestyle, Dabinovic assumed that he was a wealthy potential partner. His activities over the following two years appeared to sustain the self-salesmanship. With a loan from Banque Gonet, a small Swiss bank in Geneva, and the money from Khashoggi, Fayed had bought Favia, a small transport company, and 25 per cent of Gilnavi Spa, a company in Genoa which owned and chartered ships. Relentlessly driving himself and his brothers to find new customers and increase their trade, he decided in 1959 that, having learnt enough about the shipping business, he would fire Carasso on the ground that his services were too expensive. Carasso would allege that some of his European clients had refused to deal with Fayed and, worse, that Fayed had defaulted on the agreed payment for his business. While Carasso retired hurt to New York, Fayed bore the satisfaction of paying comparatively little for a thriving, albeit small, shipping and transport business divided among four companies.

As an import–export agent in Alexandria, Fayed had established himself as an efficient bruiser on behalf of European and American traders desperate to overcome Egypt's suffocating bureaucracy in the port. Among his customers was United Artists, the Hollywood film company producing *Khartoum*.

Understanding the Americans' urgent need to retrieve their equipment, unloaded off a freighter, from a customs warehouse for filming in Sudan, Fayed telephoned Charles Orme, the film's producer, with good news. 'It's all arrived,' he said.

'Good. We'll collect it.'

'It'll cost another $10,000,' replied Fayed. 'Extra expenses.' The money, he added, should be deposited in a Swiss bank account.

Orme sighed. The Egyptian, a fervent consumer of Royal Jelly in a bid to retain eternal youth, was a 'lovable rogue'.

Adnan Khashoggi regarded Fayed by then as an unlovable rogue. After polite but unsuccessful attempts by Khashoggi to recover the £100,000 which had, without authority, been withdrawn from his company's bank account, Fayed received in June 1958 his first writs. Robustly, he planned to ensure that Khashoggi would not pursue his claims. The subsequent agreement entirely benefited Fayed. In return for Khashoggi abandoning his claims for all the business debts, the personal loans and the £100,000 withdrawn by Fayed, Fayed promised to allow Samira her freedom to remarry and return to Egypt. As a precaution against further liabilities after the agreement was signed, Khashoggi published an advertisement in the *Al Ahram* newspaper in September 1958 warning Al Nasr's customers that Mohamed Fayed, having been 'dismissed', no longer represented the company. Calculated to cause embarrassment, it was easy retaliation from a family irritated by the debris of soured relations.

The humiliating advertisement was unhelpful when Fayed offered his help to two more of Nasser's victims – the Barcilon brothers, owners of the American-Nile Company which organized luxury cruises along the Nile and controlled two hotels, the Continental in Cairo and the San Stefano in Alexandria. Fayed's bid for the company had been rejected as ludicrously low, but the brothers agreed that his appointment in May 1960 as a director and the group's 'administrator' could be helpful.

But this defensive ruse to protect the company from nationalization failed.

In 1961, Nasser ordered the wholesale confiscation of foreign and Egyptian property. Among the casualties was the American-Nile Company. Fayed had already anticipated that Nasser was not helpful to ambitious entrepreneurs and, to avoid nationalization, had transferred ownership of his Middle East Navigation Company to Genoa, leaving behind the nascent De Castro Shipping and Tour Company, a single-roomed office under a large display sign, a forlorn token of his ambitions. In that year, he moved his home to Geneva. While he would be based in Switzerland, Salah and Ali divided the management of their shipping business between Genoa, Alexandria and Beirut. As the eldest brother, Mohamed was naturally the boss. Buoyed by new self-confidence and developing charisma, he had by 1962, thanks to his good relationship with Banque Gonet, obtained more loans to raise the share capital of the Middle East Navigation Company to £6,000 and increase his investment in the Gilnavi shipping line which, with 100 per cent loans, had bought six roll-on roll-off ferries for $120 million.

*

TEN YEARS AFTER meeting Adnan Khashoggi, the former door-to-door salesman – by means of an extravagant and enjoyable lifestyle across Europe – was cultivating the image of an immensely rich shipowner. The chauffeured limousines, well-cut suits and expensive entertainment in the best restaurants and night clubs were flaunted to give an impression of vast wealth. The truth was that Fayed had earned some money from Europe's booming economies, but success was still elusive. Unable to find partners and bankers to finance a leap into the Onassis league, he gazed enviously at Khashoggi who, within five years, thanks to Saudi Arabia's increasing oil revenues, was establishing the foundations of a multi-billion-dollar

empire as the trusted middleman between the Saudi government and American weapons manufacturers. Unlike his former
brother-in-law, Fayed lacked roots and a background to borrow the millions he sought. Effectively, he was an itinerant,
professionally and personally, burdened as the national of a
pariah state by the need to obtain visas for travel in Europe
and reliant on instinct and a 'feel for finance' rather than on
technical mastery of a balance sheet. Undaunted by those
handicaps, he sought to overcome his lack of education and
pedigree by performing an excellent imitation of a tycoon of
substance.

The ploy was not ill considered. Money attracts money and
Fayed hoped that his performance would be a magnet to those
like-minded entrepreneurs seeking partners and proposing
deals. Among the ranks of that ambitious club was Bozo
Dabinovic, the Yugoslav shipbroker turned arms dealer based
in Geneva. In his own search for wealth, Dabinovic had
alighted upon Haiti, the impoverished island in the Caribbean
mercilessly ruled by Papa Doc Duvalier, a tyrant guided by
voodoo and protected by the thugs of the Tontons Macoute.
Probing the commercial possibilities on the island, the Yugoslav, supposedly drafting a shipping law for the Haitian
government, suggested to Fayed that the Caribbean might be
something of a honeypot. Fayed's dream, following in Khashoggi's footsteps, was to find his own oil state and become a
middleman, earning commission on brokered trade. If the
Middle East was barred by his lack of connections, the Caribbean was a suitable alternative. With Dabinovic's promise of
an introduction to Papa Doc, Fayed flew to Haiti to commence
on 12 June 1964 the first major performance of Fayed the
Tycoon.

Since Papa Doc was attempting to lure international investors to his island to overcome economic sanctions imposed by
the United States, Fayed gambled on a warm welcome and,
hoping to improve his chances, risked introducing himself as a

Kuwaiti sheikh keen to invest some of the Gulf's new and growing oil wealth in the lawless country.

Fayed gazed at his potential prize with contempt. In contrast to the Egyptians with their 4,000 years of history, the blacks in Haiti were the descendants of slaves, probably sold into captivity by Arab traders. Black Africa, Fayed believed, was uncivilized and his first impressions of Haiti's deserted, crumbling capital, Port-au-Prince, did nothing to alter his prejudice. On the main road, a corpse had been left to rot on a chair by the president to warn of the consequences for those daring contemplate opposition.

Presenting the visiting card of Sheikh Mohamed Fayed from Kuwait, a relative of the Sabahs, the ruling family, the Egyptian met Duvalier in the formerly grand presidential palace. Fayed's cover story suffered no harm from that month's headline news reporting British soldiers being rushed to protect Kuwait's borders from threatened Iraqi aggression. The encounter between Duvalier, eager to embrace any glittering illusion, and Fayed, an increasingly adept conjuror of fantasies, intoxicated both men with moonshine. Vast riches, Fayed promised the despot, would follow his $1 million investment in a new oil refinery. Reporting the agreement the following day, *Nouvelliste*, the local newspaper controlled by the dictator, hailed Fayed as a blessed deliverer.

In an interview with the newspaper, Fayed boasted that General Navigation & Commerce, his latest shipping company, registered in Kuwait, enjoyed an annual turnover of £10 million (about £100 million in today's money) and transported the bulk of Kuwaiti oil around the world. His plan, he boasted, was to expand the company's activities in Haiti by building an oil refinery and modernizing the harbour. Six weeks later, after a trip to Europe, he announced in Port-au-Prince that, under the proposal he would present to Papa Doc, Haitians would be trained as welders to complete construction of the oil refinery within thirty months.

Four weeks later, in September 1964, linking up with Clemard Charles, a Haitian banker and confidant of Papa Doc, Fayed offered the dictator another proposal: in return for receiving the port's income and acting as the exclusive representative of all shipping lines in Haiti, he would dredge Port-au-Prince's delapidated harbour, improve the wharf and manage the ships' pilots. Since Fayed would receive all the commission on the freight moving through the port, the potential profits, to the fury of the existing shipping agents who stood to be disfranchised, were considerable. The dictator agreed to Fayed's proposed four-year contract for a $5 million improvement scheme and a thirty-year exclusive contract to control all the harbour's activities. The only casualty was Valentin Petroleum, an American company, whose contract with the regime was scrapped. Fayed was unconcerned. Ensconced with his brother Ali in the Chrysler building in Port-au-Prince and free to make use of the harbour's $160,000 bank deposit, he appointed an English harbour master and was soon able to congratulate himself as the first improvements – marker light and buoys – appeared.

Fayed established himself rapidly in Haiti. Delighting Duvalier's entourage with his charm and bonhomie, he had secured for himself a large house, the protection of Lieutenant Woolley Gaillard as a bodyguard, the patronage of Papa Doc's wife and a relationship with Marie Denise, the dictator's eldest daughter and a renowned temptress; most importantly, he was known as the millionaire confidant of Papa Doc himself. Daily he sent flowers to the palace and entertained the dictator's cronies. Over meals, he met other expatriates regularly, Poles and Americans, arousing the suspicions of the local American embassy and the CIA. The intelligence agency's report of a dinner party attended by Fayed mentioned that the 'Kuwaiti' had explained that he was in Haiti 'to explore oil-producing and investment possibilities'. The memorandum commented that Fayed 'strikes one as being friendly and evil at the same time'. The agency was interested enough in Fayed to make inquiries in Kuwait. Although his company was registered in that country, it was soon established that he was actually an Egyptian. Before that discovery was registered in Washington, Papa Doc had decreed that Fayed had been awarded Haitian nationality. But the naturalization did not pass smoothly. Two judges refused to approve the breach of the law requiring ten years' residence, but a third judge 'saw the light'. Fayed also asked Papa Doc to grant him a Haitian diplomatic passport. Although the Haitians were initially baffled by this request, he charmed the president's family into accepting his desire to act as a representative of Haiti. In truth, desperate to disguise his Egyptian origins in the anti-Nasser atmosphere still prevalent in the West, he needed the document as an invaluable prop for the status he craved.

His travels on that passport to Europe and the Middle East were noted by CIA stations. In the midst of the Cold War, an Egyptian posing as a Kuwaiti sheikh and travelling on a Haitian diplomatic passport would natually arouse suspicions, not least that he was possibly involved in arms deals or intelligence operations.

The halcyon days as adventurer and carpetbagger passed rapidly. To Fayed's dismay, the British experts whom he had retained in London derided his proposed refinery. Haiti's petroleum requirement, they reported, was too small and the jar of black, tarry liquid he had submitted for analysis proved to be low-grade molasses extracted from an abandoned French sugar plantation. There were no local oil deposits to exploit. Fayed's exclusive agreement at the port had been also successfully challenged by the ousted Americans. The dictator tore up his contract with Fayed.

Soon after Christmas, his relations with Duvalier soured. Consistent with their reputation, representatives of Papa Doc arrived at his office and demanded a bribe, a pittance for a Kuwaiti sheikh. 'I felt trapped by gangsters,' he would later complain, claiming that the desired bribe was $5 million. Fayed declined to pay, and Gaillard, his bodyguard, mysteriously disappeared. Understanding the omen, on 4 February 1965 he and Ali boarded a plane and fled the island, leaving behind partners whose lives were now endangered and a legend about one of the few men to have deceived Papa Doc and escaped.

In the ensuing investigation, Papa Doc's trusted police discovered that the harbour authority's bank account was empty. Fayed would deny that he had stolen £153,000 but, chillingly, Haiti's local newspapers announced that Papa Doc was seeking his erstwhile harbour director around the world, dead or alive. Privately, Fayed would claim to have lost $60,000 in the venture – later he would say $2 million – and in return only possessed a valid Haitian diplomatic passport. But that, in his opinion, was a godsend.

In the shadow of lurid reports of Papa Doc's dispatch of a hit squad to settle accounts with the duplicitous Arab, London became Fayed's refuge. Life in the capital, in the midst of the Swinging Sixties, suited his taste for fast cars and fast women. Like many Arabs eager to play, he believed that the Muslim God did not extend his gaze from the Middle East to see his children playing in London. Usually dressed in the uniform of the era – dark-blue corduroys, a black turtle-neck pullover and patent leather zip-up Chelsea boots – the slim thirty-six-year-old rented a small ground-floor flat at 60 Park Lane, bought a white Mercedes sports car and contemplated how he might expand his small shipping business. Unfortunately, unlike his Greek heroes a decade earlier, Fayed still lacked the resources, relationships and sheer ability to become a shipping Goliath.

Instead, introducing himself as Mohamed Fayed, a shipper and transporter, the self-assured workaholic was just another foreigner eager to be taken seriously and irritated by Britain's bositerous snobs. His past, Fayed convinced himself, remained his Achilles' heel. Gossip about Adnan Khashoggi's glittering parties in Paris, London and New York and stories about Samira's happiness and success irked the outsider. Unlike his former brother-in-law, Fayed still owned no property and could only boast about inconsequential, grubby business failures. Too often people had turned against him: Samira and Khashoggi, Leon Carasso and now Bozo Dabinovic and Papa Doc had bred a succession of excuses. To deflect criticism, he cast himself as the victim whose survival depended upon retaliating before he was attacked. In self-protection, it was so much easier not to allow anyone too close to understand his weaknesses, so much safer not to take the risk that they would dislike the real Fayed. These self-doubts were not assuaged by the mundane nature of his business, General Navigation and Commerce Ltd (known as Genavco), his first British company, registered in July 1965 as a specialist in forwarding freight. The company's principal employee was John Hadjiouannou, a small, bald schoolfriend from Alexandria, recruited as a clerk to liaise with Salah, who was now living mostly in Genoa. Genavco guaranteed an income but was patently not the foundation of an empire.

So far, the major casualty of his unsuccessful ambitions was Dodi, his ten-year-old son. On his occasional visits to Alexandria, Fayed could not help noticing the boy's unhappiness. Barely literate, speaking poor Arabic and uninspired, Dodi endured an isolated and loveless childhood. Frequently, he cried, and he even screamed during the night. Anguished by the suffering, the father would comfort his son in a shared bed and, the following morning, would spend over-generously on toys. Torn between earning his fortune and caring for his son, Fayed was inevitably distracted by his career. Yet he did little to alleviate the boy's misery. Until 1965, Dodi had been visited by Adnan Khashoggi's sisters – his loving aunts – and by his maternal grandmother. Briefly, he had also been reconciled with his mother. But in 1965 all the Khashoggis had moved from Egypt to Beirut, leaving the boy alone with the mercurial and unfaithful Salah and his wife, both unhelpful influences. Even Fayed's own father and sisters, living near by, were uninterested. The fracture in family relations was permanent and deep. On Aly Aly Fayed's death in 1966, the three brothers, although listed in the newspaper announcement as mourners, were unable to return for their father's funeral in Alexandria. Even Dodi was kept away. Solitary and philistine, the three Fayeds were patently unsatisfactory as Dodi's role models. Yet their detachment from their past drew the brothers and Dodi closer. Together, under Mohamed's leadership, they had after all broken free from Aly Aly's small world. The next step was more difficult.

*

CULTIVATING ONE HUNDRED contacts to find just one lucrative relationship required hard work and considerable expenditure. So much depended, Mohamed believed, on his image. Park Lane was an impressive address but his small flat was dowdy. Inspired by the flamboyance now fashionable in London, Fayed sought people capable' of transforming his surroundings. Money would not be a barrier. Minimizing his taxes by retaining his capital and earnings in Switzerland, he had accrued sufficient money in Banque Gonet, benefiting also from the 1967 devaluation of sterling, to borrow to live beyond his means, the cardinal principle which thereafter would guide his finances.

Recommended by a Hungarian carpenter, Fayed arrived at the studios of Bill Mitchell, a former seaman and self-educated sculptor and designer whose concrete murals had been praised by Lord Snowdon. 'I want you to build me a special cupboard,' Fayed told the Cockney. 'With a special drinks cabinet. Money no problem.' For Mitchell, specializing in decorated verandas and in furniture and tables adorned with etched glass, it seemed an odd request. The Arab's pidgin English, delivered in a comical tone, had an unusually endearing quality but his taste was certainly dubious. It was, mused Mitchell, debatable whether Fayed valued European culture or was simply keen to feed off it. Certainly, he judged, the Egyptian was anxious to create the image of an enormously rich businessman.

Soon after his flat was transformed, Fayed began hosting parties on a Roman scale, proferring friendship, especially among London's small Arab community. Glamorous girls, especially blonde Scandinavian models, alias 'party girls', many easily seduced, featured at his celebrations. To the bachelor the girls were a commodity and he, as the generous patron, was pleased to entertain an attractive selection. Providing a good time for his new acquaintances was an investment and an opportunity to discover secrets. Knowledge, he reasoned, was a source of power. As his guests relaxed, though puzzled by his strange habit of constantly rubbing his hands in lemon juice, he won their trust. Some, abandoning caution, laughed as he snapped photographs – sometimes in the midst of playful sex – with the newly invented Polaroid camera. It was, they reckoned, just another hilarious prank.

Among those many whom Fayed cultivated during that first year was Salim Abu Alwan, an Iraqi businessman living in Dubai, an insignificant, arid, desert outpost in the middle of the Persian Gulf. Ignored by the world, Dubai had been, in a pact of mutual dependence, ruled by the British since 1820 as one of five Trucial states. Less than one dozen British advisers, in collaboration with Sheikh Rashid bin Said al Maktoum, the ruler, controlled the kingdom's finance, internal security, shipping and defence. The state's small population lived around a narrow creek serving as a natural harbour for sailing dhows trading between Iran, India and the other small kingdoms dotted along the sandy Arabian peninsula, north towards Kuwait and Iraq and south towards Oman.

From Alwan, Fayed learnt that two recent developments augured dramatic changes in Dubai. Alarmed by Nasser's aggressive nationalism, the British feared that their considerable military and financial stake in the Gulf was threatened. Secondly, oil, already produced in neighbouring Abu Dhabi, would certainly be discovered in Dubai itself. In a short time, predicted Alwan, the featureless sandscape, renowned only for its tax-free port benignly welcoming traders, would offer attractive propositions to European businessmen. In fact, added Alwan, Sheikh Rashid, the kingdom's enlightened ruler, was by chance visiting London with Mahdi Al Tajir, his Bahraini adviser, at the end of his first trip to Europe. 'Tajir is a good friend,' added Alwan. 'They're staying at the Carlton Tower Hotel in Knightsbridge.'

'Can I meet him?' asked Fayed.

'I'll fix it,' replied the Iraqi.

'This is my friend Mohamed Fayed,' said Alwan, introducing the two men, sufficient words to dispel any suspicions Tajir might have harboured towards a stranger. Instinctively, Fayed sensed his good fortune as he shook hands with the skinny Tajir, who was three years younger than the Egyptian and smaller too. In the background, at the centre of a Majlis, the Arab's traditional forum, sat the elderly Sheikh Rashid surrounded by more than twenty people. Tajir, Fayed could see, was undoubtedly the sheikh's trusted confidant. Neither the sheikh, the inhabitant of a small fort overlooking lines of dhows moored to wooden stakes, nor Tajir could, despite the promise of oil, encourage interest in London in their wasteland. Fayed, regarding himself as the superior, sensed an opportunity and identified Tajir as one of the hundred contacts susceptible to his manipulation, and worth cultivating.

Dispatched in 1953 by the British consul in Bahrain to a training school of the Ports Authority in Preston, Lancashire, Tajir, alias 'The Director', had returned home expecting employment as a customs officer in Bahrain's port. Instead, he had been ordered the following year by a British administrator to travel 300 miles across the Gulf to Dubai to organize the collection of the creek's customs dues.

Sitting in the shade, watching the slow movement of the dhows along the narrow waterway, Sheikh Rashid became enamoured of the efficient Bahraini as he arranged the collection of taxes on gold shipped from Dubai to be smuggled into India. In a country where birth certificates had been introduced only in 1960 and where none of the 300 local families had received a formal education, Tajir ranked as the most literate courtier in the country. Despite a fire which had destroyed the customs shed, Tajir had been allowed by Rashid, as a reward for his loyalty, to accumulate his own income from the gold trade. By the time Fayed introduced himself, Tajir was not a novice in the commission business. His mentor Emil Bustani, a famed, self-made Lebanese industrialist who had built the oil pipeline across Iraq, had taught him how, in the fashion of that era, he could expect to earn personal commissions from Continental Oil once his negotiations on Rashid's behalf to extract Dubai's oil had been completed.

Knowing that Arabs still felt insignificant and isolated in London, not least because only a junior British civil servant bothered to pay his respects to Sheikh Rashid, Fayed launched himself as Tajir's host. Collecting his new friend in a blue chauffeured Phantom VI, Fayed described his plight. 'I am the son of a pasha,' he told his credulous guest, identifying himself as a member of the former Egyptian royal family, 'who fled Egypt with the king after Nasser's revolt. We lost most of our possessions. Our land, our fleet of ships, all our possessions were stolen.' As the hired Rolls-Royce swished through London, Fayed interrupted his laments about his suffering as Nasser's victim with a supposed revelation: 'Fortunately, enough money was deposited abroad. This car belonged to my dear father, but not much else of his remains.'

Fayed's distortions, a deformation of the natural Egyptian tendency to exaggerate, were more than a defence of his vulnerability or an excuse to obliterate the irksome footprints of his past. His fantasies, infected by the legacy of Khashoggi and by London's social life, were fuelled by his inferiority complex in the face of what he believed to be the paramount importance of breeding and background. Those weaknesses, however, were well concealed by powerful charisma. Fayed, in summary, had become an impostor.

Over the following days, Fayed provided Tajir with great entertainment, including a visit to Annabel's, London's premier night club, and introductions to beautiful Scandinavian girls. Every evening was enlivened by Fayed's bonhomie and jokes.

'He's a good man,' reflected Tajir, unaware that the effect upon him was calculated. 'Good company, a good friend and someone to be pitied.' Tajir could not imagine that anyone would dedicate such energy to falsify his past.

By the time Tajir and Rashid returned to Dubai, the sheikh had become enthused by a vision of Dubai's future. To capitalize on the discovery of oil along the Gulf and the certainty of more trade, he decided to commission a proper harbour. Summoning Neville Allen, the local representative of Halcrow, the British civil engineers responsible for organizing the dredging of the creek, he ordered a scheme for a four-berth port. Although unremarkable thirty years later, the sheikh's decision at the time was revolutionary. Few, including Allen, could imagine how sand dunes could be transformed into a metropolis akin to Hong Kong. Allen did, however, expect that once his plans for the small port were completed the sheikh would invite tenders from several British contractors. The engineer was to be surprised.

Tajir returned to London to fulfil Sheikh Rashid's edict: 'We are going to build a harbour. Find people who can help us.' Comfortably settled in the Carlton Tower, Tajir had naturally contacted his new friend and generous host Mohamed Fayed. 'Sheikh Rashid', Tajir enthused, 'has entrusted to me the authority to select the contractor.' Fayed watched the facilitator carefully. Suddenly Tajir had become the most significant man in his world. At last he could become the middleman, the commission man. With limited financial risk, he could, like Khashoggi, profit from the unsophisticated Gulf Arabs, uninitiated in the complexities of capital projects, by guiding them through the maze. Without hesitation, he dived at the opportunity.

Tajir himself was by no measure innocent of this sort of thinking. With Rashid's agreement, he was already earning commissions on the contracts with Conoco (Continental Oil), a major US corporation, and he would secure hefty commissions from Boeing for aircraft sales in the region and for every major import. Commissions would also be earned from the contractor selected to build the port. If Fayed smoothed the way, he could share the payments. 'Our only problem', confessed Tajir, 'is that we don't have any money.' Unknown and still penniless, Dubai had no relationship with any bank, even to borrow £1 million for the deposit a contractor would require.

'I find money,' said Fayed. 'No problem.'

With his appetite for self-promotion, Fayed had represented himself to Tajir as an international tycoon well known to the world's major banks. In reality, he had no idea how to persuade European bankers to lend money for a harbour in an unknown Third World country which he had never visited. His talent, however, was knowing people who knew people. Through his many contacts in Geneva, he met Imre Rochlitz, an American lawyer of Hungarian origin, specializing in unconventional finance. In early 1966, Fayed asked Rochlitz, a Jew, to help an Arab state borrow about £9 million. In neutral Switzerland the absurdity of collaboration between Arab and Jew prompted no comment. 'I'd love to see Israel,' said Fayed. 'Could you arrange a visit without a passport?' Rochlitz laughed, just as he had laughed when Fayed said, 'I can introduce good girls in London.'

After reading Fayed's power of attorney from Sheikh Rashid, Rochlitz agreed to assist Fayed. The jovial and easy-going Egyptian was, he judged, totally trustworthy. After securing finance first from the government of Kuwait, Rochlitz finally accepted a deal with the British Bank of the Middle East. 'Here's a draft contract with Costain,' said Rochlitz to Fayed.

Fayed gazed at the document. 'My eyes no good,' he complained. 'My eyes sensitive. I need drops. You tell me what it says.'

The garrulous trader was, the lawyer realized, incapable of

31

reading a contract. The bank, explained Rochlitz indulgently, had agreed to fund Costain as the contractor, but his selection of Costain had been fraught.

'Which contractor is most likely to be favoured?' Fayed had asked Tajir.

'Well, Costain dredge the creek, have built a dirt runway and a small airport terminal building,' replied Tajir, adding that only a British company would be considered. Although hardly a recommendation for a huge project, especially given that Halcrow opposed Costain, it was sufficient to justify selecting the company which promised to pay the highest commissions to Rochlitz, Tajir and Fayed.

Rochlitz had already approached Philip Sowden, Costain's manager of civil engineering. 'Costain will pay us between 10 and 12 per cent commission,' he told Fayed.

'Good,' Fayed replied. 'We'll divide it.' Using the potential agreement as an excuse, Fayed introduced himself to Sowden. Unaware that the Rolls-Royce parked by the kerbside was hired and that the tailored suit was Fayed's costume for the performance, Sowden had no reason to doubt that Mohamed Fayed was an immensely rich and powerful Arab broker. 'My appointment as your adviser', Fayed explained in early 1967, 'would be profitable.' In return for 12 per cent commission, he could guarantee more contracts. The English builder, with no real experience of the Arab world, was easily seduced by the forceful salesmanship, bonhomie and generous hospitality into believing that a rosy future in Dubai beckoned. He was the type whose earthly requirements were well judged by Fayed. With everyone promised some benefits, an alliance was forged. Fayed had achieved his ambition. He was a Middle Eastern commission agent.

In Dubai, Neville Allen, the Halcrow engineer, did not protest after hearing that the contract was not to be tendered. In a world where the ruler's word was the law, he understood the need for discretion. Tajir was the 'Golden Boy' upon whom Dubai's development depended. Watching Fayed with Tajir at

Rashid's Majlis, he would tell enquirers, 'The Golden Boy liked Fayed as a man after his own heart. Fayed speaks well and can persuade.' Allen was similarly impressed that Fayed, a notably elegant man, had established a relationship with Rashid. Introduced as the dispossesed son of a pasha, Fayed easily persuaded himself that the sheikh's smile implied acknowledgement of his importance for Dubai, just as he had made himself important for Costain. Allen knew better: 'The ruler suspects him, but thinks he's a good man with good intentions for Dubai.' For the sheikh, all Arabs from the north, especially Egyptians and Palestinians, were to be kept at arm's length. The foreigner was welcome but expected to behave as a servant of the local inhabitants. Cautious and sly, Rashid allowed Fayed to delude himself about his importance, but intended, to forestall excessive influence and power, to withdraw the patronage at some point in the future. In the meantime, Fayed could count his blessings that he had landed in the right place to enrich himself. Eager to ingratiate himself, he offered Neville Allen 'a chauffeured Mercedes and a good time when you're next in London'. Assuming that Fayed meant a blonde, Allen declined the offer.

In London, just one piece of housekeeping remained. Imre Rochlitz was invited by Tajir to an anonymous, private conference room at the London Hilton. 'Please promise', urged Tajir, 'that there'll be no publicity about a Jew arranging the finance.' Rochlitz nodded. Tajir's embarrassment was obvious and was enough to prompt Rochlitz to reject Fayed's offer of a formal partnership.

On 5 June 1967, the Costain contract and bank agreements were signed. Fayed's commission was worth £1.5 million – a sensational amount under any circumstances, especially for him. Although his agreement with Tajir was to share the commission – a 'greedy man', he would later complain – and others in Dubai would also expect a share, Fayed's stock had soared.

The following morning, Fayed and Costain's managers

prepared for a champagne celebration, but disaster struck. On that same day, Israel invaded its Arab neighbours and launched the Six Day War. The bottles of champagne remained unopened. Fayed's first deal appeared to have collapsed. Tantalizingly, he stood at the abyss, uncertain whether the anti-British riots in Dubai would wreck his journey to El Dorado.

*

SOME WEEKS LATER, reassured that once the Middle East had stabilized the contract would be implemented, Fayed began negotiating for more than just the commission on the construction. Costain would need to transport from Europe to the Gulf not only cement and steel but every bolt, machine, paperclip and plastic door-handle. Nothing could be bought locally. In the pre-containerization era, organizing the smooth flow of hundreds of tons of supplies to arrive on the site exactly when required was a major leap from supervising the importation of furniture into Saudia Arabia, as he had done fourteen years earlier, but Fayed convinced Costain's directors that his shipping agencies in Piraeus, Beirut and Genoa were not merely name plates on shabby offices but represented the tentacles of an empire. His task was to turn that sales patter into reality.

Through headhunters, Fayed hired Ed Brown, an expert shipper, to replace John Hadjiouannou, his schoolfriend. Simultaneously Genavco, increasing its staff from eight to fifty, moved from the City to Waterloo Place, off Piccadilly. Hadjiouannou was transferred to Genoa to work with Ali supervising the development of their shipping brokerage. By early 1968, Fayed was presenting himself as a major trader in the Gulf, securing the agencies in Dubai for Caterpillar and General Motors.

In late 1968, after the first sale of Dubai's oil and after Costain began construction of the port, Sheikh Rashid, reassured by the certainty of future finance, sent an urgent message to the airport. John Harris, a British architect known to the sheikh since he designed the country's and the Gulf's first 280-bed modern hospital ten years earlier, was ordered to delay his departure. Harris, still hugely impressed that the £6.5 million budget for the hospital's construction had been under-spent by £18, rushed to the ruler's office. 'I want you to design a trade centre,' ordered Rashid. 'It will be the tallest building in the Middle East. It will be a conference centre with shops, offices and a luxury hotel for international corporations need-ing headquarters in the Gulf.' Four minutes later, Rashid terminated the conversation. 'Go now. The plane is waiting for you.' Naturally, Tajir would implement the ruler's edict. Auto-matically, he turned to his friend Mohamed Fayed to seek the finance and to negotiate the proper terms with a construction company. Not surprisingly, Fayed was thrilled.

In summer 1969, as Harris completed the draft designs, Rashid and Tajir flew to London. Without a Dubai embassy in London and with their country still barely acknowledged by the British government, the visitors were grateful that Fayed was waiting in Heathrow's VIP lounge with 'his' chauffeured Rolls-Royce outside. To those who had scarcely shaken the sand off their sandals, Fayed seemed a smooth operator in the world's financial capital. Keeping relationships sweet was his special talent. He understood how to ingratiate himself with those upon whom he was dependent, even if they found his Arabic, spoken with an Egyptian accent, occasionally difficult to understand. But the courtier's presence was not pure servil-ity. As he hovered in the Carlton Tower, awaiting the summons to provide any service required by the ruler or his team, Fayed was acutely listening and watching, impatient to learn.

Among the sheikh's important meetings was a visit to John Harris's office near Oxford Circus on 28 July 1969 to inspect the plans for the Trade Centre. Accompanying Rashid were Tajir, Bill Duff, the British financial adviser in Dubai, Isa Gurg, a future ambassador to London, and Fayed. Arriving in Fayed's Rolls-Royce, Rashid led his small entourage into the architect's office. After all five had signed the visitors' book, Fayed stood in the background as the sheikh knelt on the floor excitedly examining reams of drawings. Observing Rashid's interest in design and construction, Fayed decided to become a similar visionary. Overnight, he adopted architecture as a passion.

The sheikh's next stop with Fayed was Morgan Grenfell, the City merchant bankers. Their contact was the Honourable David Douglas-Home, the twenty-three-year-old son of the defeated Conservative prime minister. Rashid's visit to seek a loan had been well prepared by Fayed. Douglas-Home had barely arrived from Oxford University when the son of an Egyptian pasha had been delivered to his office in a Rolls-Royce. Douglas-Home had no reason to doubt Fayed's account of his close relationship with Sheikh Rashid and his statement that a loan would be guaranteed by the British government's Export Credits Guarantee scheme. 'No risk and lots of future profits,' Fayed had enthused. Douglas-Home nodded with satisfaction. Rashid's visit had not dented that impression. Nevertheless, the sheikh's signature for the loan had been followed by a minor embarrassment.

The bank required a deposit of £700,000. Fayed had arrived with a cheque and was asked to sit in a small glass cubicle in the entrance hall. For nearly four hours, he had waited patiently while the cheque was cleared. Thankfully, sighed Douglas-Home, the Egyptian had not protested about the indignity. There was good reason. After Rashid's departure, comparatively huge sums were guaranteed to pour into his account at Banque Gonet.

In an era when the average income of Britons was £1,508 and a five-bedroom house in Kensington cost £35,000 (compared to over £2 million today), Fayed had accumulated about £2 million. On the advice of Martin Müller, his Swiss lawyer, the brothers established four Liechtenstein trusts to manage their new wealth and avoid British taxes. More certain of his destiny, Fayed planned as usual to spend more money than he possessed to accelerate his transformation from middleman to real tycoon. Oblivious to the expenditure, he would live on a grand scale. The first bauble was a Hawker Siddeley 125, a private jet to extend his reach across the world, gambling for the big prize. Business was war, and for the victor the spoils would be magnificent.

3

Fantasies and Reality: A Man of Property

AFTER A DECADE emulating Adnan Khashoggi, Fayed's new model was Mahdi Al Tajir. Since their first meeting, Tajir had invested in property tens of millions of pounds earned from commissions. In Britain, he had bought a grand house in London, an estate in Scotland and a mansion in the home counties; and in Roquebrune on the Cote d'Azur he had acquired a breathtaking villa overlooking the Mediterranean. Twice Fayed had borrowed the house for summer holidays. Now, to fulfil his dream of owning the toys of the rich, he was searching for his own. Extravagantly he also calculated that buying large houses, boats and planes would enhance his image, an essential tool for mixing with celebrities and finding new deals.

The next bauble was a Rolls-Royce Phantom VI convertible and a chauffeur, Glyn John. His second acquisition was Chalet Ursa, a seven-bedroom house with a bowling alley in Gstaad, Switzerland, owned by the Earl of Warwick. Skiing certainly did not figure in Fayed's mind when he bought Fulke War-wick's unique house, and the president of Eagles, the resort's prestigious club, did not offer to introduce Fayed to his new neighbours. Indeed, as the first Arab in Gstaad, Fayed was mistaken by habitués as a servant, especially since he neither made an effort during his first season to join the international celebrities dancing and drinking every night at the Greengo disco in the Palace Hotel nor issued invitations to his neighbours, who eventually lampooned the Arab's home as a chalet adorned in the 'New Farouk' style. But it was an ideal venue for entertaining the Swiss bankers whose continuing trust and money he required.

His more serious investment was in London, then on the eve of a spectacular property boom. During the late 1960s, Fayed had bought two more apartments at 60 Park Lane. In 1970, he began progressively purchasing all forty flats in the block, most to be rented out on short-term lets through his private company. Moving from the second-floor flats, which were allocated to Salah and Dodi, he bought two large flats on the top floor for himself and Ali, who was then living with his future English wife Tracey, a former shop assistant.

To create a luxurious penthouse, Fayed summoned Bill Mitchell and Janos Trajer, a modernist Hungarian architect. 'Change everything,' he laughed. Staircases were to be inserted, new walls built to be covered alternately with leather and illuminated perspex, ceilings would be draped with silk like a tent, and there was to be a vast cupboard enclosing a music system and bar. To Mitchell and Trajer, it appeared that Fayed's taste was undecided, especially when he ordered Ed Brown, the manager of Genavco, to buy antiques – not because he liked them, Brown reasoned, but because, like many Arabs, Fayed believed it was cheaper to buy second-hand goods.

At last, Fayed was equipped to receive Tajir as an equal. Regularly hosting superb meals in the penthouse prepared by Abdul, his Nubian cook, Fayed invited the Tajir family to exceptionally amusing lunches. The only other guests were Ali, Tracey and occasionally Salah. 'Mohamed knows how to entertain,' Tajir remarked as he departed, still chuckling over his host's jokes which, as always, were peppered with vulgarities and expletives. His obsession with sex struck his guest as hilarious. Even for a pasha's son, his lack of education was not surprising, for the sons of the rich were usually spoilt. There was no hint in those days of Fayed's contempt for the Gulf Arabs who, unlike the Egyptians, could not boast an illustrious history. Out of self-interest, he concealed his prejudice. Similarly, Tajir remained silent about his recent discovery. Fred Pennyman, a former American diplomat employed by Conoco, had telephoned with bizarre news. 'Fayed approached me to do some oil deals,' the American reported. 'So we checked him out. It seems he's not the son of a pasha and the Rolls-Royce was hired.' Tajir smiled, and said nothing when Fayed approached him, during a jocular meal in 1970, about a pressing problem.

Ever since their first meeting, Fayed had lamented the fate of the deposed Egyptian royalty. 'I have no passport,' he complained. 'The Haitian passport I've been using has expired. My brothers and Dodi have the same problem. Can you help?' Although all four Fayeds possessed Egyptian passports, Tajir understood that President Nasser's antics created difficulties for Egyptians in the obtaining of visas. In contrast, passports issued by the Dubai government were internationally acceptable, although the holders were not accorded Dubaian nationality. 'No problem,' said Tajir to his deserving friend.

Over the meal, the two plotted Fayed's new identity. 'Let's put "Al" in front of your name,' laughed Tajir. 'That'll make you important.'

'Yes,' yelped Fayed gleefully. 'Al', according to the custom in Dubai where a handful of families dominated the nation, indicated the pasha or the head of a large family.

'And', added Tajir in full flow, 'we'll say you were born in Al-Fayedia. A town named after your family.'

Fayed was overjoyed. Tajir added one more fabrication to massage Fayed's vanity. Instead of 1929, he entered his date of birth as 27 January 1933, one year younger than Tajir. Since Fayed had shed four years, his younger brothers followed suit, somewhat exaggeratedly: both reduced their ages by ten years. Birth certificates had been introduced in Dubai only in 1960, so accuracy about age was not to be expected. Gazing at the new passport, Fayed was enthralled. Although it was merely a travel document and not a change of nationality, it did bequeath respectability. Sixteen years after he had escaped selling Coca-Cola in Alexandria's dusty streets, he was finally a pasha with a house on Park Lane. But he wanted more.

Driving along the Cromarty Firth in 1972 with Ed Brown, unsuccessfully searching for opportunities to profit from servicing the offshore rigs in Britain's new oil industry, Fayed spotted the ruin of Balnagown Castle, the ancestral home since the late fifteenth century of the Ross clan. 'I wonder if it's for sale,' mused Fayed, reflecting the Arab love of traditional English grandeur.

Twenty miles north of Inverness, the thirty-room home of Sir Charles Ross had fallen into disrepair, the common fate of many Scottish estates. Near bankrupt after a hectic and colourful life manufacturing weapons, game hunting in Africa and womanizing, the twenty-first laird had faced ruin from the alimony claims of his former wives and the demands of the Inland Revenue. Only his death in 1942 had saved him from ignominy. The enormity of Ross's debts, Fayed would later laugh, had compelled the laird to live in America, only visiting his castle secretly at night. For the next thirty years, despite the sale of the surrounding estate, Ross's legacy of accumulated debts had still not been repaid.

Fayed's knock on the castle door to ask the owner if he could buy the ruin was welcomed. The estate office, he was told, was looking for a buyer. Over lunch, he was offered the ruin for £60,000. 'Done,' said Fayed, adding that the deal would be concluded through Bocardo SA, his Liechtenstein company. He returned to London as a laird. 'The Scots', as Fayed correctly said of local hostility, 'didn't believe that some bloody Egyptian would enhance their heritage when I bought the castle.' Approached by a local newspaper, he could not resist the opportunity to star in his new show. Joking about wearing a kilt – 'It's a mini-skirt' – he further embellished his biography. 'I consider myself English,' Mohamed Al Fayed told the journalist. 'I had an English nanny and I've sent my son to

Sandhurst.' Somehow the reporter for the *Glasgow Herald* also left with the impression that Mr Al Fayed 'went to a public school south of the border where he was caned and stuffed full of crumpets'.

The only truth was that Dodi had been sent to Sandhurst in a desperate bid to cure the young man of timidity, aimlessness and low intelligence. Having emerged from Alexandria as a solitary, shy youth utterly spoilt by unquestioned expenditure at the local yacht club on speed boats, sports cars and parties, Dodi's poor education in Egypt and inability to speak fluent Arabic had not been improved at a Swiss school near Gstaad favoured by the unconcerned international set for their children of similarly low calibre. But after less than one year Dodi had abandoned the school and, aged thirteen, remained at home until, thanks to Tajir's generosity, the seventeen-year-old had been granted a place in the military academy as a Dubai national for a six-month course. 'I felt sorry for Dodi,' Tajir would say of a boy who forlornly sought his father's approval but dreamt of becoming a film producer rather than a soldier. Four weeks after entering the military academy, he had begged to be withdrawn. Unable to run more than 500 yards and had been unwilling to parachute, the shy victim of divorce had disliked rising early, although he had enjoyed playing polo. To conceal his failure, he would later suggest that he had been offered a post in the air force of the United Arab Emirates (as the Trucial States became known after independence in 1971) and had been appointed an air attaché at the UAE embassy in London. Both stories were untrue. Painfully passive about his fate and defensively insisting, 'I am happy,' he appeared to those whom he encountered to be lacking both affection and purpose.

*

TO QUASH ANY DOUBTS about his own love for his son, Fayed named his latest acquisition *Dodi*. The beautiful sixty-five-foot timber schooner festooned with gleaming brass fittings, originally known as the *Sakara*, required a crew of between five and nine. Initially rented in the Mediterranean from the Earl of Warwick, this latest bauble was bought soon after Fayed had acquired the Castel Ste-Thérèse, a four-bedroom villa in the Parc de St Tropez, the Riviera resort transformed into a mecca for the ultra-fashionable by Brigitte Bardot. Built on a steep hill, the unmodernized house set in ten acres overlooked a garden tumbling 200 yards down to a beach just thirty feet wide. This was the ideal setting for Mu-Mu, as he increasingly liked to call himself, to offer endless champagne to new acquaintances encountered in Gstaad. During those balmy days and nights when Fayed enjoyed parking his car prominently in St Tropez's small harbour and flaunting the company of a small, anonymous and somewhat fat Arab woman whose qualities were not self-evident, no one queried their host's confusing description of himself as a Lebanese shipowner nor realized that his private 'fleet' comprised just two ships, the *Dalia Star* and *Mudi Star*, both bought with loans in 1972 and managed by Salah in Genoa.

Even Fayed seemed to believe his own story as he regaled his new friends while sitting on the sand with tales of how the *Dodi* had been built by his grandfather, of how he had been educated at the exclusive Victoria College in Alexandria (Khashoggi's school) and of how his family had lived in their own mansion in Alexandria for over a century. In fact, the house continued to be rented from the expelled British owner until 1972, when it was purchased for a pittance. No doubts arose because Ali and Salah, sitting near by, nodded in agreement. Mohamed, all concurred, dominated the trio. He, it was speculated, earned the money; Ali controlled the finances; while Salah spent it. In truth, Mohamed spent more than he earned, but quantifying the wealth had been deliberately made impossible as Fayed spoke about his homes in Scotland, London, Gstaad, Genoa and Geneva, and referred to appartments in Paris and New York. The impression given that the brothers ranked among the legendary rich Arabs was misleading. All their property had been bought for about £300,000, but who could doubt that Mohamed was rich when he completed his buying spree by beating the socialist politician Harold Lever in procuring Lord McAlpine's pile, Barrow Green Court, Oxted, an Elizabethan-style mansion with oak-panelled rooms and massive fireplaces set in sixteen acres of Surrey?

Entertainment, prestige and especially sex dominated Fayed's plans for the transformation of the architecturally nondescript house into a fun palace for four men: the three brothers and Dodi.

Ordering Janos Trajer to build a huge kitchen to indulge his love dream of gargantuan banquets of stews, barbecued lamb, grilled fish, chicken and pea soup, to restore the reception rooms so that hundreds could party and to redesign the bedrooms into seduction chambers, he indulged his new passions for design and architecture. 'It's all so expensive,' complained Trajer, itemizing Fayed's shopping list.

'Money is none of your business,' laughed Fayed. 'Just do. I pay.'

Paintings and statues of naked nymphs, insisted Fayed, would dominate his home. Throughout the house, he positioned large statues of semi-nude Greek goddesses. Six life-sized marble statues were bought in one session, all of slender women with large, exposed breasts. To carry the weight, the cellar ceilings were reinforced. Life-size paintings of near-naked nymphs were hung on dark papered walls. The vast new marble bathroom with its six-foot double tub and gold taps was dominated by statues of seductresses. And in Fayed's grand bedroom Trajer placed a gigantic bed, covered with black and white velvet, on a raised plinth, surrounded by paintings of more naked girls.

'Get this girl. Paint her,' Fayed ordered Trajer one Monday morning. The Hungarian gazed at the page from the previous day's *Sunday Times* colour supplement which had been thrust into his hand. A stunning blonde, with her enormous breasts exposed, had been photographed close up on a sunny, sandy beach. 'Get her,' ordered Fayed, assuming that his money could buy anything and anyone.

'She won't come,' announced Trajer one week later after encountering a sceptical model agency. 'I'll do the next best.' Giving the photograph to a painter, he handed to Fayed one month later a vague likeness in oils. Clearly disappointed, Fayed ordered the painting to be hung in Salah's bathroom.

Gradually it became apparent that the model for Fayed's sex palace was Stocks, the love nest in Hertfordshire owned by Victor Lownes, the Playboy club manager. Although he had visited the house only once and had never been seen at the raucous club near his home in Park Lane, Fayed had read the colourful newspaper reports about Lownes and his cronies ceaselessly cavorting with voluptuous Playboy Bunnies and sex-hungry starlets. Too timid to join the club, the outsider saw no reason not to emulate the scene-setters. One Sunday morning, carefully studying as usual the enviable lifestyle por-trayed in the *Sunday Times* colour supplement, Fayed saw a feature about the world's finest jacuzzi, then still a rare pos-session for the rich in America and quite unknown in Britain. The jacuzzi, big enough for twenty bathers, had been built for Lownes in a cavern at Stocks lined with delicate stone and marble with frescoes on the ceiling. Images of a Roman orgy sprang to mind as Fayed carefully cut out the photograph and summoned Trajer. 'I want this!' he cried ecstatically. 'In the stable.' The Hungarian architect, stimulated by the challenge as much as by the fees, set to work.

Recruiting Bill Mitchell to produce concrete which had the appearance of marble, the Hungarian designed a jacuzzi, lit by spotlights of changing colours to accentuate the mood of Fayed's selected tune, 'The Floating Cloud', which hummed from the music system. Above the jacuzzi would be a bar with two shock showers. Adjoining the cavern was a sauna. 'It's a seduction room I'm building for you,' laughed the Hungarian.

'No, a recreation room,' guffawed Fayed.

Soon after its completion, Fayed telephoned Lownes. 'I'm sending my helicopter. Come. Look what I've got.' Lownes, a keen skiier, had previously accepted Fayed's invitation to a free holiday in Gstaad. During his week in the mountains, chuckles and small talk had seemed to be the limits of Fayed's 'impenetrable' conversation. 'Everyone laughs, so Mu-Mu laughs,' Lownes had observed. But any doubts had been smothered by Fayed's generous hospitality. 'Take my excellent food and a free bedroom in one of Switzerland's best resorts,' he seemed to be saying, 'but don't ask for much more.' The food, prepared by Abdul, appeared to confirm Fayed's explanation to the American visitor that his wealth was partly inherited from his father, the pasha, who, after Nasser's revolt, had gone into exile with King Farouk, finally settling in Genoa. The frequent clattering of a telex machine in the hall, apparently reporting the worldwide movements of Fayed's fleet of oil tankers, seemed to verify Fayed's story. Lownes, like other visitors, who included David Niven, Omar Sharif and their wives, had no cause to wonder if their host's façade concealed any insecurity. After all, when the Fayed brothers bought neighbouring chalets – one for each brother – and then bought Olden, the town's most picturesque and popular restaurant, their enormous wealth seemed only too evident. Any doubts would have disappeared after Lownes landed in Oxted in the helicopter to inspect the jacuzzi. 'I'm very impressed,' said Lownes generously at the end of the tour. 'Lovely,' he added, thinking, 'Mine is bigger but not as grand.' It did not occur to the American that the helicopter had been specially hired by Fayed to parade his wealth.

With the turf came the girls suitable for a rich bachelor. In 1974, Fayed saw in a magazine a beautiful blonde model posing as a mermaid. 'Get this girl. Paint her,' he ordered Bill Mitchell.

'She wants a fortune,' Mitchell reported some days later.

'Don't bother. I'll negotiate,' said Fayed. The next time Mitchell saw the model, she was playing in the jacuzzi. He was not surprised. Fayed regularly entertained the most beautiful girls, especially during the month the Miss World competition was staged in London. Miss Australia was Fayed's particular favourite, while Miss Brazil and her equally beautiful companion were welcome but not allowed to swim in the pool. Sipping Napoleon brandy from a paper cup, Fayed invented an excuse about the water, disguising his own fear that the black girls might deposit germs. His phobia extended to all pools. Only recently, at the Sheraton Hotel in Dubai, he had warned John Tilman, an employee, 'Don't go in the pool. You'll get syphilis.'

'More scared of germs than people,' thought Tilman.

Most of the girls visiting Oxted, whatever their motives for coming, understood the rules. No girl was ever invited to live with Fayed, none was allowed to stay long, but few were disappointed on departing. All left, as John Blower the gardener noticed, clutching a suitcase full of expensive gifts, bought on Fayed's Harrods account. The gardener would also relate the story of three girls, invited by Fayed to the house, 'weeping because he didn't want them'. Fayed's moods were variable. But he always enjoyed Blower's account of the goings-on during his employment at Kensington Palace. As a party piece, Blower would be summoned to relate the story about his hunt for Princess Margaret's knickers in the garden after a rowdy night with Peter Townsend, her ill-fated admirer. Repetition never blunted Fayed's taste for a good sex story.

*

HIS NEW WEALTH AND STATUS, Fayed knew, depended upon maintaining a close relationship with Mahdi Al Tajir. In 1972, one year after Dubai became independent as part of the UAE, Tajir had been appointed the federation's ambassador in London, and shortly after he was promoted to serve simultaneously as the director of Rashid's office. Tajir's eminence enhanced Fayed's own potential rewards. To entertain his benefactor, Fayed would arrive for weekend parties at his partner's latest acquisition, Windlesham Moor, a fifteen-bedroom residence occupying fifty-four acres in Surrey, including a nine-hole golf course, accompanied by celebrities including, to Tajir's pleasant surprise, Michael Caine and Roger Moore, new acquaintances whom Fayed had collected in St Tropez and Gstaad. Perhaps the Egyptian had brought the film stars as proof that he could rival his host's friendship with Abdul Halim Hafez, the Arab world's most popular singer whom he had introduced to Fayed on a previous occasion. But, to Tajir's surprise, the actors called their new friend 'Michael'. Fayed, smiled Tajir, never stopped inventing a new biography and a new life. Fayed could not however rival another of Tajir's acquisitions, Mereworth Castle, a Palladian mansion bought to house his new art collection.

Tajir's enormous wealth, earned from commissions and investments and now approaching £1 billion, encouraged Fayed's optimism that he could take a bigger share. Thanks to their alliance, he had earned a hefty commission from Bernard Sunley, the British builders awarded the contract to build the Trade Centre in Dubai. But manifestly it was an uncertain income. Notably, Fayed was absent from the grand opening of Port Rashid on 5 October 1972, a signal to onlookers that commission men were creatures of whim and favour rather than necessity. Indeed, there had been a hiccup in Fayed's fortunes.

To limit Tajir's influence, Sheikh Rashid had initially excluded his senior adviser, and accordingly Fayed, from any involvement that year in the construction of the Gulf's biggest dry dock. But by the following year negotiations for the one-million-ton dock had floundered. 'You'd better get Tajir back,' Neville Allen advised Rashid. Summoned in 1973 by the sheikh, the seemingly indispensable Tajir and in turn Fayed eventually claimed the commission and the credit from Costain for the initial £91 million contract, which would expand later into a £280 million development. That year, the opportunities for profits in the Middle East once again seemed truly limitless.

In the aftermath of Egypt's surprise attack on and humbling of Israel during the Yom Kippur War in 1973, the Arab oil producers grouped together in the oil cartel OPEC (the Organization of Petroleum Exporting Countries) decided to treble prices. Overnight, Middle Eastern sheikhs, formerly ridiculed as basket cases, became the world's most coveted customers as the annual incomes of Arab oil states soared. In the race to spend the Arabs' new wealth, Fayed yearned to emulate what had become the talk of the bazaar: Adnan Khashoggi's multi-billion-dollar arms deals brokered between America and Saudi Arabia. The stratagem, he had learnt, was to elevate himself from the status of a mere commission man.

Among the many teachers Fayed cultivated in order to learn about finance and sophisticated banking was Michael Ward, a young, ambitious corporate banker at Morgan Grenfell. Fayed regularly invited Ward to spend weekends at the George V in Paris, to play and to discuss business. Over meals in the best restaurants and over drinks in night clubs while beautiful women waited patiently near by, he would pick the banker's brain about the intricacies of the big deals dominating the news in London and New York. To Ward, Douglas-Home and their superiors, excited by the potential riches of Arab petrodollars, Fayed was an enticing prospect as an introducer of new business and they signed a commission agreement to pay 25 per cent of any fees for business introduced by him. Yet the bankers harboured few doubts about their client's morality. Repeatedly, during discussions in their City office, Fayed would make unguarded comments about a partner such as, 'He thinks we're going to pay him, but we won't,' or he would say, 'We can renegotiate the contract after it's signed.' The bankers would blanche: their client was evidently a pirate and a bandit. Characteristically for that breed, his priority was to win acceptance in the City as a respected player. His vehicle was Costain.

By the mid-1970s, the construction company had, thanks to Tajir and Fayed, won contracts worth £280 million in Dubai. The company's directors had received good value for the commissions. Convinced by Fayed's prediction that his close relations with Sheikh Rashid would deliver more contracts, they welcomed his new strategy. In December 1974, he bought 20.84 per cent of Costain's shares for £4.16 million. Without any proof, the directors had assumed that Tajir was a silent partner in the deal. Five months later, Fayed was appointed a company director. At forty-six, regarded as a reliable Arab entrepreneur in London, he was an interesting prospect for British companies seeking business from the oil-rich Arabs.

Among those desperate for introductions to Middle Eastern wealth was one of London's established players, Roland 'Tiny' Rowland. A meeting between Rowland and the Egyptian was arranged by Soubi Roushdi, a lawyer and an acquaintance of Fayed's from Alexandria, employed in London by an Iraqi bank.

Buccaneer, tycoon, deal-maker and commercial terrorist, Tiny Rowland was established in London as an intrepid business baron whose charm and cultivated manner disguised a manipulative conspirator trading in character assassination to win financial and political advantages. In crucial traits, he mirrored a later Fayed: a foreign outsider and self-made multi-millionaire who was denied approval by the British establishment and so had become a rebel tycoon.

He was born Roland Fuhrhop in a British internment camp in India on 27 November 1917 to a German businessman and his British-born wife, who had been incarcerated soon after the outbreak of the First World War by the British authorities as undesirable aliens. Returning to Hamburg in 1920, the Fuhrhops prospered. Initially, after Hitler became chancellor in 1933, Nazism was so impregnated into Tiny that he was appointed leader of a Hitler Youth group. Even after moving to Britain in 1934 on his mother's orders to complete his education, Tiny Fuhrhop's Nazi sympathies and anti-Semitism were noted by his headmaster at Churchers College in Hampshire.

At the outbreak of war in 1939, the twenty-two-year-old British citizen formally changed his name to Rowland, but his loyalties remained so pro-German that he was rejected by Field Intelligence on security grounds and conscripted into the Medical Corps. Based in Scotland, Private Rowland was assigned to clean latrines and hump stores. 'The worst period of my life,' he later complained, referring to his imprisonment for twenty-seven days in Barlinnie prison after a court martial for desertion. By then, convinced of Hitler's inevitable victory, Rowland associated with prominent British Nazi sympathizers and, on hearing in 1941 that the battleships *Repulse* and *Prince of Wales* had been sunk, publicly paraded his joy. Detained as a danger to Britain's security, Rowland had been interned in the Isle of Man with his parents and other British fascists. 'A very good and loyal German,' a camp official would later describe the young Nazi.

Released in early 1945, Rowland returned penniless to London. After working briefly as a porter at Paddington station, targeting the first-class compartments for big tips, he searched for business opportunities, selling chickens to London's night clubs, dealing in army surplus stores and driving taxis at night. By 1946, Rowland had realized that his wartime allegiances were damaging his prospects. Deliberately, he concealed all his German antecedents (on his marriage certificate he would falsely name his father William Rowland rather than Wilhelm Fuhrhop), adopted the patrician air of a British gentleman with a suitably cut-glass accent and, with three partners, began manufacturing refrigerators, which were in great demand in postwar Britain. Within one year, he was driving a Bentley and a Mercedes around London. But in 1948 the business collapsed. Rowland was investigated by the Inland Revenue and ordered to repay £200,000 in taxes. Marked as dishonest, he emigrated to Southern Rhodesia, the British colony in Africa known as the 'Garden of Eden', to become a farmer.

By 1954, Rowland was broke. Returning to Europe, he

became involved in a fraud. Posing as 'Ernest Raven', he presented forged documents to a Swiss bank in Basle suggesting that he owned 620 tons of Polish copper and walked out carrying a suitcase stuffed with banknotes worth £2.3 million in today's values. The Swiss police never identified the phantom 'Raven' but arrested and jailed his unwitting partner, Dusko Popov, the famed Second World War British double agent.

Flush with stolen money, Rowland returned to Rhodesia and began investing in gold mines, car dealerships and social relationships. Investors in Rowland's first gold mine discovered that his prospectus was false, but never recovered their considerable losses. Subsequent investors in his copper and emerald mines also rued their stupidity for succumbing to Rowland's charm. In 1961, in the midst of building an oil pipeline from the Indian Ocean to landlocked Rhodesia, Rowland was recruited by Angus Ogilvy, who was seeking a wheeler-dealer to resuscitate the collapsing fortunes of Lonrho, the London & Rhodesia Mining and Land Company. 'I cleaned the pants off Ogilvy,' Rowland later boasted of his treatment of the Old Etonian. 'I had him eating out of my hands.' Ogilvy had gratefully accepted Rowland's offer of a tax-avoidance deal to enrich himself substantially. 'I was out of my depth,' Ogilvy would later confess when confronted with the dishonesty. Rowland had cheated Lonrho's shareholders by submitting false valuations of his own mines which were to be merged into Lonrho. He went on to ignore repeated accusations of criminality – including a South African arrest warrant for fraud – and the charge that he used the public company as his private piggy bank. But Lonrho's fortunes indeed appeared to revive dramatically under his management. 'Africa is down,' he told friends. 'It can only go up.' Delighting in crisscrossing the continent in his private aircraft, the lone gun stealthily peddled influence among Africa's dictators. 'There's not a single man I could not buy,' Rowland bragged. 'Every man has his price.' Corruption did not trouble the self-deprecating tycoon as he bought politicians for what were known within Lonrho as 'seeds well sown' or 'special payments'.

By 1971, surrounding himself in mystery but keen to portray himself as a modern Cecil Rhodes, Rowland was running a company that employed 100,000 people in twenty-nine countries producing or trading a huge assortment of merchandise from sugar to newspapers, platinum to beer, diamonds to railways, and motorcars to gold. Yet in his quest to build an international empire Rowland had attracted controversy, government investigations and doubts about his finances. Prevented by exchange controls from remitting to Britain Lonrho's profits in Africa, he allowed the company's assets to be overvalued for its accounts. For years, he had employed compliant accountants – 'paper merchants' he dubbed them – to massage the annual accounts and ramp up the share price. In the City, where Rowland was cast as a 'freelance vagabond' unwilling to play by the rules in his risky foreign adventures, there was neither sympathy nor support as Lonrho veered towards bankruptcy. As the share price slumped and accurate reports of Lonrho's dishonesty swept the City, Warburgs, the merchant bankers, resigned as the company's advisers. Rowland's ambitions, it was said, were misconceived. He was a deal maker, not a manager. Criticized as 'Rhodes without the vision', Rowland replied, 'Who cares about the vision as long as I build the empire?'

To improve Lonrho's status, Rowland appointed new directors, including Edward du Cann, MP, a fallen star in the Conservative Party, and Duncan Sandys, the former Conservative minister and Winston Churchill's son-in-law. When other Lonrho directors requested the details of a secret payment to Sandys, protected by a tax-evasion scheme, Rowland lied. Indignant about Rowland's dishonesty, the directors in 1973 revolted and demanded his resignation. A ferocious, public boardroom battle erupted. Each day, newspapers published stories about Rowland's perfidy, provoking unprecedented condemnation of Lonrho's chicanery from the prime minister,

Edward Heath, who castigated the company as the 'unpleasant and unacceptable face of capitalism'. Not everyone was critical, least of all Lonrho's shareholders, who flocked to the banner of the capitalist adventurer. Brilliantly, Rowland survived the coup and forced the majority of Lonrho's directors to quit. 'You're oversexed,' Rowland was told. Surprised by the accusation, he demanded an explanation. 'You like screwing people,' was the reply. Amorality had triumphed over virtue, yet the humiliation rankled ever after, tainting Rowland's opinion of British politicians, especially after Heath ordered an investigation of Lonrho by the Department of Trade and Industry (DTI).

*

ONE YEAR LATER, in 1974, Rowland was indulging in a buying spree to expand Lonrho, although, as so often, the company was short of money. To finance his ambitions, he chose to sell Lonrho shares to new investors. Targeting the newly enriched Arabs, Rowland's first successful seduction had been the Sabahs, the ruling family of Kuwait, who became Lonrho's single largest shareholder. Seeking another Arab investor, Rowland spent some time in Egypt, and eventually Soubi Roushdi suggested that Mohamed Fayed was a potential although unknown investor.

Visiting Fayed in his Park Lane penthouse, Rowland was certainly surprised. Unlike the erudite, aesthetic Rowland, the Egyptian appeared to be obsessed with sex. Scattered on the coffee table were picture books of voluptuous women in a variety of suggestive poses which the bachelor made no attempt to conceal. His spluttered, expletive-ridden English was offensive to Rowland, with his ear for the rounded sentence, and enhanced the visitor's impression that there was little to distinguish Africans and Arabs, and nothing to distinguish Egyptians from other Arabs. Rowland's genial patter, developed over twenty-five years in Africa, concealed that prejudice.

Posing as a tycoon of a major British company with vast international relationships and deep roots in the British establishment, Rowland affected his smoothest public school intonations to excite Fayed with visions of 'a triangular relationship between the Arab, African and European worlds' and a 'partnership' between equals. 'Together we can do so much,' purred Rowland. 'Invest in Lonrho. Inject your Costain shares into Lonrho and become one of our directors.' Cast in an unaccustomed role, Fayed was more than flattered by Rowland's approach: he was awed. Instead of the salesman or servant, he was the quarry. Images of banking millions of petrodollar profits flashed across his mind. 'I have much in common with this man,' he thought. Some would say that Rowland was more cunning, yet he had a weakness: he tended to trust those whom he could buy.

Enthusiastically, Fayed agreed to Rowland's offer. Under the £7 million deal in March 1975, Rowland exchanged 5.5 million Lonrho shares for Fayed's stake in Costain and paid an extra £375,000. With £3 million profit on his Costain shares, Fayed bought a further 4 million Lonrho shares and became a Lonrho director and Lonrho's representative on Costain's board.

The welcome accorded to Fayed at his first Lonrho board meeting was gushing. Sitting in the spartan conference room in Cheapside, so different from the wood-panelled boardrooms favoured by Britain's traditional companies, Fayed was introduced as 'a major player in the Middle East'. Looking at his fellow directors, he recalled how Rowland had once scathingly dubbed them 'Christmas-tree decorations'. They certainly seemed slavishly obedient. That was not objectionable. Rowland's approach to business, he believed, mirrored his own. Sending Ali to attend Lonrho's board meetings on his behalf, he would rely on Rowland while he pursued his other interests. Ali's shy, intelligent manner, which was on display even when he was attending the desultory meetings of the Anglo-Arab

Chamber of Commerce, was a marvellous smokescreen given that, in negotiation, manipulation and deception, he nearly ranked as his brother's equal.

But divorce was mentioned before the honeymoon ended. 'Everything is arranged and agreed before I even get there,' Ali griped. 'He presents us with deals and figures, wants us to nod like fools and then leaves.' Rowland, it was clear, expected silent compliance. He resented even telephone calls with suggestions for new ventures. 'He wants me to be a zombie,' raged Fayed. Another discovery was more disturbing. Rowland, he found, used Lonrho's money as his own. The company jet was frequently dispatched to Africa to collect a friend's wife or deliver a politician to his home. Lonrho was educating the children of African friends and funding 'investments in people'. Paying bribes, especially on that scale, unsettled Mohamed Fayed. 'He's spending thousands on nothing!' he exclaimed. Confronting Rowland, he demanded an explanation.

'In Africa, Tootsie,' smiled Rowland using his new nickname for the Egyptian, 'you need to invest long term.'

'But where are the profits?' asked Fayed, concerned about his personal investment.

His partner smiled but did not answer. He was, Fayed knew, syphoning off profits into a secret personal Swiss bank account.

In early 1976, Fayed's irritation with Rowland turned to alarm. Gossips in Cheapside were chanting Rowland's latest outburst: 'They're coming down against us.' Rowland's fellow directors mirrored their master's fury that two DTI inspectors were investigating Lonrho. 'That ignorant lawyer and accountant think they can understand international business,' screeched Paul Spicer, the most notable nonentity in Rowland's constellation. Inexperienced in the ways of British government, Fayed was bewildered by the jumble of accusations about the misuse of Lonrho's money. Even Lonrho's accountants, it appeared, had been deceived and the company's 1974 accounts distorted to assist the deception. 'Tyranny and madness,' complained disgruntled accountants, echoing the testimony to the DTI inspectors of former directors describing a man who 'made promises to people, sometimes fulfilled them but always made them dependent upon him'. That, reflected Fayed, was now happening to him. Rowland's extraordinary self-revelation to the inspectors – 'I always assumed my right to do as I pleased . . . I felt that the whole show belonged to me' – confirmed his lack of repentance.

Rowland's own reaction to the inspectors' investigation struck Fayed as bizarre. 'They are using unreliable evidence,' he told Fayed. 'Inaccuracies and prejudices drawn from every fragment of nastiness.' Rowland, Fayed noted, was ruthless in his determination to prevent publication of the DTI's report. Firstly, he had unsuccessfully tried to blackmail Sir Angus Ogilvy, the former Lonrho director now married to Princess Alexandra, the queen's cousin, by releasing letters proving that Ogilvy had been a party to unlawful decisions. Secondly, Edward du Cann, at Rowland's instigation, had threatened in the House of Commons to embarrass the government by revealing secret British conspiracies in Africa.

Rowland's public declaration of war against Whitehall and Westminster persuaded Fayed to disentangle himself from Lonrho. 'I've entered a whorehouse and I want to get out,' Fayed told a Kuwaiti investor. 'I'm afraid my money will disappear if I stay.' Although the Egyptian still could not completely understand the company's accounts, he feared that his precious millions were endangered. In a parallel deal on 29 May 1976, Fayed resigned his Lonrho directorship, sold his Lonrho shares to the Kuwaiti investors, and bought back his Costain shares from Lonrho for £11 million. Fayed had earned over £8 million in the deal, which minimized the acrimony as he bid Rowland farewell. The two, it seemed, were unlikely to meet again.

*

FLUSH WITH NEW PROFITS, Fayed indulged in a favoured pastime – spending. In Paris he bought a small apartment block off the Champs-Élysées, in New York he purchased a lease on 75 Rockefeller Plaza, while at Balnagown he negotiated to buy 30,000 acres around the castle for £2.3 million and embarked on a restoration programme of the building and distillery, landscaping the surrounding four lochs, restoring the Italian garden and rebuilding the stag herd. Local gossip about the mysterious Arab laird, jetting up from London to Inverness, flying to the castle by helicopter and driving along the North Sea coast in his Roll-Royce – the first of sixty-four which he would claim to own – flattered his self-importance.

Flying to Dubai in 1976, he had every reason to believe his star was in perpetual ascendant. Construction of the thirty-nine-storey Trade Centre, which would be completed in two years, had earned him a 15 per cent commission from Bernard Sunley on the £100 million contract. Negotiations were under way for a £120 million contract to build a further twenty-two berths in the port and there were plans to build a giant aluminium smelter. All, he hoped, would produce hefty commissions. Negotiation of the smelter's construction was a particularly succulent prize. Fayed had called Paul Brauner, the managing director of the British Smelter Construction Company, who had won the $1.2 billion contract. 'I want you to meet the board of Morgan Grenfell,' said Fayed. 'Come to Park Lane.'

'You can get the whole board to your office?' asked Brauner, wondering how an unknown Arab could marshal Lord Catto, David Douglas-Home and other directors and managers at his command.

'They'll come when I tell them,' laughed Fayed.

To Brauner's surprise, the whole board was indeed waiting when he arrived in the penthouse. At Tajir's behest, the bank was to be given the syndication rights to finance the smelter. Brauner unquestioningly accepted Tajir's instructions. 'Fayed's the messenger boy,' he realized. Six weeks later, accepting another invitation to the penthouse, he understood that Fayed was also a money man.

'I'll give you £1 million', offered Fayed, 'if you move the building contract from Wimpey to Costain.'

'Impossible,' replied Brauner. He nevertheless finally relented, 'in the interests of prudence', and awarded Fayed's company a minor contract worth £22 million in the smelter's construction, albeit without accepting the £1 million. Delighted to be collecting commission from both Morgan Grenfell and Costain, Fayed sent Brauner a case of 'Dodi' whisky, specially distilled in Balnagown. The only impediment to Fayed's future fortunes was a deterioration in his relationship with Tajir, whose own position in Dubai had weakened.

Accepting exaggerated descriptions of himself in British newspapers as 'the world's richest man with a £2 billion fortune', Tajir had, during his ambassadorship in London, bought thirty town houses, country mansions and castles across Britain and Europe and Texas. The 'Chic Sheikh', who blithely bought twenty suits in one visit to Savile Row, had amassed an exceptional collection of gold and silver antiques and other *objets d'art*, and had used his diplomatic status to fix commercial deals with the world's big players. But his influence in Dubai suffered as Sheikh Rashid encouraged educated young Dubaians to replace the Bahraini. To protect himself during his visit to Dubai, Fayed attempted several new ruses. Firstly, he appointed Humeid bin Drai, Rashid's boisterous head of protocol, as Costain's representative. Secondly, he offered Jabber Abdullah, the sheikh's friend and bodyguard, generous entertainment during his visits to London. But those ploys, he knew, were insufficient. Unlike Tajir, neither of his appointees was sufficiently sophisticated in business. So, increasingly desperate, he sought the help of St John Armitage, the wily British consul in Dubai, to promote Costain rather than Wimpey, a rival company. 'I've done so much for British business,' pleaded Fayed. Armitage, a former soldier, was unimpressed. In his opinion, commission agents were grubby and an Egyptian declaiming about his contribution to British business was irritating.

'The man's talking bullshit,' he told a colleague. 'He's the epitome of all the dozens of commission agents I've met. He's got no special status.' Convinced that paying commissions was 'damaging to British business', Armitage established himself as Fayed's opponent, warning British companies that the Arab lacked influence. 'Just bid with locals,' he told the directors of Wimpey, hoping that the construction company would outbid Costain.

Sensing the new mood, Fayed returned to London to ponder more bad news. His virtual exclusion from the contracts for the new aluminium smelter had reflected the fading prospect of involvement in contracts to build a new tax-free zone in Jebel Ali. Although Costain's share price was still high, its future profits were uncertain. Quietly, Fayed sold his 20 per cent stake in November 1977 for £15 million, bringing him a profit of £10.84 million. Assuming a roughly equal share on the £85 million of commissions earned with Tajir, he had earned at least £50 million in Dubai. In ten years, therefore, he had made at least £60 million, a respectable prize for a small player. His absence in 1979 from the queen's formal opening of the Trade Centre confirmed that his influence in Rashid's palace had declined. His only consolation for the end of the glory days was a twenty-year contract granted by the sheikh to manage the Trade Centre.

At fifty, Fayed was enjoying a lifestyle that suggested he was celebrating. He was occupying the entire seventh floor of 60 Park Lane, where in his latest renovation he had fitted on to the interior walls oak panels stripped from English castles. With the thick Persian carpets, this gave his home and office a sumptuous air. Few passing through this establishment could remain unaware of their host's fascination with Britain. 'I love this country,' he would repeat, his sincerity only too evident. Sitting on a low sofa in front of a small antique table, enjoying an uninterrupted view across Hyde Park through a spectacular wall of glass, he was often surrounded by overflowing filing trays and the debris of newspapers discarded on the floor –

speedily scanned for pretty girls and potentially profitable opportunities. Identical black briefcases for London, Paris, Dubai and New York stood in a precise row alongside a series of identical white telephones. 'Between the potted orchids and the perfume-injected air', wrote Tiny Rowland later, 'was the delicious smell of lots of money, and it attracted many, many influential visitors from the City and from politics.'

Below, in flat number 47, he employed four secretaries, although only his personal assistant was trusted with his cash, kept in his desk, whose key Abdul retained. Unlike other executives in London, Fayed preferred to pay in cash. Gigantic sums – brick high – in bank notes were collected from a nearby branch of the Midland Bank. It was, the Egyptian would say, 'just a practicality to facilitate my life'. Shamelessly peeling off banknotes from a wodge or plucking a brick from his briefcase, he regularly pushed the cash towards staff and others in manner characteristic of a dealer. Cash payments as a reward for service, for loyalty and even for friendship were not bribes but traceless recognition of gratitude. Solitary, occasionally reclusive and often feeling unloved, Fayed used banknotes to secure the attention, affection and indebtedness which others attracted by their character and conduct.

To swell his performance, Fayed had hired as his butler Sydney Johnson, the black valet previously employed by the Duke and Duchess of Windsor, whose arms had cradled the dying monarch. Dressed in striped trousers and black jacket, Sydney served an unusual diet prepared by the Nubian cook Abdul in Park Lane and by Abdullah, an Indian, in Oxted, which pandered to his employer's increasing terror of illness and of death. Fayed, whispered Ed Brown, the manager of Genavco, was becoming 'a bit of a hermit'.

In what would later be diagnosed as an obsessive compulsive disorder, Fayed's fear of germs had developed into a psychoneurosis. Nothing in his mind was uglier than illness and death. Gradually, he preferred not to eat in restaurants and, unless certain about his host's hygiene, preferred to decline offers of drink and food. He ate an increasingly strictly healthy diet including kiwi fruit, yogurt and goat's milk. The fear of germs had extended to his medical care. To avoid cross-contamination from the sterilized instruments used on other patients, a fully equipped dentist's surgery had been built in a room in Park Lane and for his annual medical check-up at the London Clinic he brought in aluminium suitcases the equipment the doctors would require. But his frenzy with health did not undermine the bachelor's interest in sex.

Managing his flat was a German woman, who recruited pretty young girls with the promise of good pay and accommodation to care for the three brothers and Dodi. Dressed in seductive gingham dresses with white knickers, white bras and white socks to accentuate their youth, the girls were regularly encouraged by Fayed with the admonition, 'You like working for me? You look after me and I look after you.' Surprisingly, few of the girls' bedrooms, on the floor below the penthouse, could be locked. His accumulation of girls reflected his search for business opportunities: it was a question of spreading the risk. He hoped that with ten balls in the air just one would land a new bonanza.

By 1979, the Big One in business terms was still elusive, despite Fayed's focus on oil, banking, shipping and property. Excluded from oil trading in Dubai, he negotiated with Ameress, Armand Hammer's subsidiary, for a minority stake in oil exploration in the emirate of Abu Dhabi, also part of the UAE. Any results would be apparent only years later. In banking, he paid $4.3 million for a 70 per cent stake in the People's Bank of Houston, borrowing nearly half his investment in the £50 million bank, which specialized in property loans. Serious profits could take years to materialize. His dream of building a shipping empire to rival those of the Greek tycoons had faded. In Teleprak Street, Cairo, there was an office with just one employee; Castro Shipping in Suez remained a sign without business; and there were unpolished Genavco name-plates on buildings in Piraeus, Genoa and London. Under Genavco's supervision, the Dubai Trading and Trust Centre, employing about forty people, acted as a shipping agent for the Barber Shipping Line, Lloyd's Triestino and Orient Overseas, a small business producing low profits. Fayed's major investment was the replacement of the *Dalia* and *Mudi Star* with three new German 1,600 ton roll-on roll-off ferries. Bought through the Genoan company Gilnavi with an £18 million loan, the money was secured against the Bermuda-registered ships, a customary usage in the shipping world to reduce taxation and protect the vessel from seizure for debt in foreign ports. In total, it represented a small business with no prospect of substantial growth. It was an unsatisfactory position for an aspiring tycoon, jealous of his mentors Khashoggi and Tajir and desperately searching for acceptance by the outside world.

The hard graft was finally rewarded during a visit to Paris. Fayed heard from Frank Klein, a German born near Bonn, employed as a junior manager at the George V, that Monique Ritz, the widow of Charles Ritz, was searching for a buyer for her world-famous but delapidated hotel. Walking around the building in the beautiful Place Vendôme, Fayed was excited by the possibility of combining his new passion for building and design with the notion of hosting the world's celebrities and mega-rich amid luxury. Since the hotel's past clientele included Marcel Proust, Charlie Chaplin, Marlene Dietrich, Humphrey Bogart and Ernest Hemingway, he could hope to attract similar legends. Ownership of the Ritz, he fantasized, would provide an entrée to their club. The cost was irrelevant. Somewhere, he would find a willing banker. 'Do you want to buy the Ritz with me?' he asked Tajir.

'No,' replied his partner. 'Hotels in Paris are seasonal businesses. The profits are no good. London's much better.' Profits were not on Fayed's mind.

Advised by Marcus Agius at Lazards, a banking relationship which Fayed rightly judged bestowed upon him approval and credibility, he bought the Ritz in March 1979 for £9 million, through The Ritz Paris Holding Ltd, a company based in Jersey. There was limited publicity about the purchase, but that did not stop Fayed from posing as an architectural specialist and an expert hotelier. The Fayed family, he told enquiring journalists, had great experience in the management of luxury hotels in Egypt. Shepheard's, the world-famous hotel in Cairo, was somehow associated with the Fayed family. The announcement of Fayed's purchase of Paris's 'most famous hotel' on 30 March also mentioned that over the years the new owner had built up a number of businesses in Europe and America specializing in banking, insurance and, mysteriously, the arms trade. The press release finally mentioned his pledge to spend between 60 and 70 million francs in developing the hotel, where he had stayed as a child 'for a few days' holiday with my parents'. His first appointment was Frank Klein as the new manager: despite professing great love for the British, Fayed trusted and admired most the Germanic race. A second call was to London. 'I've bought a hotel!' he shouted at Bill Mitchell, the designer, over a crackly telephone line.

'The Ritz in Paris, I suppose,' laughed Mitchell.

'How did you know?'

'It's the only hotel in the world you'd want to own.'

'Come over immediately. I need your help.'

Walking around the hotel like Napoleon after Austerlitz, Fayed regarded the debris of a once proud monument as a challenge and a victory. Fireplaces, tapestries and other fixtures had been removed. The hotel was to be rebuilt over the following six years around the customers, with plaster falling into their coffee. Appointing two firms of architects and five interior designers, Fayed intended the modernized, air-conditioned hotel to present an atmosphere of intimate luxury with silks, velvets, special wallpapers and marble. A hole, three floors deep, would be excavated beneath the hotel for a swimming pool, a health centre, a banqueting hall and a new kitchen. Money would not be an obstacle to his dream.

*

THE PURCHASE COINCIDED with Fayed's developing affair with Heini Wathen, a twenty-four-year-old Finnish model whom he proclaimed to love. Surprisingly, the Cupid had been Dodi.

Two years earlier, in 1977, Dodi had travelled through Scandanavia posing as a film producer searching for new talent. Ever since Albert 'Cubby' Broccoli, the Hollywood producer, had in 1971 invited Dodi, the friend of his daughter, to watch the shooting of the James Bond movie *Live and Let Die* in Pinewood, the impressionable twenty-four-year-old had begged his father to invest in films. Steadfastly, Fayed had refused to succumb to his son's pleas, which he judged were either designed to effect an escape from solitude or an excuse to meet pretty girls. Despite his love for Dodi, his son's sleepwalk through life was causing him concern. Compared to himself at the age of twenty-two, Dodi was unambitious, feckless and self-indulgent. At worst, he was a spoilt, petulant playboy. His fire and drive appeared to be dedicated to chasing girls in Annabel's and Tramp, his favourite night clubs, and to spending much of the following day in bed, sometimes with the girls. Rising at lunchtime, Dodi usually ate in Harry's Bar or at other expensive restaurants with friends, watched a film, ate dinner and, late at night, resumed his life in the clubs. At best, he was a Peter Pan dreamer. Thankfully, Victor Lownes had agreed to bar the young man from gambling at the Claremont, the Mayfair club. Screaming at his son and cutting his allowance had little effect. On the contrary, Dodi simply telephoned his uncle, Adnan Khashoggi, to send a jet and joined his cousins either in the Mediterranean or America, especially the Beverly Hills Hotel in Los Angeles, to continue chasing girls and occasionally taking drugs. To Mohamed Fayed's resentment, only the Khashoggis provided Dodi with any semblance of family life in their homes and on their boats. Yet it was Dodi, despite his loathsome weaknesses, who had given Fayed a glimpse of happiness.

Dodi had arrived in 1977 in Helsinki, ostensibly as a film

producer, clutching a catalogue of models represented by the Sanelma Vuorre agency and searching for new faces. Five years earlier, his father, with the help of Klaus Skold, had done the same. Posing as a film producer based at Helsinki's Intercontinental Hotel, Fayed had led young models into believing that he was casting for a James Bond film. Those who seemed interesting were invited to London, Scotland or St Tropez. Dodi was following a tested path when he met Heini Wathen, the daughter of a fish cook and boarding-house owner in Hanko, a small seaside resort sixty miles from the Finnish capital, had enrolled with the agency after winning the Miss Hanko Summer and the Miss Viking Princess competitions in 1972. After leaving school in 1975, Wathen had followed her sister Heidi to Paris to become a model and find the ideal husband. Two years later, she temporarily returned to Helsinki to compete in the Miss Finland competition. After reaching the last ten she was eliminated, but in compensation she met Dodi and received an offer of a career in films. Dodi and Heini enjoyed a friendly relationship in Helsinki and Paris, where she modelled Finnish designs, before he introduced his latest friend to his father. Excited by Scandinavian girls, especially those he met at Régines night club, Fayed was particularly struck by Heini's purity. Although the fifty-eight-year-old Arab had not altered his cavalier attitude towards women, the wounds of his divorce had healed and he was desperate for a new family. In the same year that Ali married Tracey, Fayed committed himself to Heini by inviting her to live with him in Park Lane. The reward for Dodi was his father's agreement to finance his son's chosen career.

'My son wants to go into films,' Fayed told Richard Shuttleworth, his solicitor at Freshfields, 'and I'm going to finance him.' There was also a project. Elliott Kastner, an American producer, had enticed Fayed to invest £1.5 million in his next film, *Yesterday's Hero*, written by Jackie Collins and starring Ian McShane as a football hero. Cautioning his client, Shuttleworth suggested consulting David Norris, a lawyer with considerable experience in Hollywood. The advice was judicious. Efficiently, Norris demolished the Kastner proposition as a glaring pitfall for amateurs. 'Don't touch it,' Norris warned. The £2 million budget was structured to prevent Fayed earning any profit on his investment. Appreciating Norris's talent, Fayed welcomed the lawyer's suggestion that he appoint Timothy Burrill, a talented film producer, to manage his new film company, Allied Stars, a name similar to United Star, one of his shipping companies. 'Dodi is chief executive,' Fayed announced, explaining that he would not be a director of his son's company, though it was supported by '£90 million of my own money'. Burrill agreed to become managing director after Fayed promised, 'You get ten per cent of any profits.' He then presented an employment contract for Fayed's signature. 'Don't you trust me?' asked Fayed. 'I don't think it's necessary. I gave you my word.' To the Egyptian's delight, Burrill politely succumbed. Backed by Burrill's expertise, the birth of Allied Stars in Pinewood was announced at the Cannes film festival. At last Dodi was in the film business, with an expensively furnished suite of offices decorated with sepia photographs of yachts at Cowes.

Burrill launched Allied Stars energetically into its first production, *Breaking Glass*, a musical directed by Brian Gibson. Regularly, Burrill arranged meetings with the Fayeds, proposed new projects, submitted minutes of their discussions and invited Dodi, the executive producer, to visit the set and view the rushes of his first film. After a few weeks it dawned on him that the pace of his activities was irritating his employer. Dodi Fayed was uninterested either in managing the film's finances or in supervising its artistic development. He was irked by the manager's expectation that he would put in appearances at his Pinewood office, and his four visits to the film set were notable only for his unexpected offers of cocaine. 'The screening's at twelve midday in Audley Square,' he was told by Burrill when the film was completed. 'It's just one hundred yards from your flat. You'll be there, won't you?'

'No problem,' replied Dodi, replacing the telephone receiver. Repeated calls at 11.45, at midday and at 12.15 all received the same assurance: 'I'll be there. Fine.' Dodi never arrived. Lying in bed with a woman, he was snorting cocaine. Girls and glamour were the only pursuits of a rich boy indifferent to the new toy provided by his father. Burrill and Norris had finally understood that, while the Fayeds spoke grandiosely about creating a major film empire, their finances were limited and Dodi's main interest was to bask in the spotlight. The proof was Dodi's reaction after watching, at Burrills's insistence, ten minutes of *The Long Good Friday*. As a potential investment, he declared, the film was 'boring' and not worth financing. It would become a legendary success.

Amid much razzmatazz, *Breaking Glass* was screened in May 1980 at the Cannes film festival. While Allied's employees wore T-shirts emblazoned with 'Dodi Fayed Picture Company' on the front and 'Chariots of Fire' on the back, Mohamed Fayed was ensconced on the SS *Dodi*, his schooner, in the harbour, posing as royalty-cum-tycoon, entertaining celebrities and his staff.

'Front row for me,' Fayed demanded for the screening, anxious to be seen.

'Afraid not, Mr Al Fayed,' he was told. 'That's reserved for the actors and directors.'

Undaunted, Fayed arrived with a large entourage and filled the second row. To reinforce his presence, he hosted a wild, all-night party, although, to avoid the rabble, he himself remained in an adjacent, guarded room. Critically and commercially, the film flopped. While Fayed lost about £50,000, the other financiers went bankrupt. 'It's your fault!' Fayed unjustifiably screamed at David Norris. 'You've taken bribes.' Making false accusations had become Fayed's favoured method for terminating contracts without paying compensation. His disloyalty towards honest, diligent employees as part of a bid to save money was particularly brutal in Norris's case because the lawyer had delivered *Chariots of Fire*, already destined to be a success.

Until 1979, David Puttnam, the director, had obtained no financial support for the film about two British athletes competing for the 100 metre sprint in the 1924 Olympics. Fayed was Puttnam's last hope. Unwilling to read the script, Fayed could not understand why the public would pay to see a film about two sprinters without sex, beautiful women or fast cars. A group of Hollywood executives, invited by Dodi to make a pitch in Park Lane, sat bemused as, halfway through their discussion, Fayed turned to his son and shouted, 'You're an idiot! An idiot!' Dodi, the chairman of the company, stared straight ahead in silent embarrassment. Those watching the two men understood their relationship only too well. Dodi's opinion was unrequested. To decide whether he should invest in *Chariots*, Fayed had delegated David Norris to fly to Los Angeles and deliver the definitive advice. 'Do it,' reported Norris and negotiated a deal with Twentieth Century-Fox. The guarantee for Fayed's $3 million investment was telexed by Banque Gonet. United Star Shipping, the Geneva bank assured Hollywood, 'controlled assets worth $100 million', though Fayed did not reveal that most of the company's unquantified assets had been pledged against loans. Allied Stars bought a 25 per cent stake in the film.

Fayed's hope that Allied Stars' commitment to *Chariots* would alter Dodi's life was misplaced. Regularly, in London, Dodi encouraged friends while dining in restaurants to join him in the lavatories to snort cocaine. He was thrown out of Nikita's, his favourite Russian restaurant, by the outraged owner. Undeterred, Dodi invited his friends to his flat in Park Lane. On a rare visit to the set where the *Chariots* training scenes were being shot in Scotland, he even handed out cocaine to the cast. 'Get out!' Puttnam told Dodi, forcibly ejecting the executive producer from the set. 'Don't ever come back again.'

Before the film was completed, Mohamed Fayed began to

fear that he would lose his investment and sold out with the proviso of a share of profits if the film succeeded. To his surprise, *Chariots* was the hit of 1981, winning four Oscars. 'I watched the rushes every night,' Fayed would thereafter boast, furious that Dodi rather than himself was presented to the queen at the London première. The immediate casualties had been Allied's senior staff. In a burst of pique, Fayed had fired the executives four days earlier and withdrawn their tickets to the screening. Allied collected about $6 million in profits, paid to Sprint NV, a Dutch company. The casualty was Timothy Burrill, who failed to receive his 10 per cent. His agreement with Fayed had only been oral, after all.

Chariots' unexpected success rejuvenated Fayed's interest in films. Irritated that Goldcrest, Puttnam's company, claimed the credit owed to Allied, he placed advertisements in the trade press lauding Allied Stars and announcing the first ever payment of $1 million for the film rights of a Stephen King book and the production of a new film, *The World According to Garp*. Neither investment would be a commercial success. The prospect of new deals, nevertheless, transformed Dodi's life. Although his contribution to *Chariots* had been minimal, his name as executive producer was emblazoned on the credits and on the posters. Aspiring film actresses snapped up his invitations. In a new burst of extravagance calculated to win friends and find appreciation, the vulnerable man who did not threaten vulnerable women was delighted to provide a consoling cushion for the troubled in a glamorous world. Emulating his father, the new producer sought to buy affection and friendship by recklessly indulging in expensive junkets in London, in Paris and on the Côte d'Azur, showering gifts on film actresses like Brooke Shields and Koo Stark, with no chance of earning back the money he was spending. In London, Fayed became infuriated by his son's decadence. After a series of lashing rebukes, he abruptly halted any financial support. Overnight, Dodi's credit cards were dishonoured and the payment of his hotel bills refused. The schooner *Dodi* reverted to her original name *Sakara*. The father–son relationship was frozen.

Maintaining stable friendships had always been difficult for Mohamed Fayed. Emotional and unreasoning, he was unable to ignore any irritation if money was not at stake. But the additional ingredient had been the birth on 5 December 1980 of Jasmine, Fayed's first child by Heini. Silently, Dodi feared that his unique relationship with his father was threatened. Fayed did little to reassure his son despite his apparent reluctance to marry Heini. The child's birth certificate confirmed the double life he favoured. The family's home address was given as Park Lane rather than Oxted, where Heini lived with the baby while he remained during the week in London, and Fayed did not include 'Al' in his name. His confusion of reality and fantasy, a major influence on his breach with Dodi, also fractured his relationship with Mahdi Al Tajir, still the ambassador of the United Arab Emirates in London.

*

FLYING INTO HEATHROW or Luton, Fayed had regularly used the VIP facilities provided for diplomats and heads of state. Still citing his status as Sheikh Rashid's special representative, he had claimed the privileges due to a Dubaian diplomat despite the absence of any documentary proof. Officials at Heathrow had become suspicious and eventually the Foreign Office asked Tajir to explain precisely what Fayed's status was. The ambassador's relationship with Fayed was already strained. He had deliberately excluded the Egyptian from any involvement in the development of Jebel Ali, a huge tax-free industrial zone fifteen miles along the coast from the capital. But Tajir's own star was also waning once again. During a confrontation in a Majlis, he had been accused by a younger rival of unreasonably demanding commissions and, although his denials had been accepted, Rashid's imminent death undermined his position.

When the Foreign Office's enquiry about Fayed arrived, Tajir was caring for Rashid, laid low by a stroke, in a German hospital. In Tajir's opinion, Fayed was a jester and bag-carrier whose wilful misconstruction of his past and his good fortune had become tiresome. Dictating a memorandum for circulation within the embassy, Tajir reminded his staff that Fayed was not entitled to any diplomatic privileges. A copy of that note was secretly passed to Fayed by a friendly diplomat. Insulted, and convinced that Tajir was no longer valuable, Fayed declared war. Ignoring the automatic immunity accorded to a diplomat, he impetuously issued his first writ for libel in the High Court. A new enemy had been created.

During that summer of 1982 in St Tropez, Fayed moored the *Sakara* alongside the *Nabila*, Khashoggi's astonishing 282-foot yacht. Dubbed 'the most opulent modern yacht afloat', the *Nabila* was equipped with a swimming pool, sauna, discotheque and helipad and had been used by 'Cubby' Broccoli as a location for a James Bond film. Fayed gasped and stared at the girls seductively sunning themselves on the *Nabila*'s decks. In the space of thirty years, Khashoggi had become a multibillionaire while Fayed, relegated to the periphery of Middle Eastern commerce had earned only millions.

Over a drink chilled by undisguised frostiness, the two men discussed their lives since the Fayed divorce in 1957. While Fayed led an anonymous, occasionally reclusive life, Khashoggi had become an international magnet for partying. Earlier that summer, the Egyptian had not been invited by Khashoggi to a memorable day at Ascot and a splendid party in the evening at the Belfry in Knightsbridge. The restaurant, owned by Charles Riachi, a Lebanese middleman, had been filled with the Playboy set. Khashoggi had been the centre of attraction, especially as he was entertaining the young sultan of Brunei. The closest Fayed got to that dizzying social circle was Victor Lownes's acceptance of an invitation for dinner at Park Lane with Mohamed, Ali and Tracey. Heini, Lownes had noted, had disappeared. As ever, Fayed was a loner, and Khashoggi, looking at his former brother-in-law, lacked any urge to re-establish relations. When Fayed's glass was empty, Khashoggi rose and bid his guest farewell.

If Khashoggi was unimpressed by Mohamed's achievement, Fayed hoped that Rowland might be stirred. On his return from France, he included Rowland's name as one of several hundred among the rich and famous who received small leather diaries embossed in gold with 'Hôtel Ritz, Paris' and their initials. The package also included two bathrobes, marked with the hotel's name. 'Surprised' by the gift, Rowland telephoned Fayed. After their reunion in spring 1983, Rowland appreciated that during the intervening six years Fayed had metamorphosed into a more refined businessman but was still ambitious to win social acceptance. Rowland was happy to walk the short distance from his own Park Lane apartment and, over breakfast in Fayed's penthouse, discuss transport companies and oil concessions in the Middle East, although no deal ever materialized. Predictably, just before his guest's departure, Fayed would thrust a gift at Rowland. Invariably, to the aesthete's amusement, it was a sex-toy, one of many Fayed had accumulated in his home. Among the deals Fayed proposed to Rowland was the purchase of International Marine Services (IMS), a loss-making maritime salvage company in Dubai, which Fayed had been offered by its German owners. Fayed's offer, drawing him closer towards Rowland, who was by then engaged in outright warfare against Tajir, sealed the Egyptian's fate.

A telephone call in late 1981 from Christoph Bettermann, a thirty-three-year-old German lawyer, while Fayed was working in his twelfth-floor suite in the Dubai Sheraton, introduced the new opportunity. IMS, Bettermann explained, was a subsidiary in Dubai of Salzgitter, a German state-owned steel manufacturer. Created in a reckless moment by a bureaucrat in north Germany, IMS owned thirteen salvage tugs and supply vessels servicing ships and oil rigs around the Gulf. The enormous losses, explained Bettermann, were partly caused by the presence among the 1,400 employees of a Mafia fugitive apparently protected by a power-broker in Dubai. Anxious to stem the losses and secure help from the Dubai government, Bettermann had been instructed to seek Fayed's help.

Companies in trouble always interest aspiring tycoons and Fayed's own shipping interests activated his curiosity. 'Come and see me,' he laughed. 'I'll help you.'

'I won't be able to pay you,' said Bettermann.

'Don't worry,' replied Fayed. By the end of the day, Bettermann held a list of telephone numbers of influential Dubaians in a position to ease IMS's troubles. Months later, when Fayed returned to the emirate, he called Bettermann: 'How's business?'

Reluctantly, Bettermann admitted that IMS's plight had deteriorated.

'Come and see me when you're next in London,' urged Fayed.

Early in 1983, Fayed returned once more to Dubai. Over the previous months he had been earning handsome commissions selling Gulfstream jets in the region. Once established in his Sheraton suite, he telephoned Bettermann. 'You sound unwell.'

'I've got a cold,' replied the German.

'You need right medicine,' laughed the hypochondriac, who was frequently afflicted by hay fever. 'I always travel with a suitcase full of medicines. Come to my hotel and collect the bottles. But don't come upstairs. I'll send my driver down.'

At reception, Bettermann was handed a bottle of Activa in linctus and a nasal spray.

The following morning Fayed telephoned. 'You better?'

'Yes.'

'Right, how's IMS? Is it for sale?' Fayed had decided that IMS, located in a shack in a shabby area near the creek, could be bought cheap. Although its vessels were worth $14.5 million, the company's debts were higher. Before Bettermann could react, Fayed added, 'Tell your bosses to call me.'

To avoid an embarrassing public disclosure of their losses, the German bureaucrats sought a discreet sale. While Price Waterhouse examined IMS's accounts on Fayed's behalf, Salzgitter's auditors conducted a furtive search to establish whether Fayed was sufficiently rich to buy the company. The German report concluded that, despite his Scottish castle and property in Park Lane, there was no evidence of any substantial wealth. Probably, concluded the investigators, Fayed's money was concealed in a series of secret Swiss bank accounts. Sensitive to those doubts, Fayed employed Pat Rooney, a public relations expert, to drop a myth into Bettermann's ears. 'Mohamed Al Fayed's family', whispered Rooney, 'owned the famous Shepheard's Hotel in Cairo.' The German had no reason to harbour any doubts.

In the meantime, to hammer down the price, Fayed offered Rowland the opportunity to buy IMS. Rowland's rejection, forwarded to Salzgitter, added to the Germans' uncertainty. Having reduced their original asking price from $10 million to $70,000, IMS was finally sold to Fayed for just $1. Whether that astonishing reduction was associated with the suspected employment of the Mafia fugitive was uncertain, but over the following seven years IMS would pay off all the debts and remit $21 million in profits to Fayed's Swiss bank account. That success was due to Bettermann's appointment as IMS's manager and the outbreak of the Iran–Iraq War in 1980. Damaged shipping required salvage and Fayed spurred his manager to profit from the Iraqi and Iranian attacks on ships: 'Money is lying on the street. God has given you a brain. Use your brain. Pick the money up.'

Bettermann had no illusions about his new employer's shipping experience. 'My total assets', Fayed told the German, 'are three ro–ro vessels, and one of them has been stuck since last November on a sandbank.' Bettermann had also become accustomed to his new employer's methods. Twice every week, they would discuss business on the telephone. Unwilling to read documents or leave a paper trail, Fayed encouraged the German to commit nothing to writing, agreeing everything orally; and, since Fayed's concentration span was short, their discussions were brief. Regularly, Fayed asked Bettermann to transfer money to an account at the Union Bank in Geneva and warned that, to protect his investment, auditors would visit Dubai every year.

During 1983, Bettermann arrived at 60 Park Lane. For two hours he waited watching television in a book-lined room in apartment 48, receiving food and newspapers. During those aimless minutes, he reached for a book. To his surprise, his hand was touching a false front. To his greater surprise, moments later, the bookshelves opened and through a hidden door Mohamed Fayed appeared. Fayed had another surprise for Bettermann. Thirty minutes later, the German was introduced to Michael Gillard, a financial journalist employed by the *Observer* newspaper which had recently been bought by Tiny Rowland. Fayed urged Bettermann to reveal to Gillard some secrets about Mahdi Al Tajir and the Mafia fugitive in Dubai. It was a strange introduction to a new alliance between Fayed and Rowland. The German was recruited as a tool for Rowland's vendetta against Tajir.

Angry that a potential business deal with the Shah of Iran had been sabotaged by Tajir, Rowland had ordered the *Observer*'s editor to attack the ambassador. In Rowland's view, since Fayed was also at war with Tajir he automatically became Rowland's friend. But Bettermann, unwilling to become a newspaper's source and thereby increase his troubles in Dubai, betrayed no secrets. Fayed, however, was more forthcoming. In the bid by British companies to win £2.5 billion of contracts in Dubai, he told the journalist, Tajir had earned over £75 million in commission payments, including a 'single payment of £10 million'. Although '£75 million' was an underestimate, the *Observer*'s story in June 1983 embarrassed Tajir and pleased Rowland. Warming to Fayed, the Lonrho executive calculated that the Arab could play a supporting role in another of his plots – his frustrating six-year battle to buy Britain's largest chain of department stores, the House of Fraser.

4

A Game of Chess

FOUNDED BY LORD FRASER, a brilliant Scottish retailer, House of Fraser employed 27,000 people in just over one hundred stores including Dickens & Jones, Barkers, and the Army & Navy. The jewel in the crown was Harrods, bought in 1959. Fulfilling its cable address, 'Everything London' and its motto, 'Omnia Omnibus Ubique' ('Everything for Everybody Everywhere'), Harrods' reputation was embellished by the fable of a telephone call from the office of Ronald Reagan, then the Governor of California, to order an elephant. 'Would that be the African or Indian variety, sir?' the enquirer was asked. By 1983, seventeen years after Lord Fraser's death, the building and interior of Harrods were drab and scruffy, yet, given the deteriorating finances of the group, provided about 50 per cent of House of Fraser's entire profits. The accelerating decline was the fault of his son Hugh Fraser who, enfeebled by his father's domination, had become an alcoholic and addicted to the roulette wheel. Often playing two tables simultaneously in London's best casinos, Hugh Fraser regularly ended the night out of pocket. On one memorable night, he had dropped £500,000 on number 32, his 'lucky number'. In early 1977, Fraser had needed £4 million to pay off gambling debts. His salvation was, in his words, 'a fantastic guy, just like my father' – Tiny Rowland.

Desperate to alleviate Lonrho's crippling debts, Rowland had spotted the extraordinary benefits of House of Fraser's huge cash flow for his beleaguered company. Hugh Fraser's offer to sell a stake in SUITS, an undervalued public company which owned 10 per cent of House of Fraser, was Rowland's chance to buy the whole group cheap. Unspoken was the ultimate prize, Harrods. 'If I meet the president of Venezuela,' Rowland had mused, 'and say "I own Lonrho," his eyes glaze over. But if I could say "I own Harrods" he would instantly recognize my importance.' House of Fraser, Rowland divined, was a guaranteed passport to international recognition and a cure to the City's ostracism.

Rowland bought Fraser's shares solemnly promising to remain a passive investor. Days later, he broke the promise. Launching a public bid to buy SUITS cheap, he waged an emotional battle, aggressively destabilizing the company's board of directors. Temporarily, his campaign ended in stalemate as the Labour government referred his bid to the Monopolies and Mergers Commission to consider the public interest. Convinced he was the victim of a long Whitehall vendetta against Lonrho, Rowland did not conceal his sense of grievance. 'Are you planning to bid for House of Fraser?' he was asked by the Commission.

Unequivocally he replied, 'We are not considering a bid at the moment.' Rowland's bid was approved, provided that promise was kept. Having snapped up a bargain, he raised his stake in House of Fraser to 29.9 per cent. Once again ignoring his promises, Rowland prepared to launch an uncontested bid for the whole of House of Fraser.

Rowland's plans quickly went awry. At a dinner in Glasgow with House of Fraser's directors, Rowland displayed disdain rather than charm towards twelve proud Scotsmen renowned for their feudal loyalty to their laird. Thier patent antagonism towards his bid provoked Rowland's ire. Cavalier towards his new enemies and towards Warburgs, their hostile bankers, Rowland returned to London and launched a campaign of terrorism in the boardroom and at a succession of special shareholders' meetings. Intending to destroy the opposition with threats and embarrassment, he spewed out irate telexes, abusive telephone calls, abrupt ultimatums and unreasonable demands punctuated by a flood of caustic circulars damning the House of Fraser directors. Rowland's blind rage failed to conceal the fatal flaw. Warburgs' analysis of Lonrho's finances revealed that the company was too poor to launch a bid. 'Whatever way we looked at the company,' reported Simon Garmoyle, 'it was shaky.'

Lonrho's profits were falling. Earning unremittable profits in Africa, losing money in Britain and incapable of creating original wealth, Lonrho's quest for House of Fraser was, admitted Terry Robinson, the finance director, 'a simple cash operation. There was no passion for Harrods.'

Riled by that truth, Rowland issued a deadly riposte. At a critical meeting of the House of Fraser's directors, he threatened to publish evidence which he had secretly purchased demonstrating that Hugh Fraser was personally bankrupt after incurring new gambling debts of £10 million. 'Hugh will have to resign,' said Rowland icily. Fraser's fellow directors were mortified. But, having plunged in the dagger, Rowland offered, as an act of friendship, to withdraw the weapon from the corpse. 'I felt desperately sorry for him,' he said unconvincingly when, on Monday, 26 January 1981, he arrived for a board meeting with a secret agenda – to announce a takeover bid for the group with Hugh Fraser as Lonrho's appointed chairman. To his surprise, he was outwitted. Ignoring his 'bombshell', Professor Roland Smith, the hulking deputy chairman and a professor of management science, led his fellow directors into voting for Fraser's dismissal as chairman of the board and for the rejection of Rowland's bid. Heralded by the media as 'the most extraordinary takeover battle since the war', the bid was marred by two miscalculations: undervaluing House of Fraser at £226 million and misjudging the City's and the government's reaction – another reference to the Monopolies Commission. In January 1982, the Commission ruled against the bid. Still Rowland resolved not to surrender.

The 1980s were a glorious decade for capitalists and

buccaneers. Galvanized by the Reagan–Thatcher economic boom, international tycoons exploited their access to inside knowledge. Spurred on by bankers begging to lend money and by small investors besotted by tales of mega-million earnings, all the major players were deluged with offers of deals to earn on the turn – short-term gambles to buy and sell stock and currencies. Rowland spurned most of those offers. Although he lived to deal, Rowland's opportunities, unlike Rupert Murdoch's and Jimmy Goldsmith's, were limited by the antipathy felt towards him in Westminster and Whitehall. His broken promises bolstered those sentiments.

In December 1981, Sir Godfray Le Quesne, the chairman of the Monopolies Commission, influenced by the DTI's condemnation of Rowland's dishonesty, ruled on spurious grounds that Lonrho's takeover of House of Fraser was 'against the public interest'. While newspapers condemned Le Quesne's recommendation as flawed, prejudiced and a 'disgracefully raw deal', Rowland blamed the establishment: 'They and the City don't like me and wish I would go away.' In contrast, Professor Roland Smith, House of Fraser's chairman, was 'delighted' by the report and offered his fellow directors a glass of champagne to celebrate. 'We thought it was all over,' said George Willoughby, the finance director. 'Everyone else who loses at the Commission just goes away. We didn't realize what was going to happen.'

'This is just another hurdle that we have to overcome,' announced Rowland. 'These are skirmishes. It's who wins the war that matters.' Undaunted, he continued his campaign with the growing albeit reluctant support of City investors disgruntled by Professor Smith's performance as chairman. On 6 May 1983, in another ballot of 130 million shares, Rowland lost by a mere 1.8 million votes. Yet another ballot was due at the annual general meeting seven weeks later. Victory was in sight, Rowland believed, if he organized the help of friends. Among the four chosen was Mohamed Fayed.

Rowland's resumed relationship with Fayed was as friendly as it had been before. The only noticeable change was the

Egyptian's solitariness. Compared with his behaviour in the 1970s, he appeared to be less sociable, even reclusive. 'A bit like Howard Hughes,' an associate of Rowland's noted. Increasingly phobic about the threat to his health presented by germs, uneasy in the company of strangers and conscious of his new young family (since Heini was again pregnant), Fayed was indeed more withdrawn than before. The change encouraged Rowland, over breakfast in Park Lane, to accept his host's emphasis on his trustworthiness. In his pidgin English, Fayed appeared to say that he shared so many of Rowland's aspirations, values and characteristics. Certainly, he was listening carefully to Rowland's proposition.

'House of Fraser', began his visitor, 'is a sleeping giant which the market does not properly value. The company will only change ownership once in my lifetime.' Fayed's eyes gleamed. 'Anyone buying the shares, Tootsie,' continued Rowland, with a meticulous pause after each word, 'and voting with Lonrho, will earn a good profit.' The Egyptian knew exactly what he was saying. Any doubts were dispelled with Rowland's final sentence. 'There's no risk for you, Tootsie. If the share price falls, I'll find someone to buy your shares. At the original price, no loss to you.'

'Good,' rasped Fayed. 'Good.'

The deal was done. No paperwork or record of their conversation existed to prove how Rowland had lured Fayed into his web.

Later that day, Fayed repeated the conversation to Ali, emphasizing Rowland's fateful prediction that 'The company will only change ownership once in my lifetime'. Understanding how to profit from Rowland's plot, the brothers bought one million House of Fraser shares. To disguise their ownership, the shares were bought through Credit Suisse in Geneva and registered in the name of Adriana Funaro, Salah's Italian wife. It was not a coincidence that Funaro, who had never bought shares in her life, used Strauss Turnbull as her stockbrokers since they acted for Lonrho.

Among the three others whom Rowland also recruited was Dr Ashraf Marwan, alias 'the golden child', the Egyptian son-in-law of the late President Nasser and the former chief of staff in President Sadat's private office. During the 1970s, Marwan had travelled with Rowland throughout Africa and the Arab world arranging contacts and business deals. At one stage, their partnership ended in tears when Rowland sniped, 'In terms of business, Marwan is totally unreliable.' But Rowland exuded sweetness over lunch at the Ritz in London on 10 May 1983 as he outlined to Marwan the benefits of buying the shares. Nine days later, with the help of a Rowland loan, two million House of Fraser shares were bought in Marwan's name. 'Rowland cast that fly,' commented a subsequent investigator, 'and Dr Marwan swallowed it.'

On the eve of the crucial vote, on 28 June 1983, Lonrho delivered boxes of proxy cards to the company's register. Four cards belonging to Rowland's friends, including Marwan's and the Fayeds', had been stapled together by Lonrho. To Roland Smith and Warburgs, by then convinced that Rowland was bugging their telephones and intercepting their mail, the evidence of a conspiracy or 'concert party' seemed overwhelming. Smith appealed to the government, which, on 23 August 1983 ordered a new DTI inquiry into Rowland's alleged conspiracy – which had nevertheless failed to secure the prize. Simultaneously, Conservative MPs recruited by du Cann persuaded the government to order a new Monopolies Commission inquiry into Lonrho's bid for House of Fraser. The fate of the group had become a major political and financial controversy. To Fayed, however, Rowland's interminable dispute was of little interest. Preoccupied by a burst of frantic activity, as he expanded his empire using an undisclosed source of finance, his attention had shifted.

*

AFTER 1979, FAYED's relationship with Morgan Grenfell had cooled, and he turned to Marcus Agius, the merchant banker at Lazards who had advised during his purchase of the Ritz, to discuss a series of new ventures. Like all his breed in the City, Agius saw Arab clients as succulent targets promising enormous profits and Fayed's image matched the promise. During those early summer weeks of 1983, the Egyptian seemed especially attractive as he telephoned the banker about several new propositions, including buying a controlling interest in MGM, the film studios, and two hotels, the Dorchester and the Savoy. As always Fayed's lifestyle was calculated to suggest prodigious wealth. His true worth, however, was very uncertain, since other than the commissions from Dubai worth about £50 million and his profit from the sale of the Costain shares he had not noticeably earned any huge amounts. His continuing businesses produced only reasonable profits. His refurbishment of the Ritz in Paris would mean debts until the next millennium; IMS's profits in Dubai were regular but small; Fayair and Bermair, two aircraft companies, earned annually $2 million commission from Gulfstream for sales; he had earned £1 million for introducing business to Morgan Grenfell; Allied Stars, his film production company, had earned at most $20 million; and Genavco, the shipping company with new branch offices in the Midlands, Tilbury and Ipswich, was earning modest profits by providing computer services and the hire and maintenance of executive jets in Southampton, and from a contract awarded by the Ministry of Defence to transport to the Falkland Islands the materials to build an army base, a harbour and a runway, but the company was only worth £2.5 million. Adding everything together, Fayed appeared to be worth at most £100 million, but much of that fortune had been pledged as security against loans. Thanks to his profligate spending, there was little cash. In net terms, he could barely be worth £10 million. That truth, however, was concealed. Just as he had invented a new past, Fayed had, by imposing strict compartmentalization and rigid secrecy, presented himself as substantially richer.

With characteristic braggadocio, the Fayeds would claim to

Whitehall civil servants after November 1984 that while the net worth of their commercial assets was $300 million, the true value of their total fortune was over $1,000 million. Obliquely, Fayed was admitting his penchant for huge borrowings to finance his lifestyle and business activities. So long as he paid the interest on his loans, raised in Switzerland and America, he hoped that no banker in London would spot his deception.

Until then, Marcus Agius had never queried the accuracy of the Fayeds' claims to wealth but since he had never discussed any deal worth more than £25 million he could accurately assess his client's value while listening to his boasts of his genius for buying properties at prices which in retrospect appeared low. Because the Fayeds had astutely organized their business through Switzerland to reduce their declared income to minuscule amounts in Britain and avoid paying hefty local taxes, it was easy to assume that, in the heady atmosphere engendered by the world's expanding economy, the value of their assets would automatically increase. That impression was reinforced on 25 June 1984. In a bank transfer from an undisclosed account at Citicorp in Zurich, £50.5 million was deposited in a new Fayed account at the Royal Bank of Scotland in London. At the time it was assumed that the money was Fayed's, but its arrival coincided with his successful consolidation of a relationship with the sultan of Brunei. His introduction to the oil-rich monarch looked like a stroke of luck, but in hindsight it can be seen as the climax of his costly and careful strategy.

In his wildest dream, Fayed had never imagined that Dodi, his spendthrift son, vulgarly cursed for idleness and diffidence, would raise the curtain to his fame and fortune. But a telephone call from Dodi in late 1983 had caused Fayed to tremble with excitement.

Dodi reported that Adnan Khashoggi, as ever the generous host, had invited the sultan of Brunei for lunch at the Belfry in Knightsbridge. Knowing that Dodi was in London, the Saudi had asked his nephew to join the large party. 'You were both at Sandhurst,' he said politely. 'You're bound to have something in common.'

Over the previous year, Khashoggi had introduced the sultan to the pleasures of the world: 'You've got all the money. You should spend some.' The thirty-six-year-old sultan's face was a mixture of embarrassment and gratitude. 'Take the 727,' laughed Khashoggi, referring to one of his three Boeings, 'and have some fun.' Travelling with Victor Dananza, a forty-eight-year-old New York 'Mr Fixit', the monarch had jetted around the world's fleshpots – Dananza's speciality – staying especially long in Las Vegas. Returning to Europe, the sultan offered to buy the plane, an ideal transaction for Khashoggi, who had already ordered a replacement DC8. Investing in people, as Dodi observed, was Khashoggi's talent. Addressing the monarch shyly, Dodi said, 'You know, you really should come to the Ritz [in Paris]. Our hotel is the best in the world. You'll be our guest.' The sultan's acceptance was passed on to Mohamed Fayed hours later.

Like most self-made tycoons, Fayed's success stemmed from his ability to observe and copy his models – in his case, Khashoggi and Tajir. Middlemen, he knew, were required to be ruthlessly efficient, extremely hard working, charming, extravagant and opportunistic. Travelling across the world in considerable style to seduce the courtiers and advisers of oil-rich monarchs was an expensive gamble. In recent years, the developing world's leaders had become more sophisticated, discriminatory and remote from adventurers. Fayed's approach, however, had become more refined than most. Cultivating a new image, he represented himself as the master planner and architect of Dubai. That small emirate's major developments – port, dry dock, aluminium smelter, Trade Centre and coastal free-trade zone – had been, he taught himself to repeat, inspired by his genius and initially financed by his billions. Since only a handful of Dubai's citizens knew the truth, there was little risk that Fayed's fable would be exposed. The act had now been perfected. Fayed awaited the opportunity for the performance on the perfect stage of the renovated Ritz in Paris.

Mohamed Fayed, the mega-tycoon, had attempted to meet the sultan the previous year. The occasion was a visit to the Ritz by Khashoggi and Dananza. 'Do you think the sultan would like to buy a Gulfstream?' asked the Egyptian as he showed his visitors the redecorated Imperial Suite.

'I'll ask,' replied the American unconvincingly. Fayed's motives were obvious and Dananza intended to protect his friend.

One year later, Fayed's investment in the Ritz had been repaid. Acting as the hotel owner and doorman as the sultan and his fiancée arrived in the Place Vendôme, he personally escorted the monarch to the Imperial Suite on the first floor. Over the following hours, pushing Dodi forcibly to the side-lines, he exhaustively charmed his guest. 'I built Dubai,' he gushed. 'It's thanks to me that the country has now ports and hospitals and a Trade Centre. I can do the same for Brunei. Trust me.' By the end of the sultan's short visit, Fayed had convinced the monarch of his genius as an adviser and friend. 'I'd be very grateful if you could come and help,' said the sultan.

Fayed arrived in Brunei at a fortunate moment. Like Dubai one decade earlier, Brunei was a new honeypot emerging from its colonial status, but had been struck by a disaster caused by the British Crown Agents. London's bureaucrats had misman-aged the sultan's finances, losing hundreds of millions of pounds. Fayed, like other non-British advisers, had a distinct advantage, despite the country's emotional and political links to Britain, in winning the sultan's trust.

Situated on the northern coast of Borneo, in South-East Asia, Brunei is a tiny kingdom of 230,000 people whose benign despot, blessed with considerable oil revenues, was with more justification than others renowned as 'the richest man in the world'. Owning more palatial homes scattered around the world than other mortals own shirts, the sultan was a magnet for the world's wheeler-dealers seeking to sell planes, yachts, palaces or their services to help invest his estimated $24 billion fortune. One assessment in 1984 recorded that the sultan possessed eleven Rolls-Royces and Bentleys, seven Mercedes and four Ferraris. By 1992, he apparently owned 153 Rolls-Royces. His first custom-built Boeing 727 included a jacuzzi from which, in an emergency, the water could be dumped in less than eight seconds. That was replaced by a lavishly decorated Boeing 747. His home, a palace of 1,788 rooms costing an estimated $600 million, was bigger than the Vatican. The opulent lifestyle was, according to his dissatisfied courtiers, the product of a naive mind easily misled by avaricious vultures. The mystery and challenge for all visiting salesmen was to win access to the sultan and seduce him into accepting their propositions.

Noticing the naivety of both the young sultan and Pehin Isa, his Malay adviser, Fayed effortlessly represented himself as a major player in the world with British roots: 'Of course, based in Park Lane and with my home in Scotland, I am well connected to the British government.' Repeatedly, to the Egyptian's quiet amusement, the sultan and his staff expressed their gratitude that he had so graciously offered to resolve their problems.

Over the previous four years, Fayed had assiduously wooed bankers across Europe. Introduced by Banque Gonet, the tiny bank in Geneva, and his Swiss lawyer Martin Müller as a reputable, international businessman, he had devoted considerable attention and expense to entertaining those bankers, who, beguiled by the mystery of wealth, responded well to his generous hospitality in Gstaad, in London, in Scotland and more recently at the Ritz. His immaculate performance left his guests, driven by herd instinct, with an irrefutable belief in their host's riches. Although Banque Gonet had vouched in 1981 to Twentieth Century-Fox that their client was worth $100 million, Fayed had found bankers in Geneva and Zurich prepared to accept his boasts of greater wealth. Affluent clients, as Fayed knew, found it easier to borrow money than the poor. Required to invest the huge deposits of 'hot money' in their accounts, and more adventurous than their reputation suggested, the Swiss bankers trusted Fayed, especially after seeing evidence of his financial relationship with the sultan.

Hired as the trouble-shooter, in summer 1984 Fayed was given three powers of attorney by the sultan. The first concerned a contract with Mario Lavia, an Italian marine designer for the construction of a luxury yacht. Having advised the sultan to terminate the contract, Fayed transferred $200 million deposited in Lavia's Credit Suisse account in Switzerland to his own name and would have been able to borrow for his own account against that deposit.

The second power of attorney was to resolve a dispute which had arisen between the sultan and Carl Hirschmann, a Swiss aviation engineer supervising the maintenance of the monarch's personal Boeing jets. Hirschmann and his son had been contracted by the sultan to convert a Boeing 747-SP into a transporter for his polo ponies. A sum of $100 million had been deposited in the engineer's account. But the sultan had become displeased and started legal proceedings in Switzerland against the Hirschmanns. For the Hirschmanns, this bitter blow was aggravated by the son's detention in Brunei until the sultan's money was returned and the father's claim for $48 million for work already undertaken was settled. The power of attorney required Fayed to terminate the contract and recover the sultan's money. That money, too, would be deposited under Fayed's control in Switzerland.

The sultan's third power of attorney granted to Fayed was to negotiate the purchase of a hotel in London. The Savoy and the Dorchester were mentioned. The £50.5 million transferred on 25 June 1984 from Zurich to Fayed's account at the Royal Bank of Scotland in London was the sultan's money for the purchase of a hotel.

*

ALL THAT ACTIVITY coincided with visible evidence of Fayed's close relationship with the sultan. At a formal dinner organized by the Fayeds at the Ritz Hotel to mark the award of the Ernest Hemingway literary prize, the sultan was billed as the star appearance. To the guests' disappointment, the sultan was present only on a pre-recorded video, during which, after speaking about Hemingway as if he had been a lifelong friend, he gave the diners a guided tour of his palace. The juxtaposition of a literary prize and the sultan's odd self-promotion served Fayed's purpose of displaying his intimacy with the monarch. Just two days after the sultan's £50.5 million was transferred from Switzerland to Fayed's account, the Egyptian appeared in London before John Griffiths QC, appointed by the DTI to investigate Rowland's alleged conspiracy against House of Fraser's directors. He had no intention of telling the complete truth.

Giving his address as the Trade Centre in Dubai, and not Oxted or Park Lane, and describing himself as a shipowner, Fayed had agreed with Adriana Funaro, his sister-in-law, to testify to Griffiths that they were rich, innocent foreigners. Denying any knowledge of a secret agreement with Rowland and feigning mystification about all the inexplicable coincidences linking Funaro's share purchase with Ashraf Marwan's, he pleaded total ignorance. For her part, Funaro, who lived in Italy, demurely explained that she had bought the shares after reading a tipster's column in the financial page of a British newspaper. That was not the only incredible testimony. In December 1983, Ali Fayed had 'blindly' sold Funaro's shares and, on the same day, they had been bought by Marwan. 'A 100 per cent coincidence,' Fayed told the DTI inspector. 'I'm not interested in House of Fraser,' exclaimed Fayed in a burst of apparently genuine indignation at the end of his testimony. 'I never want to hear it mentioned again.'

Griffiths, an inexperienced investigator, was easily convinced. After all, Rowland's description of the Fayeds as rich spoke for itself: 'The Al Fayeds have huge joint interests and if you make enquiries, you will hear that when in London they conduct all their business from their Park Lane apartment, and know and receive numerous visitors every day from the City. They are extremely well known, and have brought well over a thousand million pounds' worth of business to this country.'

Although Griffiths believed the Fayeds, he accused Rowland of lying. 'His wishes', he would report, 'often father his memory.' Marwan was also accused of having 'lied deliberately'. There was, concluded Griffiths, compelling evidence of a conspiracy between the two men. But Griffiths had only penetrated part of the conspiracy.

On 28 June 1984, the day after Fayed's testimony to Griffiths, he invited Rowland to breakfast in Park Lane. Sensing his visitor's vulnerability, he offered: 'I'll do whatever I can to help you.' Reminding Rowland of his participation in the concert party, he repeated, 'We helped you last year and we'll do the same again.'

'That's good of you, Tootsie,' smiled Rowland, pausing momentarily. 'Perhaps I should sell the shares to you. We could come to some sort of agreement.' As Rowland appeared to be choosing his next words carefully, Fayed's eyes sparkled. 'A temporary arrangement, Tootsie,' concluded Rowland. In Rowland's scheme, Fayed would be cast as a warehouse. The Egyptian would buy the shares while Rowland fought and won his political battle and Fayed would return the shares at the appropriate moment. 'Naturally, Tootsie,' concluded Rowland, 'like last time, you won't lose any money. We'll guarantee you a profit.' Fayed nodded enthusiastically. 'Or', added Rowland melancholically, 'perhaps we'll just sell out. Abandon the lot.'

Again, Fayed nodded. Rowland's proposition was an easy, risk-free deal. Harrods, he now knew, was an unexploited goldmine. 'I'll give you £120 million for your shares,' said Fayed. 'I've got cash, Tiny.'

'I'll think about it, Tootsie,' laughed Rowland. Surrender was far from his mind, but Fayed might be useful to him.

Fayed was oblivious to the depth of Rowland's cunning. In

the league of pirates, Fayed was a mere novice compared to his visitor. Similarly, Rowland had no reason to suspect that the well-dressed, laughing pasha's son was in fact a self-made, rough commission agent. Disarmed by Fayed's bad English, rustic mannerisms and short attention span, Rowland did not suspect that his apparent confusion obscured a razor-sharp mind. The combination of Fayed's randomness and his enthusiasm for participating in another plot sapped the maverick's customary suspicion.

Fayed chuckled: 'It's a deal?'

'We'll see, Tootsie.' As Rowland began to depart, Fayed thrust his hand into a drawer and pulled out a package. The former German roared with laughter and stuck the dildo in his pocket. 'He's mad about sex,' he grinned when he later showed it to his directors.

In the course of that day, Fayed's excitement about the possible deal was tinged by concern about his testimony to Griffiths. Less than twenty-four hours earlier, he had told the government inspector that he was not interested in House of Fraser.

During his twenty years in Britain, Fayed had learnt some of the rules. Whenever considering a questionable ploy, it was advisable to gild your deeds with the prior endorsement of a banker or lawyer. In that dying era of self-regulation, bankers and lawyers were still assumed honourably to place the public interest before self-interest. According to the unwritten rules of professional practice, the scions of the City institutions still murmured, 'my word is my bond.' Despite a rash of well-publicized scandals and alleged crimes involving famous tycoons, the banks, Lloyd's insurance market and other City institutions, Fayed believed in adhering to the rules. He therefore telephoned Edward Walker-Arnott, a senior partner at Herbert Smith, the City solicitors, for advice.

Would there be a problem, asked Fayed, if he bought Rowland's shares? Ponderously, Walker-Arnott spelled out an escape route. While, legally, said the lawyer, Fayed might be obliged to write to Griffiths, there was a danger. The inspector would feel bound to include that discussion in his report. Not only would that publicity jeopardize the negotiations with Rowland, but Griffiths might conclude that Fayed had after all conspired with Rowland. Silence, suggested Walker-Arnott, was the best course. Reassured that his new arrangement with Rowland was sanctified, Fayed's thoughts raced. Perhaps he could bid for House of Fraser. He telephoned Agius at Lazards.

'Do you realize', warned Agius, 'that if you buy House of Fraser your lives will never be the same again?' Fayed was silenced. At that time, London's newspapers had never written about him and not a single photograph was available. 'Until now you have led private lives,' continued Agius. 'Once you are known to be potential bidders, you will be in the public eye. People will want to know who you are. Your background will be scrutinized.'

Reports about the skulduggery of the tycoons – Robert Maxwell, Rupert Murdoch, James Hanson, Jimmy Goldsmith and Tiny Rowland – and investigations into alleged crimes involving Guinness and Blue Arrow had filled the media. Despite their cultivated images as respectable, family-loving citizens, many of those players were amoral bandits who had all tried, repeatedly but in the end unsuccessfully, to resist the intense media scrutiny. Since Fayed had never considered himself among that party and had only a limited understanding of Britain, he ignored the banker's advice.

The banker then moved on to the practicalities. In the light of the Griffiths inquiry, bidding for House of Fraser would depend entirely upon the attitude of Roland Smith and his suspicious directors.

Having heard the advice, Fayed moved fast. The following day, he invited Marwan, whom he had met in the midst of the share conspiracy in July 1983, to lunch. 'I'm thinking of buying Tiny's stake in House of Fraser,' Fayed said. Marwan nodded.

'Mohamed seems serious,' Marwan later told Rowland.

'Do you think it's his own money?' Rowland asked, somewhat puzzled, adding mischievously, 'I'd sell to Tootsie if he plans to bid for the whole company. But I don't think he's got the money.'

Marwan, although bemused by Rowland's logic, nodded. Fayed was unknown among London's Egyptian community, was never seen at the embassy and to Marwan seemed a recluse. 'He never goes out,' he joked to Rowland, 'and never sees anyone. But I'm sure it's not his money.'

Hearing Marwan's report, Fayed became convinced that a deal was possible if only he could persuade the Lonrho chief to take him seriously. Only months earlier, making an offer in the lift at Cheapside, Rowland had, to his embarrassment, laughed: 'You haven't got the money, Tootsie!' To reverse that impression, Ali was dispatched to visit Rowland. The younger brother produced a letter from the Royal Bank of Scotland confirming that the bank was holding £132 million for the Fayeds to buy the House of Fraser shares owned by Lonrho. The bank had also guaranteed a £80 million loan using the shares as security. Curiously, Ali refused to leave the letter. One hour later, Fayed telephoned Rowland and suggested that they meet House of Fraser's directors together. Rowland refused.

Tantalizing other players was one way the tycoon obtained pleasure. The ill-restrained glee evident in a hand-delivered letter which Fayed received from Rowland on 3 July rejecting the deal was intended to hurt. But Fayed merely laughed: Arabs know that the best deals require patience while the seller dangles the fruit to check the market. Rowland, he believed, would eventually accept. 'Just let me know when you want to sell,' he replied.

*

ON 15 AUGUST 1984, Fayed arrived in Brunei. By any measure, the visit was a milestone in his life. Having won the sultan's trust, he was to be formally appointed as an investment adviser. In his discussions with Pehin Isa and Abdul Karim, the

sultan's local financial adviser and the manager of the investment agency, Fayed explained that he had established Hyde
Park Investments, a trust in Liechtenstein, for the sultan's assets
and had set up the Alfayed Investment Trust (AITSA) for his
own purposes. His plan was to negotiate prestige acquisitions
in Britain – initially a hotel, either the Savoy or the Dorchester
– for the sultan. With that hurdle overcome, Fayed broached
the last, sensitive purpose of his visit. 'Could I use the money
deposited in Switzerland?' he asked Isa. 'Just for a short period.
You'll get commercial rates and security.' Isa, pleased to regard
the Egyptian as an old friend, could see no objection. 'It will
be returned,' said Fayed in his most soothing manner, 'within
six months. With a good profit for you.' Isa agreed.

Once the sultan's money had been transferred to an account
at the Swiss Bank Corporation in Switzerland, Fayed arranged
to borrow a similar amount on his own account against the
security of the sultan's deposit. The technical term is a fiduciary
loan. Five days later, on 20 August, Ali told Ian Sinclair at the
Royal Bank of Scotland that, in addition to the £50.5 million
already deposited in the bank, Mohamed would transfer
another $330 million from Zurich. Sums of $229.9 million and
SF156.3 million had already been deposited in their account at
Banque Gonet during the summer of 1984. On 23 August,
Mohamed Fayed left Brunei.

The new transfers to London, Ian Sinclair at the Royal
Bank of Scotland assumed, belonged to the sultan and were
connected to Fayed's interest in buying a hotel. Technically, he
was incorrect. The money belonged to the sultan but, under
the agreement, it was loaned to Fayed. Legally, it was Fayed's
money.

Long before he left Brunei, Fayed had decided secretly to
abandon his conspiracy with Marwan and Rowland. Instead
of acting as the broker or warehouser in Rowland's plan, he
would become the principal, buy the House of Fraser shares
for himself – and keep them.

Fayed returned to unexpected news in London: Lazards

were simultaneously advising British American Tobacco on whether to bid for House of Fraser. To Fayed's fury, Marcus Agius of Lazards had unapologetically resigned as his confidential adviser. It was, he wrote to the bank's chairman, 'a complete betrayal of the duty which a financial adviser owes to its clients'. The City's definition of honesty, he believed, was a warped one. On Ian Sinclair's recommendation, Fayed retained Kleinwort Benson as his new advisers, and on 28 August he was introduced to John MacArthur, the deputy head of corporate finance. This move proved to be a godsend for Fayed.

John MacArthur, aged fifty, was regarded as an honest although not particularly intelligent banker, employed by one of the pillars of the City establishment. At their introduction, Fayed and his brother struck MacArthur as 'interesting and experienced people involved in big deals'. Putting on the performance so carefully polished over the years, Fayed portrayed himself to the banker as the high roller with unlimited cash. Allaying any suspicions MacArthur might have had, the brothers spoke during their conversation of their property and shipping interests in Europe, the Middle East and America, and mentioned their bank deposits in London. Since, unlike MacArthur's other clients, the Fayeds were private individuals and the Royal Bank had confirmed a huge deposit, the banker did not ask to see the history of those bank accounts. Instead he relied upon a briefing from Sinclair, who explained that, while it would be 'well-nigh impossible to complete an accurate balance sheet' on the Fayeds' wealth, the recent deposits by the brothers had been embarrassingly high. Anticipating their 'proposed acquisition', he stated that the deal was possibly 'fronted by the Fayeds for a very substantial investor'. Revelation of the identity of the investor depended upon the Fayeds, added Sinclair, apologizing for the 'cloak and dagger' secrecy. Undeterred by the mystery, MacArthur regarded the prospect as 'just another normal deal', for which he came prepared with 'lots of experience'.

Inevitably, since Fayed had returned only five days previously from Brunei, the banker asked about the relationship. With no difficulty the Egyptian explained, 'There's the sultan's business and there's our personal business.' Told with great conviction, Fayed's story was that he would buy the House of Fraser shares through the Alfayed Investment Trust (AITSA), a Liechtenstein trust, and that any extra funds required would be lent interest free to AITSA from the family's personal fortune. Although McArthur's overriding duty was to check the accuracy of the Fayeds' assertions, the banker abandoned any thoughts of investigation. He did not enquire about the noticeable absence of a business structure which had supposedly generated £615 million in cash after tax. Nor did he think it odd that a man who had accumulated such an enormous fortune would bother to list as evidence his homes which, however splendid, added barely £10 million to his wealth. With MacArthur gullible in the face of Fayed's charm, greedy for the fees and lured by the promise of a long profitable relationship, Fayed's mention of Liechtenstein was sufficient to forestall enquiries. MacArthur simply attached Kleinwort's reputation as the guarantee to Fayed's claims.

In early October 1984, Rowland flew on Lonrho business to Africa. Before leaving, he had called at 60 Park Lane. Fayed's Jekyll and Hyde personality – the laughingly generous pasha disguising his iron determination – was as confusing as ever for Rowland. 'You can trust me,' repeated Fayed. But, unknown to Rowland, in his absence MacArthur visited Roland Smith, the chairman of House of Fraser, to suggest that an unnamed client might launch a bid using Rowland's stake. 'Another of Tiny's tricks, I suspect,' scoffed Smith.

Three days later, the banker arrived at Park Lane with Lord Rockley, the head of Kleinwort's Corporate Finance Division. Over the following two hours, the bankers and Fayed discussed the details of a bid at 295 pence a share, and worked out the strategy they would adopt towards Rowland, the

House of Fraser directors and the government regulators. Everything depended upon Rowland's attitude on his return.

Rowland was fuming. Throughout his African trip, he had been preoccupied by the bad news that the Monopolies Commission chairman had extended his inquiry by three months. 'Why don't you sell your shares?' Sir Godfray Le Quesne, the Commission chairman, had asked Rowland.

'It was the last straw,' explained Rowland subsequently. Le Quesne, he suspected, wanted time to assemble his reasons for refusing permission for Lonrho's bid. If that occurred, Rowland concluded, Lonrho would be compelled to sell the shares at a terrible loss. Just as the financial markets in London were booming and Murdoch, Maxwell and Hanson were hoovering up companies free from any government hindrance, his ambitions were gripped in a Whitehall quagmire.

Rowland's proposed solution was to sell his shares to Fayed, an ideal warehouser who, he felt, could be manipulated. Although Rowland knew little about Fayed's background other than his loyal membership of the concert party, he believed him to be transparent. He was the customer whose trust could be bought, and Rowland tended to rely upon those whom he could buy, especially those who told him what he wanted to hear. The Egyptian, he calculated, lacked sufficient money to launch a full bid and would not qualify under the Commission's criteria as an acceptable purchaser. With supreme confidence in his own judgement, Rowland met Ashraf Marwan for breakfast in a Park Lane hotel on Monday, 29 October 1984. Impatiently, Fayed telephoned both men several times. 'What does Tootsie want?' asked Rowland.

'Your shares,' replied Marwan.

'Has he got the money?'

'He says he has.'

'How much is he worth?'

'He's got at most fifty million pounds.'

'Where's he getting the rest of his money?' asked Rowland,

who agreed that Fayed was a 'fifty man'. The source, they concluded, was a loan from the Maktoum brothers of Dubai, the emirate's rulers since the death of their father Sheikh Rashid.

With Rowland's agreement, Marwan telephoned Fayed from the hotel. 'Come to me,' urged Fayed. 'We can talk.' Just before 11 a.m., the two men walked into 60 Park Lane.

There were only fifty-five minutes available for discussion. Marwan was due to fly by Concorde to New York that morning. Rowland's offer was simple. He would tolerate no haggling about price and no alterations to his timetable. He would sell his 46.1 million House of Fraser shares for 300 pence each: £138 million was to be handed over by Friday in cash. Marwan noted the three conditions in his notebook: cash, secrecy and Rowland to remain as a director of House of Fraser.

Excitedly, Fayed dived for the irresistible opportunity, inadvertantly divulging that he hoped to make a full bid. 'You don't have enough money, Tootsie,' Rowland smiled. It was agreed that Rowland would return for breakfast on 1 November to settle any snags.

As Fayed escorted his guest to the oak door, both men looked pleased. The two players had resumed their old game of chess, but this time they had unknowingly embarked upon a unique duel of attrition lasting until death. 'Tiny,' said Fayed, 'I'll give you £100 million for your shares in Lonrho.'

Rowland laughed: 'You haven't got that money, Tootsie.'

Fayed added, 'And I'll pay you £5 million a year for five years if you continue to run Lonrho's Africa division.' Rowland laughed again. Long after the lift had delivered Rowland to the ground floor, Fayed was still smiling.

*

THE REMAINDER OF that day was frenzied. As bankers and lawyers gathered in Park Lane to construct the matrix for the transaction, MacArthur broached a sensitive topic. 'You'll need to employ a public relations adviser,' he told Mohamed Fayed. The purchase, MacArthur explained, 'will plunge the Al Fayeds into a high profile situation'.

Aggressively, Fayed rebuffed the banker: 'Our privacy is vital.'

Ali agreed. Conscious of their many deceptions, he favoured the protection provided by obscurity.

The banker was persistent. 'You need someone who'll make a song and dance, Mr Al Fayed. Someone to answer the questions.'

Both Fayeds grimaced. There appeared to be no alternative. The banker's candidate was Brian Basham, the son of a butcher and a former financial journalist who could be relied upon for whole-hearted commitment to his paymaster. Eventually Basham would admit, 'I'd work against Tiny Rowland for nothing.'

The first meeting between the publicist and the Fayeds was warm. 'We want to make a huge, positive statement,' started Basham. 'We'll need to win hearts and minds,' he continued, lapsing into the jargon of the Vietnam era. 'Convincing the City that the Al Fayeds are serious. Get rid of the negatives and prove the success. Winning Hs and Ms.' Basham's patter excited Fayed's dreams of fame. 'They're blocking bids by outsiders,' Basham said of the government's attitude, 'especially by Jews. You're buying a national asset, so you'll have to prove that you're a good custodian of this national monument.'

Fayed swelled with pride. Embellishing his past had become an ingrained habit. Even more than the professional hypist imagined.

Over the previous years he had seen how British journalists unquestioningly accepted the Arabs' assessment of their own wealth. Tajir had simply mentioned one dozen homes and no journalist queried his claim to be 'the richest man in the world'. Inventing history, Fayed had reasoned long ago, was a habit favoured by Britain's most narcissistic personalities, who included or excluded events from their biographies to suit their requirements.

Telling a good story was Fayed's strength, and Basham was an eager salesman. With great swagger, Fayed spoke about his family's historic wealth, declared that Al Fayedia, the town in Egypt, was named after the family, and boasted about his homes across the world and his fleet of ships, adding that the *Sakara* had been inherited from his grandfather. (The Earl of Warwick, he knew, had died recently.) He hardly paused for breath.

By the end of his speech, Basham had crafted an image: blessed with genius, the pasha had personally transformed Dubai from a desert wasteland into a modern city and billions had flowed ever since. The Rolls-Royce, the Gulfstream, the helicopter and the Ritz were the symbols of his incredible wealth. In the heady atmosphere prevailing on the eve of his biggest deal, Fayed as the originator of a Big Lie, presenting his fable with such charm, assurance and hospitality, convinced himself that even the malicious would not probe their veracity. The notion that the government or anyone else would devote energy to investigating his past was inconceivable. In short, he believed himself to be invincible.

Fayed's expectations about Basham's reaction were not disappointed, though the publicist made one check. 'The Al Fayeds say they're worth billions,' he told Sir Clifford Chetwood, the retired chairman of Wimpey. 'How big are they?'

'They're huge,' replied Chetwood.

Later that night, Fayed was presented with the result of Basham's skills. 'The Al Fayeds', he read in a press release which Basham stressed would appeal to the City and Whitehall, were 'an old-established Egyptian family whose fortune was established a century earlier by their grandfather, who grew cotton in the Nile delta which was exported to Lancashire.' The brothers 'had attended British schools and been cared for by British nannies. While the family's Egyptian property had been nationalized by Nasser, its shipping fleet had survived Nasser's nationalization.' Their own wealth, stated to be 'about one billion dollars', was based on 'widespread international interests' which included 'shipping, hotels, construction, oil, property and the Ritz Hotel in Paris'. 'Good! Good!' exclaimed Fayed. Everything was set for the deal.

As arranged, just before eight o'clock the following morning, 1 November 1984, Rowland returned to Fayed's flat in a good mood. The Egyptian's banter reinforced Rowland's trust in his partner. 'What about the dividend?' asked Rowland, keen to get the cash to fund Lonrho's depleted bank account.

'You have it,' Fayed gushed.

On the other side of the large room, Ali was telling Sinclair at the Royal Bank that the deal was still on. The telephone was handed to Rowland. In his unmistakable voice, the tycoon corroborated Ali's message. The exchange would take place the following day.

Unknown to Rowland, soon after his departure Mohamed and Ali Fayed, accompanied by their bankers, drove to the Army & Navy Stores to meet Roland Smith for the first time. 'The purchasers', MacArthur had secretly revealed to Smith the previous day, 'are three extremely wealthy Egyptians. You'd better meet them as soon as possible.' Despite MacArthur's assurances, the professor was suspicious that, after years of warfare, Fayed was involved in another conspiracy with Rowland.

Fayed's performance was immaculate. Introduced as Mohamed Al Fayed, he oozingly reassured Smith, 'We don't want any trouble. We want the businesses to develop. All your troubles with Rowland are over. We have nothing to do with Rowland and his people. We are Egyptians. We are involved in shipping, property and especially the Ritz in Paris. We will do for House of Fraser what we did for the Ritz. It was run down and we rebuilt it.' Smith listened politely as Fayed stressed, 'We don't want any aggravation or controversy.'

'I can't stop you buying Rowland's shares,' replied Smith, 'but if you want to make a full bid you'll need the consent of the board, and that will take time.'

House of Fraser's directors were quietly summoned to meet Mohamed and Ali at 6 p.m. Showing them photograph albums of his renovation of the Ritz Hotel and emphasizing his love of Balnagown Castle in order to work on the emotions of the Scottish directors, he boasted of what he could do to improve Harrods. 'We want to make big profits using the Harrods name,' he said. 'Just like we've done with the Ritz.' Nabisco, the giant American food manufacturer, he asserted, paid the Fayeds 'millions of dollars' in licence fees for the use of the 'Ritz' name for their crackers. Sensing his audience's suspicions waning, his spirits rose. His latest fabrication was on target.

The only caution was expressed by Smith. 'We cannot support a full bid until we have seen how we work together.'

'It was a better atmosphere', confirmed finance director George Willoughby, 'than when we met Rowland at the Central Hotel in Glasgow.'

At nine o'clock the following morning, 2 November 1984, Rowland telephoned Ali Fayed. Assured that everything was in place, the Lonrho chief was suddenly caught by surprise. 'You are giving up the directorships?' asked Ali.

'Certainly not,' snapped Rowland. 'The deal is cash against documents.'

'I only raise it', continued Ali, 'because Kleinworts suggested it.'

'I'm dealing with the Fayeds and not Kleinworts. If you want we can call it all off.'

'No, no,' soothed Ali.

Without the shares, Rowland would be powerless to stay on the board. The duplicity was mutual. Rowland and the Fayeds each believed that they could outwit the other. Nevertheless, Ali's question agitated Rowland. His whole purpose was for Lonrho to retain its two directorships and wait for the DTI to withdraw the restrictions on Lonrho's bid while the

Fayeds warehoused his shares. Despite the late hour, he telephoned Marwan in New York and remonstrated. Marwan, having pacified one man, quickly called Ali Fayed and urged him not to rock the boat. 'Ashraf, they must resign,' said Ali, referring to the two Lonrho directors. To the Fayeds it was inconceivable that they would invest £138 million and not snatch control from Rowland.

'Just complete the deal,' sighed Marwan.

At noon, £138 million was transferred to Lonrho's account and the share certificates were handed over. 'He has given me the chance on a golden tray,' cooed Fayed. He had taken the first step towards his ownership of Harrods. There was no evidence either that the money was not Fayed's or that the shares were not owned and controlled by Fayed's Liechtenstein trust: the shadow of the sultan had not yet fallen across the landscape. Three hours later, one telephone conversation ignited Rowland's bitter feud against his erstwhile partner, upsetting for ever Fayed's life of secrecy and lies.

*

BARBARA CONWAY, a *Daily Telegraph* journalist, telephoned Fayed for a comment. Emphatically she was told that Rowland and the other Lonrho director were resigning from the House of Fraser board. Immediately, Conway repeated the conversation to Rowland. Infuriated, Rowland telephoned the Egyptian, who denied Conway's report. Rowland rechecked and called back. Fayed again denied Conway's report. 'You are lying,' snapped Rowland. Fayed smiled. Rowland, who prided himself on 'reading people', was hoist by his own petard: he could never tell the truth that his warehousing deal was borne on the back of their understanding in 1983. Nor could he formally complain to the DTI that he was the victim of deception. Nor did he in November 1984 suggest that the Egyptian lacked the money for a full bid. In common with all tycoons, Rowland had made and overcome one thousand mistakes in his journey to transform Lonrho's turnover in fifteen years from £1 million to £2.5 billion. Still unaware of the unprecedented circumstances of his latest imbroglio, he remained silent, albeit plaged by uncertainty, as Fayed was introduced to the media.

Wary of Fayed's bad English, interspersed as it was with frequent profanities, Basham had decided to avoid press conferences for that weekend's newspapers. Instead, he would rely upon trusted journalists conducting controlled, 'exclusive' interviews. To Fayed's satisfaction, not one of the business editors of the quality newspapers during those interviews questioned Kleinworts' description of the Fayeds as 'members of an old-established Egyptian family who for more than a hundred years were shipowners, landowners and industrialists in Egypt'. The report that Sunday in the *Observer*, Rowland's own newspaper, gave Fayed particular joy.

Michael Gillard, the financial journalist especially trusted by Rowland, described Fayed in the *Observer* as an 'undisguised Anglophile whose old-established family has been doing business with Britain for more than a century. They started shipping cotton from Egypt to Liverpool . . . The Al Fayed reputation in the City is high not least because of his success in building up Costain into the largest contractor in the Gulf.' Having exaggerated their reputation, Gillard reported that 'they are the largest shareholders in one of Texas' major banks . . . Their fortune could be worth at least £500 million. They only smile when asked to put a figure on it.'

Considering its pedigree – the endorsement of his bogus claims published with Rowland's encouragement – Gillard's report thrilled Fayed. In future, as other journalists arrived for interviews, photocopies of the articles, with Gillard's on the top, were presented as 'background facts'. The further endorsement of Fayed's story by the bankers at the Royal Bank of Scotland and Kleinwort Benson, with Lazards' scribbled approval, encouraged him into a burst of irony. 'Ethics and morals count here like nowhere else in the world,' he told the *Daily Mail*. 'When we do something in business, we like to do it with love and affection. The British have business traditions which we love.' Discovering how much he enjoyed the spotlight, Fayed fell into rhapsodies about his rich grandfather, his English nanny and his English education at Victoria College in Alexandria, the exclusive school attended by the Khashoggis. Like a religious mantra, he chanted his story so often that he convinced himself of its truth. 'Good, good,' he grunted, as the grateful departed. They had even complied with his request not to take photographs. Since no pictures existed in the normal agency files, the chance of a former friend from the back streets of Alexandria appearing to expose the impostor was minimized. While in truth employing only a handful of unquestioning clerks, who obeyed orders to destroy the paper trail reporting commission payments, bank interest and profits on 'miscellaneous one-off transactions', he had created the public image of a tycoon managing a business empire.

That Sunday, after reading the newspapers, Fayed welcomed Marwan to lunch in Oxted. Despite the *Observer*'s favourable report, a quotation from Rowland was irritating the Egyptian. The battle for House of Fraser, said Rowland, was 'not over yet' because he might repurchase the shares. 'Somehow I do not think', Rowland added, 'that Mr Mohamed Al Fayed will want to vote me off the board . . . You have only heard the beginning.'

'He must resign,' Fayed urged Marwan.

'I'll talk to him,' agreed Marwan.

But the news the following day was grim. 'Tiny's not going to resign,' Marwan told Ali.

'Then there's a problem,' said Ali, with some insincerity. A break with Rowland was important if they were to secure Roland Smith's support.

Two days later, to Fayed's astonishment, Rowland began buying House of Fraser shares from Marwan and another of those involved in the concert party. Fayed watched incredulously as Rowland accumulated a 6.3 per cent stake and announced his continued interest in either buying the store group or blocking a Fayed bid. 'He's mad,' exclaimed Fayed as the share price rose. His frantic calls to Marwan – 'He must stop' – were ignored.

The evidence of bitterness between the two men produced one advantage. Hearing reports of the row over the weekend, Roland Smith found his suspicions of a new conspiracy between Rowland and the Fayeds disappearing. Fayed exploited the professor's growing trust to embroider the stories of his fabulous wealth. 'We own a building in New York worth one billion dollars,' he claimed, hoping to overwhelm the chairman with visions of his financial resources. His ruse was successful. Smith agreed to write to Rowland demanding his resignation as a director. 'Good, good,' said Fayed as their telephone conversation ended. Days later, Rowland did resign; but by then Fayed's joy had soured.

Marwan was in daily contact with the Fayeds on a completely different matter: he was mediating a dispute between them and Carl Hirschmann, the Swiss aircraft engineer. Hirschmann claimed that Mohamed Fayed had interfered in a contract between himself and the Sultan of Brunei. In response, Fayed claimed that he was acting under the power of attorney granted to him by the sultan. To protect his claim for $48 million compensation, Hirschmann had seized the sultan's Boeing 747. Marwan's neutrality was, Fayed feared, contaminated because of his allegiance to Rowland, but he did not realize his folly in allowing Marwan to meddle in his business.

Visiting Hirschmann in Zurich days after lunching in Oxted, Marwan was growing weary with the convoluted dispute, but towards the end he was offered a tasty morsel. 'The money Fayed used to buy Rowland's House of Fraser shares', said Hirschmann, 'belongs to the sultan.'

'How do you know?' asked Marwan.

'From my contacts in Brunei,' replied Hirschmann; his source was a Brunei official, he confided. Fayed, continued the aggrieved Swiss, held a power of attorney over the sultan's money.

Although Hirschmann provided no evidence for his allegation, Marwan relayed the news to Rowland. Their belief that Fayed had borrowed the money from the Maktoums, it appeared, was wrong. After flying to Switzerland to hear Hirschmann's story personally, Rowland returned to London, 'berserk because he thought that Fayed was a friend. He didn't like being cheated.' Rowland was struck by an uncommon foreboding. Had he misjudged the Fayeds? The newspaper reports of Fayed's billion dollar fortune were odd. Naturally Rowland turned to Marwan, an Eygptian, to discover whether their 'fifty man' had genuinely accumulated that fortune since they had been Lonrho directors seven years earlier. As the former director of Egypt's intelligence service, Marwan's sources of information were excellent. Just two telephone calls, one to the director of Egypt's domestic intelligence service and a second to Mahdi Al Tajir, his neighbour in Carlton Terrace, established the truth.

Until that moment, Fayed had survived as a middleman in the jungle without obligations to anyone. Those injured by his tactics or insults were small players who accepted the risks of their secretive world. Rowland, however, was a unique, big player, and on 16 November 1984 Fayed realized that the rules and stakes had changed. Both *The Times* and the *Evening Standard* published stories that the Al Fayeds had possibly bought the shares on behalf of the sultan of Brunei. Puzzled by the disclosure, Fayed told enquiring journalists, 'We bought the shares on our own behalf,' and pondered the source of the story. The answer arrived on his doorstep the following day.

Calling at Park Lane on Sunday evening, 18 November, Marwan showed Ali Fayed a letter from Hirschmann. It confirmed his allegation about the sultan's money and empowered Marwan to negotiate a compromise settlement with the Fayeds. Ali went pale. The allegation was outrageous, he told Marwan, and motivated by spite. Amid recrimination, the mediation was abandoned. Angrily, Fayed accused Hirschmann of blackmail, issued writs for libel against Marwan, levelled a torrent of abuse on the telephone against Edward du Cann, Lonrho's chairman (which was reported to the police), and, through Basham, issued statements to the press denouncing the lies. Finally, Fayed obtained two statements from the sultan denying any link to the shares. The sultan's unequivocal denials should have been sufficient, but Fayed, conscious of his vulnerability, was now nervous.

Fearing exposure of his past and fearing fear itself, Fayed saw himself as a victim whose activities were being endangered at a particularly delicate moment. Rowland's menacing behaviour, he decided, justified proper protection. He also feared Tajir, and Papa Doc's old contract to kill him. The prospect of a physical attack, however, was only an excuse. The real threat was his exposure as a fantasist. For thirty years he had embellished his biography, and by 1984 the image bore no relation to the truth. The bluster and his fabrications had smoothly concealed a distasteful flaw: his lack of moral courage. The bubbly, self-confident businessman was insecure. The danger he feared was exposure as an impostor. Recruiting bodyguards was his remedy.

On the recommendation of Control Risks, the security consultants, Fayed held a 'beauty contest' of six former SAS soldiers who had all served in the Iranian Embassy siege. The winner, due to his additional experience in Beirut and Kenya, was Brian Dodd, a tough former member of the Parachute Regiment with considerable experience in close protection. In turn, Dodd recruited Michael Lee, a former physical training instructor in the Parachute Regiment and 216 Royal Signals. On alternate weeks, they were to accompany Fayed wherever he went.

Their recruitment in late November coincided with the sultan's arrival in London. Since his own visit to Brunei, Fayed had assiduously striven to restore the status he had craved in Dubai under Sheikh Rashid. On his entry into Heathrow's VIP lounge to await the sultan's arrival, he had identified himself as the sultan's 'Private and Personal Adviser cum Agent in

London'. Over the following weeks, he hoped, he would fulfil that ambition.

Secretly, Fayed had negotiated in his own name the purchase of the Dorchester Hotel. Unknown to the vendors, he was acting under the sultan's power of attorney and the ownership would be transferred to the monarch. To impress his new mentor, who would occupy the hotel's top floor, Fayed asked Lee to recruit more bodyguards. Six former soldiers from the SAS and Parachute Regiment, paid £60 per day by Genavco, were stationed permanently on the hotel's top floor.

Conducting the sultan around his new acquisition, Fayed spoke convincingly about his plans: 'I'll turn this into the best hotel in the world. Like the Ritz.'

'How much will it cost?' asked the sultan.

'£30 million,' replied Fayed.

A trickle of reports about Fayed scurrying from his apartment along Park Lane to the sultan in the Dorchester reached Rowland via London's gossip traders. As his master plan of warehousing the shares with the Egyptian had unravelled, he abandoned his original guess that Fayed had borrowed the money from Dubai and began constructing a melodrama to corroborate his wilder suspicions. Fayed, he believed, had bought his shares using the sultan's money under a secret power of attorney. With Marwan's help, he launched a massive investigation into his former friend's background. Fayed could not fail to see the first results. On 8 December 1984, the *Guardian* printed the first story directly linking Fayed with the sultan. Further articles appeared in the *Daily Telegraph* on the 19th and in *The Times* five days later. Fayed's only retaliation was to issue writs for defamation against Marwan. As Rowland, unbeknown to Fayed, flew for Christmas to his house in Acapulco, Mexico, with Marwan, Hirschmann and their families, Fayed focused upon spreading his hospitality to recruit friends among House of Fraser directors.

Orchestrating a show, Fayed knew, would win hearts and minds. His forceful personality was well disguised by jokes and laughter. Alex Craddock, the Harrods manager employed by the group throughout his life, had visited the Ritz and returned impressed. 'Mohamed', Craddock told his fellow directors, 'appreciates quality. He'll not terrorize us like Rowland.' Unlike Tiny Rowland, an ogre who did not love Harrods and would not invest money, Fayed was clearly a builder. Similarly Roland Smith, the company chairman, was seduced by Fayed's suggestion that his salary should be doubled with a backdated bonus. Leading his fellow directors to a reception in the Park Lane penthouse, Smith emerged charmed by his hosts and reassured by Ali's apparently thoughtful intelligence. 'It's outstandingly palatial,' gushed one director. 'I'd never seen anything like the sheer quality.' Champagne, canapés and sumptuous décor had earned the Fayeds credibility. Like the City's bankers and lawyers, the directors assumed that the opulence confirmed the Fayeds' phenomenal wealth. On 3 January 1985, the Fayeds joined the board as directors. Although without any management experience, they asked to be consulted on all decisions. The Scotsmen did not demur. The only cloud was Rowland, stirring up trouble by telling a newspaper, 'I am delighted that the Fayeds have now joined the Fraser board. Mohamed and Ali are still close friends of mine.'

Rowland's jockeying puzzled government officials. 'Is Rowland crazy or what?' asked Hans Liesner, a DTI civil servant responsible for competition policy. Both Liesner and his colleague Martin Vile could not suppress their suspicions. 'Perhaps the Fayeds are co-operating in another secret plot with Rowland?' On Fayed's behalf, the House of Fraser directors agreed to counter that mistrust. Roland Smith visited Sir Godfray Le Quesne, chairman of the Monopolies Commission, with Fayed to emphasize their co-operation. 'The directors', said Smith in a show of unity, 'are either neutral or unopposed to a Fayed bid.'

Next, accompanied by Kleinworts' John MacArthur, Fayed visited Elizabeth Llewellyn Smith, the taciturn deputy director general of the Office of Fair Trading. Bursting with venom, Fayed attacked Rowland. 'The man is mad. Mad!' he exclaimed. 'I have made much money. So much money. The sultan is . . .' Whatever Fayed was saying was lost as excitement overcame him.

Smiling weakly at the foreigner's plight, Llewellyn Smith addressed MacArthur: 'We'll need a statement that the Fayeds can finance a full bid. That'll be all. Thank you.'

Sitting in the splendour of their Park Lane penthouse, Mohamed and Ali were undisturbed as they faced the moment of truth. Glancing at a draft list of their assets presented by MacArthur, Ali's expression hardly changed as he scanned the exaggerations describing the Fayeds as 'leading shipowners in the liner trade, operating from Genoa, Piraeus, London, Dubai and Egypt', as bankers and members of 'Middle East oil exploration consortia with major oil companies', and as 'involved in many construction projects, particularly in the Middle East'. The Fayeds, Ali read, had won construction contracts worth $2 billion in Dubai for docks, a hospital and the Trade Centre. He did not blink either at the false statement that the Fayeds 'owned' 75 Rockefeller Plaza in New York. On the contrary, delighted by the audacity of their coup, Ali nodded his approval. 'The British were easily fooled,' he thought.

In his formal reply to Llewellyn Smith's request, MacArthur affirmed that the Fayeds were registered as the owners of the shares transferred from Rowland and that they controlled sufficient funds for a full offer. Denied any independent means of investigation, Llewellyn Smith unequivocally accepted the banker's assurances. The barriers were falling.

5

The Bid

MOHAMED FAYED WAS GLOWING. Preparations for a full bid
for the House of Fraser were under way. His dream of being a
tycoon, power broker and fabulous pasha were finally materi-
alizing. While assuring the sultan that his interests would be
pursued, he concealed his agenda: promoting his own importance. Perceptively, he spotted the individual who could best
advance his cause, Gordon Reece.

Flamboyant and shrewd, Gordon Reece was a political
public relations specialist enjoying a close relationship with
Margaret Thatcher, the prime minister. His easy access to
Downing Street matched Fayed's requirements. Buying introductions for access to government leaders was the usual custom
in the Middle East, and selecting Reece to lead him into
Britain's centre of power was Fayed's masterstroke. Inviting
the lobbyist to his penthouse, the Egyptian easily persuaded
Reece of his own importance and of his indispensability to the
sultan. In return for a generous fee and a flat in 60 Park Lane
at a low rent, Reece delivered awesome results.

In mid-January 1985, Reece was sitting in Thatcher's study
in Downing Street. In the midst of a financial crisis, Britain's
plight had been aggravated by the sultan's decision to transfer
the management of investments worth $5 billion from London
to New York. The prime minister, due to meet the sultan by
the end of the month, needed leverage. 'I know someone in
London who is very knowledgeable about Brunei,' offered
Reece. 'He's very well connected to the sultan. In fact, he's

complained about a problem with the renewal of the sultan's British passport. There's a Foreign Office cock-up.' Thatcher summoned Charles Powell, her trusted foreign policy adviser, and ordered him to solve the passport problem. 'This man Al Fayed,' said Reece, 'he might also be able to help with the sultan's switch from sterling.' Those few words uttered by Reece established Fayed's credentials in Britain's most important office. The big performance in Park Lane had elevated an unknown Arab middleman, one of thousands passing anonymously through London to offer their services as intermediaries, into a player at the centre of power.

Automatically, Powell, who had never heard of Fayed, telephoned the co-ordinator at the Foreign Office. 'Is anything known about Mohamed Al Fayed?' he asked. That simple question activated routine searches through the files of MI6, the foreign intelligence agency; of MI5, the domestic counter-intelligence organization; and throughout the Whitehall network. The negative response cleared Fayed for an approach which transformed his status and wealth. Powell telephoned Fayed and invited him to Downing Street to discuss the sultan's visit.

No man crosses the threshold at Number 10 without feeling exhilarated, but the experience for Fayed was especially pertinent. For over thirty minutes, he spoke about Brunei as the sultan's representative. His advice was deemed by officials to be 'helpful but not especially important'. By the time he stepped out of the building, having emphasized to Charles Powell his love of Britain and his desire to assist the government, Fayed's swirling fantasies had placed him at the core of Britain's political life.

On 29 January 1985, the sultan met Thatcher in 10 Downing Street. The prime minister pressed her guest to transfer his money back to London. For his part, the sultan complained about Britain's withdrawal of the Gurkhas stationed in his kingdom. By the end of the visit, both sides agreed to reverse their decisions. Although no one saw Fayed in Downing Street during that encounter nor ever found his name on that day's

Downing Street visitors list, Fayed spread the news that he had indeed accompanied the monarch and had been introduced to Thatcher as the sultan's adviser. Since Thatcher never publicly denied the claim, it was accepted as true. The next step in Fayed's equation was self-serving: 'I've done a favour for Britain, now Britain owes a favour to me.'

Using the sultan to serve Mohamed Fayed's interest, John MacArthur and his chairman Michael Hawkes were introduced to the monarch at the end of that same day. In the allotted twenty-five minutes, the bankers sought to win for Kleinworts the management contract of the sultan's $3 billion portfolio. Visibly unimpressed with British bankers after the Crown Agents had lost a fortune on Brunei's account, the monarch never bothered to reply to Kleinworts' offer and letters, nor did Fayed bother to argue his bankers' virtues. His purpose had been to impress the bankers with his own importance.

Even Fayed, however, was surprised by the influence of Reece. A telephone call to Park Lane from Field Marshal Sir Edwin Bramall, the chief of the defence staff, exceeded his expectations. There was a problem, explained the senior officer, who wondered whether he might call at Park Lane with Michael Heseltine, the secretary of state for defence. Ecstatically, Fayed agreed. Shortly afterwards, the two men passed through the armour-plated glass vestibule guarded permanently by two men, crammed into the small lift and ascended to the penthouse. Fayed welcomed his guests boisterously. The 'problem', it transpired, was the sultan's decision to switch a £500 million order for defence equipment from British manufacturers. Anxious to restore the British contract, Bramall had been smoothly assured by Gordon Reece that only Fayed could influence the sultan. 'I will do it. You can count on me,' pronounced the pasha to the grateful supplicants. 'I love Britain and will do whatever I can.' As the two visitors squeezed back into the lift, the field marshal murmured, 'He's "own troops". He's going to help.' With very little effort, Fayed delivered what they wanted. To embellish his feat, after Bramall and

Heseltine had offered their sincere thanks, the sultan's representative also arranged for the monarch to donate 'hundreds of thousands of pounds' to the Army Museum and the Imperial War Museum. 'I've done more favours for Britain,' was Fayed's calculation. 'Now Britain owes more favours to me.'

Only one person was tarnishing his glory: Rowland. Pursuing his quarry, the Lonrho executive had discovered the sultan's connection to the Dorchester transaction and had passed the secret for publication to the *Daily Telegraph*. 'Another pinprick,' cursed Fayed. Issuing an inaccurate public denial and serving another writ on Marwan, his sense of invincibility was nevertheless undiminished. Having just bought 55 Park Lane, a block of flats adjacent to the Dorchester Hotel, for £37 million, he appeared to be funding an expanding empire, especially in the short-term renting of luxury flats. In reality, the purchase was financed by a massive loan from Credit Suisse whose repayment Fayed could never afford. Secrecy still protected the ambitious Egyptian.

Anticipating increased agitation from Rowland, Fayed summoned Mick Lee, his senior bodyguard. Two men, he complained, were insufficient for total protection in Park Lane, in Oxted and while he travelled. Avid to build a large organization, Lee exploited his employer's eagerness. 'Tried by twelve and carried by six,' he murmured, repeating a regimental motto. 'Twenty-four-hour protection, every day,' he calculated aloud like a barrow boy in a street market, 'will cost you thirty men.'

Rather than blanching at the prospect, Fayed's eyes gleamed. 'Where you get from?' he asked.

'Mates,' replied Lee. 'I'll find 'em.'

The notion of a band of bodyguards appealed to Fayed's self-regard. As a child, he had seen the rich racing through Alexandria surrounded by bodyguards and he aspired to the frisson and prestige that his passage surrounded by protectors would excite. On the grapevine, Lee's offer to ex-soldiers, in the Military Police, the Parachute Regiment and the SAS, especially those trained in close-escort protection, spread quickly. During February, twenty former members of Britain's elite regiments, trained to kill, were recruited to protect the pasha. On Fayed's instructions, Lee sought another twenty.

Tony Evans, a former Para, did not accept the job only for the money. The introductory pay, through Genavco, Fayed's shipping company, was only £100 per week. Instead, it was the glamour, the good food and the promise of more money if he performed. At the end of the first month, a wodge of bank notes was pushed into his hand. 'What's this for?' he asked, counting out £1,000 in fifties.

'Don't you want it?' scoffed Lee. 'It's for doing your job and keeping your gob shut.' Understanding his employer's mentality, Lee added, 'Don't think about what goes on here, or think about what he asks. Just do it and take the money.'

Spotting the guns lying on a table in Lee's office scarcely hidden by a cloth, Evans asked if he too could be armed. Like many soldiers, he loved guns and was attracted to the possession of a revolver in London.

'No problem, mate,' replied Lee.

Like the other recruits, Evans aspired to membership of the 'Good Boys Club', the five senior bodyguards who grabbed all the foreign trips and the extra wodges of cash.

Concealed under his jacket, Lee was carrying a Walther PPK, the handgun favoured by professionals. Dodd was carrying a 38mm gun. In Dodd's opinion, proper protection without a gun was impossible because an assailant could be armed. His employer was easily convinced. With Fayed's agreement, his private army had been armed, tucking Smith & Wessons and 38mm revolvers into the waistband of their trousers or in pouches as they accompanied him in a haphazard manner around London, in the countryside and on his plane. His armoury in Oxted even included a shotgun disguised as a walking stick. Bob Curry, a former SAS soldier, was handed a Model 40 Smith & Wesson, featuring a concealed hammer, designed for firing from a pocket without the risk of jamming. Fayed's justification for having four armed men accompany him around London was not only the presence of guns on Rowland's Gulfstream but his desire for the companionship of unquestioning fans, smiling in approval whenever he raised his eyes.

At the end of February 1985, in the early hours of a Sunday morning, Bob Curry drove for the first time to Oxted, alias 'Fort Apache', carrying a box of tea bags from Park Lane and the Sunday newspapers bought at midnight at King's Cross station. During the previous two weeks, Lee had created an 'Ops Room' in Barrow Court. In two lockers, he had stored a 32mm machine gun obtained from the Middle East, semi-automatics, revolvers and several pump-action shotguns. The low fences installed eleven years earlier had been replaced by eight- and ten-foot fences. Curry was among the first to witness a further refinement. Radioing his arrival in advance, he stopped outside the newly installed high gates and extinguished the lights. Stepping out of the bushes, a guard, his face blacked out, wearing combat uniform and black gloves, levelled a shotgun at the window. 'Drive up to the house,' he ordered in succinct, military style. 'Stay in the car until further orders. The rottweilers are loose.' Curry drove 300 yards, past a new necklace fence, to a side entrance and stopped. A door opened. A dim light shone on to dogs being tethered to the outside wall. 'Okay,' he was ordered. 'Come in.' Carrying the tea bags and newspapers, Curry entered the new Ops Room.

The sight that met his eyes was starkly familiar. Dressed in Parachute Regiment uniforms with polished boots, Fayed's bodyguards stood silhouetted against an electronic panel erected along one wall. Flashing lights identified the locations of sound sensors and light beams guarding the fence and the grounds. In the event of an alarm being triggered, the position would be illuminated, hastening the arrival of four armed men. 'Good. Good,' Fayed had said, reassured by the spectacle of military discipline transforming his home into a fortified camp. 'You stand in my presence,' he commanded, resisting the urge to demand salutes as well. In his vicinity, he was satisfied to notice, the trained killers seemed to shrink; he felt himself an equal, a man's man. The guards would carry shotguns as he walked, fastidiously dressed in garish shellsuits and white gumboots, across the one-mile cycle track, across the gallop constructed of rubber and sand, into the isolated fields of his estate. Although drilled to obey without question, all his bodyguards regarded an attempted murder in the midst of the Surrey countryside as less than probable and could only speculate about the feared assassin's identity. 'He says there's a contract out on him by Papa Doc of Haiti,' remarked Lee, interested in his employer's murky past. 'Seems he did some business and vanished taking the money.'

The security arrangements had changed Fayed's family life in Oxted. The birth of Jasmine in 1980 had been followed in September 1983 by that of Karim, a son. Although they were registered under the surname Wathen-Fayed, the children's illegitimacy was a source of grievance to their mother. Living with his many idiosyncrasies – his extraordinary obsession with germs, his variable moods, his expectation that she remain isolated in the country while he spent the whole week in London, his insistence that they sleep in separate bedrooms – imposed unrelenting pressure upon the former model. His latest habit, emphasizing the differences between Arab and Scandinavian culture, was to isolate himself every morning in his personal gin palace, a large, heated marquee erected in the garden. Fitted with Persian carpets on slats and comfortable wicker chairs, Fayed sat surrounded by telephones in a coat and hat in winter or tracksuit in summer, ignoring both the howling wind and the sunshine, wilfully oblivious to the bulldozers carving a disfiguring path for the M25 motorway through his estate. Enveloped in romantic dreams, he was the desert pasha constructing his kingdom. Outside his command post, he expected that his underlings – family and employees, especially his bodyguards – were waiting in fear and anticipation of his whims and moods.

*

THE NEWS FROM LONDON was mixed. Whitehall's bureaucrats, reassured by his bankers and lawyers, were inclining to
favour Fayed's bid, if only to spike Rowland. To Sir Gordon
Borrie, the director general of the Office of Fair Trading (OFT),
Rowland and his team 'weren't a pretty sight. Not like the
normal smooth merchant bankers. Rowland was red toothed
and raw.' More important than personal antipathy was a
change in government policy. Breaking with socialism, Norman
Tebbit, the secretary of state for trade and industry, had
announced that takeover bids would no longer be referred to
the Monopolies Commission to investigate 'the public interest'.
That change of policy prompted Sir Godfray Le Quesne, the
Commission's chairman, to announce at the end of February
1985, that 'circumstances have changed' and Lonrho could
after all bid for House of Fraser. Fayed had lost the political
advantage.

But Rowland was not jubilant. The stakes had utterly
changed. His original bid at 150 pence was too low. The new
minimum, £3 per share, was far beyond his debt-stricken
company's limits. Thwarted, he plotted a scenario based upon
hope rather than reality.

Since a British public company like Lonrho, he reasoned,
had been subjected to a rigorous inquiry by the Monopolies
Commission, it was inevitable that a Liechtenstein-registered,
off-the-shelf company called the Alfayed Investment Trust
(AITSA), with three unknown Egyptian brothers listed as directors, would also be investigated by the Commission. Once the
reference was announced, he believed, the share price would
collapse and Lonrho could buy the store group cheaply.
Fayed's treachery would be avenged.

Critically, Rowland's sources of information for that conclusion did not include a well-connected merchant bank or
anyone enjoying an amicable relationship with Borrie or Tebbit. Instead, he relied upon a gaggle of compliant lawyers and
brokers and Edward du Cann, the shady MP whose relationship with Thatcher had faded to antipathy. None of them

realized that under Tebbit's new directive 'the public interest' would no longer prevent a takeover.

'We can do it now, let's hit it,' urged John MacArthur, convinced that Fayed's route was clear. Assiduously, Fayed had been cultivating Roland Smith, evoking a halcyon future of complete autonomy and huge investment under his owner-ship. Richer than he anticipated because the pound had sunk to an all-time low against the dollar, he offered a phenomenal £4 per share in cash for the remaining 70 per cent of the shares. The total investment would be £573 million. To remove any doubts he promised House of Fraser's directors higher salaries and secure contracts. On 4 March 1985, with the directors' support, Fayed publicly announced his intention to bid. Rowland was shocked. Accurate rumours suggested that somehow the Fayeds had found a further £435 million in cash, which valued the group – after the rise in value of his shares since their purchase in November 1984 and the drop in ster-ling's value – at £615 million. Since there was no history of their fortune before December 1984, and he was convinced by the circumstantial evidence of the powers of attorney, Rowland swore, 'It must be the sultan's.' There was no proof the sultan had financed the purchase, so the monarch's spokesman nat-urally denied any involvement.

Fayed knew that Rowland and du Cann had been pouring vitriol over his reputation. In particular, the two had lobbied Alex Fletcher, a junior minister at the DTI. But Fayed was unaware that the tycoon and Marwan had earlier flown to Marbella, Spain, for lunch with Adnan Khashoggi, the living witness to his lies. Solemnly promised confidentiality, Fayed's former brother-in-law had revealed the truth. 'He's not the son of a pasha,' laughed the billionaire, 'but the son of a poor education inspector who lived in a dirty house in Alexandria.' Rowland had passed on that revelation to Fletcher. 'The Fay-eds' claims of wealth cannot be true,' he seethed, setting out his research. The Ritz Hotel was fully mortgaged; the Fayeds did not 'own' a block in New York's Rockefeller Center, but only a minority interest which was subject to a lease; and their 'fleet of ships' was just a few barges and three roll-on roll-off vessels. 'The tale MacArthur and Basham are peddling is rubbish,' Lonrho's executive told Fletcher. 'We would expect a level playing field,' added du Cann, whose own credibility was even less than Rowland's. The minister's distaste for du Cann was equalled by his distrust of Ashraf Marwan, who at Rowland's request had sent the politician an allegedly signed copy of the sultan's power of attorney to Fayed dated 23 August 1984. Neither Fletcher nor Borrie was impressed by Marwan's suggestion that Fayed was lying. Five months earlier, Marwan had been judged by John Griffiths, the DTI inspector, to be a liar. The only effect of the denunciation was to boost Fayed's status, robustly embellished by MacArthur.

On 6 March Alex Fletcher invited MacArthur to his office. 'Are the rumours about Fayed and the sultan true?' Fletcher asked. 'We are satisfied', sang the banker from Fayed's song sheet, 'that our clients are using their own money, have got enough money and are acting on their own behalf . . . One shouldn't draw any inferences because they were acting for the sultan in the Dorchester.' The minister was satisfied. Nevertheless, as a safety check, the Fayeds' bankers and lawyers were asked to produce another written statement verifying their wealth.

The Fayeds had taken great care since the previous summer to cultivate their advisers, who gathered compliantly on the evening of Friday, 8 March 1985 at 60 Park Lane to produce that statement. The existence of Fayed's cash was indisputable. Earlier that day, $474.7 million had been transferred from the Swiss Bank Corporation in Zurich to London. Described as a fiduciary deposit, the source of the money was disguised, but Fayed's money had been borrowed from the Swiss banks against the security of a huge deposit by the sultan. Yet the Fayeds' advisers, mesmerized by the opulence of Park Lane, had been conditioned to avoid inquiries about the background of the transferred money. Cheerfully, under the chairmanship of

Richard Fleck, a solicitor from Herbert Smith, they read out a list of the Fayeds' assets, and with each item one of the brothers chirruped its value. Unchallenged, Mohamed indulged his fantasies once again while Ali calmly produced bank statements to substantiate their exaggerated claims. One banker glanced at a paper passed by Ali. '160 million,' Ali read, before adding, 'dollars.' In fact, the sum was Swiss francs, amounting to just $60 million. If the banker had given it more than a cursory glance, he would also have noticed that the statement reflected a mere thirty-two-day fixed-term deposit. The magic sound of very large figures caused their advisers to forget that the statement was not proof that the money actually belonged to the Fayeds. Totting up the list at the end, MacArthur announced, 'One billion dollars.' Seduced by the Fayeds' performance, not one of the professionals paused to confront the truth: that the brothers' claims were hugely exaggerated, that their own property was already pledged as security against loans and that their business could not have generated £615 million in cash. 'The Fayeds have more than adequate funds of their own to finance the offer,' MacArthur would tell the government's officials the following week, in a way that suggested he had scrutinized their accounts. Foolishly, the so-called professionals had been led by the nose – though the Fayeds' task had been greatly eased by the general hostility towards Rowland.

Gordon Borrie, the director general of the Office of Fair Trading, did not trust Rowland's motives. Twice the Lonrho chief had been condemned as a liar by DTI inspectors; he had organized a concert party; he had sold his shares to Fayed; then he had bought a 6 per cent stake from other members of the concert party; and finally, cleared by the regulators to launch a counterbid for House of Fraser, he had done nothing. He had not even bought more shares. Rowland was dangerous trouble, Borrie concluded. Whatever Fayed's background, if he could pay cash for the shares the bid would not be blocked.

*

As Fayed's advisers left the penthouse that Friday night, prepared to launch the bid when the stock market opened the following Monday, Brian Basham outlined to the Egyptian his plan for the weekend's news coverage. Critically, that would establish the atmosphere in Whitehall. 'Journalists', said Basham, 'will undoubtedly raise Rowland's claim that you're acting as a front for the sultan. What's your answer?' Unblinking, Fayed replied, 'Our fathers met many years ago at the Ritz in Paris.' As always, the fantasist had blurred the truth.

Before the journalists arrived to be briefed, Basham copied down Fayed's denial. 'Mr Al Fayed's long-standing relationship with the sultan', wrote Basham, 'was a continuation of a relationship cemented between their fathers. It is absolute nonsense that the money is coming from Brunei. It is coming from the Fayed family funds that have been accumulated over generations and been wisely invested.' Basham had no trouble convincing the two important journalists about his employer's veracity.

The first was Ivan Fallon, an uncritical business columnist of the *Sunday Times*. Well rehearsed, Fayed described to his visitor how the cotton, plucked by his great-grandfather's serfs in the Nile Delta, had been shipped to Lancashire's mills. Operating on him like a drug, Fayed's lies only encouraged him to utter greater fabrications. In a burst of colour, the Egyptian added that in 1966 he had offered to build Sheikh Rashid a port in Dubai because, 'My ships carrying pilgrims could not get in. There was no proper harbour, just a creek.' In his article Fallon described the Fayeds' fabulous riches: 'Already wealthy when they left Egypt, the Al Fayeds have multiplied their fortune many times since.'

*

To Ian Watson, the business editor of the *Sunday Telegraph*, who followed, Fayed augmented his exaggerations. 'Kleinwort Benson', the editor would report, 'has had a relationship with the Al Fayeds for several decades. The bank will show Tebbit and the OFT this week that the Al Fayeds have about $1 billion of free wealth over and above the £615 million they have currently put on the table for House of Fraser. This is a lot more than the debt-ridden Lonrho could produce.' Neither the Fayeds nor the bank pointed out to the journalist that their relationship had been born only weeks earlier or that he had doubled their fortune to $2 billion. By then, MacArthur had fallen completely under Mohamed's spell, a condition induced by a combination of remarkable charm and the theatrical performance of a mega-tycoon. His credulity was only too manifest when MacArthur appeared that Sunday on television.

Fayed watched delighted as MacArthur, interviewed by John Plender of the *Financial Times*, confidently spoke of the Fayeds' 'net worth of several billion dollars'. The banker repeated that the Fayeds' money came from 'their own resources, which stem from their family businesses going back several generations, founded in Egypt some one hundred years ago and since then developed outside Egypt post the Nasser period'. No one, least of all the government officials who were also watching, suspected that Fayed might be telling audacious lies. He had successfully inspired confidence in himself and hardened doubts about Rowland's motives.

The single sceptic that weekend was Melvyn Marckus, the *Observer*'s City editor. Urged by Rowland to report Fayed's deception and his link to the sultan, Marckus had eagerly repeated Fayed's propaganda about accompanying the sultan to Downing Street, which he had every reason to believe. Yet Marckus, concerned by his proprietor's interference and doubtful about the scale of Fayed's deception, limited his article to a suggestion of dishonesty. Even that terrified Fayed. Incapable of controlling or even anticipating the effect of his reactions, he responded with a sledgehammer, inflicting enormous damage upon himself. On Monday morning, he issued a writ alleging defamation. Marckus, who believed his article to be 'objective', was, he told colleagues, 'surprised, astonished and furious. It's a gagging writ.' Having tried to keep some distance from Rowland, Marckus was galvanized by Fayed's writ into searching for real truth, so driving the *Observer* into Rowland's camp.

*

AT EIGHT O'CLOCK on Monday morning, 11 March 1985, while the Fayeds sat nervously in Park Lane, brokers began offering £4 for each House of Fraser share. But there were no sellers. Everyone was holding back in the expectation that Lonrho would be making a rival bid and that the price would zoom. Instead, there was a shattering surprise. Just before midday, Rowland sold his 6.3 per cent block to Fayed. Lonrho's second sale seemed to be the signal that Rowland had abandoned the quest. But the transaction was Machiavellian. Convinced that the Fayed bid would be blocked by Tebbit, Rowland had sold in the expectation of buying the shares back cheap. By 1 p.m., the Fayeds owned more than 50 per cent of House of Fraser.

The brothers' first visit that day was to Elizabeth Llewellyn Smith, the deputy director general of the Office of Fair Trading. Over the weekend, the quiet official had become slightly sceptical of the Fayeds' claims. To satisfy the OFT, she had told her visitors, they needed to provide assurances that the Fayeds' funds were acquired legally and to state whether an unknown third party was involved.

To reinforce his case, Fayed had earlier telephoned John Fryer of the builders Bernard Sunley, whom he had represented in Dubai. 'Say I got you five hundred million pounds' worth of business,' he urged. The builders undertook to tell the OFT that Fayed had secured contracts worth £400 million. In truth, the figure was about £260 million. Fryer, it was agreed, would tell the inspectors that Sunley had paid Fayed £40 million in commissions, although according to their accounts the company had paid him £22.5 million.

Fortunately for Fayed, Llewellyn Smith, blind to the web

of deception, asked imprecise question. By contrast, her visitors gave hard, emphatic answers. In the Fayeds' presence, Mac-Arthur repeated his belief that the brothers possessed assets worth $1.1 billion, 'including the Ritz Hotel in Paris'. The official's notes mysteriously inflated even the Fayeds' exaggerations. Listing their assets, she scribbled that they were worth $1,150 million plus the £450 million cash (an inexplicable sum) for the takeover, more than the value of British Airways. Like all her colleagues, she never queried how a man of Fayed's pedigree, claiming to possess over $1 billion and resident in London for twenty years, had never paid British taxes. To suffocate any residual doubts, the solicitor Edward Walker-Arnott pompously asserted, 'Herbert Smith do not take on cases which do not hold water.' In a letter which would subsequently be condemned as 'untrue, incorrect, seriously exaggerated or otherwise misleading', Herbert Smith wrote, 'We are . . . entirely satisfied . . . as to the accuracy of the instructions given to us by the Al Fayed brothers.'

Fayed's next stop the following morning, 12 March, was Norman Tebbit. The secretary of state had been reminded by Gordon Reece, the Conservative Party's adviser, that Fayed, unlike Rowland, was 'a friend of Britain'. His presence at 10 Downing Street, continued Reece, had assisted Thatcher's negotiations with the sultan, while Rowland had embarrassed Britain in a row about enforcing oil sanctions against Southern Rhodesia in the 1960s. Considering Fayed's 'enormous wealth', there was no reason, he concluded, to believe Rowland, an established liar. Since Reece and Tebbit knew each other well, the politician was naturally influenced by those arguments, bearing in mind that since January 1984 the *Observer* had been publishing embarrassing claims that Mark Thatcher had earned commissions from British companies for contracts in the Gulf by immorally exploiting his relationship with the prime minister. Accompanied by MacArthur and Professor Smith, the Fayeds were shown into the secretary of state's office. Sitting near Tebbit were Alex Fletcher, Gordon Borrie and Martin Vile, an assistant secretary at the DTI. Tebbit had been advised by Borrie that Rowland, condemned for dishonesty by two DTI inquiries, was untrustworthy. Kleinworts and Herbert Smith, Borrie believed, could not have been duped by Fayed and morality was irrelevant: 'It's a cash bid and as long as the shareholders receive their money, the OFT has no further interest.'

Tebbit agreed. 'I didn't care who owned Harrods or House of Fraser,' he would say. 'I was only interested in takeovers on competition grounds, and there was no competition element involved.' Both sides were invited to argue their case. Tebbit's principal concern was whether the Fayeds possessed the cash for the acquisition.

Martin Vile had been particularly impressed by Mac-Arthur's confident television appearance and by the bankers' repeated assurances of the Fayeds' independent wealth. 'Is it your own money?' asked Tebbit. With massive sincerity, Mohamed Fayed endorsed MacArthur's assurance that 'more than $1 billion is available' and the banker's estimate that the Fayeds possessed forty liners. 'We have major shipping interests,' Fayed told Tebbit, looking straight into his eyes. 'For fifty years. All around the Mediterranean.' Even that shrewd politican, forewarned by Rowland, could not have imagined that Fayed owned only three cargo vessels.

'Are you acting on behalf of the sultan of Brunei, Mr Al Fayed?' asked Tebbit.

'No,' replied Mohamed, deciding nevertheless to admit one truth at last, 'I've acted for them in other businesses like the Dorchester, but this one is mine.'

'Why is Alfayed Investment Holdings owned by a company based in Liechtenstein?'

'That's simply for tax purposes,' replied MacArthur.

To double-check, Tebbit asked the Fayeds to leave and turned to Professor Smith: 'What checks have you done on the Al Fayeds?'

'I've been more concerned that they'll be good for the

business than discovering where their money comes from,' replied Smith. 'But I'm satisfied that they are very rich.'

Tebbit remained wary. Heedful of Rowland's menacing warnings, he appeared to require more checks and proof. 'You've had since last November to investigate their background,' complained George Willoughby, the finance director. 'It's a bit late to raise that question now.' Tebbit did not reply.

As the Fayeds were led out through one door, the Lonrho delegation entered from another. Rowland's attitude to Tebbit was uncomplicated: he hated British politicians. Inscrutably, the secretary of state sat listening to Rowland and his advisers as they argued that Fayed was not using his own money and required investigation. 'What does it matter who brings in the money,' asked Tebbit, 'providing it's brought in?' Po-faced, he asked the clinching question, 'Why don't you counterbid? Or make a conditional bid?' Rowland sat silent. Tebbit had called his bluff. Here was a man who ranted and raved against Fayed one moment yet the next sold him the shares twice over and thereby delivered the company into his hands.

Nevertheless, as an unusual precaution, Tebbit telephoned Michael Hawkes, the chairman of Kleinworts. Despite his title, Hawkes, a compromise candidate after an internal feud in the bank, could not boast the most astute mind in the City. But even he understood that Tebbit's call was designed to place the responsibility for any future imbroglio firmly on the banker. Explicitly, the secretary of state asked him whether the government could rely upon Kleinworts' assurances about the Fayeds. 'We haven't known the Fayeds long,' replied Hawkes, 'but we've had satisfactory assurances from the Royal Bank of Scotland and we have no doubt that sufficient funds are held on their behalf in Switzerland.'

'But are they acting for the sultan or themselves?'

'My reasoned judgement is that it's for themselves. It does not make sense that the sultan would use them as a front. There would be no reason why he could not buy it on his own behalf, quite openly.'

Tebbit saw the strength of that argument.

Over the following three days, Fayed worked furiously. Anticipating Rowland's moves to expose his lies, which included Marwan's delivery of the Egyptian family records which proved the Fayeds' poverty, he engineered laudatory letters to Tebbit from the British contractors working in Dubai and gave more interviews suggesting that to find against him would be racist. 'I know people think I'm just a bloody Egyptian,' he told journalists. But his most effective agent was once again Gordon Reece.

The lobbyist, indebted to Fayed's generosity having accepted the flat in Park Lane serviced by his benefactor's staff, called Downing Street to secure a seat for his client on 14 March at the prime minister's dinner for President Hosni Mubarak of Egypt. Charles Powell, eager to find suitable Egyptians to fill the sixty-six chairs, was willing to oblige. As usual, he made some checks, especially with the DTI. According to that department, 'Fayed's big in the Gulf, involved in the Dubai Trade Centre and certainly acceptable for the dinner.'

For Fayed, it was an astonishing coup. Not only had he rarely returned to Egypt since 1958, not even for his father's funeral, but he remained ostensibly the sworn enemy of the Nasserites who had overthrown the pashas. He enjoyed no status in Britain either. Yet Reece had secured his invitation to the dinner to be seated next to Carol Thatcher, as well as an introduction that same evening to the prime minister. For Fayed, seen in animated conversation with Mubarak, a man he had never met before, the event was another step in his bewitching of the British establishment. Thatcher was his latest and biggest prize. Observing that he seemed intimate with both the sultan and Mubarak, she overrode Lonrho's objections. Subsequently, she would explain to du Cann that the dinner invitation had been sent out at the behest of the Foreign Office, but no one was fooled. Fayed had charmed, cajoled and finally bought his way into a second visit to

Downing Street. The politicians no longer harboured any doubts about their choice.

Like a roll of drums, Tebbit's announcement on 14 March that the Fayeds' bid would pass uninvestigated heralded the defeat of Rowland's seven-year battle for the House of Fraser. Fayed was the victor. He was no longer a commission agent, a middleman, a servant and a groveller to kings and sheikhs. He was a principal with the power to say, 'I don't need that person.' Privately, he understood the audacity of his coup. In the face of adversity, he had surmounted the near impossible. Publicly he boasted, 'The British government, they gave me House of Fraser in only ten days because they know who is Mohamed Al Fayed.' As he repeated that pronouncement, he convinced himself of its truth and of his own importance. 'I love Britain,' he proclaimed with mock sincerity. But a newspaper headline – 'First Suez, Now this. Nothing is sacred' – reflected the British distaste for the sale of a 136-year-old institution to a foreigner. Leonidas, the chocolate concessionaires at Harrods, discovered that their Jewish customers preferred to buy at Selfridges rather than in an Arab-owned store. The outsider was determined to reverse that antagonism. Just as he had bought the professionals to deliver him House of Fraser, he would bribe the British to love and accept him. Like all hard men, he was innocent of sin. Never growing weary of trying, he believed that he would soon belong.

6

Harrods

THE EARTH DID NOT MOVE as Mohamed Fayed entered
Harrods for the first time as the owner. Unrecognized among
the thousands of shoppers, excitement understandably surged
through him as he walked inside the world's most famous
store, frequented by Britain's aristocracy. 'All this belongs to
Mohamed Al Fayed,' he intoned. Surrounded by his armed
bodyguards, only the cognoscenti would notice a change of
posture, an unmistakable swagger marking the newly bestowed
mantle of fame, power and prestige. Instinct and bravado had
been rewarded. No longer the mere employer of fifty shipping
clerks, he now controlled the fates not only of 27,000 House
of Fraser employees but also of thousands of suppliers to his
one hundred stores across the country. At the age of fifty-six, a
time when most men contemplate retirement, he was embarking upon a new life. The scale of his success – the journey from
the backstreets of Alexandria to Knightsbridge – would remain
resolutely concealed. But the inbred attitudes, the morals and
the methods of the bazaar would be mercilessly deployed.
Adopting the style of the varying despots – of Duvalier, Rashid
and the sultan – he would expect total obedience to his
commands. Discussion, self-criticism and compromise were
alien weaknesses. Taking the lift to the fifth floor, he was
greeted by Alex Craddock.

Entering Craddock's office, Fayed found himself quivering
before the visual evidence that Harrods offered a passport into
British society and the royal family. Four royal warrants granted

by members of the royal family were hanging on the wall. Surely there would be no objection to their transfer to the new owner. A photograph of the queen was a reminder that, since 1982, Harrods had also sponsored the Windsor Horse Show, where Prince Philip was both president and competitor. Fayed could expect to receive that year's invitation to sit near the queen in the royal box. Harrods reeked of celebrity, respectability and grandeur. Intoxicated by his surroundings, it seemed to him that his ownership was an inevitable destiny. Whether others would accept his transformation did not intrude into his thoughts. His priority was to regenerate the business.

Both the stores' staff and their directors were exhausted. Shell-shocked by their battle with Rowland, the House of Fraser board had lost the spirit to manage and develop the business. Recruitment of new executives had been sabotaged by the struggle. Investment had been stymied. Hopelessly outmoded compared to Manhattan's major stores, especially in its fashion department, Harrods was dilapidated, trading on its reputation rather than on innovation. The fabric of the building was also lamentable. During the 1960s, plastic had been stuck over elegant cornices and ugly glass covered the marble, but nothing concealed the dirty, crumbling brickwork, the oxidizing metal, the gloomy lighting and the poor wiring. In the patchwork repairs of the Fraser era, space had been wasted and the walls of the famous Georgian restaurant had been covered by seventeen layers of paint. One of the capital's most famous destinations was dying. The blame, Fayed knew, was borne by the same directors whose virtues he had sung over the past four months. First he would reward all of them with bonuses and 50 per cent salary increases – not least because Craddock was encouraging the staff to sell their share options to Fayed – and then he would expel the ageing fossils.

Touring the shop floors, the new owner did not encounter an obvious welcome. Although relieved by the end of the uncertainty and the unexpected delivery at their homes of exhortatory brochures from Rowland, the excitement of the battle among the staff had palled long before. They were not interested in City affairs, and regarded Harrods not merely as an employer but as a way of life. The years of disturbance, they hoped, were over.

Selling clothes or washing machines five days a week to strangers may not appeal to most, but for the elite of professional retailers employed at Harrods providing good service to their customers was a skill to which they had dedicated their lives. Ambitious teenagers with limited academic qualifications were eager to rise up the ladder to become Harrods buyers, departmental directors and even members of the board. No other store offered the atmosphere, the style and the certainty of meeting the famous. The world of Harrods was not only a place of work but also the hub of social life. Friendships and marriages were forged in the shop, in the canteens and in the well-equipped staff sports club in nearby Barnes. Camaraderie and unusual loyalty sprang from the pleasure derived from outsiders' recognition of the world's most famous store. Telling any stranger on a beach in Benidorm or even in Brazil, 'I work at Harrods,' won instant appreciation. 'If I was cut, I'd bleed green,' was a common joke among the many who had served twenty years and more in the store. Loyalty was their creed, a quality which Fayed claimed, in broken English, 'I value very important.'

'I want to transform Harrods into the best store in the world,' enthused Fayed to Craddock. Recognizing his own inexperience in managing such a revolution, he asked Craddock to find someone to mastermind the cure for the whole House of Fraser group. 'I want the best man in the world,' he exclaimed. The glamour of Harrods and the chance of a Rolls-Royce job would, he confidently expected, attract the best.

Unable to find this paragon in Britain, Craddock approached Brian Walsh, a 'highly recommended' Australian retailer. Glancing at Walsh's CV, Fayed exclaimed, 'Here's the man who can do it!' – a phrase often heard by his subordinates. One man, he believed, could implement his dream. Initially uncertain about the offer, Walsh was eventually enticed by the challenge presented in a Price Waterhouse report which described the group's vulnerability if radical revitalization was not undertaken. 'You'll be in charge of everything,' said Fayed. 'I'm surrounded by idiots.' Promised a long leash, Walsh agreed to start in mid-1986 on the promise that he was employed by 'an enlightened family-owned business where the concepts of excellence and the bottom line do not conflict'.

In the early months, that claim was borne out. With no interest in board meetings or feeling under any obligation to notify the directors of his proposals, Fayed would walk into their board meetings late and depart early. Habits learnt since Alexandria were not a blueprint for either teamwork or the smooth control of a widespread corporation. Unaware that a strategy should not be a matter of impulse, Fayed returned to Park Lane hardly attempting to consolidate his control over the group. Restraining his instinctive irritation with the calibre of people employed, he allowed Ali, a polite manager, to become the chairman of House of Fraser and shunned publicity himself in an attempt to avoid Rowland's ire. In truth, he trusted only a handful of people: his two brothers, Martin Müller, his Swiss lawyer, and two Swiss bankers privy to the fiduciary loan.

In private, however, Fayed could not restrain his boasts about his success and his genius. In June, three months after buying Harrods, he was invited to Carlos Place, in Mayfair, to meet Shri Chandra Swamiji, an Indian guru also known as the Swami. Wearing a gold necklace and holding court on a bed covered in tiger skins, the Swami encouraged Fayed to express his sentiments freely and to describe his relationship with the sultan. Uninhibited and unaware that their conversations during his three visits were being recorded, Fayed spoke about his intimacy with and affection for the monarch, admitted controlling some powers of attorney, exaggerated his own wealth, but emphatically denied that the House of Fraser had been purchased either with the sultan's money or on his behalf.

That denial, accepted by most observers in London, was endorsed by the government. At the Windsor Horse Show in May, Fayed was presented to the queen. He bowed, proudly, and to disguise his flawed English, he merely mumbled. Understandably, the monarch's smile was worth a fortune to the Egyptian who, during the show, was seated some distance from her. Winning acceptance was not as uncomplicated as he had hoped, although there remained some housekeeping to complete.

The publicity, which had provoked enquiries into his life, highlighted potential sources of embarrassment, not least his matrimonial arrangements. Hitherto, the existence of Heini and their two illegitimate children had been unnoteworthy, but Heini was now pregnant with their third child. To aggravate his predicament, in gratitude to Great Ormond Street hospital where his son Karim had been successfully treated for severe meningitis, Fayed had anonymously contributed £100,000 to a new Karim Centre for Meningitis Research. But, irritatingly, journalists had asked about the benefactor. The press was also asking about his family relationships. Although he remained unenthusiastic about marriage, he resolved that there were advantages in legitimating his ten-year relationship with Heini.

Accompanied by Ali and by Gunilla Martinson, Heini's cousin, Fayed and his bride-to-be arrived on 11 July 1985 at Westminster Register Office having told Paul Fairhurst, the deputy registrar, that there were to be no leaks to the media. In a swift, businesslike ceremony, devoid of observable emotion, Fairhurst completed the legal procedures initiated by an application that was strewn with fabrications. Fayed had described his father as a 'shipowner' and entered his age as fifty-two rather than fifty-six. Unlike the listing on his children's birth certificates, he entered his own profession as company director rather than shipowner. Significantly, to avoid prosecution for making a false entry, his name was simply 'Fayed'. The 'Al' was omitted. If, as Fairhurst uttered the formal declaration that Mohamed and Heini were 'man and wife', the married couple kissed, the registrar missed that fleeting moment. As they left the building, Fayed hissed to Brian Dodd, his bodyguard, 'Never mention this day again.' Denied any ebullience on that special day, Heini could console herself that her new husband was genuinely besotted by their children.

Parts of Oxted had been converted into a children's dream world. Two Wendy houses and climbing frames had been erected, a complete fairground was being designed and the first of twenty children's electric cars waited permanently charged in the garages. In the stable block, ponies were carefully groomed to introduce the children to the delights of riding while inside the house was the plunder of a toy store. Regularly, Fayed's helicopter and car returned from London filled with the latest toys, teddy bears and gadgets scooped up from Harrods. Among his early plans was to build the finest Toy World in the store, an indulgence for his children, compensation for his own deprived childhood and a way of redeeming his conscience for his shortcomings towards Dodi.

*

MENDING THE RIFT with Dodi had begun the previous summer. An early-morning call reported that two days earlier, during a 2 a.m. frolic with a girl, Dodi had fallen from a cliff-top restaurant in Sardinia on to rocks and had broken several ribs. He was taken by helicopter to Khashoggi's yacht, on which he was holidaying, whereupon the *Nabila*'s resident doctor had dispatched the injured patient by helicopter to Berne for treatment. Fayed had flown to Switzerland and there, inevitably, met the mother of his son. The reunion was tense. Fayed had not been invited earlier that summer to Dodi's engagement party to an Iranian girl at Cap Ferrat organized by Samira. Nor was he encouraged to stay long in the hospital. But, by the time the three met again at Samira's suggestion in Paris in summer 1985, father and son agreed to heal the four-year breach. Dodi, complained his mother, was relying exclusively upon the Khashoggis for financial support. Regularly, their son received tens of thousands of pounds from his uncle and cousins while living in Khashoggi's homes in Spain, in the South of France, in New York, on the *Nabila* or on chartered yachts in the Caribbean. Yet he desperately needed his father. Among the Khashoggi family, it was agreed that Mohamed had put the fear of God into his son. 'Dodi even squeezes lemon on to his plate and cutlery like his father,' sighed Samira. Her son had become acknowledged as a 'great listener'. He would sit in night clubs listening to women's tales through the night, hoping for a reward at six o'clock in the morning. Dodi was an amiable man but, it was whispered, not a great sex act. It was time, said Samira, for reconciliation. Fayed should support Dodi financially and rebuild their relationship. The father agreed, but in return ordered Dodi to break off relations with the Khashoggis. Dodi undertook to do so and returned to London. Fayed expected no different.

Fayed was enjoying his new autocracy. Bewitched by the meteoric rise in his financial and social status in Britain, he had become accustomed to an exhibitionist lifestyle, especially in France. Flying from London by helicopter, usually with Katie Manning, his attractive blonde secretary, and four bodyguards, he would board his Gulfstream unquestioned, knowing that gifts given by his staff guaranteed that he would not be stopped or searched. Landing at Le Bourget fifty minutes later, and again waved through the normal controls, he would be driven to the Ritz for dinner, then a visit to a night club and finally to his flat off the Champs-Elysées. France, he felt, was more congenial to his methods. Sympathetic to secret understandings and with a respect for money, the local politicians responded uncritically to the generosity he could offer at the Ritz.

Handing out presents to powerbrokers was an instinctive part of Fayed's style, and few in Paris were more important than Jacques Chirac, the Gaullist mayor. In the Place Vendôme, Fayed had encountered a major problem and only Chirac could produce a solution.

FAYED

A proposed pedestrian precinct barring access to the hotel was certain to be vetoed, but there had been a damaging court decision in April 1982 ordering that the reconstruction of part of the hotel should cease. To transform dowdy attics into luxury apartments, Fayed had without permission replaced eight historic windows with substitutes and skylights that were three times larger than permitted. He had also removed protected chimneys to build vents for the air conditioning. The inspector general of the commission of major historic buildings had obtained a court order to compel the restoration of the historic façade. Fayed had disputed the order and the commission had appealed to Jack Lang, the minister of culture, to enforce the judgement. Two years later, the minister had failed to act and the Court of Appeal had agreed to repeat the order. Again Fayed failed to comply with the judgement, as he would once more in 1986. His certainty that he was immune was founded on his appeal to Chirac. Fortunately, the mayor was receptive to his eulogies about the hotel and the city, and naturally Fayed, grateful for the mayor's support, was prepared to contribute legitimately to his party's election fund. The Egyptian made regular trips, accompanied by two bodyguards and driven by Christian Stanneck, an Austrian, or Josef Goedde, a German, to arrive at the Hôtel de Ville. Unusually, his burgundy, black or gold Samsonite briefcases would not have been placed on the back seat. Instead, his hand would firmly clutch an ordinary black leather case as he walked alone through the courtyard into the grand building. Thirty minutes later, he would reappear – without the briefcase.

To those still suspicious about the source of Fayed's funds, there were eyewitness accounts of his conversations that month with the sultan, who occupied a permanent office and suite at the Ritz, adjoining the garden. Standing amid the excavations in the basement, the site of a future health centre and swimming pool, the sultan made his irritation plain. 'You told me this would be finished three months ago,' the sultan said reproachfully to Fayed. The completed pool had been ripped apart after leaks had been discovered. In a manner which the bodyguard Bob Curry would recall as 'grovelling', Fayed asked to be forgiven. Shortly afterwards, he presented the monarch with a new armoured Mercedes. The cost was £145,000. 'It's the sultan's own money,' sighed Frank Klein at the Ritz bar to a bodyguard. 'We'll need more money to finish. We'll ask the sultan.' Fayed's extravagant loss of control over the hotel's finances was recorded in the company's accounts, but he appeared indifferent to the consequences of his profligacy. While retaining the legal ownership of the hotel, he seemed to rely entirely upon the sultan to finance his ambitions.

From Paris, Fayed flew to St Tropez. Among his entourage was Petra, a beautiful eighteen-year-old German employed as a maid in Park Lane. To Fayed's delight, his new status had enabled him to surround himself with attractive employees and others. Women like Petra, he hoped, would be attracted to money and power like moths to a flame.

The routine after the Gulfstream landed at Nice had been refined. The waiting Mercedes drove Fayed, Petra and the bodyguards to the harbour where the couple, welcomed by the Italian crew, boarded the *Cujo*, a former US Coastguard cutter, to speed across the bay to St Tropez.

The Castel Ste Thérèse was under reconstruction. Fayed slept on the *Sakara*, the schooner, while his guards were lodged in a house. The following morning, Petra was sunbathing topless on the beach. Furious about what he considered her indiscretion, Fayed ordered that she return to London immediately. The Gulfstream was to bring Heini from London. She would sleep on the *Rameses*, a new yacht bought by Fayed from the original owner, Gerald Ronson, watched by cameras and monitored by bodyguards sleeping in the rear. Fayed would sleep on the *Sakara*. To allay Fayed's fear of an assault in St Tropez, the six-foot fence surrounding the property had been reinforced, new shotguns were stored in the bodyguards' operations room and two rottweilers were chained to posts near the entrance. Concern for his security preoccupied Fayed's evenings in the village. After lunching on the *Sakara*, the schooner sailed to St Tropez and moored in the best position opposite the Café de Paris. Driven from the villa to the port, Fayed and Heini would board their boat and eat dinner, occasionally before the gaze of gawking tourists shuffling past. To forestall an invasion of his privacy, Bob Curry and another bodyguard stood at the foot of the gangplank. 'No photographs,' Curry ordered, even occasionally snatching the camera of a disobedient foreigner. Hidden near the gangplank was a holdall with a Remington, a short-barrelled Defender pump-action shotgun. As an additional precaution, the town's police chief was induced to provide a regular patrol to pass his ship.

Few visitors called on the Fayeds that summer to join the celebration of his business coup and his secret marriage. The only break in their solitude was the occasional visit of a neighbour, Christopher Hanbury, a tall, retired cavalry major employed by the sultan as his private secretary in Britain. Discreet and loyal, Hanbury had met the sultan at Sandhurst and liaised on his behalf with Fayed.

Hanbury's employer that summer was 650 miles south in Marbella, the Spanish playground for super-rich Arabs. He was one of Adnan Khashoggi's 400 guests at a million-dollar party celebrating his fiftieth birthday on board the *Nabila*. Those guests who had not arrived in their personal aircraft had been ferried into the resort in Khashoggi's fleet of jets for a two-week bacchanalia. Hollywood stars, European royalty, famous politicians and fellow tycoons had flocked to join the spectacular. Few of those invited would speak about Fayed and few would even know of his existence. By contrast, Khashoggi was described as 'the richest man in the world', controlling an international empire worth £2 billion.

Gazing at the shimmering Mediterranean, excluded from those celebrities, Fayed became consumed with resentment. Whatever his destiny and regardless of his achievments, he was regarded by that crowd as inferior. In the evenings, as he waddled through the streets of St Tropez, dressed in blue shorts and a coloured shirt, he grew bitter about the lack of recognition of his achievements and wealth – especially from Khashoggi. Hearing shortly afterwards that the Saudi had sailed the *Nabila* to Brunei to complete its sale to the sultan, Fayed swore revenge. Contacting the sultan, he warned, 'Khashoggi has tricked you. The boat is the target of Iranian terrorists. Sell it immediately.' The *Nabila* was resold to Donald Trump at a $20 million loss, permanantly damaging Khashoggi's relations with the sultan. As usual, Fayed had not anticipated the results of his impulsive venom. Khashoggi fell easily into Rowland's dragnet.

7

Bribes and Lies

'Tiny's gone mad,' shrieked Fayed. During the summer of 1985 the *Observer* had published a series of defamatory attacks on the Fayed brothers. Rowland's newspaper campaign, his international dragnet to unearth his past and his bombardment of politicians were far beyond Mohamed Fayed's experience. Successful as a fighter and survivor in a small arena, he could not understand why Rowland, unlike other players, refused nobly to accept defeat. Fayed's past was no preparation for Rowland's cunning and malice.

'I've been cheated by a crook,' Rowland had told his directors after Fayed's bid had been approved by the government. 'I don't even want House of Fraser any more. I don't want someone else's mistress. I just want justice.' In fact, Rowland wanted revenge. He had declared war against Tebbit, Thatcher and the Fayeds. In a feud which would cost £20 million and permanently cripple the *Observer* and Lonrho, he turned the fate of a shop in Knightsbridge into an issue to destroy politicians and destabilize the Conservative government. His intention was utterly to ruin Mohamed Fayed.

The calm of Mohamed Fayed's honeymoon had first been ruffled in May 1985. A temperate article written by Duncan Campbell-Smith in the *Financial Times* suggested that the Fayeds' description of their wealth had been greeted in the City with 'some disbelief'. Based on original interviews in London and across the Middle East, the article concluded that the credibility of the Fayeds' and of Kleinworts' statements was doubtful.

Fayed wanted to ignore the defamation but Kleinworts, sensitive about the serious allegations, sought reassurance from him that House of Fraser had been bought with the brothers' own cash and without loans. Fayed's reply to John MacArthur conjured a new fantasy. 'We lost a lot because of Nasser,' he claimed, 'but we had moved to the Gulf and had £20 million there.'

'A sort of war chest?' asked the banker.

'Yes,' agreed Fayed eagerly, reminding the banker that after 8 March 1985 AITSA, his Liechtenstein trust, had $474.7 million in its account.

'What about your relations with the sultan?' asked MacArthur.

'I know the sultan for many years,' repeated Fayed, suppressing the weak man's doubts. 'My own father knew the sultan's father. They even met at the Ritz in Paris.'

Reassured by his client's statements, MacArthur protested to the *Financial Times* editor while Fayed threatened a writ unless an immediate retraction was published. Simultaneously, Brian Basham issued a threatening press release: 'The Fayed brothers are advised that any allegations that they are not acting on their own account are defamatory.' Within hours, the *Financial Times* editor surrendered and published an apology. *Le Figaro*, which had republished the article, also printed a retraction, stating that the piece 'wrongly referred to the mysterious and even suspicious origins of the Al Fayed family'. That, smiled Fayed, marked the end of any journalistic investigation.

Two weeks after his wedding, Fayed discovered his mistake. His Sunday mornings were ruined by the *Observer*'s relentless reports about his dishonesty; brazenly, the newspaper was even publishing lies. The first was a facsimile of 'the sultan's power of attorney to Fayed to buy the House of Fraser'. Fayed was astonished by the forgery. The following week, Donald Trelford, the *Observer*'s editor, quoting false information planted by Rowland's Israeli lawyer in a New

York Jewish newspaper, denounced Fayed as an anti-Semite. Only two years earlier, Fayed bitterly recalled, the editor had blithely accepted a weekend's free hospitality at the Ritz and had charged 10,000 francs 'spending money' to buy luxuries for himself in the hotel's shops. The prevailing rule in this war was the doublecross. Although Trelford would subsequently apologize for both false allegations, Fayed had been harmed. Rowland had a brilliant weapon with which to wage war.

Rowland, the Egyptian rightly suspected, was trawling the world for information. Using private investigation agencies, the *Observer*'s more deferential journalists and his own network of relations, Rowland was determined to unearth dirt; the newspaper's campaign was merely a public sideshow to the serious lobbying in Westminster. Sir Edward du Cann, Lonrho's unctuous chairman, was constantly asking questions and agitating among ministers in the House of Commons. Irritatingly, he appeared to have secured the sympathetic support of other MPs, including Teddy Taylor, David Ashby, Sir Peter Tapsell, Charles Wardle, Kenneth Warren, Anthony Nelson, Sir Robert Sheldon and Sir Peter Emery. All of them, it seemed to Fayed, had joined Rowland's campaign to drag his name through the mud. 'You're going to have to defend yourself,' Brian Basham told his client, who bizarrely still professed to 'like' Tiny. 'Let's see what we can find out about the vermin,' urged Basham, convinced that no one could become a multi-millionaire without covering up evidence of wrongdoing. 'You should know your enemy. We'll just look into Rowland's life. We know so little about him. We'll get Arthur Young to investigate his own finances and business. When we find something, we'll hit back.' At that stage, Rowland's army record, his wartime internment for his Nazi sympathies and his other dubious activities remained concealed. Even the condemnatory DTI report into Lonrho had been blurred by myths and distortions. 'I've just met someone who might help us,' suggested Basham in an attempt to persuade his client of his strategy.

AN UNCERTAIN BEGINNING
Mohamed Fayed with Dodi at his fourth birthday party.

Dodi and Samira, his mother, in the
same year. Fayed's influence prevented
a deep relationship.

The earliest published photo of Fayed
in uniform in 1964 when he held a
Haitian diplomatic passport.

THE FAYED DYNASTY

Ali, Salah, the Egyptian ambassador, Mohammed and Dodi have always appeared to be extraordinarily close, sharing everything. Mohammed Fayed, however, is the undisputed leader.

Adnan Khashoggi

FRIENDS BECOME ENEMIES

Mohamed Fayed's talent to charm was the foundation of his fortune, yet he turned his mentors, Adnan Khashoggi, his former brother-in-law, Mahdi Al Tajir, his benefactor from Dubai, and Tiny Rowland, his ally after the 1974 partnership, into bitter enemies. Only the Sultan of Brunei, after a frosty interlude, has remained loyal.

Mahdi Al Tajir

Tiny Rowland

The Sultan of Brunei

PLAYBOY
Dodi enjoyed wearing military uniforms and jetting around
as playboy and film producer.

CELEBRATING SUCCESS

Fayed at the reopening of the Windsor villa in Paris in 1989, accompanied by
Earl Spencer, his wife Raine, Madame Chirac, Jacques Chirac, then mayor of
Paris, and Sydney Johnson, the Duke of Windsor's valet, which triumphantly
confirmed his tenacity and skills. Similarly, his celebration in 1990 with
(*left to right*) Ali, Michael Cole, and Dodi on the fifth anniversary of his
take-over of Harrods proved his resilience to criticism.

THE SHOWMAN
Summoning the cameras Fayed
enjoys dressing up as the owner of
Harrods: as a cook, a boy scout and
a grocer; promoting the unsuccessful
Harrods' beer; and as a pharaoh despite
his pledge against returning to Egypt.

THE CELEBRITY HUNTER
Fayed made great efforts to be photographed with the Queen at the Windsor Horse Show; and similarly enjoyed using the launch of the Harrods sale to pose with celebrities: Gary Lineker, Cliff Richard, Dame Edna and Tony Curtis. Many celebrities were invited to stay in his homes.

THE FINNISH WIFE
Heini Wathen, posing (*left*) as a
beauty queen for the Miss Finland
competition in 1977, was introduced
to her husband by Dodi. Twenty years
later, at the Harrods Christmas
show (*below*), she appeared as
the loyal wife.

Ali Fayed, at the Windsor Horse
Trials with Tracy, his wife, who now
lives in Connecticut.

Not quite convinced, Fayed pondered his plight. His vulnerability had come as a shock to him. Having to conduct his
business under rules requiring sensitive disclosures was a chill-
ing development. Publicity and open warfare offended the
habits of a lifetime spent in the shadows. His life's success
owed more than was healthy to what his competitors might
damagingly describe as deception and manipulation. The journey from dissolute Coca-Cola vendor to owner of the House
of Fraser stores had left behind some unforgiving casualties.
Khashoggi, Papa Doc, Tajir, Marwan, not to mention Rowland, were unlikely to forget their injuries. In the jungle, there
was no mercy. Partners had been casually transformed into
opponents. Hitherto he had rarely flinched from confronting
his enemies. But, just as he had exploited his knowledge of
their weaknesses, he suddenly felt vulnerable in the spotlight
which fame had focused on him, revealing blemishes that could
not be glossed over. Exposed to the public gaze, he feared
retribution. There was every reason to expect his enemies to
use his own methods on him. He had scored points over many
whose names were long forgotten. There were no moments of
regret for those people. Throughout his life, he persuaded
himself, he had suffered as the victim of malicious forces
unwilling to accord him the respect he deserved. Revenge was
not unattractive for a man who believed that he was a martyr
of an injustice. His bodyguards provided physical protection
and this time he was not ready to surrender and lose the prize.
While the notion of hiring a private detective appealed to his
appetite for secrets and power, the dangers of Basham's proposal might be outweighed by advantages. 'Who you got?'
asked Fayed. Basham's nominee was Richard New, a former
special investigator for Customs and Excise who had retired
and joined Network, a private investigation agency.

Fayed was uneasy during his introduction to New. Uncov-
ering Tiny's skeletons could provoke lethal retaliation. Only
that month, a journalist had written after an interview that
Fayed had graduated from the University of Alexandria with a

degree in economics and was proud that he had not relied on his family. Rather, he had set off 'to prove I could make it on my own'. Protecting his fantasies against Rowland's inevitably damaging attacks, he decided, would crush suggestions that he was inferior. Richard New was hired to launch the counter-offensive.

The irony of Fayed and Rowland both nursing grudges amused New. After years of targeting senior corporate managers, he could tell that their row was the result of a falling out between conspirators. Whether Fayed had doublecrossed Rowland and whether their agreement was illegal was irrelvant. The investigator calculated that Rowland's own campaign was subject to the danger of self-incrimination.

'I'll find out Rowland's real background,' said New, holding a two-year-old *Sunday Times* news item which hinted at tantalizing details about Rowland's hidden past. 'The best start would be to get his army record.'

'I'll pay whatever it costs,' interrupted Fayed, convinced that, just as in Egypt, all British government records were obtainable for a price.

'Then,' continued New, 'we'd better investigate his African activities and go through his DTI report and get information on his aircraft's movements.'

New's appointment hardened Fayed's conviction that attack was his best defence. The prospect of discovering Rowland's secrets fed his desire for more sensitive information and for an organization to fight a long war. On 1 September, he recruited Royston Webb, a Welsh barrister previously employed by Nabisco, the food giant, as his general counsel. Basham and New were to report to Webb.

*

SEPARATELY, HE SOUGHT supporters to fight Rowland at Westminster. At least ten detailed anti-Fayed submissions had been sent to ministers by Rowland and by sympathetic politicians. Teddy Taylor, the Conservative MP for Southend, had asked twenty-three critical parliamentary questions. Newspapers carried reports of their demands for a government investigation of the Fayeds' bogus background and for an order for the divestiture of House of Fraser. Infuriatingly, no one was arguing his case. His one supposed ally, Sir Peter Hordern, House of Fraser's paid parliamentary consultant, was outrageously lame. 'I pay him £40,000 a year and he never asks a question to help me or attack my enemies,' he griped to Lord King, the chairman of British Airways, at a reception. 'He says he sympathizes. No good to me.' In full flow, Fayed continued, 'Tiny has all these MPs like du Cann who are paid to ask questions. I need someone in parliament.'

'You should use Ian Greer,' recommended King. 'He's very good. Knows a lot of the right people.'

'I'm thinking of hiring Ian Greer,' Fayed told Hordern, who in fact was paid £24,000 a year.

'I wouldn't advise that,' replied Hordern scornfully. His advice was ignored. Fayed entered the turbulent cesspit of Britain's politics. He was no longer simply a businessman.

On 28 October 1985, the diminutive Greer was ushered past the bodyguards and accompanied in the small lift to the seventh floor of 60 Park Lane to meet Mohamed and Ali. Unlike so many others, Greer was not asked to wait, nor was he treated with disdain. For the two Egyptians, Greer was welcomed as an important ally.

In every respect, Greer was the type of Englishman Fayed detested. Small, delicate, self-important and, worst of all, an effeminate homosexual, Greer was the antithesis of his prospective client's taste. 'Shirt-lifters', 'cock-suckers', 'poofters', Fayed had used every slang expression to vent his violent homophobia. 'You gotta fight the shit with shit,' he would indelicately proclaim. Sitting with Greer, however, he repressed his prejudices. There was no alternative. The lobbyist's well-rehearsed sales pitch – his client list included British Airways, British Gas,

Cadbury Schweppes, Asda and Philip Morris – and his close relations with senior Cabinet ministers could not fail to impress the outsider.

Translating Fayed's broken English, so staccato and without inflection that it was impossible to gauge the man's sentiment, Greer observed his prospective client's charm and humour turn to anger. 'I do so much for this country,' cursed Fayed, employing his customary vulgarities, 'I bring so much money here. Now that madman pours shit on me.' Greer could not fail to understand that the Egyptian felt unloved, misunderstood, abused and persecuted. 'I want people to know how I and my family are committed to Britain. This is our home.' Greer was not allowed to depart without hearing Fayed mention his two visits to Downing Street and his trusted relationship with Margaret Thatcher. 'She knows who is Mohamed Al Fayed,' he repeated twice, once more posing as a pasha. His fist crashed on the table. 'I brought £5 billion to Britain. The sultan is my friend.' Britain's debt to Mohamed Al Fayed had not been repaid. An expression of sympathy spread across Greer's pixie face. Lobbyists seeking accounts are easily converted to their client's cause. Rowland was indisputably spiteful and vile, and Fayed was indisputably a friend of the Conservatives.

Greer's promise of action packaged in respectability exactly met the client's demands. 'I can offer a carefully prepared programme to gather support among backbenchers to put maximum pressure on Leon Brittan to take quick and decisive action,' offered Greer, refering to Tebbit's successor as secretary of state for trade and industry. His efficiency was obvious to Fayed. To avoid aggressive haggling and risk losing the appointment, Greer agreed an annual fee of £25,000, considerably less than his other clients were charged.

Thirty-seven hours after Greer had walked out into Park Lane, Fayed's reservations evaporated. A hand-delivered letter from the lobbyist suggested that his money was producing fast results. 'I have spoken to Neil Hamilton,' wrote Greer, 'who has agreed to table a question.' Fayed grunted in satisfaction. His contract with Greer had already found a supporter.

Born in 1947 in a small Welsh mining town, Hamilton was an ambitious, right-wing Conservative barrister elected to parliament in 1983 for Tatton in Cheshire. Defamed in a BBC documentary for his alleged neo-Nazi opinions, Hamilton's successful libel action against the Corporation suggested a self-righteous streak which suited Fayed. More pertinent was Hamilton's position and activities as a vice-chairman of the Conservative Party's Trade and Industry Committee (not to be confused with the all-party select committee covering the same subject). In February 1984, the politician had been introduced by Sir Peter Hordern over lunch at Harrods to the directors of House of Fraser and was converted to the anti-Rowland camp. Rowland's verbal abuse of the store group's directors, his venom towards Thatcher and his breach of the promises guaranteeing the *Observer*'s independence had offended many MPs, including Hamilton. Supporting Fayed's cause was an automatic reaction. The source of Fayed's money, Hamilton believed, was irrelevant; and, if Fayed had lied about his past, he was no different to Rowland and many other self-made tycoons. His first parliamentary question, in November to Leon Brittan, asking whether the secretary of state was satisfied that the *Observer*'s independent directors could protect the newspaper's integrity, even passed unnoticed in Rowland's camp. Only Fayed, reading the House of Commons' order paper, was satisfied that a counterattack had finally been launched.

The parliamentary printed record was posted to Fayed by Greer. To convince his client of hectic activity on his behalf, he enclosed a note: 'I am anxious that the major investments made by you in Britain are fully appreciated and that we quickly achieve a greater understanding of the commitment your family has made to the United Kingdom.' His plan, the normal practice among lobbyists, was to introduce Fayed to other sympathetic MPs.

First to call in at Park Lane was Gerry Malone, the

parliamentary private secretary of Leon Brittan. His chief had already rejected Rowland's request that the Monopolies Commission investigate Fayed's ownership of House of Fraser. Then Fayed met Sir Michael Grylls, the chairman of the Conservative backbench Trade and Industry Committee. Well groomed and precise in his speech, Grylls's manner reassured Fayed of a solid supporter.

The third Conservative politician introduced to Fayed was Tim Smith, an accountant formerly employed at Peat Marwick Mitchell. His credentials as a sympathizer were impeccable. In October 1971, he had been hired to investigate Lonrho's accounts. Struck by the 'Byzantine complexity' of the company, his suspicions were confirmed by the DTI's report about Lonrho in 1976. 'I was puzzled', he told Fayed during their first meeting, 'that Rowland was not prosecuted after those findings. There was so much dishonesty.'

Fayed beamed. Another supporter. 'We paid cash for House of Fraser and the shareholders accepted our money,' he told his new confidant. 'It was approved by everyone. You've got to stop Rowland. He is attacking my dignity, my honour. Integrity means everything to me.' Fayed's words were spoken in earnest, but on his lips they bore a meaning that was different from the way others would understand them.

Shortly after the politician left, Fayed sat drinking a glass of Sakara, his special blend of whisky produced in a distillery close to Balnagown. The video of a Hollywood thriller was flickering on a big screen, while his fingers were selecting meat and smoked salmon from a large plate. Pieces of food fallen from his mouth, the shells of half-eaten nuts and paper tissues used to wipe away an unseasonal attack of hay fever were scattered on the thick royal-blue carpet. For an obsessive in cleanliness, the debris was extraordinary – except that pashas rely on donkeys to clean up. Bitter distaste drove the strategy of a man for whom no one – other than those paid to do so – seemed to care. Money had bought supporters: Gordon Reece, Brian Basham and Ian Greer were undoubtedly among Britain's best lobbyists; and there were four MPs, all now pledged to fight his cause. A fifth, Sir Michael Grylls, had pledged loyalty but had explained that he preferred to work in the background, orchestrating his junior colleagues, Hamilton and Smith. The reticence of a politician anxious to please appealed to Fayed's harsh understanding of *Realpolitik*. Nevertheless, he wilfully ignored Grylls's latest truthful advice. 'Mohamed,' the tall, silver-haired Conservative had said, 'don't worry what the *Observer* publishes. Nobody reads the newspaper.' Fayed never listened to opinions contradicting his own beliefs. Despite all those donkeys and all his money, Rowland always sprang surprises.

*

A REPORT THAT EVENING from Richard New unleashed trembling fears. Over a gossipy drink with Nicholas Vaffiadesis, alias 'Nick the Greek', another private investigator employed by Network, New learnt of an alarming development. Rowland, it appeared, had hired an expert to intercept Fayed's telephone calls illegally. With effort and some persuasion, New had traced David Coghlan, the expert, and eventually enticed a sworn affidavit out of him. At Rowland's request, according to Coghlan, he had been hired in September 1985 by Ashraf Marwan, who, after speaking three times on the telephone in the technician's presence to Rowland, explained their requirements. Six weeks later, Coghlan had delivered eighteen hours of Fayed's tape-recorded conversations intercepted in a junction on the street. Rowland had been disappointed: nothing incriminating had been recorded. But the development filled Fayed with horror. Rowland had escalated their feud to unimagined heights. This was no longer an unpleasant spat between rival cronies. This was real war. Until then he had never contemplated bugging telephones, but his duty was self-protection.

Graeme Arno, who as a British Telecom engineer had regularly serviced the telephones at Park Lane, was offered an unbelievable salary. 'You will report only to me,' ordered Fayed. 'Only you are allowed to touch the telephones. Find the bugs. Talk to no one else.' The telephone lines in all the flats at 60 Park Lane – the whole block by then belonged to Fayed – were rerouted through a monitoring system installed in a riser cupboard on the second floor. Tape recorders, a spectrum analyser and clips had been fitted by Arno close to the switchboard so that every telephone line could be tapped. At the same time, the whole telephone network at Harrods and at the headquarters of House of Fraser in Victoria were rerouted to identical monitoring systems which, activated by voices, could simultaneously tap four conversations. All Fayed's employees, from humble salesman to his top management team, became vulnerable to his eavesdropping. In the Egyptian's mind his bugging was further justified by the news that Mahdi Al Tajir's brother had been kidnapped in London and released only after payment of a $3 million ransom. Fayed was frightened. His personal security required complete reconstruction.

Forty bodyguards had been recruited by Mick Lee, but the organization was sloppy. Every month, he was handing out thousands in cash – so much that bodyguards laughed that they could not fold their wallets – but he resented the poor value he was getting for his money. Searching for a replacement, he telephoned Lord Bramall, recently retired as chief of the defence staff. 'I need someone to reorganize my personal security,' he told the soldier. Bramall's recommendation was Jonathan Heywood, a former major in the Grenadier Guards and a commanding officer of the SAS's G Squadron.

Soft spoken and dressed in an anorak and jeans, Heywood's image as he lounged in Park Lane did not appeal to Fayed, but, as Bramall had pointed out, his candidate's credentials were impeccable. Five years earlier, Heywood had been involved in the televised siege of the Iranian embassy in Kensington, the SAS's most heroic exploit at that time.

'Tell me what's wrong,' asked Fayed.

'I'll talk to the men,' replied Heywood.

Over the following two weeks, Heywood unearthed the chaos and unscrupulousness festering beyond Fayed's control. The accounts were inaccurate, the organization was slack and the proliferation of guns was alarming. Bodyguards racing around London Ulster-style with Walther PPKs hidden in Bianchi pouch bags or stuck into their trousers was a reckless procedure. The reality of armed bodyguards walking through Harrods behind Fayed was positively frightening. 'Lee and Dodd will have to go,' pronounced Heywood.

Fayed agreed, but decided that both would receive £25,000 in cash to ease their departure. 'But you take over,' offered Fayed. Heywood accepted on condition that he was allowed to impose mass dismissals. The handful of survivors would call that weekend 'the night of the long knives'. The new recruits would be paid £19,000 per annum through Balnagown Estates, about 30 per cent above the normal rate. On Fayed's orders, Dodd handed over his 38mm gun and ammunition to Heywood personally.

'The guns will also have to go,' said Heywood.

'No,' replied Fayed. 'I need them for my protection.'

Heywood compromised immediately. 'We've got to make it legal,' he insisted. The handguns were unacceptable. All the Smith & Wessons, the Walther PPKs and the machine gun, he insisted, were to be destroyed. Collected in London, he watched as their barrels were sawn off and ordered that the debris be dumped in the River Wye. Their immediate replacements were Mosberg model 500 shotguns registered with the police as sporting guns. To instruct the new militia – recruited as before from the SAS, Paras and Military Police – in close protection and to supervise the reconstruction of the Operations Room, Fayed hired two retired American Secret Service agents previously attached to President Reagan's personal security group. Former SAS soldiers would be based in Park Lane, while the ex-Paras would be assigned to Oxted.

'Now, I want you to wear this when you travel,' said Heywood, holding up an armoured vest. 'It's worn under the shirt.'

'You're mad!' shouted Fayed. 'I'll be seen a mile away.'

'I'm wearing one now. You can't see it,' said Heywood.

'No,' snapped Fayed. 'No.'

'I'd like you to wear this earpiece.'

'No!' shouted Fayed. 'Stick it up your arse.' Heywood was startled. 'And no donkeys in my car,' ranted Fayed. 'Only the chauffeur.'

'Glyn John will have to go,' said Heywood passively, referring to Fayed's trusted driver. 'He talks too much and he's not trained. You need a driver who can ram and jam and get through an attack.'

'Bah,' said Fayed dismissively.

Fayed's violent reaction bewildered Heywood. The soldier failed to understand the Egyptian's real requirement: the donkeys were retained not as bullet-stoppers but to reinforce his sense of power. None of his enemies would fire bazookas at his bullet-proof car driving through Hyde Park, nor were they likely to shoot him while he crossed a London pavement from his car to a building or walked through Harrods. The presence of four huge men was at best a precaution against verbal assault. More importantly, they were living proof that someone cared for Mohamed, and they dissipated another of his complexes – his size. Disliking small men, he enjoyed badgering his hefty protectors. To his delight, the donkeys used the codename 'Lion' for him. 'The lion leading the donkeys,' he laughed, telling himself that he possessed the power of a godfather, dictating the fate of thousands and defying other mortals. The proof was demonstrated in New York, where, bored in his suite at the Pierre Hotel, he had left his personal assistants Katie Manning and Alison Bozek in the hotel while he, despite the dangers, walked at midnight into Central Park surrounded in box formation by four bodyguards. 'He pushed his luck,' the guards would later complain. 'The gangs were circling.' Fayed chortled. He was king.

The illusion of power grew from the new security routines devised by Heywood. Instead of simply walking across the pavement in Park Lane to his waiting car, his progress from the penthouse was reported by bodyguards whispering into throat microphones. In a synchronized manoeuvre, the Mercedes drew up at the kerbside and alert bodyguards outside murmured, 'All clear.' Four more bodyguards spilled on to the pavement to surround the target as he walked twelve feet from the building to the kerb. Ensconced in his car, he was thrilled by the uninterrupted drive through Hyde Park to Knightsbridge thanks to newly learned tactical driving drills. Leapfrogging with the Mercedes, the back-up Range Rover blocked other traffic, reinforcing his sense of importance. Nevertheless, to bolster the pretence that these were vital security routines, the back-up car's trunk carried his survival equipment: a medical chest, oxygen mask, stretcher, trauma kit, saline drips, a neck collar and equipment for breathing through the throat.

'The Lion has left Papa Lima,' announced Alpha team leader, 'and we are proceeding on red route.' In the Park Lane operations room, dominated by a large colour-coded map of London's streets hung on a wall behind Perspex, the hum of codenames followed the progress of the white armoured Mercedes through the capital. 'The Lion is arriving at the Corner Shop.' Four bodyguards awaited Fayed in the Harrods delivery bay. Rather than go direct to the executive offices, he had adopted the practice of touring the store in a manner akin to a royal procession. Accompanied by his posse of bodyguards, some secretly armed, he passed through the departments greeting customers and occasionally speaking to his staff. The presence of his protectors warned those contemplating an injudicious word of the risk. Indispensability suggested power and, to confirm his own supreme authority, he allowed no one to doubt that everyone was dispensable. Whether someone stayed or departed was irrevelvant because others were always available. 'The donkeys like working for me,' smirked Fayed, 'but they need to have respect.' His own fears were invisible to the casual observer.

Rubbish, he muttered, too much rubbish. The tour's purpose was to understand Harrods' problems and, pending Brian Walsh's arrival, to consider improvements. So many of the staff frustrated his desire for perfection and his ambition to transform the store into the world's best. Through head hunters, he had already found Stan Frith, renowned as a personnel director at Texas Instruments, to clear out the dross and hire a new generation. Allowed to name his own price, Frith had been glowingly introduced to the board: 'He's the man. He'll report to me every day.' Heading Frith's hit-list was the directors' dining room on the top floor, where white-gloved waiters served food on Royal Doulton china while the other staff ate in a gloomy area amid creaking pipes. Soon Frith would be damned as the 'Angel of Death'.

Inevitably, during those tours Fayed noticed the large number of attractive young girls employed as sales assistants. Stylishly dressed in starched white blouses and dark suits – many smiling as he passed – their fresh youthfulness and well-behaved middle-class backgrounds suggested obedient sexuality. Bursting with vanity and testosterone, Fayed easily misinterpreted the smiles greeting his procession as an acknowledgement of his attractiveness. The joke about the Sloane girl's answer to what she did in the mornings, 'I either go home or go to Harrods,' had caused convulsions of laughter. He had not been slow to notice that sexual relationships permeated the store. Ambitious women employees reporting to male managers often welcomed the opportunity for intimacies, even within the store itself. Gossips spoke of finding a Father Christmas with his pants down in a cupboard and of discovering couples in dark basement stairwells. There is Allah the Almighty, Fayed reasoned, and then there is Me. Women, he believed, would now worship him. 'That girl in the fashion department,' he told the personnel director, 'she should work in my office.' Many Fionas, Charlottes and Victorias of Kensington and Chelsea seized the opportunity to escape the shop floor and head for the executive suite.

Melanie, a blonde, buxom former airline hostess, eagerly accepted the offer to transfer from the shop floor to Park Lane. Soon after, her appearance was transformed. 'Daddy will look after you,' promised Fayed, handing her six fifty-pound notes. 'Buy yourself some new clothes.' Melanie also enhanced her looks with expensive cosmetics and a gold Cartier watch given to her on her second day. Paradoxically, Fayed saw no incongruity in attempting to suborn girls with cash and promises. The man who would endlessly pontificate about the insult to 'my dignity, my integrity, my honour, my family' believed it natural to offer to buy a woman's compliance. Even if she refused his offer, he never grew tired of trying. 'Find me another Melanie,' Fayed repeatedly ordered to successive personnel directors who understood that beautiful young blondes should be recruited to work in his private office. The lure for the most favoured was a convertible Volkswagen Golf or BMW. Money made men behave in odd ways but, to Fayed, offering money to women was as normal as squeezing lemon all over his food and surrounding himself with bodyguards. The security, he believed, guaranteed him immunity to any retribution.

'We'll need camera surveillance throughout Park Lane,' recommended Heywood.

'Good,' replied Fayed.

'And we'll reinforce the doors.'

The nine existing security cameras connected to monitors in the Operations Room were to be doubled. Bullet-proof doors were to be installed in Fayed's apartments and on the new connecting door leading into 55 Park Lane. Security circuits would be installed on door locks to block access to unauthorized bodyguards. Park Lane was his private club where, with unlimited money and new fame, he expected unsupervised liberty.

To confuse any intruder, the existing penthouse was to be rebuilt and a new penthouse erected on the roof. A maze of new corridors and doors would be constructed to allow his own movement between the flats and the floors in 55 and 60 Park Lane to pass unobserved by the miniature cameras and microphones installed in the ceilings by ADT, the security company. But the tyranny of his security system denied him total secrecy.

The names of most visitors entering Park Lane were carefully recorded before Fayed's express approval was given for entry through the bullet-proof glass doors. Even those whose names were deliberately withheld were soon identified by the curious bodyguards, often assisted by members of the Egyptian's domestic staff. Watched by the security guards on the monitors, a succession of beautiful young women, from lunchtime until late in the evening, entered the penthouse flats of Mohamed, Ali and Salah, remaining until the early hours. Fayed, with his fetish for privacy, expected them to pass unseen or ignored by discreet bodyguards and domestic staff either grateful for cash payments or threatened by legal reprisals. Wagging his forefinger, he regularly warned his bodyguards about the risk of fraternization: 'You're fired if I see you talking to my girls.' Unlike Khashoggi, who had famously entertained eight prostitutes in one evening in a jamboree in his Manhattan triplex, the Fayeds wanted secrecy.

Among the bevy of attractive women was Claudia, a long-legged German girl, often dressed in leather, who officially was given a single bedroom off the Rotunda, a living room constructed with false ceilings. There was Jill, usually wearing leather too, known to the guards as 'All the kit'. And there was Vanessa, a well-built blonde, found once at 4 a.m. on Fayed's staircase, 'delivering sandwiches'. The procession of women eager to enjoy an experience with the famous Fayeds was dizzying. Most were destined to visit Salah Fayed, codenamed 'Gaddafi' because of his nasty, explosive temper, or 'Fruitbat' because he only came out at night, whose sexual appetite seemed to be insatiable. One of the few non-blondes was a Chinese girl, alias the 'Masseuse', who would arrive in a Volkswagen and was known to be delivering drugs to Salah. Other girls, including another Chinese, were seen on the monitors entering Ali's flat. Bona-fide masseuses or physiotherapists visiting Mohamed Fayed would be directed to his special massage room adjoining the Blue Room, a guest bedroom.

The Fayeds' exuberance was shared by Dodi. Since their reconciliation, Mohamed had restored his thirty-two-year-old son's £150,000 monthly allowance; his free accommodation in Park Lane, Paris, St Tropez and the suite at the Pierre in New York; and his personal fleet of cars, a Mercedes, a Lagonda and two Aston Martins. Either unaware or heedless of the effect of bestowing unaccountable wealth upon his son, Fayed encouraged Dodi to share his own ambitions in Britain. 'You've got to become English,' Fayed urged his son, speaking as usual in Arabic. Dodi approved of his father's agenda. His mother had so often spoken of the advantage of knowing the right people and marrying into the best circles. Then tragedy struck in March 1986. Drinking excessively and swallowing too many barbiturates, Samira suffered a mild stroke and died of a heart attack. The Khashoggis blamed a doctor's treatment and the broken heart she had suffered after her third husband, employed by Adnan Khashoggi in Spain, had squandered millions of dollars and eloped with another woman. Devastated, Dodi planned to fly to Cairo for the funeral. His father, loathing the Khashoggis, discouraged the journey. Insisting that his son was too distraught, Mohamed Fayed exerted overwhelming pressure on his son. Dodi obeyed. The Khashoggis were hurt but not surprised. Ever since the reconciliation between father and son, Mohamed had forbidden Dodi to meet or speak to his cousins, and Dodi had yielded to his father. In the same vein, he accepted his father's strategy that polo matches were ideal venues for the family to shine.

In sponsoring a Harrods trophy for polo at Cirencester Park in July 1986, Fayed knew that among the benefits would be an introduction to Prince Charles and Princess Diana and a further meeting with the queen. To smooth his chase for 'incredible royal connections', Dodi nurtured his father's ambitions by courageously improving his polo, while Mohamed Fayed, standing in the special enclosure, often announced donations to charities at the end of the day. The Egyptian believed that playing polo with the royals and even selling shirts to Prince Charles through the newly acquired Turnbull & Asser in Jermyn Street implied social acceptance. His generosity, he was sure, such as hosting a lunch at Harrods for holders of the Victoria Cross when others had refused sponsorship, proved his commitment to Britain. His imagination was limitless.

Imitating his father, Dodi also welcomed any opportunity to exploit the fame and wealth which had followed in the wake of the House of Fraser purchase. While producing two F/X films in Hollywood and planning a production of *Hook*, based on *Peter Pan*, whose rights his father had bought at a low price from their owner, Great Ormond Street Hospital for Sick Children, he indulged his dream of becoming a macho-man by driving an 1100cc motorbike or, dressed as a US naval officer or wearing US combat fatigues, flying his father's helicopter. But even as a fantasist he could not match his father. His helicopter flying ceased after one occasion when the craft's perilous rotation over the Battersea heliport was only just brought under control by the professional pilot. His yearning to be physically strong was reflected in an expensive private gym in Park Lane. 'I graduated from Sandhurst, you know,' he boasted to a bemused bodyguard, a former Para who had yomped across the Falklands. 'Let's go for a run.' Breathless after a 400 yard jog in Hyde Park, he spluttered, 'Have we run a mile yet?' Returning to his flat and the unused gym, Dodi consoled himself with innumerable model aircraft, videos of the James Bond films, military regalia, a Beretta pistol and action-man magazines – all feeding his dream and justifying the presence of a bodyguard permanently waiting downstairs.

Supposedly vulnerable to kidnapping or assault, he had been assigned Bob Curry as a bodyguard.

The former SAS soldier pandered to his employer's vanity. Daily, Curry would visit the restaurant chosen for that night's dinner – Miyama, the Japanese restaurant off Berkeley Square, San Lorenzo in Knightsbridge or Harry's Bar in Mayfair – and hand over an envelope filled with fifties to guarantee an effusive welcome from the cloakroom attendant, waiters and the manager. The envelope guaranteed a centre table where Dodi was certain to be spotted by other diners. Using the bodyguard as an actor in his own performance, Dodi paid to be noticed and invariably declined invitations to eat in private homes. Glamour lay in entertaining Brooke Shields and Marie Helvin to dinner in public with a bodyguard in tow.

The procedure was repeated late at night as Dodi led the procession of freeloaders to Annabel's and Tramp. Joined in those clubs by the singer Tom Jones or by Johnny Gold, Tramp's unmistakable owner, ordering bottles of Stolichnaya vodka for £110, he gloried in his guests' illusion that the bodyguard watching from the bar was detailed to protect him from an assassin. Augmenting his fantasies, Dodi paid Curry an extra £150 in cash every month to carry a loaded gun. 'Watch my glass whenever I leave the table,' he instructed his protector. Even that precaution against poison was not deemed sufficient. On his return to the table, he would order a new bottle of vodka, the seal to be broken in his presence. His guests seemed impressed, but they were the types to be equally charmed by his small talk if, in return, they received free accommodation at the Ritz or free holidays in St Tropez.

Unthreatening, desperately seeking relationships, Dodi required protection from solitude. 'I don't want to be alone anywhere,' Dodi told Curry as he was lifted drunk from the lavatory floor at Tramp.

'Don't forget this, sir,' replied the bodyguard, picking up a wodge of fifty-pound notes and pushing it into his client's pocket. Holding Dodi with one arm, the bodyguard left the club clutching a Tesco carrier bag of porn videos handed over by the barman. Waiting outside was Dodi's green soft-top Aston Martin, identical to the model used by James Bond in *Living Daylights* with the registration number CIA 208. A broken wing mirror, clipped while brushing a skip, was testament to a previous night's drunken excess. Insisting on driving, Dodi felt safe because a monitor built into the dashboard was connected to a CCTV camera beamed from the boot: anyone following would be seen.

Obsessive security had even been extended to Fayed's young children, including Camilla, his baby daughter born in February 1985. Each child had been assigned a bodyguard with the order to expect a phone call from the father at any moment demanding the infant's precise location. More guards had been placed across the estate at Oxted, even hiding in the bushes, to respond instantly to any entry. Additional protection had been arranged for Jasmine, his five-year-old daughter attending a local school. In an unusual arrangement with the head teacher, Fayed had inserted a bodyguard, posing as the school janitor and gardener, to patrol the premises. Counter-surveillance car patrols and motorcyclists cruised through the area to spot potential kidnappers. On their father's orders, the children were growing up fearful of assault in the midst of the Surrey countryside.

Since the discovery of Rowland's telephone taps, Fayed had increased his security in Oxted by installing cameras and sound detectors in the trees, and ordering more rottweilers. Even Sunday walks across his estate had become mini-military operations. Thirty minutes in advance, bodyguards were dispatched along his route to check that no landmines had been planted, that no assassins, having scaled the chain fence and avoided the dogs and infrared cameras, were concealed in bushes. Accompanied by two armed men, Fayed would walk up the wooded hill to his favourite bench. Along his route, other armed men waited in hiding. 'If anyone attacks, you kill them,' he had ordered.

'We'll have a problem with that,' replied his bodyguard.

'Then shoot them in the legs,' scoffed Fayed, clearly displeased.

The fantasies of self-importance which explained Mohamed Fayed's preoccupation with bodyguards and security were now being augmented by his real fear of Tiny Rowland. Although he would often chant, 'I fear nobody. I fear only God,' the truth was that he was terrified of Tiny. Gradually, his status was being corroded as Rowland's propaganda connecting him with the sultan was slowly establishing itself as the truth. Chain fences, cameras, rottweilers and guns now offered Fayed protection from Rowland's revenge. But during 1986 he realized that his private army could do nothing to influence Rowland's pursuit of a legal solution: his intensive lobbying of the DTI to strip Fayed of House of Fraser. The first step, the Lonrho chief was urging, was an inquiry by the Monopolies Commission. Weekly, in support of Rowland's campaign, the *Observer* published false allegations about 'criminal conspiracies' between Conservative ministers and DTI officials; 'authenticated transcripts' of non-existent conversations; a false report that the Fayeds had not held Egyptian passports since 1960; and a piece reporting the delivery to the prime minister of a transcript of the secretly taped conversations between Fayed and the Swami in Carlos Place in June 1985. Enclosed with the transcript was a letter from Rowland inaccurately alleging that Fayed had paid the Swami $500,000 for an introduction to the sultan. Unmentioned was Rowland's own payment of $5 million for the tapes. The most wounding allegation had been published on 12 January 1986. Donald Trelford, the *Observer*'s editor, had reported that Fayed and Mark Thatcher had secretly travelled together to Brunei in October 1984. Trelford's account, supported by eyewitness statements and documents, suggested that Margaret Thatcher was a party to the sultan's secret funding of Fayed's purchase of House of Fraser.

Fayed had good reason to feel outraged by the *Observer*'s

allegations. Most were untrue. Trelford's account of the trip to Brunei, as the editor later conceded when confronted with sworn affidavits from Brunei officials, was based upon forged documents; the tape recording of Fayed's conversation with the Swami had been edited and failed to substantiate Rowland's allegations; while the Swami's account of the 'introduction' to the sultan was subsequently admitted by Rowland to be phoney when he sued the guru to recover his $5 million. The only truth was a visit to Oxted by Mark Thatcher on a Sunday morning. That encounter, however, had not been leaked to Rowland.

*

UNTIL JUNE 1986, Fayed had hoped that Ian Greer would recruit sympathetic politicians to neutralize those embarrassments and mount a counter-campaign.

At the beginning of the year, after the publication of the Mark Thatcher story, he had met sixteen peers and fourteen Conservative MPs all resentful about Rowland's use of the *Observer* to embarrass Mrs Thatcher. To reinforce his case, he had at Greer's suggestion invited Tim Smith, Michael Grylls and Neil Hamilton to lunch at Harrods on 10 March 1986. Despite his eccentric manners during the meal and his irritating habit of never listening and only lecturing – 'I am fighting for my dignity, my integrity, my honour, my family' – their polite response to his vulgar condemnations of his foe and tactless demands for questions in parliament and representations to ministers had encouraged Fayed's assumption that his guests were unquestioning supporters. After they had departed clutching presents from their host, he waited for action. He was disappointed. Paul Channon, the new secretary of state for trade and industry, refused the MPs' request for a meeting. News of that failure coincided with the publication of the latest *Observer* exposé.

On 15 June 1986, a Rowland torpedo scored a devastating hit. That Sunday, the *Observer*'s article 'In search of the fabulous Pharaohs', exposed the brothers' false account of their wealthy pasha family. Based upon intensive research in Egypt by Peter Wickman, a respected independent journalist, it was the first true account of the Fayeds' humble origins.

'Ian,' Fayed shrieked at Greer early that Sunday morning, 'they're shitting on me from a great height.' Defenceless, Fayed knew that Rowland would the following day find tame MPs to circulate the article around Westminster and propose a Commons motion to enshrine the article in Hansard, the official parliamentary record. His enemy was so well entrenched – 'He's got so many MPs in his pay,' he shouted at Greer – that any MP who dared voice support for the Egyptian himself was instantly attacked by Rowland's press machine. More than ever, Fayed was desperate to secure committed supporters in the Commons who agreed that exaggerating your past was not a cardinal sin.

Fortuitously, two months earlier, Tim Smith, the Conservative MP for Beaconsfield, had lodged a request for a debate in the Commons to attack Rowland's misuse of the *Observer*. It was due to be held just three days later, on 18 June 1986. In anticipation, Fayed invited Smith to his office.

After thirty-five years in the bazaar, taking commissions and handing out bribes, Fayed could usually smell whether a person's honour was affordable or beyond even his resources. He would agree with Rowland, a profligate corrupter: 'The definition of an honest man is when his price is too high.' Watching Greer and his coterie of MPs, dressed in badly cut suits and a mite too eagerly eating his food, Fayed suspected cosy relationships cemented by financial arrangements. After all, he paid Greer and he imagined that the lobbyist cared for his contacts. In Fayed's world, money was the natural glue for holding relationships together.

But even the Egyptian had not realized the full extent of the dishonesty. Secretly, Greer was paying Grylls and Hamilton commissions for introducing clients to his agency. Grylls had received at least £86,000 from Greer for encouraging corporate executives to retain the lobbyist. Neil Hamilton had received at least £15,000 for introductions but had requested Greer, to evade income tax, to launder the payments through paintings, airline tickets and garden furniture purchased by Christine Hamilton, his wife, at Peter Jones. In the opinion of those politicians, Fayed was a typical rich Arab useful for satisfying their greed for money.

Sharing commissions, providing generous hospitality and offering thank-you payments had been as natural to Fayed since his apprenticeship with the Khashoggis in Saudi Arabia as was his irritating habit of renegotiating signed contracts. The refinement of his bribery during the early 1980s stemmed from the growth in the number of employees. Whereas previously he had handed out cash among the Genavco clerks, his secretaries and the bureaucrats helpful to his small shipping, film and hotel business, the new political battle required different stakes. The wodge of fifties in his pocket was no longer sufficient. Instead, he always travelled with two leather briefcases, both secured by combination locks: one for his business documents and the other for the fifties. Neatly wrapped £1,000 blocks filled the locked case carried by his bodyguards and positioned every day in the same precise spot in his home, in his helicopter and in his office. Habitually, on arrival in his office, he personally placed the bribing briefcase on a table near to his chair.

When Tim Smith entered Park Lane in June 1986 to discuss the imminent Commons debate, Fayed identified the MP as the only politician in his armoury who was challenging Edward du Cann and the Lonrho army in Westminster. That nonentity, confused about his role as an MP and with limited ministerial future, he realized, was his only hope in stopping Rowland's war of attrition. Watching Smith, an awkward, friendless, forty-year-old accountant, listening patiently to his familiar rant, Fayed felt a mixture of gratitude and desperation. His hand moved towards his open briefcase. Lifting a white envelope, he thrust £5,000 towards the politician. 'From Mohamed.

Present. It's nothing.' Startled, Smith pushed the envelope aside. 'I couldn't,' he spluttered. Fayed's response to that embarrassed refusal, repeated on countless occasions with men and women, was well honed. Exploding in a phoney burst of grievance about spurned generosity, he persuaded Smith to retain the paper brick. Smith lacked the courage and character to refuse, and merely murmured his thanks. 'Just between you and me,' twinkled Fayed, reassuring the politician of secrecy. The animal savoured his kill. In Fayed's mind, he had dispensed a thank-you gift, the largesse of a rich man buying friendship and loyalty, similar to many other wodges he had thrown at his senior executives. The corollary was that those accepting Mohamed's gifts belonged thereafter to Mohamed.

Hansard's report of the debate on 19 June 1986 satisfied Fayed that he had received some value for money. He did not read all the small print but he sensed the gist. Smith had criticized the *Observer*'s independent directors for not stopping Rowland's campaign against the Fayeds and he had sponsored two critical early-day motions. The target, Fayed believed, had been finally hit. In gratitude, he invited Smith and Greer to lunch.

Sitting in the centre of his own universe, vague about the political environment and bereft of any profound observations about the world he sought to influence, Fayed sermonized once again about 'my dignity, my integrity, my honour, my family'. Blinded by egotism, he could not imagine any perspective on the saga other than his own. With implacable faith in his ability to win, he urged Greer to organize delegations: 'I want processions in the parliaments. Processions.'

Greer grimaced. 'We need information about Rowland, Mohamed,' he replied.

'I've got,' cried Fayed. The first rewards of his own investigations into Rowland's affairs had been delivered, albeit under constrained circumstances.

'I don't want anything obvious,' Fayed had ordered Royston Webb, his lawyer. 'Not too dirty.' Interpreting his orders faithfully, Webb had told Richard New, their investigator, 'We don't want to do anything illegal.' Lonrho employees were not to be offered bribes to secure sensitive information. New was perplexed. He was bribing air-traffic controllers to obtain a daily account of the movements of Rowland's plane; he was paying money to discover the secrets of Rowland's health; and he was offering large sums of money to secure Rowland's confidential army records. But, to avoid embarrassment, he was forbidden by Webb to travel to Africa. Instead, he was to rely upon an incompetent investigator.

Dozens of eyewitnesses and the DTI inspectors' report about Lonrho had recounted episodes of Rowland's immorality in Africa – his widespread bribery and his suspected provocation of a geologist's suicide – but no one was prepared to swear an affidavit. Undiscovered was Rowland's murky, murderous world – in particular, to secure oil and diamond concessions, his support of and supply of arms to the rebel army fighting in the brutal Angolan civil war; and also the provision of his Gulfstream jet and pilot to transport a four-man murder squad from Britain to Spain on behalf of a Brazilian tycoon to eliminate a rival. The scale of Rowland's machinations was beyond Fayed's comprehension and, unlike Rowland, he lacked the subtlety and the relationships to gather useful information. 'Go and see Jimmy Goldsmith,' Fayed had ordered New. 'He knows a lot about Tiny.' Flying to New York, New had expected major revelations. Instead, after a long wait, Goldsmith appeared, harassed by a major business deal and, in a brief outburst, declared, 'Rowland is a truly evil man.' The tycoon had then abruptly departed. Fayed, it was clear, could expect no support from other players.

New could console himself with other successes. Affidavits obtained by the investigator from former British soldiers described Rowland's glee in 1941 on hearing the BBC radio report of the sinking of the British battleships *Repulse* and *Prince of Wales* by the Japanese. His Nazi sympathies and his desertion from the British army were confirmed as the reasons for his detention until 1945. New had also discovered that Tiny's jet had flown occasionally to Libya, which was branded as a terrorist state. A search of all companies connected to Lonrho revealed Tradewinds, an air freight company whose co-directors were Ashraf Marwan and a Libyan intelligence chief closely connected to Colonel Gaddafi. With the help of a CIA source, New could prove that Rowland was involved with two former CIA officers in illegal arms trading with Libya.

More denigratory revelations were provided by Dan Mayers, an eccentric gem prospector and a former partner of Rowland's in Africa. Mayers produced documentary evidence of Rowland's lack of candour towards Lonrho's shareholders, of a tax evasion deal through Liechtenstein and of an indictment for fraud by the South African government against Rowland. The discovery that Rowland had been arrested by customs officers at Houston airport for carrying guns on his Gulfstream was a bonus.

Fayed's forlorn struggle to secure favourable newspaper coverage was suddenly over. Friendly journalists were always grateful for scoops and the *Sunday Times*, with Rupert Murdoch's blessing, began publishing a succession of damaging articles about Rowland based upon New's investigations. Fayed convinced himself that the revelations, repeated by Greer's team in the Commons, would swing public opinion against his enemy. But the excitement passed. The stories were too obscure to arouse public or political disquiet. His campaign was faltering at birth. New proposed a fresh tactic.

The investigator had discovered Francesca Pollard, an unstable thirty-seven-year-old housewife living in a dirty London council flat and already engaged in an active vendetta against Rowland. Pollard's complaint was credible. As the granddaughter of Walter Williams, the founder of the Israel-British Bank, she was the principal beneficiary under his will. But in 1974 Harry Landy, a director of the bank and, as her uncle, a trustee of the will, had defrauded the bank and so caused its collapse. In 1979, Landy was convicted of perpetrating a £27 million fraud and sentenced to five years' imprisonment but, thanks to Rowland, he appealed on a technicality and was eventually acquitted. Thereafter, he was employed by Lonrho to manage a property subsidiary. Blaming Rowland for helping her dishonest uncle, Pollard regularly and noisily demonstrated outside Lonrho's offices in the City to embarrass the tycoon. By chance, she was spotted by New and invited to meet Fayed.

Oozing charm and sympathy, Fayed greeted Pollard at their first meeting as a lost daughter. The plan, proposed by New and Royston Webb, was for Pollard, continuing to pose as the poor, protesting housewife, to smear their mutual enemy in an intensified public campaign. 'Good. Good,' cackled Fayed. To the impoverished woman, the millionaire's offer was irresistible: 'I give you £25,000, expenses, a driver, a car and money for your lawyers to fight your uncle.' His support, however, would remain a secret. Neither the public nor Rowland were to know that the clumsy woman was Fayed's tool. Delighted that someone espoused his most precious cause with one hundred per cent commitment, Fayed thrust some fifties into New's hands and demanded instant results.

Therefore I accuse . . ., a four-page glossy pamphlet written by New and Webb but signed by Pollard, was produced two weeks later. Adopting Rowland's tactics, it was a caustic, defamatory attack on Rowland delivered to thousands of prominent Britons. A bewildered Rowland was reluctant to issue a writ against a penniless woman.

'I'll demonstrate outside Cheapside,' said Pollard, working on Fayed's frustration.

'Good, good,' enthused the store owner, relieved by Pollard's enthusiasm for embarrassing his enemy.

Driven to the City in an anonymous van by New and two bodyguards, the bedraggled woman stood outside Lonrho's headquarters in Cheapside with a placard denouncing 'Tricky Tiny' and 'Robber Rowland' for fraud. To Fayed's surprise,

the publicity aroused Rowland-haters. Hundreds of sympathetic letters from Westminster, the City and respected professionals arrived at her council flat. 'Baby One,' purred Pollard
during her regular telephone conversations, 'what is Baby One
doing about the Pig today?' Their code required no translation.

'A gift from the gods,' Fayed told his confidants, ignoring
the uncomfortable truth that his new weapon was anti-Rowland rather than pro-Fayed. 'What you do to make things more
bad for him?' asked Fayed.

'I'll call on Spicer at home,' she replied, referring to Paul
Spicer, an insipid Lonrho director particularly close to Rowland. 'That should be a fun afternoon. And I'll call on his
neighbours too.'

Fayed roared with laughter. With luck, a lot more money
and the discovery of more dirt on Rowland, the Tiny–Tootsie
feud might become more balanced. In the meantime, his regular
flights to France promised relief and reassurance.

*

'PLANE SECURE,' announced the bodyguard. Fayed had
walked three yards from the Mercedes to the Gulfstream at
Luton airport. Seated in his throne-like chair in the new aircraft
while the bodyguards strapped themselves in at the back – the
area designated for donkeys – he smiled at the young blonde
secretary near by. This trip to Paris, he anticipated, would be
quite special. He had even convinced a former Royal Military
Policeman to carry a gun.

Awaiting the Gulfstream at Le Bourget was a specially built
Mercedes four-wheel drive, protected by armour and with slots
for guns. The owner was thrilled by an additional feature: a
pan, attached underneath the car, was filled with tacks to
demobilize a pursuer. Seated in the front, Fayed grunted as the
rear door closed. In the mirror he observed the blonde girl's
awe as the police escort on motorcycles, arranged by Josef
Goedde, the German head of security at the Ritz, signalled
their departure.

The refurbishment of the Ritz had won accolades. The recognition of his political adeptness was Jacques Chirac's agreement that he should receive an award, La Grande Médaille of the City of Paris and the presentation by the mayor of the Légion d'Honneur for his contribution to the city. Invest a lot, get back even more, had been his successful recipe in Paris.

Ingratiating himself with Chirac had delivered another prize. Over the years, Fayed had been persuaded by Sydney Johnson, his valet previously employed by the Windsors, that the villa and its contents in the Bois de Boulogne occupied by the former king and his wife for forty years, were unique. In 1953 the Windsors had been granted a lease of the house, built at the turn of the century by the Renault motorcar family. But during the duchess's long terminal illness the house had fallen into disrepair and many of the Windsors' belongings – especially historic mementoes – had either been sold to finance her medical care or been stolen. Excited by the prospect of another project which would bring him closer to the British royal family, Fayed began negotiations in late 1985 for a lease on the villa at a peppercorn rent in return for funding its restoration. To Fayed, the *nouveau riche* aspiring architect, the notion of living in the house inhabited by the Windsors offered itself as an automatic passport to fame and social acceptance in Britain. 'The abdication', he would tell inquirers, 'had a big influence upon me.' Considering that he was eight years old at the time, and only four according to his phoney date of birth, the idea that the abdication had influenced a child's life in Alexandria's back streets was far-fetched. Even if he spoke the truth, he had utterly misunderstood the position. The British royal family had deliberately shunned the Windsors, especially after the duke's expression of sympathy for Adolf Hitler. Anyone perpetuating the Windsors' legacy was unwelcome.

Oblivious to history and fired by his imagination, Fayed energetically planned an approach to Maître Suzanne Blum, the Windsors' intelligent lawyer and ferocious defender, with an offer to buy the remaining personal effects in the villa. Fayed calculated that Blum, aged eighty-seven, only two years younger than the ailing duchess and suffering creeping blindness, would be susceptible to an emotional rather than a financial offer. Sydney Johnson, a unique intermediary, had arranged to meet Blum in the delapidated villa in late 1985. Mr Al Fayed, his new employer, explained Johnson, had become attached to all things British while a child in British-ruled Egypt and retained a particular fascination for the Windsors. Mr Al Fayed, continued Johnson, would like to discuss with Blum the creation of a permanent memorial to the Windsors. Blum nodded approvingly.

The duchess died on 24 April 1986 and shortly after the funeral Fayed began negotiations with Chirac for the villa's lease and with Blum for the Windsors' possessions. Of special importance was the duchess's jewellery, which Blum conservatively valued at £6 million. Fayed, she believed, had agreed to that price, but on the day of signing the contract the Egyptian arrived with a revised offer. As far as Fayed as concerned, he was dealing with an old woman who could be snowballed. A confidential opinion of jewellery experts, he explained, valued the duchess's treasures at £4.2 million. Adopting a method so favoured in the bazaar, he offered the lawyer £5 million. Astonished, Blum refused to sell the jewels to him. Instead she would offer them for sale by auction. Nevertheless, she sold Fayed the contents, and he had secured the house.

Business complete, Fayed returned to London to prepare for his holiday in St Tropez. Unlike those of other families, the Fayeds' journey had become something of a military operation. Three nannies and eight bodyguards accompanied the Fayeds and their three children. To provide for all their requirements, an advance lorry with over eighty suitcases would leave England two days before. In anticipation, Fayed indulged in an eccentric spending spree.

Accompanied by his posse of bodyguards, Fayed toured the Harrods Food Hall for one hour dictating a shopping list. Fish, meat, vegetables and fruit were ordered in massive quantities. Pointing at the smoked salmon, cheese and peppered gammon, Fayed told the bodyguard scribbling his order that everything was to be sliced to his precise thickness. Heads would roll if a slice was a fraction too thick or too thin. The foibles of a tycoon were to be satisfied. Everything was to be packed in vacuum boxes with dry ice and loaded on to the Gulfstream. In additon, large quantities of his special pistachio nuts, Glacier mints, shampoo and Harrods biscuits were to be packed. He eschewed ordering jam and pasta. Sydney made better plum jam than Harrods supplied and the pasta would be brought from Italy. Finally he ordered five dozen boxes of Perrier and Evian water. The bottled French water would also be flown on the Gulfstream to France. Unmentioned were the huge cartons of Kleenex tissues and the specially prepared lavatory paper favoured by Fayed. 'Have you got my prawns, you fuggin' donkey?' asked Fayed the following day as he stood on the villa's patio overlooking the Mediterranean drinking a beaker of Perrier brought from London. 'Yes, sir,' replied the guard. Fayed grunted. Humiliating his staff was a temporary emollient to the discredit which Rowland was once again heaping upon him.

*

HIS ENEMY'S ARMOURY had increased after his successful bid in August 1986 for the *Today* newspaper. Fayed had considered launching a rival bid but, warned that potential proprietors are subject to investigation by the Monopolies Commission, he abandoned the idea. Angered and frustrated by his powerlessness, he returned to London and directed his venom at Ian Greer. 'I want processions in parliament to stop that crook,' he screamed, oblivious that the Commons was in summer recess.

'It doesn't quite work that way, Mohamed,' said Greer. 'We've got to calmly persuade MPs and ministers of our case.'

Patience was a quality unknown to Fayed. He wanted action – bulldozing action. 'I want processions,' he growled.

Greer agreed to ask Smith and Hamilton to protest to Channon about Rowland's abuse of his newspapers. Only Smith undertook to do so. When parliament resumed in the autumn, he promised Fayed, he would ask more questions. The Egyptian felt helpless, especially since Rowland's latest campaign had again hit its target.

In a letter to Paul Channon, Rowland had urged that Fayed's takeover of House of Fraser should be referred to the Monopolies Commission, which could recommend the compulsory sale of the company. New information, wrote Rowland, obtained from the company's latest accounts, proved Fayed's dishonesty. Increasingly cowed by Rowland's terrorism, the civil servants had no alternative but to examine his latest torpedo.

Fayed had hoped to preserve the secrecy of his finances but, on the insistence of his professional advisers, he had been obliged to reveal that soon after his purchase he had pledged all the House of Fraser shares as security for a loan of £425 million. Rowland's interpretation of that discovery was that contrary to their assurances, the Fayeds had borrowed all the money to buy House of Fraser. They had not used their own cash for the bid, Rowland told Channon. That was perfectly true.

The original purchase in March 1985 had been funded by a fiduciary loan from the Swiss Bank Corporation, but one year later, on 3 March 1986, Samuel Montagu, acting on behalf of thirteen banks, had syndicated a seven-year loan of £425 million to the Fayeds. The loans were secured against the House of Fraser shares. The refinancing of the loans was uncomplicated and suspect.

John MacArthur, then a respected Kleinworts banker representing Fayed, had approached Ernest Cole, a senior corporate banker at Samuel Montagu. The Swiss Bank Corporation, explained MacArthur, had loaned Fayed the original purchase money for House of Fraser. SBC's loan was expensive, said MacArthur. Could the Fayeds enter into a new arrangement? Cole was receptive. Samuel Montagu was owned by the Midland Bank, which had traditionally lent money to House of Fraser under its previous owners. Those loans remained outstanding and the Midland's managers were keen to reorganize all the loans from twenty-six other banks to the Fayeds under one umbrella. Accordingly, MacArthur had no difficulty in switching the loans from the Swiss bank to a consortium in London and simultaneously increasing the loans to the Fayeds. That of course begged the fundamental question. In March 1985, Fayed had insisted that his purchase was funded by his own cash. How, he was asked by his advisers, were they to explain his huge new debts?

Fayed's initial explanation for the new arrangement appeared to its author incontrovertible. After the original takeover, he said, the brothers' ownership had been transferred to a British company to allow interest payments on the subsequent loans to be offset for tax purposes against profits. 'We need our money for other purposes,' Fayed had replied, 'and we like borrowing.' As evidence, he produced statements showing that AITSA, Fayed's Liechtenstein trust, possessed fiduciary deposits worth $291 million. The truth about his loans had been, he hoped, disguised.

The credibility of that explanation was weakened after another discovery. In 1986, the House of Fraser group lost £20 million and the losses were set to continue in 1987 at £18.6 million. The group's finances seemed precarious, yet Fayed insisted that there was no mystery. The losses were simply a legitimate device to avoid paying tax. 'More than that', insisted Fayed, 'I refuse to say.' He could, he told his advisers, rest on a negative. 'No one has disputed my ownership of House of Fraser and no one has claimed any rival interest in the money used.'

Demolishing Fayed's negatives was the reason for Rowland's visit with two fellow directors and his lawyers to Roger Allen at the DTI. The civil servants who had approved the takeover had since moved to other departments. Allen, as a public servant, was obliged to listen to Rowland's argument that the onus lay on Fayed to prove the history of his fortune. Presenting a copy of the *Observer*'s article exposing Fayed's real Egyptian background, Rowland sat back, allowing his lawyer to argue that the implication of Fayed's silence was that his alleged fortune in truth belonged to someone else, probably the sultan. 'How', asked Rowland, 'could Fayed, a poor boy from Alexandria, have earned £615 million without paying any tax?' Allen showed no reaction. 'I think the Inland Revenue should investigate Mr Al Fayed,' added Rowland. 'After all, he's lived in Britain for more than twenty years and yet gives his address as the Trade Centre in Dubai. Odd, isn't it?'

In fact, Rowland had already taken the initiative, and the Inland Revenue's inquiries were causing Fayed embarrassment. The approach to the DTI achieved similar consequences. The reorganization of his finances, Fayed heard from his bankers, had surprised government officials. John Fordham, Rowland's solicitor, had presented a file to DTI and OFT officials outlining the flaws in Fayed's claims about his background and wealth. The immediate result was a letter written in July by Llewellyn Smith, the deputy director general of the Office of Fair Trading, to Michael Hawkes at Kleinworts querying the Samuel Montagu loan and a new document she had received from Lonrho. The document purported to prove that in August 1984 Fayed had controlled $1.5 billion belonging to the sultan, and that in June 1985 he still retained $200 million of the sultan's money.

'Rowland has been on to the OFT,' Michael Hawkes told Fayed. 'He claims you used the sultan's money.'

'Tell them that the sultan has denied any ownership,' said Fayed.

Hawkes replied to Llewellyn Smith that the purported power of attorney was a forgery and that the loan organized by Samuel Montagu was calculated to minimize British taxes. In November 1986, Hawkes telephoned Fayed again. The news was good. Rowland had met Gordon Borrie claiming to possess the sultan's power of attorney. 'Let me see it,' challenged Borrie. Rowland had refused. Borrie's increased distrust of Rowland should have pacified Fayed, but his rival's operation was unsettling him.

The sultan was displeased by Rowland's denigratory attacks and by Fayed's sharply escalating costs for rebuilding the Dorchester and the Paris Ritz. At the Dorchester, Alistair McAlpine, the contractor, was battling with 'a nightmare' as Fayed's original £70 million budget, more than twice the first estimate, soared above £100 million. First, Fayed had ordered that the hotel's quality should resemble that of the Ritz; then, to reduce costs, that it should be the equivalent of a Holiday Inn; and then, as it neared completion, the new work was ripped out and the hotel rebuilt to match the Ritz. The monarch decided to distance himself from the source of his over-expenditure and embarrassment. That autumn, Fayed flew in his Gulfstream to Brunei to negotiate an amicable settlement. Besides Katie Manning, his secretary, he was accompanied by four bodyguards and Josef Goedde, his German chief of security at the Ritz. At the end of one week, after waiting endlessly for meetings and emerging tense from negotiations, Fayed agreed to resign from the board of the Dorchester, to repay some loans and to terminate other agreements. Since the purpose of the relationship had been achieved, the breach was not damaging, unlike his worsening position in London.

In the House of Commons, Rowland's troops were ceaselessly asking embarrassing questions; weekly, the *Observer* linked Fayed with the sultan and Mark Thatcher; and worst of all, in early December, Rowland met Channon. After a presentation marred by Channon's artlessness – 'The blind must be leading the blind,' thought a member of Rowland's entourage – Rowland's demand for a Monopolies Commission inquiry was refused but, for the first time, the possibility of another investigation was not excluded.

Fayed's advisers had already sensed the change of mood. At the beginning of the month, Gordon Borrie, the OFT's director general, had asked Michael Hawkes to explain his certainty about the Fayed's wealth.

'Effectively,' summarized Borrie, 'you relied entirely on RBS [the Royal Bank of Scotland] and the Fayeds, didn't you? You made no enquiries of your own?'

'That's correct,' replied Hawkes.

Borrie reported to Channon on 11 December that while a Monopolies Commission inquiry was unjustified – because no competition issue was involved and the management of House of Fraser was satisfactory – the doubts about Kleinworts' assurances could justify an inquiry.

A meaningless series of indecent words burst from Fayed after Royston Webb revealed the latest blow. Imprisoned by his lies, Fayed's defence was to attack. Only Tim Smith, a lone voice crying out against Rowland's thunder, was openly pledged to fight Fayed's corner. To prove his value, the MP would submit thirty-seven questions to ministers, write four letters to the secretary for trade and industry and join four delegations. Gratefully, Fayed had continued the cash payments. If they did not meet, he suggested, he would leave the fifties in a white envelope at the Park Lane reception. The politician did not demur. Fayed was satisfied. How else could he secure support in parliament?

By then, paying for favours, support and silence had become a regular habit. Every week two bodyguards collected between forty and fifty thousand pounds in cash from the Royal Bank of Scotland or the Midland Bank in Park Lane. At least once a month, two bodyguards were dispatched on the so-called 'Bung Run'. Entrusted with about twenty white envelopes, each filled with £50 notes, they drove around London under strict instructions that the delivery was only to be undertaken if the addressee, invariably a pseudonym, personally accepted the envelope. Among regular recipients living in West London and Islington were journalists and a French woman living near Harrods. If money could halt Rowland's vendetta, Fayed reasoned, he would happily pay out a fortune to achieve that end. So much, he moaned, was going wrong.

That Christmas, he travelled to his chalets in Gstaad. Ten specially prepared turkeys had been packed at Harrods and entrusted to Tony Harris, a bodyguard, to drive to Switzerland in a lorry carrying £4,000 worth of provisions from the Food Hall. French customs had confiscated the load. 'Send the Gulfstream,' ordered Fayed, determined to have turkeys for Christmas. Heini was also complaining. 'That man can't do the black runs,' she complained, irritated that a bodyguard detailed to accompany her skiing was too slow. Momentarily, Fayed looked dismayed: a detail had been overlooked and he was to blame. Quickly he would recruit a former Marine trained in Norway.

To get some peace – since he hated skiing – Fayed ordered two bodyguards to accompany him on a walk carrying a collapsible chair and a rucksack filled with drinks. Their shot-guns were carried in a second bag. High up in the snow-covered Alps, the silence was broken only by Fayed's belches, until suddenly he became agitated. Unlike himself, his guards were not wearing yellow Timberland boots. 'Buy for all the boys,' he directed, pointing at his feet. 'Yessir.' Late that afternoon, the order was received at Harrods. By the following morning, a consignment had been transported to Switzerland on the Gulfstream. 'Very good. Very good,' puffed Fayed as he gazed down at his escorts' identical feet and up at their matching Barbours. Then he screamed again. At his expense, Dodi had rented a chalet in Vail, Colorado, for Christmas. Unannounced, he had married Suzanne Gregard, a model, whom he had met in 1984 in New York. Incapable of ration-alizing his son's unexpected decision as an impromptu reaction to his mother's death, Fayed yelled about the insubordination and the insult to his own dignity. Retribution was considered. Perhaps he should stop Dodi's cheques and refuse to pay the credit card account. Instead he uncharacteristically, and temporarily, restrained his spleen.

Fuelling his anger was fear: fear of embarrassment, fear of Rowland, fear of the unknown. Better protection was his answer. The videos showing President Reagan surrounded like an envelope were his model. Jonathan Heywood, his SAS-trained bodyguard, might be able to disappear into the desert or jungle, but he looked irritatingly stupid inside office blocks. No doubt he could read a map in Iraq, but he got lost driving around London. Always he was talking about 'surveillance for a potential assassin', when what Fayed wanted was more protection from the *Observer*; and the people he was hiring, according to the graphology reports submitted by Guildford expert Erik Rees, were the wrong types. Heywood was to be fired. 'He's a homosexual,' Fayed amazingly told his body-guards on the morning that Heywood disappeared from his flat in 55 Park Lane. 'It's true,' he swore, feigning sincerity in a bid to support his utterly dishonest accusation. 'A man was found sleeping in his bedroom.' The man, innocently staying overnight in London, was a fellow ex-SAS officer and a friend who had been seen by a housemaid. He had spent the night in a sleeping bag on the floor.

Before 1985, dismissing employees had not preoccupied Fayed. On the rare occasion that a secretary or clerk was dismissed, there were few repercussions. But, with his huge payroll and with his conduct exposed to judgement, Fayed's humiliation of his employees had become a way of life. For someone whose image relied upon inventions, it was painless to invent accusations against those whose removal he deemed necessary. Intimidation, he calculated, would not only forestall unpleasant, retaliatory counter-accusations but would enhance his own control over the remaining employees. Cravenly, the weak would not dare to dispute his outlandish fabrications.

Fayed, perpetually embittered by the attacks on himself, was mastering the art of denigrating others. His invention about Jonathan Heywood's homosexuality served its purpose.

'You tell everyone Heywood was queer,' Fayed ordered Mike Waller, recruited as Heywood's replacement. The mild-mannered former Special Branch officer, responsible for Margaret Thatcher's protection in Downing Street, had been headhunted by Sir David McNee, the former commissioner at Scotland Yard. Attracting the prime minister's chief bodyguard as his own head of security, Fayed believed, was a major coup.

'But there's no corroboration,' replied the former police officer. Heywood's bed linen had been checked and Waller had searched through his predecessor's personal belongings. 'There's no evidence that he's queer,' insisted Waller justifiably.

'You're fuggin' stupid,' snapped Fayed. 'I'm telling you and you can't see.'

Waller could never quite understand his new employer's requirements. 'You should be like Adolf Hitler,' Fayed had ordered Waller on his appointment. 'Ruthless.' Expecting Waller to be ruthless was akin to expecting Hitler to become a rabbi. 'I want the men armed,' ordered Fayed, ignoring the illegality. Unwilling to argue that bodyguards were deterrents and bullet-catchers, but not gunmen, Waller half satisfied Fayed's demand for armed protection around London. A bodyguard was dispatched to John Slough in Hereford, the SAS's base town, to purchase six Czech model 85 9mm handguns with extended magazines and some 38 Specials. To legalize their possession, Waller created and registered with the Metropolitan Police the 'Park Lane Gun Club'. The revolvers were stored in a locker in Park Lane. Shooting practice for the bodyguards was organized at a range in Billericay and at another under the arches at Waterloo station. On Waller's strict orders, the guns were not to be carried on duty. But, unknown to Waller, Bob Curry, in return for extra cash, did pack a handgun into a pouch. His self-justification was simple: 'Lose your client, lose your job.'

The guns enhanced Fayed's sense that he was safe from Rowland's tightening noose. Reports in January 1987 suggested that Roger Allen and other DTI officials were sifting evidence verifying Kleinworts' incompetence. 'Why they pick on me?' hissed Fayed to Royston Webb. 'I do no different to everyone else. Everyone deals this way. They after me because I'm Egyptian.'

To forestall an investigation, Fayed launched an attack against Rowland. In a letter to the DTI on 2 February 1987, he listed the DTI's own findings on Rowland's dishonesty and corruption after its investigation of Lonrho. The DTI's curt reply was to summon Michael Hawkes for further questioning. Anxiety fizzed among Fayed's advisers. Mohamed and Ali, Royston Webb and Edward Walker-Arnott gathered in Park Lane to stiffen Hawkes's resolve. The banker's submissiveness was not reassuring. The same feebleness which had unquestioningly repeated the Fayeds' claims two years earlier could not be transformed into an advocate of aggressive defence. 'You must tell the DTI officials', Hawkes was instructed, 'that it was a cash bid. Where their money came from and any questions about the Fayeds' childhood and background is therefore irrelevant and unjustified.' Hawkes did not inspire confidence. 'A weak, vacillating nonentity,' concluded Royston Webb.

Hawkes's embarrassed report about his meeting with Sir Brian Hayes, the DTI's permanent secretary, justified Fayed's pessimissm. 'I want to know precisely the source of the Fayeds' wealth,' Hayes had demanded. From the banker's dithering reply, Hayes had extracted damaging admissions of ignorance. Besides Fayed's assurances, Hawkes had admitted, he relied upon a solitary telex from a Swiss bank. 'Hawkes has done us no good at all,' Webb reported. 'He's put up a bad performance.'

Cursing the banker's ineptitude and swearing revenge against all his enemies, Fayed turned to Gordon Reece for help. His lobbyist's close relationship with Margaret Thatcher, the Egyptian hoped, could forestall any reference to the Monopolies

Commission which threatened his ownership of House of
Fraser. Reece failed to respond. He turned to Alistair Mc-
Alpine, the Conservative Party treasurer.

To strengthen his link with the Conservatives, Fayed had
responded positively when approached in 1985 for donations
to the Winter and Blue balls and to requests from constituency
chairmen. His initial donations had been small but, as his
problems increased during 1987, he became more generous.
He had however never contributed large sums of money to
Alistair McAlpine, the contractor rebuilding the Dorchester,
with whom he had argued. He would claim to have transferred
£250,000 to McAlpine, but could never produce a receipt or a
bank document to prove the massive payment. Nevertheless,
Fayed calculated that for his money he should receive something in return. But McAlpine, like Reece, failed to satisfy his
request to intercede with Thatcher. His only ally was Ian Greer.

Alarm now permeated Fayed's telephone calls to Greer.
'More MPs,' he shouted. 'I need more MPs. More processions.
Go to the minister.' Greer was anxious to oblige. Without
making any overtures, Fayed had won the support of Dale
Campbell-Savours, an impeccably honest Labour MP, appalled
by Rowland's manipulation of the liberal *Observer*. Campbell-
Savours's flurry of questions and early-day motions condemning Rowland had been helped by Webb's provision of written
drafts, but Fayed could not rely upon a man he had never met
and whom he was not 'thanking' financially. He wanted politicians committed to himself not guided by mere principles. In
particular, he wanted to replace Peter Hordern, House of
Fraser's lacklustre parliamentary consultant, who refused to
adopt du Cann's aggression.

'I'll ask Tim Smith,' replied Greer. Smith, however,
declined. 'We can use Tim Smith in other ways,' wrote Greer,
adding that Andrew Bowden, the fifty-six-year-old Conservative MP for Brighton Kemptown, seemed keen. 'At last we
have a campaigner,' Greer wrote. 'I have known Andrew for

twenty years and can depend on him. He is without doubt the right person.'

After his introduction to Bowden on 18 February 1987, Fayed asked, 'How much you want?'

'£50,000 a year,' replied Bowden. Fayed was not averse to the deal, especially after the politician suggested that Michael Land, a friend formerly employed by Lonrho, could provide embarrassing information about Rowland. That was exactly the attitude Fayed appreciated. Land would be paid £1,500 in cash by Webb, to be collected in brown envelopes from Park Lane. But formalizing an arrangement with Bowden, it was agreed, was best delayed until after the general election in June.

Since the government's term of office was likely to end in four months, a year earlier than necessary, Fayed expected the momentum to fizzle out. The opposite occurred. The civil servants, especially Sir Brian Hayes, Roger Allen and Sarah Brown, who had met Hawkes and Rowland, hastened the issue towards a decision. Their department had recently been involved in so many business scandals that further delay was unpalatable. An early decision, Hayes told Channon, was necessary. A meeting was convened under Channon's chairmanship on 27 February 1987, attended by Michael Howard, the junior minister responsible for corporate affairs, and the civil servants. The politicians were told that according to new evidence Fayed and his representatives had lied about his wealth. Agreeing the government's policy, however, was not straightforward. Channon directed Allen to submit a memorandum listing the options.

Roger Allen's task was made easier by Tebbit's statement in 1985 approving Fayed's bid. 'In considering whether to make a reference [to the Monopolies Commission],' Tebbit had stated, 'I took into account the statements made and assurances given by the Al Fayed family about the offer ... [and] the support given to those statements and assurances by Kleinwort Benson.' The source of Fayed's wealth, the politician had admitted, was material. Since a belated investigation by the Monopolies Commission was ruled out, the only options, Allen advised Channon on 4 March, were either to take no action or to appoint two DTI inspectors. Whether the inspectors would discover the truth about the Fayeds' finances was questionable. Channon and Howard decided to ask the brothers for more information.

Once again Hawkes was summoned by Hayes. 'It appears', said Hayes, referring to the loans organized by Samuel Montagu after the takeover, 'that the secretary of state was misled. Possibly he was given false information about the Fayeds' wealth. I need clear evidence that it was their own cash.' The banker was asked to submit a new statement setting out the Fayeds' provable wealth.

On his return to Park Lane, Michael Hawkes's account of the meeting incited Fayed to frenzied action. To embarrass Rowland, he had commissioned Arthur Young to investigate his persecutor's personal finances. Unfortunately, the auditors reported, they were shrouded in impenetrable foreign trusts. But Lonrho's accounts were easier to criticize and, with Basham's help, Fayed financed an embarrassing demonstration. Orchestrated by Royston Webb and Richard New, actors and actresses had been scattered among the thousands of eager shareholders at Lonrho's annual general meeting and their questions, publicly revealing flaws in the company's massaged accounts, had undermined du Cann's normal smooth performance. The tactic had succeeded, but only momentarily. Although Basham had persuaded journalists to report the discrepancies, they were quickly forgotten.

Everything, Fayed realized, depended upon his MPs lobbying Channon. On 2 March, he had invited Tim Smith to a meeting with Webb. Excitedly, Fayed recited his services to Britain. 'Margaret Thatcher', he expostulated, 'invited me to Downing Street and thanked me for influencing the sultan to leave £10 billion in Britain.' No one mentioned that his figure had doubled from the original £5 billion. 'There were smiles of gratitude to Mohamed Al Fayed from Margaret Thatcher.' Smith and Webb nodded. 'Charles Powell thanked me several times.' More silent nods as Fayed continued, 'Field Marshal Bramall was sent by the prime minister to Mohamed Al Fayed to persuade the sultan to place a £500 million defence order. Heseltine personally visited Mohamed Al Fayed to thank him for his services.' Exhausted by his speech, Fayed looked at the politician: 'Britain's leaders owe me.' Smith understood what was wanted: another question in the Commons. By then, Webb had left and, as the politician rose, Fayed walked to his cupboard and withdrew a white envelope. 'For you,' he said, handing over £2,000. It seemed to him, though not to Smith, that he had set a rate for a parliamentary question.

In a neighbouring room, Ali was compiling with Hawkes, MacArthur and other advisers a revised statement of the Fayeds' wealth. As Mohamed discovered when he joined his brother and Webb, the bankers had become somewhat more demanding. Their new statement suggested that the Fayeds' assets were valued at $760 million, considerably less than the original $1.150 billion. In his accompanying letter to Hayes, Hawkes insisted that the discrepancy was not material and that no third party had been involved in the takeover. Both Fayeds and Webb were optimistic that their submission would neutralize the antagonism. But, thanks to Rowland's pressure on the civil servants, they were disappointed. 'Their latest memorandum', commented Roger Allen, 'conspicuously fails to substantiate the claims of 1985 . . . [and] makes it harder to give the Fayeds the benefit of the doubt.' With the DTI now roused by 'intensified' doubts, Allen continued, the 'onus [was] firmly on them to substantiate their claims'. Urging that Channon 'cannot let the matter rest', he recommended that inspectors be appointed.

On 30 March 1987 Channon chaired another meeting. Although Michael Howard was not present, he had read all the documents and like any astute politician readily accepted the recommendations on an issue of alleged dishonesty. Yet

Channon delayed his decision. With an election looming, it was advisable to consult his colleagues before launching an investigation into a Conservative Party supporter.

For the same reason, Fayed also discounted an imminent announcement. But, he pondered, it would not be damaging to proclaim his prominence in Britain by celebrating his recent successes in Paris. Despite the strong objections of the 16th Arrondissement in Paris at a meeting on 22 September 1986 to the transfer of the Windsor villa to an unknown, private person, Chirac had agreed with Alain Juppé, his representative on the council and the politician responsible for the district's financial affairs, to approve Fayed's wish. Just eight days later, without any explanation, which 'baffled' the locality, Fayed was granted a twenty-five-year lease on the villa for 1 million francs per annum, on condition that he spent 30 million francs renovating the house.

Over the previous months he had indulged his fascination for the Windsors, planning the villa's restoration and boasting his motives. 'Britain is my second home,' he told one newspaper. 'I feel I have a duty to keep together a collection that otherwise would have been dispersed for ever.' The queen, he announced solemnly, would be offered the table on which her uncle had signed his abdication in 1936. Although an anonymous courtier disparaged the idea that the queen might accept – she needed the table 'like she needs a hole in the head' – Fayed had lured Prince Charles to the house to inspect the contents. 'I just wanted to see if he had got any of our things,' admitted Charles, who accepted as a memento a small needlepoint cushion hand-stitched by the duke. The queen, however, would reject all offers of mementoes. 'No gratitude,' cursed Fayed, not understanding that the royal family wanted to forget the disaster.

The villa, as Fayed had suspected, was nevertheless a magnet for the celebrities he eagerly sought. Important guests at the Ritz were encouraged to request a visit to the villa. Ralph Lauren was among many who were driven to the Bois de Boulogne, escorted on a private tour and allowed to select one of the duke's jackets in the cupboard to wear in the house. Restoring the villa to its former glory, Fayed reasoned, would also produce commercial and political advantages. On the evening of 1 April, he telephoned Greer. He was in the midst of bidding against fierce American and Japanese competition at Sotheby's two-day auction in Geneva for the Windsors' possessions. Fayed discussed with Greer whether he might use his new acquisitions to enhance his position in Britain. Eager to please, the following morning Greer sent written invitations to Neil Hamilton, Tim Smith, Michael Grylls, Andrew Bowden and Peter Hordern to spend the weekend of 25 April with their wives at the Ritz and visit the villa. Stressing the privacy of the invitation, Greer concluded, 'I would therefore be grateful for it being kept as such.' By the end of that day, Fayed had completed a £3 million buying spree for the Windsors' swords, seals, sporrans, buttons, buckles and silver. He had paid $352,000 for a photograph of the duke as a young man in naval uniform in a silver-mounted alabaster frame, and $220,000 for a photograph of the couple bathing in the South of France. Fayed failed however to buy the duchess's jewellery, which was sold for £31 million, £25 million more than the price Blum had quoted. His failure to buy the jewellery, he would later explain, was his own decision after deciding that the pieces were 'modern, gaudy and unimportant'.

Six days later, on 8 April 1987, at the end of a Cabinet meeting, Channon walked up to Margaret Thatcher. Standing near the entrance to the Cabinet Room, the prime minister was speaking to Charles Powell. 'I've decided, prime minister,' said Channon, 'to order an inquiry into the Fayeds and House of Fraser.' Even in normal times, a DTI inquiry was of little interest to a prime minister. With an election looming, even one which the Conservatives were certain to win, the Fayeds were irrelevant to her. She merely assented. Three days later, Channon formally announced that two DTI inspectors were to be appointed under section 432 of the Companies Act 1985 to establish whether the affairs of House of Fraser had been conducted fraudulently or unlawfully, and whether the directors were guilty of fraud, illegality or misconduct.

Overnight, Fayed's world turned upside down. Despite House of Fraser's official reaction – 'we welcome it as an opportunity to clear this matter up once and for all' – the investigation promised Fayed a perpetual nightmare. Emotionally and intellectually he was ill-prepared to sustain the pressure. Publically he complained that the decision 'cast a shadow on my dignity and my honour. I can live without riches. I cannot live without a good name. A dog barked and the ministers listened.' But in private he collapsed. In his fevered imagination, he convinced himself that the threat that the *Observer* would publish more embarrassing stories about the Thatchers and their alleged corruption during the election campaign had dictated the decision. Summoning Mike Waller, he ordered his security chief personally to deliver a letter to Margaret Thatcher.

'I can't do that,' replied Waller.

'She's your old boss,' snapped Fayed. 'You do.'

Bewildered, Waller tried to explain that even he could not just walk into Downing Street and hand the prime minister a letter.

'Go,' ordered Fayed, displeased. Not only Waller, but Tim Smith and all the other MPs had failed, he believed. Gordon Reece and Alistair McAlpine, despite his payments and gifts, had vanished. Friendless and alone, he had no choice but to rely upon Greer, who remained loyal and represented his only leverage within the government machine.

Anxiously, he invited Greer and the politicians to Park Lane. There, first Smith, then Hamilton, encountered a disappointed man. The old mantra – 'my dignity, my integrity, my honour, my family' – interlaced with references to his services to the sultan, Britain and Mrs Thatcher, preceded a desperate entreaty to each man. Smith nodded vigorously, promising his help. At once grateful and angry, Fayed stretched his hand into his briefcase. Considering the stakes – retaining House of Fraser and protecting his reputation – a few thousand pounds was a minimum investment. The brick of fifties was handed over. On his arrival, Neil Hamilton appeared similarly keen to support Fayed against Rowland. The politician sympathized with Fayed's lament about his victimization by Rowland and unreasonable DTI officials. To encourage Hamilton to plead his case, Fayed proferred another wodge of fifties. Instinctively, the politician refused. Fayed's vehement insistence that it was merely a gift, a display of gratitude, appeared to have defeated the politician's insincere resistance. 'Go, talk to Channon,' urged the Egyptian. 'Tell him it's no good.' Lobbying Channon to reverse a public announcement, Hamilton knew, was pointless. Yet, having accepted money from Fayed and Greer, there was an obligation to perform. On 13 May, Hamilton, Smith, Grylls and Peter Hordern met the secretary of state and departed empty-handed.

Five days later, Greer asked Ali Fayed for contributions to his personal election campaign chest for Conservative candidates. In a written reminder to Ali ten days later, Greer commented, 'I spoke to you last week and you said that you would kindly speak to Mohamed about the possibility of helping one or two Conservative Party candidates during the election campaign. I think a cheque for £6,000 would be sufficient. If you are able to help perhaps you would be kind enough to make a cheque out to Ian Greer Associates. I will let you have a note after the election is over of who was assisted.' Later, Greer requested and was sent a further £12,000 for distribution to Conservatives. To the Fayeds, the money was irrelevant. The politicians had failed. Despite his proven dishonesty, Rowland wielded extraordinary influence in Whitehall and Westminster. Conventional resistance had proven ineffectual. Aggressive self-defence was their next choice.

To Mohamed Fayed's astonishment, Rowland had recruited Kenneth Etheridge, a former Scotland Yard detective chief superintendent as his personal investigator. Fayed's surprise was understandable. Etheridge had been hired by Rowland while he was conducting the official investigation into the tycoon's alleged frauds exposed by the DTI inquiry into Lonrho. Despite the evidence, Rowland had not been prosecuted – to avoid, it was said, publicizing his bribes to African heads of state. After retiring from Scotland Yard, Etheridge was using his contacts among Britain's police force to spearhead Rowland's investigation of Fayed. Even for Fayed, accustomed to bribery and sharp practices, the recruitment of former senior police officers to undertake dubious activities was a bewildering escalation of the war. First there had been the discovery of Rowland's bugging operation and now Rowland had apparently commandeered the secret resources of the national police force. Convinced that he was the victim of intrigue, espionage and unimagined skulduggery, he consulted Sir David McNee, the former commissioner at Scotland Yard. McNee recommended John Macnamara, also a detective chief superintendent in Scotland Yard, who had just completed twenty-eight years' unblemished service in the Fraud Squad. Appointed head of security for House of Fraser, Macnamara, a small, weasel-like, efficient Scotsman, accepted that he was to be Fayed's weapon against Etheridge, a contemporary whom he loathed. He was the protector of a man under siege.

Security was, once again, intensified. Under Macnamara's supervision, a panoply of new checks was marshalled to protect House of Fraser and Fayed. Normal references for prospective employees were deemed to be insufficient. There would be checks in the secret computer registers controlled by the police and all the credit agencies. Telephone taps were to be increased. Staff were to be secretly monitored even outside the buildings. Macnamara was the King of Digging Dirt. Life at Harrods was being revolutionized.

8

Storekeeper

'HE'S TIPPING EVERYTHING upside down,' complained David Hedges, a dedicated Harrods employee since 1957. Hedges' anger was directed at Brian Walsh, the Australian who was completing his first year as manager of House of Fraser. With skill and passion, Hedges had risen through the ranks to become the manager of Harrods' tie department, which attracted worldwide admiration and loyal customers. 'I love ties,' said Hedges, a traditionalist 'prepared to die for Harrods'. But after two years of the Fayeds' ownership he had become bitter: 'Under Walsh everything black is becoming white.'

Sheepishly, Alex Craddock, who had nominated Walsh, conceded that his choice had been a mistake. 'He's destroying Harrods' culture,' he complained helplessly to Fayed. 'I can't believe he's doing this.' Fayed was indifferent. Intent on junking sentimentality, he shared the Australian's impatience with civilized relationships. Instilling fear, both agreed, was a certain method to achieve their goals.

Denigrating the traditionalists as 'useless', Walsh had introduced himself dramatically at a series of crowded meetings. With disdain he mentioned the closure of Harrods' kennels, where white-coated attendants cared for customers' pets; he castigated as 'useless' the lending library for the wealthy; and he spoke scathingly about the huge banking hall where society gals and their parents met but never spent any money. As the gulf between himself and the store's loyal employees widened, he humiliated his audience by requiring each to 'stand up and tell us about your job'. During their replies, Walsh judged which of 'the old dross' were to be dismissed. Harrods employees, he scoffed, were soft prima donnas mouthing quaint jargon about 'shopfitters' rather than 'visual merchandising directors'. House of Fraser, he believed, reeked of history and of dirt. Rubbish was strewn everywhere.

Creating a luxury store brimming with excellence and offering enjoyment would, Walsh understood, irritate many, but Fayed had supported his philosophy that shopping was no longer a chore but an entertaining pastime. 'I want a show,' Fayed repeated, adopting Walsh's thinking. 'I want the staff to jump and greet our customers. Don't just say Sir or Madam any more. Repeat the name on the credit card.' His 'fantastic business' would earn more millions if merchandise, branded with one of the world's most famous names, was sold worldwide. That, Fayed acknowledged, required a revolution. Walsh and his team of Australians were eager to sow convulsion.

Scrutinizing the profitability of the group, Walsh froze all capital expenditure, sold the funerals business and ordered the sale of over twenty House of Fraser stores. As an innovation in Britain, every cash till was linked to a central computer to produce instant information about sales; drastic changes were introduced in ticketing, layouts and fixtures; and opening hours were extended. Harrods' younger managers were invigorated by Walsh's honest, unfussy rampage through the cosy club, his termination of the jobs-for-life culture. But, for the traditionalist majority, Walsh's most radical innovation, the centralization of all buyers in an office distant from the shop floor, transformed the innovator into an exterminator.

Traditionally, Harrods buyers also sold their merchandise to customers in the shop. For David Hedges and his fellow buyers the virtue was to understand their customers' changing requirements. Under Walsh's revolution, Hedges was forced to sit in an isolated office, separated from the shop floor. Demoralized by the feeling that three decades of personal service were deemed worthless, thirty-four buyers resigned three months after the reorganization. Over two hundred more, including Hedges, followed in the next two years. Rather than cherishing its staff as a devoted elite, the envy of Britain's retail trade, the store became a cauldron of mutiny against foreigners – Australian and Egyptian – who ignored the Harrods way. Cast in the newspapers as a 'Bully Boss', the mercenary provoked an unprecedented strike. Fayed was contemptuous. His employees were donkeys expected to obey his orders unquestioningly. Complaints about Fayed drew the same riposte: 'It's my shop.'

By autumn 1987, Brian Walsh had forgotten that it was Mohamed's shop. He had not read the sign on his employer's desk: 'Remember the golden rule. "He who has the gold makes the rules".' After nearly two years, Fayed was no longer dazzled by Walsh, and the feeling was reciprocated. Walsh's respect for Fayed had been diminished by the difficulty his employer had in understanding a balance sheet and by his uncontrolled rages when he burst into board meetings interrupting sober discussions. 'We're in the stone age,' Fayed frequently screamed with bulging eyes. 'We don't know what's going on.' The directors stared, intimidated and amazed. Someone had got at Mohamed, put a flea in his ear. They silently agreed that it was pointless and possibly dangerous to say anything. After a five-minute rant, Mohamed Fayed would depart and Ali would look up. Bland faces stared back as if nothing had happened. Only Walsh dared utter a long, sarcastic: 'Oh boy.' But now that licence had expired.

In Fayed's opinion, he had reached the end of a steep learning curve and now understood retailing. Unknown to those who queried how a Middle Eastern commission agent could know anything about retailing in Knightsbridge, he was learning from a small army of hired advisers and consultants, especially Americans. The most trusted was Stanley Marcus, mastermind of Nieman Marcus, one of America's premier stores. After two years of listening, Fayed assumed that he had the expertise to perform everyone's job. He and Walsh had agreed that Harrods required new air conditioning, escalators and restaurants, but disagreed about the distinction between luxury, opulence and vulgarity. While Fayed, like most Arabs, loved glitter and gold, Walsh prefered plain surfaces and spaces. Their differences erupted as they stood together in the Food Hall. Looking at bunches of bananas hanging on Fayed's orders from a chandelier, Walsh scoffed to his employer, 'Are you crazy?' Resenting the public chastisement, Fayed's fury was compounded by Walsh's desire for the limelight. In interviews, Walsh mentioned only himself as 'the director' and, aggravatingly, Fayed was paying the bills for Walsh to entertain in London's best clubs and restaurants. In a collision of egos, only Fayed could win.

The final showdown broke out in the Man's Shop. With Walsh's approval, the department had been redesigned, and thirty-six leather armchairs, specially manufactured in ebonized wood, had been carefully positioned. 'What are these doing here?' growled Fayed, spotting the armchairs one hour after their arrival. 'And what are people doing fuggin' sitting down?' His voice rose. 'People should be fuggin rushing round, fuggin' spending money, not sitting on their fuggin' wallets.'

'It's for their wives,' explained Dwane McCulloch, the Australian designer hired by Walsh. 'To sit while their husbands are buying.'

'Bah,' spat Fayed. 'Out. I want them out.' With Walsh and McCulloch in tow, Fayed rushed into the street to look at the window displays. 'They're fuggin' empty,' he screamed. 'I want fuggin' more.'

'But less is more,' said Walsh. 'It's sophisticated.'

Fayed turned and stared. 'Sophisticated' was foreign to his vocabulary. 'Fuggin' rubbish,' stormed a man greedy for control. No Australian was going to teach him about selling any more. He was unimpressed and unnerved by talk of 'distinction'. His own ideas, generated by personal taste rather than market science, would guide the store's destiny. Unceremoniously, on 12 October 1987, Walsh was fired; McCulloch also departed. The dismissal was Fayed's most popular decision since the takeover. To calm any unrest, he distributed white envelopes containing £2,000 in cash. The pattern was established. Fayed never thanked those whom he dismissed for their efforts, but bribed those who remained to stay loyal. After Walsh's departure, Fayed moved permanently into Harrods as the hands-on chairman.

*

ENSCONCED IN HIS new suite of offices on the fifth floor, managing by convulsion, Fayed was immune to any antagonism caused by his edicts. He was protected by an electronically operated door at the front entrance to the suite, with four bodyguards waiting in a room ten yards from his corner office, and another bodyguard seated directly outside, guarding a second electronically locked door. Despite the tranquil appearance of his small, decorative office – tasteful flower arrangements offsetting the Louis Quatorze cabinets, round tables and sofas – the room represented the aspirations of a man anxious to establish his status. The bookshelves were lined with leather-bound volumes – 'I've read all of them,' he told visitors; an ornate silver Georgian inkstand was described as 'a gift from my father'; and twin gold Oscars for *Chariots of Fire* were said to be 'won by me', although both were replicas, the originals belonging to David Puttnam. On the walls were photographs of himself with the queen at Windsor and with Ronald Reagan. In his tidy zone of fantasy, there was no noticeable photograph of his parents.

Despite his offer to visitors of exquisite tea specially imported from Paris and the refined appearance of the attractive young women he personally chose to attend his needs, the Lion King was the isolated conductor of a sharply compartmentalized world singlemindedly dedicated to his pursuit of absolute control and financial success. Senior executives had learnt that at Mohamed's medieval court their survival required affirmations of utter loyalty, whispers of praise and a drip of salacious gossip to sow doubts about rivals. To assuage his own insecurity, Fayed had created a jungle. Contemptuously categorizing those who resisted his desires as disloyal, the entrepreneur, glorying in his increasing celebrity, behaved like an autocrat. To defy his enemies and reassure himself that despite the appointment of DTI inspectors his dignity and authority were unquestioned, Fayed's tours around the store increasingly became aggressive assertions of his passion for excellent merchandise, well-groomed staff, impeccable service and draconian security.

He would be preceded by two bodyguards pushing customers to the side, with two more following, each equipped with a pencil, notebook, portable telephone, dictaphone and occasionally a revolver, to record the commissar's diktat. 'Fire that man,' he told a bodyguard one day, pointing at a black employee in the Food Hall. 'He's badly dressed and I saw him picking his nose.' The salesman had clearly been scratching his face. Fat people, Fayed appeared to believe, were lazy, and blacks offended his idea of aesthetics. Fat black women rated near the top of his hate list. 'It's no good', he grumbled, having approved a £167 million improvement programme, 'to spend all that money on the building and have ugly people serving.' The bodyguard noted the order.

Suspecting that a customer was not being served properly, Fayed interrupted the tour with a screaming outburst. Eager to improve the store, his proposals were dictated by emotions rather than pure commerce. 'Why are the lights switched off outside the store at night?' he asked.

'To save money,' replied a manager.

'I want them on. Looks good.'

'It'll cost a fortune.'

'It's my money,' snapped Fayed. There was no riposte. Fayed's desire for perfection became his considered strategy.

As he moved on, pushing a fifty at a shop assistant who particularly pleased him, he encountered Bill Christie, the director of menswear. Christie had announced he was taking a new job at Aquascutum. 'If you go,' warned Fayed, wagging his finger, 'we'll close the Aquascutum concession in Harrods.' Undeterred, Christie resigned. Aquascutum would open its own store one hundred yards away.

Suddenly a customer's hand stretched out to greet the famous shopkeeper. Fayed proffered his hand, smiled, uttered an effusive greeting and hurried on. The forced smile evaporated as he extended his arm backwards. Micro-seconds later, a purple perfumed Roger & Gallet wipe was thrust into his outstretched hand by a bodyguard. Rubbing it vigorously over his palms to eradicate the foreign germs, he sped forward, giving the used tissue back to his escort.

'Lollipop,' he ordered, seeing a child. Instantly, the burly bodyguard produced the sweet, usually accepted in gratitude. On this occasion, Uncle Mohamed's gesture provoked a terrifying 'No thank you!' from a condescending upper-class voice as the mother snatched her four-year-old towards her in horror. 'I'm trying to teach him not to accept anything from strangers.'

'Bastards,' squirmed Fayed. A whole packet of Roger & Gallet wipes could not expunge the humiliation. Fayed did not see his bodyguard's smile. The previous day, the guard had been 'publicly bollocked' in the store for not carrying enough lollipops. 'No more lollipops,' ordered Fayed as they entered his executive offices. He hated the public. If only Harrods could survive without shoppers. Occasionally, he wished it could also survive without employees.

None of those customers, smelling seduction in the perfume department, wealth in the jewellery section and delicacies in the Food Hall, could have guessed that five floors above, in his guarded bunker, Fayed was fretting that within that vast emporium his employees were stealing and engaging in corrupt relationships to defraud his company.

Fayed's fear was 'shrinkage', the traditional peril of shoplifting and thefts by staff. Most stores tolerated 2 per cent losses, but in House of Fraser, with turnover of over £400 million, that was too much for Fayed. 'It's my money,' he shot back angrily whenever an executive sought to tolerate the losses. 'I don't want theft.' Too many commercial empires, he knew, had collapsed because their owners neglected small details. Monitoring his employees as closely as his customers, Fayed became convinced that all his staff were dishonest.

One spot-check had revealed that dozens of former employees were still receiving salaries because their names had not been removed from the register; a bugged conversation exposed a maintenance engineer plotting to receive bribes in return for a contract with a supplier; while another inspection disclosed that the staff canteen was patronized, especially for breakfast, by many local residents grateful to eat a good, cheap meal. But Fayed's greatest preoccupation was his staff's loyalty. Paranoid about treachery, especially inspired by Rowland, he no longer cared to rely entirely on telephone taps. After a director of the children's wear and toy departments had been recorded on her telephone complaining that she was being followed home every night, Fayed assumed that the most dangerous plotters would be wary of speaking openly, while those followed out of the store to their homes by his detectives might be too canny to betray their dishonesty. His solution was to insert spies into the store.

His first contingent were two sisters, Rita and Georgette Hadjiouannou, the daughters of John Hadjiouannou, his friend from Cairo employed by Genavco. The intelligent young women, posing as normal shop assistants, were deployed by Fayed to work in departments which had aroused his misgivings. Unknown to the staff, the Hadjiouannous listened, watched and reported on the performance, prejudices and loyalty of their unsuspecting colleagues. Dubbed after their eventual exposure 'the Greek Gestapo', the Hadjiouannous possessed that rare privilege in Harrods of unquestioned access to Fayed himself, a right denied to the representatives of his employees.

*

TRADE UNION ACTIVITIES in Harrods scarcely existed. Rigidly structured in 'ranks' rather than grades, employees were expected to heed Harrods' traditions rather than seek the protection of employment laws. Fayed's initial reaction to that relic was a complete lack of interest. Since buying Harrods, he had regarded labour relations and the minutiae of Britain's industrial laws as irritating nuisances which did not warrant his attention. Employees would need to understand that they survived from day to day at his will and would disappear if his displeasure was aroused. Rather than contemplating any improvement in industrial relations, he preferred to abolish them completely. 'Fix their telephones,' he had ordered Graeme Arno. The telephones of USDAW, the shop workers' trade union, were bugged. Eavesdropping on the trade union officers' telephone discussions with their members and lawyers would give him an unusual advantage, especially after he had decided that employees' contracts should be short – three months if possible – and that those seeking compensation for unfair dismissal should suffer torment to deter them from pursuing their claims. Firing employees without agreed compensation and forcing them to fight in tribunals for their legal entitlement caused a stir throughout the store. If, in isolated cases, those tactics failed to deter the persistent few, he could always pay the compensation just prior to the tribunal's hearing. His own parroted mantra – 'my dignity, my integrity, my honour, my family' – was inapplicable to discarded employees.

Fayed's senior personnel directors, Jeremy Nordberg at Harrods and Stan Frith at House of Fraser, knew the store-owner as a man of extremes: hugely generous and remarkably charming, he could tilt into a rage of vindictiveness if the chemistry of the relationship had, in his opinion, soured; at once he would declare that the employee's 'time is up'.

'I can't dismiss that man,' complained Jeremy Nordberg to Fayed. 'He's done over twenty years of good service and his colour is not a reason for dismissal.' Firing employees on grounds of their appearance or manner of speaking offended the personnel department's sense of decency. The consequences of dismissal for those aged over fifty were serious. Not only would dismissed employees have difficulty finding new jobs, but their pension was reduced for the remainder of their lives. But Nordberg and his subordinates had discovered that their Arab employer spoke scathingly about all minorities. In Fayed's lexicon, 'lazy bastards' included Indians, Arabs and blacks. Jews were simply damned as clever or greedy. To avoid employing blacks, Harrods required applicants to submit photographs. If the black applicants' qualifications were too good to ignore, a personnel executive briefed interviewers to ask the job-seeker, 'Can you speak Japanese? It's a requirement for this post.' With great efficiency, the number of blacks employed by Harrods was limited to half the number in other London stores. As a token gesture, two blacks had been promoted, one as the buyer in his favoured toy department, allowing Fayed to dismiss allegations of racism as unfounded.

'Out! I want him out,' shouted Fayed, his smiles giving way to rage. 'He was badly dressed.' Hating trade unions and scathing about employees' statutory rights, he regarded black trade unionists as devils.

'OK, Mohamed, if you insist,' said Nordberg. 'But don't complain when in three months' time you are forced to appear as a witness in the industrial tribunal. They'll offer you a cold cup of tea and give you hell.' Fayed glared at him. With all his millions, thought Nordberg, it was easy for Mohamed to be well dressed.

But Fayed's rage was spiralling: 'Fire him!' Appearing at an industrial tribunal aroused no fear in him: he would make sure it never happened. Instead, he opted for attrition. The notion of the brotherhood of man never clouded his thoughts. Nordberg and Frith, talented and conscientious personnel directors, could not defy him. Needing to survive, they developed an unemotional compliance with Fayed's forceful methods. Bonds of loyalty towards those ordered to be dismissed simply evaporated.

Acts of kindness did something to mitigate the outrage provoked by Fayed's stunts. Even cowards have a sense of duty and, like many tyrants suffering guilty consciences, the Egyptian was occasionally overwhelmed by the sight of the lame and afflicted, especially children. After further treatment of Karim's meningitis at Great Ormond Street Hospital, he had contributed £3 million for the purchase of a scanning machine and again insisted upon anonymity. Despite the favourable publicity he could attract by revealing his donations to 160 other charities – for poor children, for medical research and for victims of natural disasters – he had demanded that all his donations be kept secret. Within the store, he was also known to be generous. A tea lady, suffering from terminal cancer, was employed on full pay while she underwent treatment. The fatally sick son of Martin Mower, a bodyguard, received the most expensive treatment thanks to Fayed. Sincere condolences followed the boy's death – yet Mower was still dismissed when Fayed tired of his face. The dispensability of loyal donkeys was Mohamed's recipe for survival. Finding replacements was never a problem.

Harrods' prestige remained a magnet for those invited to enter Fayed's world. 'Here's the man!' exclaimed Fayed, who had been looking for Walsh's successor. Michael Ellis-Jones, the managing director of Harvey Nichols, the neighbouring store in Knightsbridge, was selected in October 1987 to wave his magic wand. A relaxed, urbane, experienced retailer, Ellis-Jones moved into his new offices, ordered a drinks cabinet and pondered his strategy. Walking through the store as the new managing director he was easily beguiled by his new authority. But Ellis-Jones was caught breathless by the new regime. Fayed had become resentful of any employee, even an experienced retailer, who started to believe in his own importance, and he had become rapidly irritated by Ellis-Jones's style: he failed to stay in the building from dawn to midnight six days a week; worse, at the end of the day he invited his senior managers for a drink to discuss business. Three weeks after his appointment, the honeymoon was over. Ellis-Jones did not meet Fayed's requirements. His emphasis on glamour and designer labels offended against the Egyptian's latest eccentricity. The man, Fayed complained loudly, was a time-waster. 'I run the business,' he told the new managing director. He could contradict orders given by senior managers. He would no longer delegate his authority, he had decided. Impulse and instinct dictated the strategy. In Fayed's eyes, Ellis-Jones also suffered a physical impairment: he was short, and the store-owner, a squat man forever craning his pasty face upwards, classed small men as poor performers. 'Mohamed is a man of iron whim,' griped Michael Ellis-Jones as he hurried from the building eight weeks after his arrival. 'You can't run this place like a harem. The men aren't eunuchs and the women aren't serfs.'

Complaints about Fayed's management style provoked him into questioning his victim's integrity. 'Loyalty. That's what I demand,' he scoffed, falsely labelling Ellis-Jones as a drunkard because the door of his drinks cabinet was open. 'Sometimes people let me down,' he explained soon after the dismissal. 'I try to make them better people, better to work with, better for their families. I fire them gently. I do this because the only thing you have in your life is your integrity. You must never lose it.' The opposite was the truth. Fayed was effusive in his hiring and ruthless in firing, delegating lawyers to complete the process. Fighting for his own dignity meant never losing. Ellis-Jones left feeling betrayed and demeaned, especially after hearing reports of Fayed's denigatory inventions, designed to destroy an honourable reputation.

The replacement in January 1988 was Paul Taylor, a modest but successful managing director of Dickens & Jones. Since two managers had recently been fired, Fayed chose to ignore Taylor's handicap – his small stature – but demonstrated his displeasure by reducing the new arrival's formal title to 'deputy' managing director. Taylor was briefed to pursue a fresh strategy. Since profits were falling and costs were rising, Fayed ordained that the store should increase the volume of sales, ignoring the insiders' complaint that Harrods was going downmarket. 'There's a lot of lazy people here too,' added Taylor, 'and they're spending too much.' A culture of nervousness was introduced.

Among the early casualties of that destabilization was Terence Schaeffer, the promotions director hired from Bloomingdales, the Manhattan store. As a chosen son, Schaeffer, a talented marketer, had been blessed by the King with 'the whole treatment': a flat in Park Lane, a big car and unlimited expenses. 'He wants a suite of offices,' an accountant had complained to Fayed. 'The cost is enormous.'

'Let him have it. It's my money,' snapped Fayed.

'His expenses are huge,' moaned Paul Taylor soon after his arrival. 'He flies first class, stays at five-star hotels, eats in the best restaurants and only drinks the most expensive wines.'

Fayed ignored these excesses. 'Putting Harrods on the map costs money,' Schaeffer had said, and his Edwardian Christmas theme had attracted generous applause. 'Schaeffer', it was whispered, 'is close to Mohamed.' But, at the court of Fayed, wars among employees were endemic and conflict had erupted between Taylor and Schaeffer. Fayed heard accusations that both men were having affairs with members of staff. Names were mentioned, and he mulled over his options. Prudishly, he had pronounced that sexual relations among his staff were banned and a cause for dismissal. Several bodyguards had been dismissed for having affairs with his domestics, nannies and secretaries, and those continuing their secret relationships understood the terminal risk. Hypocrisy was natural to a king. Enjoyment of young women employees was an exclusive privilege. He was minded, however, to ignore wild reports of Schaeffer's trysts until another whisper revealed that the American had bought his suits at Anderson & Sheppard, the Savile Row tailor owned by Tiny Rowland. Disloyalty was a capital offence. 'The man's out of control,' screamed Fayed. 'He's costing too much. The promotions are too expensive. He's spending my money. Out!'

The new turbulence within the fifth-floor executive suite was concealed behind the new glamour of the store, as Fayed imaginatively rebuilt, modernized and improved the building, the displays and the merchandise. For years, he had sought to associate with celebrities. Now it was part of his life. Alerted in advance, Fayed, like every diligent shopkeeper, would rush to greet visiting royalty and the famous personalities whose patronage made Harrods special. For those customers, like the family of the Sultan of Brunei, who were known to spend $1 million in one visit, or Princess Diana, a visit was welcomed either before or after normal hours. Accompanied by Fayed's envoy, their shopping would be untroubled by the public. Occasionally, they were greeted by Fayed himself.

The Egyptian's tendency towards autocracy flourished in that secret and fractious world. Dazzled by the glitter of the world-famous store and remote from the real world, he had created a lifestyle that fed his fantasies. Now the consequences of deceit were altering his personality. Hurt by the scrutiny and damnation recounted each week in 'Tiny' Rowland's *Observer*, Fayed relied for survival as much upon aggressive, venomous counterattacks against his employees and critics as upon his stubborn unwillingness to confess his fabrications. Brazen defiance had triumphed in the past and fearlessly he resolved to defeat his latest adversaries by sheer bravado.

9

The Reckoning

THE TELEPHONE CALL IN early September 1987 from Neil
Hamilton came as a relief. The ebullient politician, always
offering a sympathetic ear to Fayed's tirades, wondered whether
he might resuscitate an earlier offer and stay with his wife at the
Ritz in Paris. Fayed was delighted to agree. Freeloaders had
become a part of his life. Visitors to Harrods and the Ritz all
appeared to presume that their host would present a gift or a
free meal. Depending on their usefulness, Fayed, naturally
generous, tried not to disappoint those expectations; and Hamilton was special. Increasingly isolated and nervously awaiting
his first meeting with the DTI inspectors, the store-owner had
every reason to provide hospitality to one of his few life rafts.

Following the disappointing failure of his four MPs –
Grylls, Hamilton, Smith and Hordern – to persuade Paul
Channon on 13 May 1987 to cancel the DTI investigation,
Fayed had urged his sympathizers, in the wake of the Conservatives' June election victory, to make another attempt. To
create the appropriate mood, Hamilton had, in mid-July, tabled
a motion in the Commons condemning 'the continuing barrage
of libellous and vicious propaganda being sent by Tiny Rowland'. Greer had praised Hamilton's attack as 'very strong'.
The next day, 15 July, Hamilton had arrived at Park Lane with
Smith and Hordern to discuss a meeting planned with Lord
Young, the new secretary of state at the DTI. Deluding himself
that a new minister would take the political risk of halting a
formal investigation, Fayed lectured his team, all of whom

were now on his payroll, about the justice of his cause. All concurred. Eight days later, Hamilton had even written to encourage the Egyptian's expectations: 'I have now been elected secretary of the Conservative Finance Committee, all of which gives me a better position from which you [sic] to act on your behalf. Previously as PPS it was less easy.'

Inevitably Lord Young refused to consider the politicians' entreaty, but Fayed, grateful for support, agreed in early September that Hamilton could arrive at the Ritz on the 8th and stay 'for a few days'. In his telephone call to Frank Klein, Fayed added that the politician should be given some money. Klein understood. Giving 'spending money' to his employer's guests was not unusual. Of course, Hamilton could have refused to accept the hospitality but good living at others' expense had, for him and his wife, become a hobby.

Reading the daily reports from the hotel, Fayed saw that the politician was a professional freeloader. Not only did he stay for six nights, at a notional cost of over £2,000, but he and his wife ate every meal, drinking the best wines, in the hotel, accumulating a further bill for £2,121. Frank Klein's call one week later, reporting that Hamilton had telephoned to ask whether he and his wife might stay at the Ritz on the return journey from their holiday in southern France, aroused his anger. 'Tell them the hotel is full,' Fayed instructed Klein. It was the eve of his first meeting with the DTI inspectors. Despite all the payments he had received, Hamilton had failed to prevent the investigation.

Ironically, the inspectors' appointment had inflamed the suspicions of both Rowland and Fayed. 'Everyone hates me,' Rowland moaned to his lawyer. 'They're certain to be in Fayed's pocket. They'll write a whitewash. Or, worse, investigate Fayed's allegations of my frauds.'

For their part, Fayed's advisers were stunned by the appointment of Philip Heslop QC as an inspector, given that the barrister was even then being hired by Rowland to represent Ernest Saunders, the dishonest Guinness executive. Convinced that the appointment proved the government's desire to please Rowland, the advisers protested. Heslop was replaced by Henry Brooke QC, the son of an unpopular Conservative home secretary and regarded as pompous and as blessed by no more than ordinary ability. The accountant appointed as the second inspector, Hugh Aldous, was considered in the City inoffensive and second-rate. If appointed in New York, the inspectors would have been intelligent, educated, ambitious, aggressive and fearsome. But the two London inspectors, Aldous would self-effacingly admit, although not 'the greatest brains on earth', were 'determined to be the most efficient'. Nevertheless, they wielded awesome powers. Acting as detectives, inquisitors, advocates and judges, the inspectors could rely upon unproven hearsay evidence delivered in secret without the swearing of an oath – all inadmissible in a normal court. In a further breach of natural justice, the Fayeds would have no right to know the identity of any witnesses and would not have the right of cross-examination. At the end, the inspectors would be free to pass unfettered judgement on personalities and events regardless of proof. Had Fayed been educated and alert, he might have outsmarted the second-rate professionals. Instead he believed that the tricks learnt, practised and tolerated among Arab wheeler-dealers would allow him to trample all over his investigators in Britain.

The inspectors and the Fayeds' lawyers had first met in June 1987. Edward Walker-Arnott, who had acted for the Fayeds in the original negotiations, and Richard Fleck considered themselves, as senior partners at Herbert Smith, to rank among the elite of London's solicitors. Unusually, they had decided not to retain barristers to argue their client's cause but to use Fleck as the advocate. That decision, approved by Mohamed Fayed and Royston Webb, alleviated an unspoken but pertinent fear – namely that while the two solicitors, having pledged their reputation on the truth of the Fayeds' story, had a vested interest in maintaining the sanctity of the original version, an independent QC introduced into their camp might threaten to upset their pact if he did not believe that story. Mohamed Fayed concurred without understanding that Fleck, an indifferent advocate, might not appeal to Brooke. At least, that was how Royston Webb in hindsight explained the decision.

During his first meeting with the inspectors at the Mayfair International Hotel, Fayed oozed charm and sincerity: 'We come from a town called Al-Fayedia near the Suez Canal,' he said of his ancient and wealthy family. 'We owned 12,000 acres of land producing many crops. Our grandfather grew cotton and used his own boats to ship the cotton to England.' Warming to his theme, and unable to recall his earlier versions, Fayed regaled his audience with tales about his family's empire of shipping fleets, road transporters and a hotel chain. 'All taken by Nasser. All taken by Nasser,' he repeated. Even the family's concession to distribute Singer sewing machines throughout Egypt had been lost, he added, drawing upon his employment as a door-to-door salesman. Some £20 million, he concluded, had been salvaged from Egypt to rebuild their fortunes. At the end, Fayed, filled with self-satisfaction, felt sure that his story had been believed. Asked about the descriptions of his family background published in 1985, he quipped: 'I have no comments on any reporter or on journalistic hallucination or sensational writings. It is up to them. I have no comments.' The inspectors nodded. 'The Fayeds' case', interjected Walker-Arnott helpfully, 'is that their investments do not produce conventional profits but dramatic increase in value.' The inspectors appeared happy to accept the argument.

As his self-confidence grew, Fayed spoke as eloquently as his English allowed about his achievements in Dubai, winning for British construction companies orders worth £2 billion. Thanks uniquely to Mohamed Al Fayed, Dubai had built a thirty-five-berth deep-water port and so much more. His fortune, he explained, was partly based upon commission earned from that £2 billion. He hoped that his confident manner had removed all doubts. Instead, the inspectors explained that the brothers would be required to prove that their own money had financed the takeover. That issue, said the inspectors, had been important when Tebbit considered the Fayeds' bid.

The Fayeds' lawyers protested. The evidence, they insisted, pointed the other way. Tebbit had cleared the bid on the ground that competition policies were not infringed. Kleinworts' assurances about the Fayeds' wealth were irrelevant because the brothers had paid cash. Moreover, the inquiry was restricted to the affairs of House of Fraser Holdings, a Fayed vehicle, and did not cover the Fayeds' personal circumstances.

The inspectors were unimpressed. To Mohamed Fayed's alarm, they declared that their sole priority was to discover how the Fayeds had accumulated £573 million. By the end of the meeting, the atmosphere had noticeably cooled. Rowland, fumed Fayed, had won: the issue was the source of his money. In a subsequent letter, the inspectors described their purpose as testing the 'accuracy and reliability' of six categories of statements by the Fayeds about their family background, their wealth and their source of money. They wanted nothing less than the full story of how the brothers had since 1958 earned and accumulated $1 billion in unencumbered cash. Or, put simply, they wanted proof of MacArthur's assertion on television that the Fayeds had a 'net worth of several billion dollars'.

Some would say, 'Mu-Mu panicked when he heard about that letter.' Others would say, 'He raged and cursed.' Whatever the truth, his fury subsided when his lawyers explained the limitations of the inspectors' powers. They could demand the Fayeds' personal bank accounts but were powerless to enforce their demand. The Fayeds' co-operation was voluntary. Mohamed's behaviour had been appositely summarized by G. K. Chesterton: 'The poor have sometimes objected to being governed badly; the rich have always objected to being governed at all.'

Underestimating his investigators, Fayed's response to their first list of questions was a thin envelope containing a schedule of his assets (valued again at over $1,000 million), some balance sheets and some bank accounts listing the general movements of cash after 31 October 1984. The documents showed that on 31 October, besides £50.5 million and $330 million deposited at the Royal Bank of Scotland, there was $229.9 million and SF156.3 million at the Banque Gonet in Geneva. On 8 March 1985, AITSA, their Liechtenstein trust, controlled $474.7 million deposited at the Swiss Bank Corporation and Banque Gonet. A letter from SBC confirmed that the money had been held for the Fayeds. 'There can be no justification', wrote the Fayeds' lawyers, 'for any suggestion that the monies did not belong to the Al Fayed brothers.' The lawyers added that none of the details of the Liechtenstein trust accounts would be disclosed, nor would the accounts of Park Lane Investments Inc., a group investing in America. In fact, they refused to reveal any details of the brothers' finances before 31 October 1984, especially how Mohamed had raised loans against the sultan's money.

Two weeks after receiving the statements, in mid-September, the inspectors complained about the inadequacy of the Fayeds' answers to the most pertinent question: how had the Fayeds earned or obtained their money? Examination of the meagre balance sheets provided by the Fayeds revealed a fundamental flaw in the brothers' proposition. Their great wealth was not generating profits or even any income. They claimed to have spent $125 million in the previous year on developing International Marine Services in Dubai, on rebuilding Park Lane and on other investments, but there was no obvious source of finance. Even Genavco's balance sheet showed that it was worth only £149,801 and had, between 1979 and 1983, lost £220,130.

Two transactions, wrote the inspectors, raised fundamental doubts. The annual profits flowing through the account at Banque Gonet were never more than $10 million. Yet $330 million had been deposited in the account on 31 October 1984.

That left a 'quite enormous' gap between reality and their claims of wealth.

Secondly, the inspectors doubted the Fayeds' crucial proposition: that in 1978 they had controlled $220 million and that by 1985 their fortune had grown to $500 million. If that was true, the inspectors asked, how could the Fayeds explain the fact that on 8 August 1984 they had negotiated to borrow £100 million from the Royal Bank of Scotland to finance their proposed but unfulfilled £180 million acquisition of the Savoy; yet two weeks later, on 22 August, they had deposited $330 million at the same bank. Where, the inspectors wondered, was the money coming from? 'We just want to see the origins of the money before October 1984,' said Hugh Aldous in a telephone conversation with Walker-Arnott. 'Show us the documents proving the history of how they came to control the cash.'

Posed in a single sentence, the question seemed simple to answer. But to the Fayeds, it threatened nothing less than Götterdämmerung, the end of the world. This was the decisive moment for the brothers. The management of Harrods was temporarily abandoned as Mohamed secluded himself with his lawyers. 'There are going to be specific questions, Mohamed,' cautioned Webb. 'Unless we can prove the truth of your replies, it will be better not to speak.' For a fleeting moment, there was an option of abandoning the story contrived by the Fayeds over the years and aggressively circulated by Brian Basham. Despite the inevitable embarrassment, some formula might have been negotiated to curtail public humiliation. But there was no pause for consideration before Fayed brushed aside that option and Webb's warning. Surrounded by bodyguards, greeted by the famous and the servile and blessed by royal warrants, he considered himself immune to damage, impervious to criticism and destined to survive despite the threats of mere functionaries. Speaking in Arabic to confuse any bugging devices, Mohamed and Ali contrived a plausible answer for their still unsuspecting lawyers. They would resist any co-operation. 'They're in the midst of litigation with Rowland,' Walker-Arnott eventually told the inspectors. 'They fear that any information they supply might be leaked to their adversary.'

Given their history over the previous decade, that statement was superficially credible, but in truth Fayed was convinced that the inspectors, in common with other British officials, could be duped. Walker-Arnott was persuaded to tell the inspectors that 'the terms of inquiry do not impose any duty on the Fayeds to show how their funds were generated'. That was questionable. Walker-Arnott's second reply was inaccurate. The terms of the Fayeds' bid for House of Fraser, he stated, contained no claims about the 'manner in which they have generated their wealth'. But it was true that no one else had claimed to have lent the Fayeds the money; and the sultan had expressly denied any involvement. 'His Majesty', said the latest denial, 'gives an unequivocal assurance that he had no part in the House of Fraser acquisition nor did he provide funds to the Al Fayeds to help them secure the House of Fraser.'

The inspectors were in a quandary. The sultan's promise to testify had evaporated and Fayed offered no further information about the source of his cash other than two balance sheets of his Liechtenstein trust. On 8 March 1985, the deposit was apparently $474.7 million, while on 30 June 1987 it was $291 million. Those unverifiable and confusing revelations raised more questions than answers, but suggested that the Fayeds had briefly borrowed money to sustain a suitable bank statement, and had then repaid the loan.

*

STILL CONFIDENT, Fayed arrived for the second meeting at the Mayfair International in early December. Although the dismissals of both Brian Walsh and Michael Ellis-Jones since their last meeting were likely to prompt new questions, he had not anticipated the chilly atmosphere. Minutes after Fayed had seated himself once more in the uncomfortable chair, his face fell. Impervious to his charm, the inspectors had become stubbornly antagonistic. The two grey men, he realized, suspected the pasha of lying. The cause was quickly evident: it was Rowland's work. Somehow, during the intervening weeks, Aldous and Brooke had been persuaded to pursue the trail pointed out by Rowland. As Aldous would later say of the Lonrho chief, 'The man's larger than life. Such a fascinating strength of character. Such a delightful sense of humour.' Rowland, it appeared, had outwitted his adversary. His tactics had proved his superior cunning.

Convinced that the inspectors were insufficiently obedient to his wishes, Rowland had intimidated them by distributing a public attack on their competence. Rather than being angered by this, Aldous had confessed to Rowland's lawyer how enthralled he had become by his client's 'remarkable force of determination'. Aldous's admiration had cost Rowland £2 million in expenses. The results of his investigations were proffered by Brooke to Fayed. A bundle of photocopies of official Egyptian documents – the Fayeds' birth certificates and their school records – confirmed their family's poor background. The original documents used to establish the Fayeds' first shipping corporations in Lebanon in the 1950s bore their real dates of birth. The most embarrassing revelation was a photocopy of their father's obituary notice published in *Al Ahram*, Egypt's leading newspaper, damningly stating their real names and their father's profession. 'These are forgeries!' shouted Fayed. The inspectors smiled in disbelief.

'This surely is outside the ambit of your inquiry,' protested Fleck. Whether a man lied about his childhood, continued the lawyer, had no bearing on a commerial transaction; after all, Rowland himself had fabricated and concealed many details about his own past. The inspectors' stony faces suggested the contrary.

'He can have teams of people in his offices to forge all these documents,' bellowed Fayed, suspecting the source of the information. 'Marwan can bring anything. He can do anything.' Fayed's identification of Rowland as the source was correct.

At Rowland's instigation, the inspectors had been introduced to Ashraf Marwan. Smoothly, the Egyptian convinced the inspectors that he had been grossly maligned by John Griffiths' judgement that he was a liar and party to the original conspiracy. More importantly, he persuaded the inspectors that even he was surprised by the Fayeds' sudden wealth. 'He was a fifty man,' said Marwan. Impressed by the evidence about Fayed, the inspectors did not query Marwan's lack of surprise when the brothers in November 1984 had paid £138 million for the original stake in House of Fraser. Marwan's confirmation of the authenticity of the Egyptian official documents was accepted. The inspectors' next revelation stunned Fayed.

Days earlier, it appeared, Adnan Khashoggi had been rushed to London. The Saudi had met Henry Brooke at the Kensington home of Charles Riachi, the Lebanese businessman. Sitting with Khashoggi were John Beveridge QC, Rowland's trusted lawyer, and Rowland's accountant, who was acting as Brooke's impromptu secretary. Responding to Beveridge's questions, Khashoggi guided the silent inspector through ninety-six pages of documents and photographs starkly contradicting his former brother-in-law's version of his childhood in Alexandria. Khashoggi's roar of laughter when Brooke handed him a photograph of the Alexandria mansion which Fayed claimed as the family's ancestral home was particularly damaging. 'He bought that in 1971,' guffawed Khashoggi, endorsing the *Observer*'s description of Fayed's childhood as having been spent in an impoverished tenement. 'You see, Mr Brooke,' smiled Rowland later, 'Fayed is nothing more than a commission agent who has deceived at each stage to get what he's after.'

As the inspectors' prejudice emerged in the conference room at the Mayfair International Hotel, Fayed exploded with anger. Trembling, he spat expletives at the two men who had dared question his integrity. Khashoggi had even produced the records of the University of California which showed the date of Ali's birth as 1933. In his Dubai passport, Ali's date of birth was declared to be 1943. Khashoggi had paid for Ali's education in San Mateo and knew the truth.

Even as he shook with indignation, Fayed understood Khashoggi's motives. It was pay-back time. Fayed had exploited the divorce to keep Khashoggi's loan; he had turned the sultan against Khashoggi in 1985; and he had prevented Dodi from attending his mother's funeral. Khashoggi, who had recently borrowed about $9 million from Rowland, was not averse to righteous revenge. But in Fayed's mind it was unforgivable treachery and confirmed another suspicion.

Reports days earlier from his bodyguards about five men – two on foot, two in cars and one on a motorbike – seen monitoring his Park Lane building worried Fayed that Rowland had inserted bugs in the building. Although a dispute among his security team about the credibility of the danger – 'It's all bollocks,' Macnamara had declared – confused matters, Fayed became certain that Rowland had masterminded a giant plot and that Khashoggi was a party to the conspiracy.

'Can we have an adjournment?' asked Fleck, concerned that the explosion of anger over the revelation of trivial lies heralded unforeseen complications.

'Racist bastards,' cursed Fayed as he stepped into the corridor. Watched by his bodyguards, he continued, 'I, Mohamed Al Fayed, will destroy them.'

Walker-Arnott wagged his finger at his client. 'Don't ever speak like that again,' he warned. There was, he knew, no easy recovery from the appalling impression the Egyptian had made upon Aldous and Brooke. Indeed, the inspectors had concluded that 'Mohamed's skill in exaggerating the truth before an audience whom he believes to be ignorant of the true facts was clearly apparent.'

Edward Walker-Arnott was confused. In his early dealings

with Fayed after November 1984, his client had appeared to be unusually candid, once even spontaneously inviting the lawyer to listen to a conversation when Rowland had unexpectedly telephoned. Like Fayed's other bankers, accountants and lawyers, Walker-Arnott had never voiced any criticism about his client. On the contrary, the Egyptian's hurt response to Rowland's attacks had persuaded Walker-Arnott of his innocence. The blame for this sudden crisis, he felt, lay in the inspectors' naive surrender to Rowland's influence. Not only had the inspectors, accused Fayed, breached an explicit promise not to show documents provided by Fayed to Rowland during the inquiry, but their investigation was relying on evidence provided by Lonrho. They had exceeded their powers and were pursuing Rowland's agenda.

Surveillance on Terry Robinson, Lonrho's finance director, and on Lonrho's lawyers – John Beveridge and John Fordham – seemed to Fayed to confirm his accusations of a conspiracy. Regularly, Rowland's henchmen were seen visiting Aldous's office to 'take the inspectors through the evidence'. Even Edward du Cann, stoking Brooke's growing suspicion of the Fayeds, was, according to eyewitnesses, warmly thanked for presenting new evidence. Not all Rowland's 'evidence' was delivered discreetly. In a burst of activity, the Lonrho chief had published three glossy brochures: *Enter a different world: Harrods created by Fayed* alleged that Fayed's assurances about his inherited wealth were bogus; a fourteen-page brochure suggested that the Fayeds had possessed only £43 million in 1984; and *The sultan and I* published an edited transcript of the Carlos Place conversations between the Swami and Fayed. Unsolicited, 40,000 so-called opinion-formers across the world received each of these brochures. Darkly, Rowland hinted that he possessed new evidence proving that Fayed had bought House of Fraser with a power of attorney for $1.5 billion provided by the sultan. The sultan, wrote Rowland, was 'at the root of the worst fraud of the century'.

'Do urge Tiny not to be so aggressive,' Aldous urged

Fordham. 'He's pushing at an open door.' In the aftermath of that protest, Rowland had used Lonrho's research in Egypt, Haiti, Israel, Switzerland, the United States, France and the United Arab Emirates to persuade the inspectors to widen their inquiry. They should rely upon witnesses discovered by Rowland's investigators, he urged. The inspectors complied.

Ashraf Marwan, funded by Rowland, was leading the inspectors by the nose. In Egypt, he and Peter Wickman, the journalist, were introducing a DTI investigator to hostile witnesses. In London, Marwan had offered $2 million to the Haitian ambassador to obtain unfavourable evidence against Fayed. Although the ambassador had replied that Fayed was innocent and was 'not blamed for the circumstances which led to his departure', the inspectors preferred the testimony – witnesses and documents – provided by Sam Evans, Rowland's American lawyer, that the Fayeds had been involved in criminal activities. Under the rules, the Fayeds could not scrutinize or cross-examine the evidence, which would have been inadmissible in a court. Rowland's lawyers were thrilled. Hugh Aldous in particular, they reported, was 'naively excited' by the attention Rowland offered and preferred to discount the sultan's latest denial of any involvement published in the *Sunday Telegraph*.

Secluded in Park Lane, Fayed unleashed expletives. 'Tell them to bugger off,' he shouted at Royston Webb.

'Brooke's a second-rate medical-negligence lawyer,' declared Webb sympathetically. 'What does he know about international business?' Turning to Ali, the lawyer asked about the discrepancy in the dates of birth.

'Oh, they're wrong,' replied Ali.

'Why don't I go to California and get the truth?' offered Webb, still convinced of his employer's honesty.

'Oh no,' replied Ali. 'Just tell them to bugger off.'

The inspectors, the brothers insisted, did not have the right to investigate their private lives. Edward Walker-Arnott was more insistent. 'I think we should produce an independent report of your life in Egypt,' he suggested. 'We'll send Richard Fleck.'

The idea appealed to Fayed. 'I will arrange everything,' he smiled.

Defiantly keen to prove their wealth and their ability to raise loans, in December 1987 the Fayeds bought 10 per cent of Sears, the owners of Selfridges, for £215.7 million. 'It's undervalued,' John MacArthur had advised. 'It's a sound, long-term investment.' Fayed was persuaded that combining Harrods and Selfridges would produce 'synergy'. Bankers in the City took a different view. Since the £2 billion total value of Sears was far beyond Fayed's means – having bought the shares, he pledged them against a loan for the entire cost – and since the world's stock markets had just crashed, the deal made no commercial sense. In fact it exposed the Fayeds' severe limitations. Stepping into an unknown world, the Fayeds were ridiculed. The most interested critics were the inspectors. Unimpressed by the Fayeds' financial resources, they discovered that the deal had been approved only retrospectively by House of Fraser's directors. The brothers were clearly insensitive to proper business conduct in London.

*

JUST AFTER CHRISTMAS, the inspectors issued a final demand for an explanation of how £20 million, allegedly rescued from Egypt in the 1950s, had grown to over $1 billion. The Fayeds faced the charge of making 'false and fraudulent assertions' to the government. Detailed answers were required, otherwise the inspectors would be entitled to conclude that the money to buy House of Fraser had belonged to someone else. 'I do need an answer, Mohamed,' Walker-Arnott implored. Fayed seemed unconcerned. His imagination had never failed to produce a plausible answer.

There were, as Fayed discovered from the flow of letters dispatched by the inspectors, several reasons for their new aggression. Firstly, they had embarrassingly rebutted his valuations. His claim that he would earn $200 million in future profits by franchising the 'Ritz' trademark to Nabisco, the manufacturers of 'Ritz Crackers', was rebutted as pure invention. Similarly, his valuation of the Ritz Hotel at $107 million was double any objective assessment. His valuation of his shipping, aircraft and film companies at $373.7 million was hugely exaggerated: their real worth was $101.6 million. Finally, Ali's inconsistent assessments of their wealth – $1.15 billion in 1985 and $750 million in 1987 – was self-destructive.

'The first figure', Ali had sighed, 'was more or less an assessment at the moment.'

'You talked it up?' asked Brooke.

Ali had shrugged.

The second embarrassment was the report by Richard Fleck about his research in Alexandria. Fleck returned to Britain convinced that, thanks to his brilliant sleuthing, he had discovered the truth. The lawyer had interviewed the 'son of the family gardener employed in the family mansion' since the beginning of the century, and had spoken to a sailor at the Yacht Club who swore that the schooner *Dodi* had been owned by the Fayed family since 1913 – though its original name was the *Sakara*. 'The random appearance of the witnesses', he convinced himself, 'proved the absence of Fayed's manipulation.'

To Fleck's embarrassment, his evidence was exposed as unsound by the inspectors' own investigations and, more importantly, by an extensive report, supported by original documents, produced by Vincent Carrateau, a private investigator retained by Rowland. Exhaustively, Carrateau had gathered statements from dozens of eyewitnesses and from Egypt's official gazettes since 1925 proving that within Egypt's small cotton and shipping hierarchy there had been no trader or owner called Al Fayed. Other documents revealed the true history of the 'family mansion', their yacht *Sakara* and their 'huge fleet'. It was simply a 'will-o'-the-wisp' which Fayed had never anticipated could be uncovered by research.

Convinced that the Fayeds' story was 'a pack of lies', the inspectors travelled to Dubai and, after interviewing twenty-eight witnesses including St John Armitage, Neville Allen, Paul Branner and Mahdi Al Tajir, returned convinced of the falsity of Mohamed Fayed's claims to have earned 'hundreds of millions' as a reward for investing his own money. The inspectors concluded that Fayed's stories were 'either quite untrue or were exaggerated versions of the truth', and that British companies would have won the contracts 'regardless of any influence Mohamed Fayed might have brought to bear'. Fayed, they guessed, had earned at most £90 million in Dubai. Although exaggeration was not an offence, Fayed faced an accusation of deliberate deception, especially after three Morgan Grenfell bankers testified, '[we] just do not believe that [Fayed] had the monumental monies later ascribed to him'. In 1985, he was worth at most, estimated the bankers, 'between £20 million and £50 million'.

Mohamed and Ali Fayed were grappling in an alien environment. Exaggerated self-salesmanship was being painted as a heinous crime. On 26 February 1988 the Fayeds were asked to rebut the accusation that they lied about their background and wealth. Unable to ignore the inspectors' complaint about their 'deafening silence', they agreed to return to the Mayfair International Hotel on 8 March 1988 for a two-day session.

Neither contrite nor conciliatory, Fayed sat in the conference room stubbornly refusing to oblige his interrogators. Oblivious to shame, non-cooperation was his best and only protection. 'No one on earth has the right to invade our privacy,' he puffed crudely. The brothers, he insisted, were not a company but private individuals, 'without auditors or balance sheets'. They 'have made no statements or representations as to the source of their wealth', the statements given to the media by the banks in 1984 were uttered without their knowledge, and they were 'immaterial [since] nobody relied upon them'. Media inaccuracies, he lamented, were 'a regrettable fact of life'.

The inspectors' evident incredulity and their mention of Ashraf Marwan triggered an explosion. When Fayed heard Henry Brooke refer to Marwan's testimony about a conversation with Fayed, he shouted, 'Lies!' Lies!'

'But, Mr Al Fayed, we've heard the tape recording of the conversation.'

The tapes, said Fayed derisively, had been fixed. 'All forgeries.' Challenging the authenticity of his own voice, clearly audible on the tape, undermined his perfectly justified attack on Marwan's credibility. Even worse, it prejudiced the inspectors in their approach to the critical question, the source of their funds.

'I do need an answer, Mohamed,' Walker-Arnott implored.

'Oil,' Mohamed smilingly told his advisers. 'Oil trading in the Gulf, but I can't tell you the details. Secret.'

His lawyers did not conceal their frustration. Pleas of sensitivity, even if true, they pointed out, were unlikely to convince the inspectors.

Fayed remained impervious. 'Tell them anything,' he snapped. Oil could have been the source of his fortune if only Tajir had been more amenable. But Fayed's attempts to find oil in Abu Dhabi had by 1985 earned at most $8.4 million. Nevertheless, his obedient lawyers, in a new memorandum, invited the inspectors to assume that in 1978 the Fayeds controlled $220 million and that by 1985 the sum had accumulated with tax-free interest to over $500 million. The remaining $400 million had been earned in secret oil deals in the early 1980s.

'We mustn't give them any information, Mohamed,' cautioned Walker-Arnott, 'unless we're sure it's true.'

'Sure,' replied Fayed.

'Don't forget,' continued the lawyer, 'that Rowland was nearly prosecuted after the DTI inspection for false statements.'

'Sure,' waved Mohamed, glancing at Ali for a sign of agreement. There would be no loss of face.

Richard Fleck addressed Brooke and Aldous. Between 1979 and 1984, he stuttered, the Fayeds had been members of a consortium buying oil from the Gulf emirates and their 'very substantial profits' had been deposited by the partners in a joint bank account in the Swiss Bank Corporation. When the consortium was dissolved in summer 1984, the Fayeds' share – £50.5 million and $330 million – was transferred to the Royal Bank of Scotland. Here was the source of their wealth to buy House of Fraser. 'There are no written agreements', continued Fleck without noticeable conviction, 'evidencing these arrangements. And the Al Fayed brothers have no documentation relating to oil trading itself.' Any breach of the secrecy would produce 'the gravest consequences' to the brothers. No further information, he said, would be offered.

'Who were the partners?' asked Brooke. Fleck admitted his ignorance. In their enthusiasm to expose the Fayeds' dishonesty, the inspectors had recruited 'oil experts' to establish that no Gulf state during the 1980s had secretly supplied sufficient quantities of oil to non-traditional customers to earn those customers huge profits. Fayed was challenged to contradict those experts. The session adjourned until the following day.

'We must have names, Mohamed,' insisted Walker-Arnott that evening, fearful for his own reputation. 'Names, Mohamed.'

With a theatrical flourish, Fayed announced hesitantly. 'I tell names but you must never reveal and not ask them.' With apparent reluctance, he mentioned famous Arabs and Americans. Walker-Arnott moved his head sagely. Fayed had spoken with sufficient menace to persuade his lawyers to refrain from making embarrassing checks. None of them suspected that the list of names might be fantasy. 'Just say we're afraid they'll tell Tiny the names,' suggested Fayed.

Creating an atmosphere of mystery the following morning, Fleck defended his clients' right to 'total confidentiality'. The Fayeds, he said, had been involved in secret, special contracts with immensely powerful individuals who 'could not even be talked about'. With that, the Fayeds flounced out of the hotel, repeating their latest mantra: they were under no obligation to reveal how they had earned their fortune. Later, their lawyers would claim that all the Fayeds' files relating to the House of Fraser takeover had been 'destroyed' and that the Fayeds' instructions to transfer $400 million of their oil trading profits into their Zurich bank account 'were given to Citicorp orally'.

The inspectors concluded that the Fayeds had lied, because their answers were 'vague, shifty and, in part, plainly untrue'. The claims about enormous oil profits were rejected as 'manifestly untrue' and 'dishonest'. If they had indeed earned $400 million in five years of oil trading, they might even have perpetrated 'a fraud'.

*

JUST FOUR WEEKS LATER, on 12 April 1988, the Fayeds' lawyers received Brooke's and Aldous's provisional conclusions. The 500-page draft, the Egyptians' lawyers complained, was strewn with errors. Money stated as dollars should have been pounds, and vice versa; dates and chronology were inaccurate; quotations, frequently to the Fayeds' detriment, were carelessly cited; and some analysis of company accounts was confused. Worse than the errors for the brothers was the evidence of the inspectors' hostility.

The inspectors claimed that Norman Tebbit had allowed the Fayeds' bid on the basis of their phoney family history, yet the politician had not been questioned. By ignoring Tebbit's two statements, 'I didn't care who owned House of Fraser,' and 'It was the shareholders (including Lonrho) who sold their shares, not the government, who were responsible for the Al Fayeds' successful acquisition,' the inspectors clearly disregarded the Fayeds' principal arguments. They had also taken no notice of the Fayeds' complaint of their favourable attitude to Rowland.

Throughout their draft, the inspectors quoted the *Observer*'s reports uncritically, relying on the journalists' 'verification process' as if the newspaper was independent, and quoting forgeries and inventions such as Mark Thatcher's visit to Brunei as established fact. Their lengthy examination of the Fayeds' activities in Haiti in 1964 confirmed their prejudice. Twenty-four years after the event, without visiting Haiti but relying entirely upon evidence provided by Rowland – Papa Doc's newspaper reports and alleged 'eyewitnesses', some even anonymous, who had not even lived in Haiti – the inspectors condemned Fayed's conduct on the island. According to the inspectors, he had 'bought' the wife of Baby Doc, the dictator's son, he was accused of being 'a man capable of deceiving others with false and fraudulent representations' and he 'stole' $187,500. Among the alleged thefts, according to the inspectors, was $2,000 spent on furniture, cleaning, telephones and electricity. Those items, wrote the inspectors, were 'not normally associated with the day to day expenditure of a harbour company'.

The most embarrassing conclusion was the inspectors' uncritical acceptance of Rowland's evidence about the sultan. Their draft repeated the Lonrho executive's fanciful tale that Kleinworts had become fund managers for £3 billion of the sultan's funds, and stated that Fayed had bought House of Fraser under the sultan's power of attorney. Yet the inspectors were unable to produce a copy of the power of attorney and ignored the *Observer*'s admission that the newspaper had published a forgery. Compounding those omissions, they cited the testimony of Donald Trelford, the *Observer*'s editor, and Carl Hirschmann, the aggrieved Swiss aircraft engineer flown to London by Rowland. Both told the inspectors that the sources for their claims about the sultan connection were anonymous 'Swiss bankers'. Not only did the inspectors accept those two uncorroborated statements – ignoring Hirschmann's original assertion in 1984 that the source of his information came from Brunei – but they discounted without explanation the sultan's repeated denials. Clearly, their understanding of Fayed's relationship with the sultan was confused. Erroneously, they accepted Rowland's speculation that Fayed's dealings with the sultan had ended, yet Fayed was still in regular contact with the monarch, meeting him for lunch in London and Paris during their investigation. Hence they were unable to explain why the sultan would admit his use of Fayed in purchasing the Dorchester but conceal his role in the House of Fraser deal. 'The sultan has no evidence', his spokesman repeated, 'that the Fayeds used the power of attorney granted in connection with the Dorchester hotel to further their business interests.' The inspectors had heard too many lies from Fayed to believe any evidence submitted in his favour.

Expletives and uncontrolled fury were directed at his grimacing lawyers when Fayed saw the thick document. 'This is about my dignity,' he cried. Although he had not read the whole report, he had seen enough to know that it was the product of forgery, revenge, commercial opportunism, dishonesty and, above all, a conspiracy. In summary, it sabotaged his life's ambition: acceptance by society. 'My honour, my pri—' Fayed could not get the last word out. The lawyers, each listening at £200 per hour, sought to understand their client. 'Pri—' His eyes bulging with anger, Fayed stuttered again. His audience leant forward. 'Pri—' he stammered. Finally they understood. Fayed was talking about his 'principles', which had been offended by the inspectors' unequal treatment of Rowland and himself. Not only had they acknowledged Rowland's lies about the Swami, but Fayed's own published investigation of Rowland had exposed his accuser as dishonest.

After one year's investigation and considerable expenditure, Richard New and Royston Webb had written *Fair Cop Fuhrhop: The True Story of Tiny Rowland*. For the first time, Rowland's distortion of his past was exposed. Distributed as a letter from the vengeful Francesca Pollard and adorned with a swastika on the cover, the pamphlet provided the evidence of Rowland's Nazi sympathies during the war, the perjury on his marriage certificate (his father was falsely named Rowland instead of Fuhrhop to disguise his German birth) and Lonrho's tax evasion. Fayed was sure that the 40,000 of 'the great and the good' who received the exposé would conclude that Rowland's campaign was at best hypocritical. Although many were influenced, the inspectors, his most important target, were unimpressed.

The two men had given the Fayeds until 15 May 1988 to reply to their draft. Walker-Arnott asked for the deadline to be extended. Reluctantly, the inspectors agreed. The lawyer's tactic, to disrupt the inspectors' prejudices and impose a burden of fairness, was to deliver a 900-page submission. Fayed used that delay to urge his MPs to intensify their lobbying of Lord Young.

Commuting between London and France, Fayed cursed his failure to bend the system to his will. All Greer's efforts to halt the campaign against him had failed. Hamilton's protests to Young about the 'twentieth-century Spanish Inquisition' and 'a monstrous injustice' meted out by 'determined, powerful and unscrupulous organisations' had not stopped the inquiry. All his money to Tim Smith appeared to have been wasted. If the inspectors publicly branded him a liar it would be disastrous, but worst of all would be the retention of one short sentence in the draft report stating that House of Fraser was 'unable to meet its obligations'. The inspectors' untrue assertion of financial problems, Fayed feared, could persuade Lord Young to order a Monopolies Commission investigation followed by the compulsory sale of House of Fraser. It would be possible to prevent that, Fayed calculated, only if the report's credibility were undermined before its delivery.

Individually, Hamilton and Smith were summoned to Harrods. Genuine supporters of Fayed's cause, both agreed with his strategy. At the end of lunch with Hamilton, Fayed showed his gratitude in his traditional way by passing over a thick white envelope. 'Thank you, Mohamed,' said the politician, whose wife, just days earlier, had spent £1,000 at Peter Jones at Greer's expense. Shortly after, Hamilton wrote to Lord Young protesting about the inspectors' investigation of Fayed's personal life, which had 'no conceivable direct relevance to the Lonrho accusations', and demanding an investigation into Lonrho's 'many nefarious dealings', including a tax fraud unearthed in Liechtenstein. To maintain the pressure, co-ordinated by Greer, on 12 July Hamilton and the other MPs, put down questions and a motion criticizing Rowland. Three days later, Walker-Arnott delivered his submission to the inspectors.

Condemning the inspectors' reliance upon tainted witnesses, speculation and forgeries, the lawyer attacked their misunderstanding of international business. 'Borrowing does not imply a need on the part of the borrower,' wrote Walker-Arnott accurately, and if shipping companies lose money it does not mean they are unprofitable but may simply be avoiding tax. Those arguments were undermined, however, by the lawyer's unconvincing claims that the Fayeds had not intended to mislead the authorities about their wealth.

Denied access to the Swiss bank accounts, the inspectors chose to ignore Walker-Arnott's massive submission. Based simply upon conjecture that the flood of money deposited in the Fayeds' bank accounts during summer 1984 followed Mohamed Fayed's visit that August to Brunei, they concluded that it 'looks not only possible but probable' that Fayed had used the sultan's money. 'The evidence', the inspectors stated, 'that they were telling lies to us was quite overwhelming. But they were still determined to counter-attack and try to pretend that they were the innocent victims of some gigantic conspiracy against them.' They finished their report with the assertion that the Fayeds' deception had festered in an Alice in Wonderland world where 'lies were the truth and . . . the truth was a lie'.

*

ON 24 JULY 1988, their report was delivered to the DTI. The following day, Fayed again appealed to Hamilton for help. Three days later, on 28 July, he received the sycophantic sympathy he desired. On crisp House of Commons notepaper, Hamilton lamented that the inspectors' report would 'add insult to injury' after their 'distasteful and unwarranted intrusion into your private life'. Accompanying the letter was a copy of another letter the politician had sent to Lord Young complaining about Lonrho's suspicious accounts and the DTI's failure to investigate the company's activities. The Fayeds, Hamilton wrote to Young, were victims of 'injustice and oppression' because of the 'wholly irrelevant . . . obsession' with their background which had nothing to do with the 'legitimate public policy question of competition'. The inspectors, he complained, had become 'a tool in Tiny Rowland's vendetta', an 'incredible' reliance upon an 'untrustworthy' man.

In public, Fayed concealed the turmoil within him. Displaying remarkable resilience, he stood beaming beside Dame Edna Everage at the opening of the Harrods summer sale. 'I'm looking for a Wedgwood chamber pot for my incontinent mother,' Everage giggled. On the same day, the inspectors' report was handed to Young as he boarded an aircraft at Auckland airport, New Zealand, for the return flight to Britain. Settling into his first-class seat to spend the flight reading 'the yard thick typescript', Young knew that no advantage could be won by espousing Rowland against the Egyptian, whom he, as a former chairman of the Conservative Party, had occasionally met.

The inspectors, in their introduction, had sought to anticipate one criticism. 'We started our investigations', they wrote, 'with a predisposition not to trust' Rowland and Marwan. But by the end they had concluded that 'it was safe to rely on much of what those two witnesses told us . . . We uncovered more and more cases where the Fayeds were plainly telling lies.' The Fayeds' version, said the inspectors, was 'unreliable', 'untrue' and 'bogus'. By the time he reached the end of the first page, as the plane flew over the South Pacific, Young sighed, 'They've bought Rowland's story.'

To pre-empt that charge, the inspectors admitted that their inquiry had been established as 'a consequence of two years' unrelenting pressure by Lonrho', but they denied that they were Rowland's tools. 'The direct part which Lonrho and Mr Rowland played', they wrote, 'was a comparatively small one.' Young saw the disingenuity in that statement after reading their claim that Fayed had 'treated Rowland very badly over the share sale'. In Young's opinion, the inspectors had been supine in accepting that Rowland was 'motivated by a sincere belief that the Fayeds were not telling the truth in very major respects'. The inspectors' report, he concluded, was a 'hatchet job'. The protests of his parliamentary colleagues could not be ignored. On his return to London, he discovered that his dissatisfaction was shared by his officials. 'It's surprising', Hans Liesner said, 'that the inspectors failed to ask Rowland why he had twice sold the House of Fraser shares to Fayed. Especially because he wanted to buy the company.'

Rowland, suspecting that the report was satisfactorily critical, judged that Fayed's fate lay on a knife-edge. The deadline for a reference to the Monopolies Commission to consider divestment 'in the public interest' was 22 January 1989. To tilt the balance finally in his favour, he circulated on 4 September 1988 more than 80,000 copies of another damning glossy pamphlet, the latest development in a campaign which by then, including advertisements in the national press, had cost Lonrho shareholders £20 million. Called *The Hero from Zero: The Story of Kleinwort Benson and Mohamed Fayed*, the 185 pages of sarcasm and vitriol described for English, French and Arab readers the 'corrupt life of Mohamed Fayed'. 'I never bear a grudge,' said Rowland, announcing the publication of an accompanying brochure alleging that Fayed had evaded income tax, 'I share it with as many people as possible.'

The massive scale of Rowland's latest bombardment devastated Fayed. Everyone of any importance in Britain had received the bacillus, blending truth and lies. Lurching across the roof terrace outside his Park Lane penthouse with Bill Mitchell, his designer, Fayed showed that he was uncertain how to react. 'Don't bite back,' cautioned Mitchell, watching his emotional employer charging back and forth. 'In this country you wait. The public feels a need for fair play.' Fayed was deaf to that advice. No one in his world understood fair play. Only retaliation counted. But his counterattack could only be puny. At best, as a humiliating gimmick, he could send Francesca Pollard to perform a citizen's arrest of Rowland at Cheapside – a ruse which failed. Sometimes he wished he had installed in his new, private bathroom a lavatory with Tiny's face engraved on the bowl. It would have been such fun to shout, 'I've shit on Tiny!' His only serious hope was Ian Greer's footsoldiers. Their report was encouraging. Having heard Rowland's demands personally, Lord Young was prepared to meet Mohamed and Ali.

Accompanied by Peter Hordern, Fayed prepared himself for an outstanding performance. Carefully briefed, the two brothers sat across the secretary of state's desk pleading in uncharacteristically modest language that he should ignore Rowland's vendetta and accept their version of events. Inevitably, Fayed's pleading included the mantra: 'my dignity, my integrity, my honour, my family'. Equally inevitably, he failed to mention that by family he did not mean his loathsome father and stepmother. Yet, as so often, the apparent sincerity of the mantra appeared to have registered with its target. Influenced by Hamilton and his colleagues, Young was certainly impressed by the 'Fair Cop Fuhrhop' evidence that Rowland was a liar pursuing a dishonest campaign.

Days later, Young's opinion was endorsed by Gordon Borrie, the director general of the OFT. Although Borrie accepted that the Fayeds had lied, he believed that the prospect of unravelling the Fayeds' ownership of House of Fraser to satisfy a Nazi sympathizer was too appalling to contemplate. 'The Monopolies Commission', he advised Young, 'does not exist to punish people for lying. The shareholders got the cash. Morality is irrelevant.' On 22 November 1988, he formally recommended that there should be no reference to the Monopolies Commission. Three days later Young agreed. He was minded, he told his officials, not even to publish the report.

Fayed had reason to be delighted. He had much to thank Greer, Hamilton and the others for. The few thousand pounds he had scattered among the politicians had secured for ever his £1 billion business. His exaggerations about his life had secured House of Fraser and could be blamed on Brian Basham's excess of enthusiasm rather than on his deliberate dishonesty. 'Harrods will be in my family for a thousand years,' he smiled. 'I know that and so does Tiny Rowland.'

Hamilton naturally shared Fayed's delight. He had received so much from Fayed in cash and hospitality that he wanted to express his gratitude. Three weeks later he arrived at Harrods carrying a Christmas present. He presented to the millionaire, with his fetish for immaculate clothes, a gold-plated set of cufflinks engraved with the portcullis motif of the House of Commons. 'Thank you,' Fayed said, glancing distastefully at the tacky cardboard box. Hamilton, he knew, would expect more cash in return for the success. 'We'll deliver something soon,' he mumbled.

As Hamilton left, Royston Webb entered. Fayed's eyes were blazing. 'Hamilton has just gone,' he screamed at his lawyer. 'Look what he's given me. Cheap, fuggin' gold plate House of Commons cufflinks. I give him thousands of pounds. For what? A pair of rubbish cufflinks! They're all fuggers, these politicians. Corrupt! Here, you have them!'

'They'll never do what you expect, Mohamed,' cautioned Webb, pocketing the box and ignoring the 'hot buttons' currently enraging his employer. 'They're just using you.' Fayed listened. Of all his entourage, Webb was one of the few he trusted. Not only did the Welsh barrister seem to be genuinely fond of his employer but he also insisted that they pursue a legal solution whenever Fayed's inclination to disregard terms in contracts or break agreements clouded his judgement. 'The politicians won't help you, Mohamed,' repeated Webb, recalling that Andrew Bowden, the Conservative MP, had taken over £5,000 of Fayed's money from Greer for election expenses for 1987 and then disappeared. ('What happened to Andrew?' Webb had asked. 'He was too greedy,' Greer had replied.) 'Forget it, Mohamed,' Webb repeated.

This lack of gratitude reflected Fayed's permanent dissatisfaction. Terrified of Rowland's persecution, he wanted the utter destruction of those who had caused him distress. Yet, in the brief moments when his anger lapsed, Fayed knew that money and not truth had prevailed. His payments to Greer and the MPs had probably tilted the balance against Rowland and his own paid politicians. Lord Young, he was assured, would not publish the inspectors' report. The inspectors' condemnation would remain secret. House of Fraser belonged to him. Rowland had not won an overwhelming victory and the store was beautifully decorated for Christmas.

10

The Dark Side

ISOLATED FROM THE NOISE and odour of Christmas shoppers cramming into his store, Mohamed Fayed's portly body rocked slightly. Guffawing with laughter, he offered Mark Griffiths, his neat personal assistant, a package. 'Christmas present,' he smirked as Griffiths, whose unquestioning obedience was becoming increasingly useful, began unwrapping his surprise. Innocently he gazed at a wooden model of a friar wearing a habit. 'Push lever,' barked Fayed. His employee obeyed. A penis shot out through the friar's habit. Fayed roared with laughter and snatched the gift from the startled recipient. Repeatedly jerking the lever in and out a score of times, chortling uncontrollably as the penis mechanically re-emerged, he wanted to share his amusement. Rushing out into the corridor, he spotted a matronly kitchen attendant. 'Look!' he shouted. The middle-aged woman was uncertain of the desired reaction. Luckily for her, Fayed was too intent on his own enjoyment to notice her disapproval.

Few of those employed by Fayed or accepting his hospitality knew more about the laughing Egyptian tycoon than had appeared in newspapers. Most still distrusted the denigratory reports published by Rowland and preferred to rely upon their own experience. Fayed, the jolly and generous Arab, always with a laugh and a vulgar remark – 'How's your cock? A man can live without everything, but no cock is bad' – beguiled all but the most cynical into believing that, despite the tantrums and malice, the man possessed a heart of gold and was the master of retailing. For over thirty years, Fayed had entertained guests and cultivated the rich and celebrities with generosity and showmanship. Over the previous three years, he had posed as the Harrods doorman wearing a green uniform and top hat, he had dressed as Father Christmas, and he had donned an apron and straw boater to serve in the Food Hall. Newspaper photographers were summoned not simply to record publicity stunts but to register his love of Harrods and his big heart. 'Harrods', he would say with relish, 'is a palace of romance, fantasy and history.' But, within the store, whispers reflected unease about the Fayeds. In particular, there was gossip that all the Fayeds, the three brothers and Dodi, were indulging in unsavoury antics.

In recent months, Fayed had been enjoying edited highlights of his employees' secretly recorded conversations about their sex lives. One of many sources of the tapes was Bob Loftus, a former major with twenty-eight years' service in the army, including the Military Police, appointed as Harrods' head of security by John Macnamara. Loftus's zeal won Fayed's trust. 'Report to me directly,' Fayed had ordered. 'Only to me.' Occasionally working late, Loftus listened to the tapes of the employees targeted by himself, Macnamara, Griffiths or Fayed and delivered the results the following day. Sitting in his electronically locked office, often alone, Fayed gurgled with delight as his unsuspecting employees, men and women, discussed their intimate desires and bedroom activities. Few were spared his prying, which intruded into the lives of Andrew Jennings, the managing director of House of Fraser, and Stephen Taylor and Stan Frith, both personnel directors. Fayed's private stimulants belied the public image he cultivated. His laugh as he eavesdropped on his unsuspecting employees mocked the innocent and the loyal.

In Fayed's life, there was only one victim of injustice: himself. Those who suffered his displeasure at Harrods were not victims but traitors deserving summary dismissal. Discovering disloyalty had become a compulsive passion. His tools were telephone taps and surveillance over employees inside and outside the building. On Fayed's orders, John Macnamara and Bob Loftus had transformed the abnormal and outrageous into the normal. As more rumours spread about the store's unusual security, a sour atmosphere spread from floor to floor. Happily for Fayed, not one of his senior managers objected to Macnamara's and Loftus's activities. Security was an accepted necessity in any shop and the personnel directors, financial staff and store managers collaborated with the new requirements. Fayed expected no different. The discovery of a single act of dishonesty substantiated all his suspicions.

Just before Christmas, Bob Loftus reported that a menswear buyer, followed from Harrods, had been observed accepting a box of Havana cigars from a supplier. Ignoring the employee's tearful pleas that he was innocent, twenty-eight years of faithful service were damned by Fayed's triumphant boast that his methods were proven to be justified. The blatant contradictions – Fayed's own cash payments to politicians and others – did not encroach upon his conscience. On the contrary. Preoccupied by enhancing his wealth, he appreciated that Loftus's operation could increase his profits.

Fayed had become ever more irritated by the compensation payable on dismissal. Redundancy payments were wasted money. Removing at no cost those whose loyalty he suspected or whose faces prompted his irritation was possible if there was good cause. Among that group were the personnel officers reluctant to implement Fayed's prejudices.

After twenty years' employment at Harrods as a departmental personnel director, Fiona Walsh* proudly boasted green blood in her veins, but she opposed his policy of employing few blacks. To facilitate her dismissal, she was accused of approving the employment of a sales assistant known to be a prostitute. Walsh was appalled. Not only was the charge untrue, but the existence of a prostitution ring operating in the perfume depart-

---

* Not her real name.

ment was well known to Fayed. According to folklore, if the top three buttons of a shop assistant's uniform in the department were undone, the woman was available. After a *Daily Mirror* exposé, Fayed had voiced his outrage and demanded an apology, but his bluster was quickly forgotten. Walsh appealed to Stephen Taylor, her superior, but he ignored her telephone calls. Relying upon tape recordings provided by Loftus and Eamon Coyle, a security officer, Taylor had fired many women accused of having affairs with other members of staff or contractors, while concealing his own affair with a personnel manager who had previously enjoyed a relationship with a security officer. Those affairs all contravened Fayed's instruction that sexual relations among staff were forbidden. On the store-owner's orders, Walsh was fired and, like so many of those deemed by Fayed to be disloyal, was utterly squashed. Long before Walsh had been escorted from the building, Fayed had forgotten the casualty. There were so many, especially in the senior grades, that only the victims recalled the circumstances. The telephone taps were producing suspects and reasons for dismissal.

'Listen to her,' Fayed ordered Loftus. The target was Carol Peters, a successful merchandising executive and a casualty of Fayed's sudden, unexplained dislike. Days later the security chief returned. Peters had been overheard discussing with a dismissed employee where he might look for work. 'Find a reason to dismiss her,' Fayed demanded. Loftus returned satisfied. Overheard on Peters's telephone was her acceptance of an invitation to the opera from a supplier. 'That's against the rules,' pronounced Fayed, who had imposed an unwavering instruction that no employee was to accept any gifts or favours from contractors or suppliers. Conflicts of interest were outlawed unless approved by himself. 'Out,' he ordered.

Harrods' senior executives were told about the plan. Peters would be followed to the opera and fired the following day. Like so many decent Harrods employees, the executives faced an unpleasant choice. Either they could warn Peters and risk dismissal, or they could remain quiet, compromising their integrity. Bludgeoned by Fayed's witchcraft, all chose silence. Their lives with Fayed were too exciting and lucrative to bear the sacrifice even for a respected friend. Accepting Mu-Mu's money implied agreement with his methods. Fayed's plot passed unchallenged.

Accompanied by a personnel director, Loftus arrived in Peters' office and announced her dismissal: 'You will immediately gather your personal belongings, you are forbidden to speak to anyone and I will escort you from the building.' Humiliated and too fearful to plead that she had not consciously committed a wrong, Peters hurriedly shuffled her possessions into a green plastic bag. A pariah now, Fayed's victim was escorted into Knightsbridge and abandoned. Those left behind did not protest. Equally, those refusing to applaud Fayed's ploy on the ground that it was immoral feared accusations of disloyalty. Loftus had proved his loyalty. The reward was commensurate. 'Have you got my expenses?' Loftus had, like many others, learnt to ask.

'How much I pay you?' replied Fayed.

'Five hundred,' replied Loftus.

Fayed's hand disappeared into his pocket. Ten crisp fifties were peeled off a wodge.

'Thank you, sir,' said Loftus.

*

GIVING PRESENTS was Fayed's way of buying support. On his orders, dozens of Harrods hampers, some worth over £1,000, had been delivered to newspaper editors and City journalists. Others would be entertained at the Ritz. Driving around London one day just before Christmas were two bodyguards, delivering twenty-two white envelopes. Fayed knew no better way of finding and keeping friends. One of the envelopes was addressed to Tim Smith. On their return, the bodyguards were ordered to cash a cheque for £8,000 at the nearby Midland Bank. On Fayed's orders, the Papa Lima bodyguard team protecting Park Lane were to be be given £300 bonuses. Also at Fayed's suggestion, Macnamara had invited police officers at Vine Street station for drinks at Harrods. Some departed with a hamper and the chairman's thanks. In turn, Macnamara was welcomed at the police station's Christmas party. Despite his spotless record at Scotland Yard, Macnamara was becoming indoctrinated by a new credo. Objective when he had been recruited, he had been persuaded not to question Fayed's orders.

Bonhomie was certainly on Fayed's mind when he flew to Scotland that Christmas. As usual the Gulfstream had been packed with boxes of food personally selected in the Food Hall. A lorry with other supplies had been dispatched to the north. Heini and the three children had flown separately. His children were the only uncontrolled customers allowed in his store. Watching them run riot around the new Toy World, randomly choosing whatever they liked – from toy soldiers to pinball machines costing £2,000 – caused him genuine pleasure. Usually their haul was sent to Oxted by helicopter. This Christmas he had chosen the latest electric cars, costing £9,000 each, and electronic games among their presents. Mentally, everything had been ticked off as the Gulfstream landed at Inverness and he caught sight of the waiting helicopter for the final hop.

Unexpectedly, while climbing the four steps into the helicopter, his placid expression turned to rage. 'Where?' he screamed. 'Where pistachio?'

His bodyguards looked pained. 'No one told us,' they cried. Fear that his imminent 'bollocking' could lead to dismissals gripped the four men trained in deadly warfare. 'No one said you wanted nuts,' they pleaded.

Fayed stared contemptuously. 'Send Gulfstream. Now! Get me nuts.' Men accustomed to hide for days and nights in Ulster's mud to ambush terrorists scurried like helpless puppets. While one made frantic telephone calls to Harrods begging that bags of nuts – 'tons of 'em' – be sent immediately to Luton airport, the Gulfstream was ordered to return 'as fast as you fuggin' can' southwards. To avoid the loss of precious minutes at Luton, special clearances were negotiated for landing and take-off. Four hours later, as Fayed lay in his vast marble bath with gold taps, the helicopter landed at Balnagown's pad carrying its special cargo.

Conversion work on the castle had started. Balnagown's eight-foot-thick walls would be rebuilt and painted pink, the authentic colour to match the original sandstone, and the whole interior was being gutted and rebuilt. The mammoth and expensive undertaking gratified Fayed's eye for beauty and his lust to live, amid splendour, as a nobleman. His ambitions inevitably inspired boasts. Meeting a Scottish landowner, the Egyptian regaled him with stories about the excellent stag hunting across his estate. In reply, the Scotsman proudly admitted that the bag on his estate was 100 stags every year. That, he quietly believed, compared well with Balmoral's annual tally of 200. The royal family's shoot, not surprisingly, was considered the best in the country. 'How many head do you shoot in a year, Mr Al Fayed?' he innocently asked.

'Ten thousand,' replied Fayed without a blink.

Across Britain on Boxing Day families and friends meet for a convivial day's shooting. Since Fayed had invited no one, he was shooting duck alone with two bodyguards. Swinging his shotgun wildly, he blasted at two mallards. Both fell. 'How many you kill?' he asked.

'None, sir,' replied the guards self-interestedly. Two ducks lay on the ground.

'Bloody soldiers!' laughed Fayed, unaware that, while he had missed, the two men behind him, shooting simultaneously, had massaged his ego. Stacking the odds in his favour was natural for Fayed. Fishing in his loch had been simplified by the gillie regularly stocking the waters with 200 trout and placing two huge worms on the laird's hook before casting. This time, the shooting was interrupted by a high-pitched scream. Heini had arrived.

To outside observers, the Fayeds' relationship did not seem

one of conventional bliss. Gradually, the attractive, soft spoken former model had become anxious and slightly aggressive, disliking the presence of the bodyguards and the constraints on her life. Some detected a rift between Mohamed and Heini reflected in the absence of common interests and his restlessness to return to business. On this occasion, as so often, Heini was dissatisfied with a triviality. The following day, to prepare for the Harrods sale, Fayed returned to London. A brilliant campaign slogan – 'There's only one Sale. There is only one Harrods' – had attracted attention and Fayed added to the glamour by inviting a major celebrity to open the event. Tony Curtis, Larry Hagman and Diana Ross would be among his stars. Inevitably, the image belied reality.

'I need a manager for Harrods,' sighed Fayed. His confidant was Christoph Bettermann, the German manager of IMS, the Dubai salvage operator. 'Find me someone in Germany.' Fayed had tired of Paul Taylor. He was small and he lacked class. Image was everything and small people, he convinced himself, were inadequate people. Self-disdain influenced the Egyptian, who was just two inches taller than Taylor. Fayed's current faith was in Germans. Bettermann, an expert in the salvage of ships, was dispatched to find an expert in retailing. 'Here, have some spending money.' Fayed's hand dipped into the leather briefcase. His manicured fingers emerged clutching a wad of fifties. Momentarily, the smile disappeared from his eyes. Peeling off paper was an act. 'Buy clothes,' laughed the benefactor, handing over four crisp ones.

There was so much enjoyment as the donkey gushed, 'Thank you, Mohamed.'

Despite the inducement, Bettermann returned to London without any candidate. No one qualified was prepared to work for such a small business, he reported. 'Go to Japan,' ordered Fayed. Bettermann was to negotiate with Mitsukoshi the terms for franchising Harrods shops in Japan. Travelling with Clive de Boer, a young manager, Bettermann completed the negotiations and, on his return, reported to Fayed in Oxted. Sitting in the tent, Bettermann encouraged Fayed to consider de Boer as Taylor's successor. 'Nah,' said Fayed, unconvinced. 'Too young.' Trusting only Betterman, he made an unexpected offer. 'You come as holiday relief. For two weeks.' The absurdity of appointing a salvage expert to manage Harrods did not discourage Fayed. Bettermann was the missing son whom he trusted and could train. 'I'm not a retailer,' said Bettermann. 'Nor am I,' replied Fayed with unusual candour. He was, he confessed, a trader rather than a retailer. 'You'll get £2,000 extra.' The hand had already passed through the briefcase and the fingers held a white envelope. 'Pocket money,' he laughed. Forty crisp ones, Bettermann later counted. The training started immediately.

Daily, surrounded by bodyguards, Fayed walked his latest protégé through the store explaining the detail he expected. At the end of two weeks, the schooling was extended. Entranced by the challenge of managing the world's most famous store while commuting between Dubai and London, Bettermann was cast as Superman. Like so many anointed by Fayed's trust, he became convinced that only a great visionary, guided by consumate genius, could have recognized his own talent.

Sucking bedazzled employees into his orbit, securing their unconditional gratitude and neutering their independent judgement was Fayed's method of management. Achieving utter control of people, Fayed schemed, was won by lavishing cash and by a mixture of familiarity, remoteness and threats. But, to confirm his choice, he insisted that Bettermann live rent-free at 60 Park Lane. Eavesdropping on the telephone calls would confirm his loyalty. Sending him to the Ritz Hotel to check whether Frank Klein was selling rooms at unauthorized cheap rates would also compromise his employee's integrity. Initiating Bettermann into his world of surveillance by revealing the operations of the 'Greek Gestapo' and the telephone taps guaranteed that the German, like the others involved, performed his duties with unquestioning loyalty.

Bugging, bribing and constant surveillance had become, in

Fayed's increasingly insalubrious imagination, his secret weapon and protection against his enemies. The visual manifestation was the further transformation of Park Lane into a fortress. Vectors, ground sensor alarms and passive infrared detectors had been installed in additon to closed-circuit cameras, to cover every entrance, roof, window and wall. Every external door and the new internal double doors were reinforced to resist bullets and were connected to proximity switches activating an alarm in the Operations Room if any movement was detected. Access to his own quarters had been restricted further by new codes. The only possible intruder was Rowland's vitriol.

*

FAYED HAD GOOD REASON to fear Rowland. To undermine his foe, the Lonrho chief was inundating House of Fraser's staff at their homes with circulars and had scored a success. Surveillance had exposed a buyer in the Harrods menswear department offering to assist him. Knowing how Rowland had used bribes and blackmail in Africa, Fayed was understandably concerned to minimize other threats. His operations in Dubai were particularly endangered by the testimony of the twenty-eight witnesses to the DTI inspectors, and Dubai's new generation of bureaucrats, offended by Mahdi Al Tajir's wealth, had been influenced by local criticism of Fayed. The Maktoum brothers, the successors to Sheikh Rashid, he also knew, had been unamused by the unwelcome publicity arising out of his unsuccessful libel action against Tajir and his boasts to journalists and the inspectors that his genius and money had transformed the desert kingdom into a modern state. A personal visit to the Maktoums, he hoped, would safeguard IMS, the salvage company, and the Trade Centre, which were, thanks to the Gulf War, generating substantial tax-free profits. Those millions, vital for his financial survival because House of Fraser was losing money, were at risk if the Maktoum brothers terminated his special status.

Accompanied by Alison Bozek and Katie Manning, his secretaries, and Sydney Johnson, his valet, Fayed insisted that his arrival on the Gulfstream G3 at the airport on 4 May 1989 should resemble a state visit. Michael Cole, his new press spokesman, was sent ahead to negotiate his reception.

Born in 1943, Cole's recruitment had been a coup for Fayed. Employed by BBC TV News for twenty years, the prize-winning reporter had until recently reported as the Corporation's royal correspondent. Unfortunately, a betrayal by another journalist of his indiscreet mention of the Queen's Christmas message had caused a minor sensation and his reassignment to mundane reporting. Piqued, he had been receptive to Fayed's offer.

Cole had met Fayed while reporting for a thirty-minute television documentary on the Sotheby's sale of the Windsor possessions. While filming in Villa Windsor in Paris, he discovered that the *Daily Mail* had been allowed to borrow the Duke of Windsor's bed for the Ideal Home Exhibition. 'Have you considered what Her Majesty the Queen would think of that?' Cole asked Fayed in an urgent telephone call, anxious to protect his exclusive. 'She'd hardly approve.' Instantly, Fayed cancelled his agreement with the newspaper and subsequently appreciated that his image would be enhanced if the whole-some, well-spoken Englishman, trusted by BBC viewers, was appointed as his spokesman. For £80,000 a year, a high salary at the time, Fayed had hired the appearance of respectablility. 'He can deal with the English,' he said. 'He speaks the language so well. And the English like his type.'

Fayed dreaded visiting Dubai. Not only was the town boring, but he feared arrest or even murder. In these lawless Arab states, he persuaded himself, a man could disappear at the wave of a hand. Normally unwillingly to take physical risks, too much money was at stake not to attempt reconcilia-tion. Although the identity of his prospective assailant was never disclosed, he had ordered Mike Waller and five body-guards to bring substantial quantities of surveillance equipment and had arranged for the loan of guns. Michael Cole, he hoped, would deploy the same efficient energy which he had previously exerted for BBC News to win the Maktoums' agreement to two symbolic gestures: that Fayed's jet could be parked in the rulers' personal hangar and that the Maktoums' yellow Rolls-Royce with the memorable numberplate '50' would be provided during his visit. After hearing Cole's satisfactory report, Fayed, ensconced in a suite at the Intercontinental Abu Dhabi unsuccessfully offering to sell the rulers an aluminium smelter plant, was confident that the style of his arrival would help protect his investments. In his luggage was an oil portrait of Sheikh Rashid leading his people into the desert. The formal presentation to his sons, he hoped, would pacify the rulers.

As his aircraft taxied towards the rulers' hangar, Fayed saw that the preparations had gone awry. Michael Cole was waving his arms at stony-faced soldiers unwilling to allow the Rolls-Royce to drive on to the tarmac, while Mike Waller gesticulated helplessly, lacking his two-way radio. The radio equipment, it transpired, had been confiscated on arrival. Yet Fayed's eventual journey in the yellow Rolls-Royce, past the Trade Centre, surely the Eiffel Tower of the Gulf, to his compound on Chicago Beach, reinvigorated his spirits. On the eight-acre site, a gift from Sheikh Rashid, Bettermann had built twelve four-bedroom villas, surrounded by green lawns, with spectacular views across the blue sea. The best two villas were of course Fayed's. The lawn sprinklers were immediately turned off. Their water was interfering with the security sensors, installed just before his arrival. His private pool would remained unused. Fayed feared germs in the water. Within the first hour, a former bodyguard of Sheikh Rashid on Fayed's payroll arrived and emptied the contents of a pillow case on to the table. Three guns – a 38 Special, a Luger and a Walther PPK 7.62mm – gleamed as the Arab placed ammunition and magazines alongside. 'You must make sure I am 110 per cent safe,' Fayed ordered Waller. The former Special Branch officer assented.

'The threat is greater here than in the UK.' For Fayed it was imperative that any potential assailant should be shot dead. Such was his control over all his employees that they shrank from questioning his orders. Whether they would perform the ultimate act was less certain.

Fayed's arrival that night at the Maktoums' mansion was given added drama by the presence of his bodyguards. As far as he was concerned, one potentate was visiting another. His intermediary, Jabber Abdullah, Rashid's trusted bodyguard, had arranged the meeting. After the traditionally warm welcome by Sheikh Maktoum al Maktoum and the presentation of the painting, Fayed felt sufficiently confident to ignore the criticism of his false claims to the DTI inspectors and violently attacked his Dubaian critics. Maktoum hardly responded, but two days later Fayed received the answer to his complaint.

On the orders of Humeid bin Drai, the voluble chief of protocol, the Rolls-Royce was withdrawn and replaced by a hired Mercedes. Bin Drai's orders frightened Fayed. Until recently, the garrulous Dubaian had visited him regularly in London and Oxted and had enjoyed the women provided. Bin Drai had also profited as Costain's representative in Dubai, a sinecure which Fayed had arranged. Yet suddenly his friend was acting like a stranger. Clearly, the rulers had intimated that Fayed was to be punished. 'You're vulnerable here,' Bettermann warned. 'You haven't a local ID card or a licence to trade.' Fayed's riposte was to order Michael Cole to film a video portraying himself as the architect of Dubai's prosperity. But, hard though Cole tried to coax Fayed's employees in Dubai to attest on camera to the Egyptian's genius, the accolades markedly lacked spontaneity. Fayed, the self-proclaimed architect of Dubai's revolution, was being airbrushed from history.

11

Conspiracies and Concubines

'LIES, LIES, LIES!' thundered Fayed. The walls of his tent on his Oxted lawn seemed to flap in the turbulence sparked by its occupant's rage. Embarrassment, humiliation and fury continued to contort his features. 'He bribed someone to get it,' he added, accurately enough. Gripping the telephone, Fayed had been horrified to learn of Rowland's latest coup. His foe, he was being told, had printed that Thursday morning a special edition of the *Observer* publishing the inspectors' report. Under the huge headline, 'Exposed: the Phoney Pharaoh', there was a damaging opening sentence which stated that the Fayeds had been officially condemned for obtaining House of Fraser 'by fraud and deceit'. That he would read the inspectors' damning conclusions about his dishonesty for the first time in Rowland's propaganda sheet compounded his wrath. Once again, the Lonrho executive had outwitted the Egyptian.

Only twenty-six days earlier, on 4 March 1989, Lord Young had faced down loud protests against his refusal to publish the report. 'There is clear evidence of wrongdoing,' he told a radio interviewer, 'and publication would prejudice police inquiries.' All Fayed's efforts to prevent publication seemed to have succeeded. Then, inexplicably, Rowland had managed to acquire a supposedly secret document. The government had been sullied by an impudent, malicious plot.

Fayed's life was once again in turmoil. Across London, everyone was talking about Rowland's coup, grabbing copies of the *Observer* handed out on the streets before the government's law officers could obtain an injunction. By then it was too late. Rowland's vitriol had been officially validated. The serene enjoyment of Fayed's life, the mystery and secrecy which had given him immunity from censure, was lost for ever. Nothing had prepared him for this unsparing humiliation of constant battle with an army of enemies. While most mortals, stunned by the publication of the inspectors' censure, would have slunk into obscurity, forsaking the honour of welcoming royalty and mixing with celebrities, and expecting to surrender the royal warrants hanging proudly in his name in his office, Fayed resolved to flaunt himself unabashed. Thick-skinned and tenacious, he knew no shame. He would silence his critics and survive.

Having summoned Michael Cole, and Tim Bell, a fashionable and influential public relations expert, to orchestrate a counter-offensive, his first performance was to pose in a Harrods restaurant, surrounded by boy scouts, wearing a boy scout's uniform, including the cap, and eating ham sandwiches. 'Only God can take Harrods away from me,' Fayed told journalists, playing the defeat as a victory. 'I paid cash for the store and my cheque did not bounce. I own this place. I am making plans to be buried on top of the building. I will have the tomb on the roof.' Stirred by his own defiance, he challenged the government: 'Does anyone have the right to ask you from where you get your money?' The answer was yes but Fayed was unconcerned. He had declared war against the corrupt system which had allowed Rowland illegally to obtain the inspectors' report. Quietly, in Park Lane, a group of bodyguards were ordered to transport several black plastic bags of documents to Oxted. 'Burn them,' they were told. Before the flames destroyed the papers, Tony Evans glimpsed bank statements, correspondence with foreign companies and letters on House of Commons stationery.

Telephone calls to Greer and Hamilton reassured Fayed that the crucifying publicity had been offset by hostility towards Rowland, especially for his wanton destruction of the *Observer*'s independence. In parliament, Dale Campbell-Savours, the Labour MP, gathered substantial support criticizing Rowland, while Buckingham Palace confined itself to a discreet request that Fayed absent himself from that year's Windsor Horse Show to avoid embarrassing the queen. The royal warrants would not be withdrawn and the celebrities would not shun the shopkeeper. Officially, it appeared, there was little to fear. 'The dogs bark,' scoffed Fayed, resolved to display no weakness, 'but the caravan passes on. Why should I raise my blood pressure? Let them scream and bark and howl. We shall be around for one thousand years.'

The dogs continued to bark. Every week, quoting the stolen DTI report, Fayed was lambasted in the *Observer* as a fraudster and tax cheat. The accusation about the Fayeds' taxes hit a vulnerable target. Rowland's complaint had alerted the Inland Revenue that Fayed, resident in Britain since 1964, had not paid British income tax. In reply, Fayed claimed that while living in London he had not been 'domiciled' in the UK, which required a minimum stay of 180 days. The explanation was deemed unsatisfactory. In the global tax settlement now negotiated with the Inland Revenue for the three brothers and Dodi to limit British income tax, it was agreed that Harrods dividends could be remitted to Alfayed, another offshore company in Liechtenstein, and taxes would be paid on money brought back into Britain. That annual amount, subject to income tax, would be regularly negotiated. In settlement in the late 1980s of unpaid past taxes, the Fayeds agreed to repay about £20 million. To protect their financial affairs from future investigation, they created a new layer of ownership. AITSA, the Liechtenstein company, was made into a subsidiary of two other companies, Cenpar in Panama and Altrafin Investments in the British Virgin Islands. The Fayeds' true wealth and debts had become impossible to determine.

Another of Rowland's glossy brochures touched another nerve. Titled *House of Commons*, Rowland published an open letter to Tim Smith, attacking the Conservative politician as Fayed's lackey. Although Rowland did not know that Smith had received any payments from Fayed, he had visited the Beaconsfield politician as a genuine constituent to warn about his MP's unhelpful partisanship. Alarmed, especially by the DTI's revelations, Smith told Fayed that his support was terminated: 'I am getting a lot of hassle from other colleagues.' To his colleagues, he expressed his 'shock' that the Fayed brothers had lied about their origins. The loss of one politician was serious for Fayed but not as terrifying as the latest spectacle of Rowland's power. In retaliation for a hostile bid for Lonrho mounted by Alan Bond, an Australian tycoon, Rowland had singlehandedly pushed Bond into personal bankruptcy and had obliterated the Australian's worldwide empire. Fayed feared that he, a minnow compared to Bond, was vulnerable to similar demolition. His defences against Rowland's plan to force the government to expropriate House of Fraser were weakened when Derry Irvine QC advised that an application to the courts for judicial review of the inspectors' report would fail. His only public friend was Neil Hamilton, lashing out at Fayed's enemies in parliament. In gratitude, Fayed paid Hamilton more money and offered the politician a holiday at Balnagown.

Pleasingly, extra money was not the only way to secure the loyalty of his staff. Both Michael Cole and Royston Webb, although given hefty increases in their salaries, believed in their employer's honesty. Both intensified their efforts to establish him in the media as a victim of injustice. Cole's appointment had proved especially opportune. 'Mohamed wants this done,' he would effuse, his hair perfectly styled, injecting urgency among his staff to translate Fayed's wishes into action. Educated and informed, Cole enjoyed writing stinging rebukes in Fayed's name to newspapers and politicians. The former journalist's apt phrase offered for quotation steadily humanized the expletive-uttering Arab in newspaper columns. 'I am inspired by a man who was the victim of severe racial prejudice,' he carefully repeated from Cole's script after buying for £25,300 at Christie's the Olympic medals of Harold Abrahams, the Jewish hero of *Chariots of Fire*. 'I am fascinated by the story of a man subjected to great prejudice and English snobbery yet who triumphed.' Under Cole's aegis, he embarked upon a concerted campaign to win public approval. Few ploys were more important than the invitation to 150 journalists, MPs and the Earl Spencer and his wife Raine to visit Paris on 10 December 1989 and celebrate the completed renovation of the Windsor villa. The Spencers, especially Raine, had become unquestioning allies, always eager to accept Fayed's hospitality.

In Fayed's scenario, Jacques Chirac, the mayor of Paris, would greet the guests and present the Plaque de Paris to 'the Man of Vision'. Unfortunately, Chirac seemed unwilling to comply, partly because on 31 January 1989 the appeal court had confirmed Frank Klein's conviction for the unauthorized modifications to the Ritz, imposed a 5,000 franc fine and ordered Fayed to restore the building as previously. Once again, Fayed overlooked the judgement and boasted about his investment in the hotel's reconstruction, although the amount he claimed to have spent varied widely between $75 million in July 1986, $30 million in 1989 and $150 million in 1992. 'Tell that bastard to come,' a bodyguard overheard Fayed hiss at Frank Klein. The innuendo was unmistakable: Chirac owed Fayed. Some insiders would say that the contrary was true. Fayed had secured a soft loan to renovate the villa, although it proved to be inadequate. The mutuality of interest between Fayed and Chirac guaranteed Klein's eventual success, but many of the Egyptian's guests remarked that the mayor appeared distinctly uneasy during the celebration. Fayed ignored Chirac's mood. All that mattered was the mayor's presence for the photographers. Those in London who had rejected the hospitality would receive Harrods hampers and a souvenir of Fayed's success from Michael Cole. Half of Fleet

Street, it seemed, were receiving hampers that Christmas from Cole. The effort stemmed the poison. Many journalists, despite the report, remained sympathetic to his cause.

*

OVER CHRISTMAS in Scotland, irritated that the initiative always rested with his enemy, Fayed impatiently awaited Rowland's next move. Also on his mind was the fate of Dodi, a boy whom he loved but whose behaviour aroused his fury. Neither the best qualities nor the worst sins of the father had been visited upon his son. Unambitious and lacking any worthwhile skills, Dodi could be caring, unvindictive and generous. But bedevilled by his own fantasies, his virtues were outweighed by his colossal extravagances, which even his father, usually stricken by guilt, found intolerable.

His son's ten-month marriage to Suzanne Gregard had collapsed amicably in October 1985. Fayed, it was rumoured among the Khashoggis, had paid the woman $1 million to settle without a court battle. Returning to London, Dodi had reverted to his old habits, charging £60,000 every month on his Platinum American Express card for lunches and dinners with celebrities, drunken nights at Tramp and Annabel's, after which he regularly remained in bed with girls until lunchtime, and for frequent trips to St Tropez. Among the women he had taken on board the *Cujo*, his converted coastguard cutter, was Brooke Shields, wearing Dodi's swimming costume but making clear, like most of the famous actresses in his company, that theirs was a strictly platonic relationship. Confiscating his credit cards, Fayed knew, had little effect: Dodi would simply stage a disappearing act. In America where he could indulge his passion for a macho image, his insecure son had become intensely possessive about those women whom he desired. Subjecting them to his strange fantasies, he intimidated one with the Beretta revolver he kept near his bed and impressed others with the constant presence of a bodyguard. Several times, the Beverly Hills Hotel had complained that his son, having failed to pay his bills at Bungalow Nine, had vanished. Intoxicated by wealth, Dodi never changed. One telephone call to the suite at the Pierre in New York unearthed his fugitive, drugged son and his meek return home. 'No one pick up Dodi at Heathrow,' commanded Fayed. At the last moment, he always relented, but the consequences were predictable. Back in London, the cycle of night clubs and girls recommenced. Too often, Dodi disappeared again, abandoning a girl in his Park Lane flat. 'Tell her the decorators are coming,' yelled Fayed to clear the woman out.

Even the father accepted that his domination over Dodi had created a purposeless, terrified son. Sending him to a London psychiatrist, he hoped that the twenty-four-year-old might shed his cocaine-induced delusions and become respectable. Summoning Graham Jones, the fifty-year-old Australian chief financial officer of House of Fraser Holdings, who tactfully told Fayed exactly what he wanted to hear, he ordered that Dodi was to be taught accountancy and retailing. A special office on the fifth floor was furnished and a detailed plan of education was compiled by the executives and the personnel director. To protect Dodi from exhaustion, he would be expected at Harrods only two days a week. But during the second week, hearing monologues about balance sheets, inventories and cash flow, Dodi's eyes glazed over. Designing men's clothes, he suggested, might be a more exciting way to justify his recent appointment as a member of the Harrods board. 'Where the fuggin' hell is he?' shouted Fayed when his son failed to appear in the third week. 'He's fired!' Dodi, it was agreed, was unsuited to becoming a store magnate.

Jones, by then disliked by Ali for lunching too frequently, accepting excessive entertainment and, irritatingly, being discovered with a woman on his office floor, was finally targeted by Mohamed. 'Fire him,' he ordered. One hour later he revoked his edict. Dismissing a finance director, he was told, would alarm his City bankers, who were owed £901 million. Instead, Jones was appointed the director of corporate strategy and planning, tasked with searching for acquisitions. His most important purchase was a new venture for Dodi.

Walking up and down his Park Lane appartment wearing a baseball hat and waving a large Cuban cigar, Dodi ignored the bank statement on his desk announcing a credit of £1.75. In anger, his father had as usual cut off his son's allowances, and Dodi was living on his credit cards until the flow of cash was restored. Graham Jones was listening. 'I was speaking last night in Tramp's to Tim Jefferies,' said Dodi, referring to the millionaire husband of Koo Stark, 'and he told me about a Ferrari business for sale. That's just what I want.' Dodi had recently bought a Ferrari Testarossa, which was parked in the garage at Park Lane alongside his two Aston Martins.

Ferrari cars had enjoyed a decade of extraordinary popularity, and some second-hand Ferraris were selling for the same price as new cars. Many Ferraris were serviced and resold through Modena, a showroom and garage in Horley, Surrey, established by a group of owners. Dodi's interest in Modena had soared when Nick Mason, a drummer in the Pink Floyd rock band, was revealed to be one of its principal shareholders. 'It's a good deal,' Dodi gushed to Christoph Bettermann. 'Prices will go up and we'll make profits on the cars in stock.' His excitement was endorsed by his cousin Mudi Fayed, the eldest son of Salah, the Fayeds' latest candidate as a potential successor to Mohamed and Ali. Mohamed Fayed was convinced of the investment value of classic cars. Recently, he had spent £1 million on Rolls-Royces which were garaged at Oxted. Acting on those orders, Graham Jones began negotiating the purchase of Modena.

'Why are we buying this company?' Royston Webb asked Jones.

'Dodi wants it,' replied Jones.

'Is it in good shape?' asked Webb.

'Very good. The stock is undervalued.'

'You're sure? If anything goes wrong with Dodi involved, you'll carry the can.'

Jones smiled. He had commissioned a report by Peat Marwick, the auditors. Peat had validated Modena's accounts. Although the auditors had included a caveat that the accounts for three months of 1989 were 'not available', there appeared to be no cause for suspicion.

On the eve of signing the deal, Mohamed Fayed became nervous. Instinctively, he disliked the deal. The car business was feckless; his son was not a businessman; and House of Fraser's declining turnover showed that the country was heading towards recession. Modena was nothing more than an unauthorized second-hand dealer and Ferraris were overvalued. He wanted to abandon the deal, not least because his own finances were deteriorating. Ali agreed. 'Dodi', he shouted at his elder brother in anger, 'is too stupid. He can't run a business. His Testarossa cost £145,000 and he can't resell it for more than £120,000.' Dodi's pleas, however, were unusually persistent. Reassured by Graham Jones that Modena's assets were guaranteed, Mohamed recanted. Borrowing £7 million against IMS's assets and future earnings over the following three years, he signed the deal.

Days after the purchase, the truth about Modena's unaudited accounts for the three-month gap erupted into the open. Over £2 million had been removed by a director. The company was not only grossly overvalued, it was possibly worthless.

'Robbed! I've been fuggin' robbed!' Fayed bellowed. Borrowed money had been lost. Everyone was a culprit, except himself. Suspecting everyone of fraud, his desire for vengeance was uncontrollable. Dodi was hit first. Resenting his son's recent credit card expenditure showing that over £100,000 had been wasted entertaining Bruce Willis, Joel Silver and other Hollywood types in an extraordinary splurge at the Byblos Hotel in St Tropez and in London's clubs, he ordered his cowering son, 'Cards. Give me your fuggin' cards. No more.' Dodi was grounded. Penniless. 'He's gone ballistic,' Fayed's minions shuddered.

Fayed's monster venom was directed at his employee.

'Jones', he screamed, 'took bribes. Get him out!' Hurriedly throwing his personal possessions into a black plastic bag, Jones was escorted out of the building. Quietly, however, recognizing that Jones was not entirely to blame, Royston Webb responded to the dismissed executive's plea of poverty. Jones would be loaned £500,000, much more than he was entitled to under his contact. 'I'm so grateful,' gushed Jones to Webb. 'I'll always support you.' Pledges of loyalty were of no interest to Mohamed Fayed. Jones, he was convinced, was not an incompetent man who had made a mistake but a conspirator with Modena's directors to defraud the Fayeds. Prejudice rather than provable facts influenced Fayed's belief. Jones, the source of his embarrassment, could not be allowed to escape unpunished. He would ruthlessly persecute the offender. His weapon was John Macnamara.

As Fayed's appetite for control and revenge increased, Macnamara had become indispensable. After twenty-eight years' service at Scotland Yard, Macnamara's network of contacts throughout Britain's police forces and private detective agencies smoothed his access to the most confidential information about any Briton, especially from the files of the national police computer. Recruits to House of Fraser were increasingly approved only after Macnamara had checked the applicant's background on the police computer. His approaches for assistance to serving policemen were greeted with the respect which an honest, retired senior Scotland Yard officer could expect. Those police officers were unaware that Macnamara, susceptible to Fayed's generosity and only too ready to accept his employer's complaints of persecution, had compromised his professional judgement when it came to assessing the credibility of an accusation. Accordingly, when Macnamara contacted Guildford police on 29 January 1990 alleging that Graham Jones had been involved in a fraud, Fayed's security officer was believed. Suspiciously, Jones had also disappeared. In fact, he had flown home to Australia. In his absence, a note was filed. Fayed's anger about Jones festered, but remained a sideshow compared to his new hostility towards the government.

*

THROUGH SKILFUL DETECTION, Macnamara had obtained a tape of a conversation in a pub between Tim Hutchings of Network Security and a serving Fraud Squad officer. The policeman was recorded admitting that he had given Rowland the DTI inspectors' report. Forensic examination had confirmed that Rowland had indeed used copy Number 26 of the report, which had been delivered to the Fraud Squad. Never had Fayed imagined that Britain's police were so dishonest.

A telephone call from a German arms dealer shortly afterwards revealed that Rowland had intended to post 1,000 leather-bound copies of the DTI report from Bangkok to Britain. The German told Macnamara that, since Rowland had failed to pay the agreed £30,000 for the copies, he would sell his evidence to Fayed. To link Rowland with the theft, Royston Webb and Macnamara flew to Thailand in November 1989, protected by Mike Waller from threats, they believed, of murder by the German. Their operation ended in farce. The German refused to sell his information and Waller disappeared, reported by Macnamara as 'kidnapped'. Hours later, Waller returned after a night's drinking with the German in Bangkok's clubs. Evincing a talent for turning an innocent misjudgement into scandal and conspiracy, Macnamara denounced Waller to Fayed. Waller was fired, while Macnamara, awarded the epithet, 'Mac the Knife', slipped into Fayed's inner circle.

Macnamara had good reason to believe that the dossier he had handed to Scotland Yard about Rowland's conspiracy, supported by the tape recording of Detective Inspector Kenneth Morgan's confession, would ruffle feathers. But, to Fayed's surprise, there was no reaction. Rowland's contempt for the law was ignored. 'He's the Al Capone of the City,' declared Fayed, using Michael Cole's imagery. Despite Hamilton, Hordern and the other MPs on his payroll pressing Nicholas Ridley, the new secretary of state at the DTI, to suppress the inspectors' report, its official publication had become inevitable. In anticipation, Fayed paid Greer £13,333 to care for his interests until 30 April 1990, showed his personal gratitude to Hamilton by agreeing that the MP and his wife could stay at his private apartment in Paris and prepared for a familiar ritual, a celebration of the anniversary of his purchase of Harrods, to coincide with the report's publication. On 12 March 1989, five days after the 752-page document was released, 500 guests were invited to a party in the Georgian Restaurant. Only 150 of the faithful arrived, including the Earl and Countess Spencer, Jocelyn Stevens, Sir Peter Hordern MP and retained bankers and lawyers. Undaunted by the snub, Fayed repeated his current mantra, 'We're here and we're going to stay here for the next thousand years.'

Despite the embarrassment of banner headlines repeating the inspectors' pulverizing verdict, Fayed had cause for relief. Thanks to his loyal MPs' pressure, Sir Patrick Mayhew, the attorney general, had announced that there was insufficient evidence to prosecute the Fayeds. Two officers of Scotland Yard's Fraud Squad had flown to Cairo, sat in the sunshine by a hotel pool and returned to London. Fayed's lies, the director of public prosecutions had decided, were not criminal. The same afternoon, Ridley, an unusually unsmooth secretary of state at the DTI, resisted ninety minutes of fierce barracking in the Commons for refusing to disqualify the Fayeds as directors and establish a benchmark for business morality. Lazily calling the affair 'a freak', he told David Ashby, who demanded the Fayeds' deportation as 'undesirable aliens', 'I am not prepared to give the reasons for the decision I arrived at.' Obeying the DTI's lawyers' brief to prevaricate, he added, 'The allegations in the report haven't been substantiated in a court of law.' Ashby, who would subsequently be humiliated by newspaper accusations that he was a liar and a covert homosexual, was dissatisfied. 'There is a deep sense of frustration', he complained, 'that these crooks should be allowed to get away with it . . . We don't want these crooks.' His condemnation of the government's impassivity was endorsed by the House of Commons Trade and Industry Committee: 'It is especially scandalous that the taxpayer has had to pay £1.5 million for the House of Fraser inquiry.'

Fayed felt no gratitude for his escape. He had long ceased to care about parliament. After twenty-one meetings with Hamilton, nineteen with Smith and innumerable conversations with Greer, he decided that he could expect nothing more for his money. 'I am a taxpayer in this country,' said Fayed, inventing a new mantra, 'I have brought £600 million to this country. I am employing thousands of people. I am sacrificing everything for Britain.' The notion of 'sacrifice', an invention of Cole's, pleased Fayed. No one else equated earning millions in profits with 'sacrifice', but the Egyptian blithely did so. He assumed that when he, as a multi-millionaire, spoke, an audience listened. He also assumed that British politics was utterly corrupt. Practically every politician who spoke in his favour had been paid, and he suspected that the critical MPs were funded by Rowland. 'Investigate him,' he ordered whenever he read of an MP demanding retribution. Teddy Taylor, the Conservative MP, was placed under particular surveillance. 'He must be paid by Tiny,' spat Fayed, without a scintilla of evidence, as Taylor repeatedly voiced his condemnation in parliament. Richard New was ordered to comb Taylor's post and telephone records, to see in particular if he could find a record of a call from the politician to Rowland followed by a call to a Swiss bank. New's failure, unsurprising since Taylor was innocent, did not comfort Fayed. Taylor and Tiny's other politicians were, he concluded, just too clever to be exposed – with the exception of Edward du Cann. Paid £400,000 per annum, the ringleader in the House of Commons proved vulnerable.

In 1974, du Cann had been criticized as 'incompetent' by a DTI report investigating the politician's activities as a director of the bankrupt Keyser Ullman bank. For some time he had been on the verge of personal bankruptcy. Unable to repay a personal debt of £516,000, he owed the Inland Revenue £511,000, and had issued several cheques which had bounced. Fifteen years later, Richard New discovered that du Cann had just resigned as the deputy chairman of Homes Assured, a small finance company which had crashed owing £6 million. Two directors were charged with fraud but du Cann, innocent of any crime, had even escaped censure. The hypocrisy, Fayed protested, was unjust. While du Cann had aggressively lobbied for Fayed's punishment, the politician was, Fayed contended, himself dishonest. Worse, Fayed found it difficult to publish his assertion. In the aftermath of the DTI report's publication, even those journalists who had been amenable in return for a bottle of champagne, a side of smoked salmon and a white envelope delivered to their homes by a bodyguard were becoming unwilling to use his latest offerings. Although du Cann's bad judgement was finally published, forcing his resignation as Lonrho's chairman, Fayed was too tarnished to win credibility.

'Give up the battle, Mohamed,' urged Royston Webb, masterminding the anti-Rowland campaign. 'You've got Harrods and the rest. Just enjoy it and forget Tiny.' Fayed was unconvinced. So often when Webb sought to reason with Fayed, there was an interruption. On this occasion, two of the store-owner's children burst into his office. Clasping their booty snatched in Toy World, they danced through the office towards their father. Hugging both, Fayed sat on the floor playing. The public's image of the liar evaporated amid his yelps and laughs. Webb had lost the opportunity to argue for peace. The distraction was shortlived. Ten minutes later, weary of the disruption, Fayed's obsessive mistrust revived. Although he authorized the release of Michael Cole's homily in his name – 'Life is too short to be angry. If God is there to bless you, if you do good, you hurt no one, life will be kind' – his hunger for revenge was a permanent affliction.

*

SNOOPING HAD BECOME a major preoccupation. Security cameras around 60 Park Lane had spotted an Espace van. By chance, undercover journalists researching an article for the *Mail on Sunday* about 'The Bugging of Britain' were taping Fayed's own conversation inside the building transmitted by a concealed 400 MHz radio. Fayed exploded with anger when told of the discovery. Convinced that the journalists were employed by Rowland, he told Macnamara to improve his eavesdropping operation.

'Send over Del,' ordered Macnamara. 'I've got a job for him.' 'Del' was Derek Healey, a veteran of the Oman War who, with Andy Black, planted invisible bugs in telephones, in lamps or under desks for Fayed's operations. As an additional refinement, the waiting rooms in Fayed's offices were also bugged. Visitors would be asked to wait, especially before business discussions, to allow Fayed to eavesdrop on their discussions in the hope that they would reveal their negotiating tactics.

'I want videos too,' ordered Fayed. The latest miniature cameras were installed. Secret filming was a natural progression in a huge security operation. Ever more greedy for information, Fayed told Macnamara to plant bugs outside beyond the confines of his own buildings: in the rooms used by the Brompton Place Residents Association, whose protests to Kensington Council about Harrods' developments irritated Fayed; in the homes of contractors; in the telephones of those being sued to recover the Modena payments; and, most importantly, in Rowland's premises. Fayed's justification was self-defence against a conspiracy, a notion fuelled by Francesca Pollard.

Under Bob Loftus's protection, Pollard had been provided with a van and the presence of two bodyguards to conduct her guerrilla operations. With the public unaware of Fayed's sponsorship, Pollard's solitary protests – carrying slogans on billboards and distributing leaflets denouncing Rowland and Lonrho, all written by Michael Cole, Royston Webb and

Richard New – had won some public sympathy. But it was her regular telephone calls, reporting alarming examples of Rowland's chicanery, which fed Fayed's suspicions. 'I've just got evidence that X is being paid by Lonrho,' she would say with certainty, adding another target for his vendetta.

Heading his new hit list was Dr Barry Rider, an adviser to the Select Committee on Trade and Industry investigating the House of Fraser and suspected to be sympathetic to Rowland. 'Get her to sign letter,' Fayed told New. The letter to the Committee's chairman, written by New, complained that Rider's appointment was 'simply staggering' since he had been dismissed the previous year from the crime unit of the Commonwealth Secretariat for 'alleged fraud, fiddling expenses and threatening staff'. The denunciation, signed by Pollard, was untrue, as was her letter, written by Fayed's staff, that Henry Brooke QC, the DTI inspector, had been compliant towards Rowland because Lonrho's 'dirty tricks department had happy snaps of the comings and goings of poor Henry in relation to a certain "club" – of the nature usually referred to by the tabloids as "rough trade"'. Eagerly, Fayed authorized the defamations, including letters sent to Margaret Thatcher, since Pollard's gung-ho activities – 'I'm now off to demonstrate outside the House of Commons' – reassured the store-owner that he was striking at the heart of a rotten establishment. It was the start of Fayed's campaign against the Conservative government.

For Fayed, simple but true explanations for events were inadequate. Rather, he favoured Pollard's convenient but sinister interpretation for the commissioning of the DTI report. 'You're the victim of a conspiracy,' she told Fayed. 'It's all about a secret link between Michael Howard and Tiny Rowland.' Fayed's mind was filled with infantile conspiracies.

Unimpressed by the governance of Britain, Fayed had become convinced that the DTI investigation had been sanctioned only because of a bribe paid by Tiny Rowland. After all, he reasoned, if Norman Tebbit and Leon Brittan had rejected Rowland's requests for an inquiry, why would Paul Channon reverse the policy unless for a bribe? His own experience made this fanciful scenario plausible to him. Rowland's objections in March 1985 to Fayed buying House of Fraser had been neutralized by his own paid contacts; and in 1989 his team of paid politicians and Greer had influenced Lord Young to ignore the inspectors' report and to refuse a reference to the Monopolies Commission. That decision had been upheld by Ridley only after Hamilton's latest approach. Money had bought him access. Therefore, it was plain to Fayed that just as Rowland's money had influenced the inspectors during the investigation, his money had also initiated the investigation. Bribes explained everything. Yet his conspiracy theory would have been stillborn if the supposedly bribed minister had been Channon, an ineffectual, wealthy member of the Guinness family. Only because the junior DTI minister responsible for corporate affairs was Michael Howard could the jigsaw be completed.

Pollard revealed that Harry Landy, her uncle employed by Rowland after his conviction as a fraudster, was Michael Howard's second cousin (Landy is Howard's mother's first cousin.) New's research revealed that Howard, the son of a Romanian Jewish refugee who had changed the family name from Hecht, had grown up in the same Welsh village as the Landys. That was sufficient for Fayed to construct a sinister scenario of Rowland using Landy to bribe Howard to initiate the DTI investigation.

'Keep a watch on Howard,' Fayed ordered his investigators, New and Macnamara. To discover his private home, Bill Dunt, a bodyguard, was ordered to follow the minister from Whitehall on a motorbike. After establishing the address in West London, a round-the-clock surveillance operation was mounted to discover how often the minister met his cousin. 'If Howard can change his name from Hecht,' he scoffed to himself, 'why does the DTI condemn me for adding Al to my name?' Attempts were made to intercept Howard's post and pry into his financial affairs. Publicly, with the help of his obedient entourage – Royston Webb, John Macnamara, Richard New, Brian Basham, Mark Griffiths and, especially, Michael Cole, the voice of the BBC – he launched a defamatory campaign against Howard.

Endorsing Fayed's version as the truth, Cole began seducing chosen journalists with a credible scenario. Howard and Landy, explained Cole tirelessly, had grown up as childhood friends in the same street of a small Jewish community in Llanelli, South Wales. The Landys, he continued, had helped Howard's father to escape from Romania before the outbreak of the Second World War and Landy's brother, a rabbi, had married Howard's parents. Hence, Landy was Rowland's perfect vehicle to pay the £500,000 bribe into Howard's suspected Liechtenstein account. All that was missing was the proof, but Howard's silence, despite Pollard's staged confrontations outside Howard's country home, orchestrated after Cole had alerted local newspapers and TV companies, reinforced Fayed's belief that his suspicion was the truth. In Fayed's world, it only required one of his festering suspicions out of a hundred to be proved correct, and the other ninety-nine were deemed automatically to be true. That single confirmation occurred in mid-June 1990.

Fayed heard from Rosemary Thorne, Harrods' financial director, that Graham Jones had just telephoned. Not suspecting that she would feel compelled to report the call, Jones revealed that he had returned to Britain and sought a private meeting with her. Fayed now suspected Jones not only of fraud involving the Modena purchase, but also of joining forces with Rowland. The evidence was a private letter, sent by Jones to the governor of the Bank of England, denouncing the Fayeds' management of Harrods Bank. Fayed had obtained a copy from a journalist whom Jones had mistakenly trusted.

Fayed knew that his management of the small but profitable bank, serving fewer than 8,000 customers, was vulnerable. Several times, he had used 'pressure and harassment' to persuade

Rosemary Thorne to accept a £100 million deposit by the sultan, which was larger than authorized by the Bank of England. 'I can't do that,' Thorne had insisted on each occasion. 'It's illegal.' Occasionally, she had complained about Fayed's pressure to Graham Jones and Jeremy Nordberg, the personnel director. Although Fayed had always retreated, the disputes and the sensitive information which Jones possessed about House of Fraser's finances were cause for alarm.

Fayed's predicament was worse than he imagined. In April 1990, Jones had contacted Rowland and, in return for an initial payment of £100,000 deposited in an account in Liechtenstein, had promised to provide not only confidential information about Fayed's finances but also, posing as an honest, outraged employee, to complain to the Bank of England's supervision department. Two months later, Jones had returned to London to approach Fayed's main bankers, including Ernie Cole at Samuel Montagu and Clive Badcock at the Midland Bank. Both bankers had earlier complained to Jones about the Fayeds' finances. Furtively, Jones warned the bankers that House of Fraser was indeed nearly insolvent. Exploiting that mischief, Rowland, who eventually paid Jones £555,418, published and circulated to his 40,000 personalities a new brochure, *A financial assessment of the consolidated personal and commercial interests of the Fayeds*, describing Fayed's financial plight. Unpublished, because it was so defamatory, was Jones's four-page brief describing the relationship between Fayed and Alistair McAlpine, the treasurer of the Conservative Party who had accepted, according to Fayed, £250,000 for the party's election fund in return for unfulfilled promises. The climax of Jones's visit to Britain was a secret session with the House of Commons Trade and Industry Committee chaired by Kenneth Warren. House of Fraser, Jones told the MPs, was in 'very serious financial trouble' and even on the verge of insolvency because the banks would withdraw their support within eighteen months. 'The Fayeds', he continued, 'are men whose lack of probity and integrity is abundantly clear and it is inconceivable to me that they could be permitted to remain as holders of a banking licence.' After news of that testimony was leaked to Fayed, he classified Jones as a time-bomb requiring radical treatment.

Knowing only that the Australian was somewhere in London, Richard New was dispatched to unearth the quarry. Simultaneously, Macnamara alerted John Bates, a former detective superintendent operating as J&B Security, a private agency, to obtain details about Jones's background from searches in a national computer. In the past, Bates had proved reliable for obtaining bank statements and criminal records and identifying the owners of cars from number plates. On this occasion, he found Jones himself within one day. 'He's in the Tower Hotel,' Macnamara reported proudly to Fayed.

'Get him,' ordered Fayed omnipotently. Other businessmen and store owners might have hesitated, fearing an impenetrable legal maze. Fayed was undaunted. Nothing could stymie his wishes. Macnamara could be relied upon to squeeze the traitor. But there was a hiccup: Jones had disappeared.

Macnamara contacted Guildford police. Graham Jones, the former chief superintendent told his police contact, was a criminal avoiding arrest and he was about to flee the country. By then, another of Macnamara's private detectives had traced Jones on the Qantas ticketing computer and discovered that he was due to fly to Sydney that day. Encouraged by Macnamara, the Guildford police rushed to Heathrow, boarded the Boeing 747 – fully loaded and on the verge of take-off – and in humiliating circumstances ordered Jones to leave the aircraft. After his luggage had been retrieved from the hold, he was taken under arrest to Guildford police station. While Jones was questioned for one hour and forty minutes, Webb and Macnamara sat in an adjoining room. Three hours later, he was released. No evidence of fraud had been produced by Macnamara. At Heathrow the following day, Jones read a report in the *Daily Express* supplied by Michael Cole. Under the headline, 'VATmen's flight inquiry flattens Graham's Champers take-off', the story was contrived to embarrass Jones and terminate his new employment at Qantas.

*

FAYED'S EMPLOYEES understood the significance of his successful pursuit. Through New and Macnamara, their employer could gain access to Britain's network of private computer data and to police officers who were obedient to his interests; and, through Cole, he could place defamatory reports in the national newspapers. Dominating and embarrassing employees was a way of palliating his own humiliation. Money, he reassured himself, bought him power.

That summer, emerging from his tent on a Sunday morning, Fayed ordered his bodyguards to seize Wally Whiting, a former Military Police officer and bodybuilder. As the bodyguard lay pinned down on the lawn, Fayed urged his children to pour honey over the man's face. Roaring with laughter, the storeowner was testing Whiting's fear of losing his job. Even as he gasped for breath, the bodyguard did not flinch or complain. As he rose and walked with his stunned colleagues past the swimming pool, their employer suddenly pushed Martin Mower, another bodyguard, fully clothed into the water. Fayed guffawed even as Mower's portable telephone settled on the bottom of the pool. His children giggled. Humiliation of the donkeys was fun. His loyalty tests were as brutal as his dismissals.

The new tyranny extended to John Blower, his loyal horticulturalist and gardener at Oxted. After retirement, Blower had remained in the area and enjoyed giving speeches to local societies, especially Rotarians, describing his cultivation of orchids. His speeches were illustrated by slides of the flowers he had grown in Fayed's garden. On Fayed's orders, Macnamara, accompanied by Norman Bartholomew, a former officer in the Royal Military Police and a trained bodyguard who had been promoted to replace Mike Waller, visited Blower. After threatening him with unjustified arrest, Macnamara demanded the slides. The intimidated gardener complied.

Confusing autocracy with charisma, Fayed used similar tactics towards young women. The physical attractiveness of a plump sixty-one-year-old was negligible, but, as in any business deal, he never grew tired of trying, having calculated that if twenty attempts produced one willing girl the investment was worthwhile.

Shamelessly, Fayed used the daily tour through Harrods for what the sales assistants dubbed 'babe-spotting'. He preferred tall blondes with good figures, but dark-haired girls, if attractive, would not be ignored as potential recruits for employment in his office. As he walked past the designer boutiques – Armani, Versace, Ralph Lauren and Calvin Klein – the irony that millions had been spent on developing those images of style and purity did not occur to the predator. A short conversation established whether the girl was suitable for the executive-suite treatment. His precise descriptions in a telephone call to the personnel officer prompted the arrival one hour later in his fifth-floor office of a thrilled young woman. The routine rarely varied. 'Get good clothes,' he would say, peeling off five fifties from the wodge. As the girl smiled gratefully, Fayed would judge whether she might be amenable.

For those like the tall, red-haired, sophisticated graduate who had responded to Fayed's offer to become a 'chairman's babe', the temptation started with a surprise. 'Go home and pack,' he would announce. 'We're off to Paris.' Countless bodyguards had watched scores of 'poor, sweet, innocent girls' settling down in the Gulfstream, excited by the unexpected trip. Once again the pattern hardly changed: the girl would receive money for shopping in the afternoon; there would be a candlelit dinner at the Ritz, a drink in a night club, a swift Mercedes ride to inspect the Villa Windsor and an invitation to sleep in his flat off the Champs Elysées. The body language the following morning would reveal the outcome. 'Did you get him?' a bodyguard might ask.

'It was pathetic,' one girl replied. 'He ran a big bath, opened champagne and said "Let's drink together." A joke.'

'Heavy,' smiled a second bodyguard. 'She won't come again.'

The red-haired graduate was different. She had accepted Fayed's offer and after a holiday in St Tropez returned to London physically transformed. Replacing her Debenhams suit and Marks and Spencer shoes, she was wearing a designer-label black dress and expensive court shoes. Her nails were manicured. She was wearing two Cartier rings and a stunning gold necklace with a diamond. While her predecessor, a striking six-foot-two blonde receptionist on the fifth floor, had been forced to leave her house in Fulham, she was promoted to manager and housed in Fayed's special flat in Lisson Grove, on the border of St John's Wood. Regularly, Fayed drove to the flat at 10 p.m. to 'tuck her into bed' as he joked to her flatmate.

No opportunity was missed by the employer. The dismissal of two in-house lawyers who had incurred his anger meant that replacements were required. Royston Webb had mentioned to Fayed his interview with a twenty-five-year-old solicitor working in House of Fraser. 'She's too inexperienced, Mohamed,' reported Webb, dismissing the woman as unsuitable.

'Show photograph.' Unexpectedly, the lawyer was a tall, attractive woman. 'She's good. Bring her.'

To Francesca Armitage's surprise, as she walked into her flat the telephone rang: her employer had summoned her.

'How old?' asked Fayed at the beginning of a seven-minute interview. 'You English? You qualified? Write letter!'

'What sort of letter?'

'Anything.' Just enough, he thought, for the graphologist. 'Go have medical.' Discovering whether the lawyer suffered a sexually transmitted disease was essential.

Trudie Myerscough-Walker, his trusted PA who would marry the BBC radio disc jockey Bob Harris, understood the ritual. An appointment was made with Dr Jane Reffell near Victoria station. 'I'm also testing you for Aids,' said the doctor, who understood what Fayed required. Shocked, but fearing that she would otherwise not be employed, Armitage agreed. 'Half of London is infected with Aids,' avowed Reffell, 'and most don't even know it.' Without further explanation, Reffell began an exhaustive gynaecological examination. Armitage was puzzled by the connection between her fitness for childbirth and her employment as a solicitor. Other female lawyers, she later discovered, had not been subjected to these sensitive tests. Her report was sent to Alison Bozek, Fayed's secretary.

Over the following weeks, Fayed frequently summoned the young lawyer to his office. Closing his door, he would brush against her body, often putting his arms around her shoulders and touching her breasts. 'Don't be silly,' laughed Armitage, anxious not to risk her job by rebuffing her employer. Fayed was undeterred. As his familiarity with any 'babe' developed, he used the opportunity when alone in his office to grope her. Without warning, his hands would touch her bottom, her thighs and her breasts. Stunned by the unexpected attack, most sought to laugh it off. Rejection bounced off Fayed. Complaints to personnel officers about Fayed 'stuffing money into my cleavage' were always ignored. 'He stuffs fifties everywhere else, why not into their tits,' chuckled some personnel directors. Sitting down behind his desk, Fayed appeared set to discuss legal matters. 'Did you have a good fug on Sunday?' he asked. Armitage smiled meekly. Unabashed, her employer issued orders about contracts of employment, licensing agreements and disputes about franchises in the store. 'Sue them,' he ordered, referring for example to a sex bar in Bangkok that was calling itself 'Harrods'. Then he returned to his favourite theme. 'How many men you have at the weekend?' Armitage looked silently back at him. Fayed's hand was fumbling in his pocket. The bundle emerged. Four fifties were peeled off. 'Good!' he exclaimed.

'Thank you, Mr Al Fayed,' said Armitage, who over the previous six weeks had received one Cartier and two Harrods watches.

In June 1990, Fayed entered Armitage's office. 'You go for medical!' he cried, before abruptly walking out again. Armitage gazed open-mouthed. The brutal instructions, reinforced by the accompanying, omniscient bodyguards, were difficult to resist. 'But I had a medical nine months ago,' she told Alison Bozek, Fayed's assistant, minutes later. 'And I was perfectly healthy. Why do I need another one?'

'Those are my instructions,' replied Bozek, surprised by the retort. She chose Ann Coxon in Harley Street, another trusted doctor preoccupied by Aids.

Armitage returned to her office, puzzled that no other women in her department had been directed to have medical examinations. Coxon's report, sent to Fayed, was satisfactory: Armitage suffered no sexually communicable diseases.

'We go to Paris,' he ordered, allowing no time for protest. The Mercedes drove to Battersea helicopter terminal for a flight to Luton; champagne was served on the Gulfstream to Paris; a Mercedes drew up at the aircraft steps; passports were not required and, in bad traffic, there was a police escort for a fast drive to the Ritz. Sitting in the front of his Mercedes, Fayed watched two burly, leather-clad police motorcylists, illuminated by their flashing blue lights and preceded by blaring sirens, wielding their batons and boots to force a path through hesitant rush-hour traffic in a manner fit for a pharaoh. The contrast with his treatment in Britain was irksome, not least because staff at the Ritz, alerted by his bodyguards to his imminent arrival, would receive their master like royalty. Displays of his power and a candlelit dinner at the Ritz, he hoped, would seduce Francesca Armitage.

On the arrival at Fayed's flat, Armitage was separated from Katie Manning, his secretary, whom he had recently visited at the London Clinic. The Egyptian showed his lawyer into her bedroom and departed. At 1 a.m. he returned, wearing his dressing gown, and placed himself on the bed. In a panic, Armitage rushed into the bathroom and, from behind the locked door, beseeched him to leave. He agreed. The following morning, without mentioning the failed seduction, he gave her £300. 'You go shopping,' he ordered, giving the same amount to Katie Manning. At the end of the day, the group returned to London.

Undeterred, a few days later, Fayed telephoned Armitage at her home at 8 p.m. 'Come immediately,' he ordered. 'Work.' The telephone was cut off. Uncertain, Armitage arrived at Park Lane and was escorted to his bedroom. Sitting on a sofa, Fayed played his 'pity' performance. 'Life is so hard. All lies, lies, lies in DTI report.' Armitage nodded. Suddenly she shrieked. Fayed had stuck his hand down the front of her dress and grabbed a breast. 'I need the loo,' she cried. Locking the door, she shouted, 'I think I have to go home.' When she emerged, Fayed pointed at a door. 'A bedroom for you whenever you want. Let's watch TV.' A click on the remote and *Miami Vice* appeared on the wide screen. Thirty-five minutes later, Fayed accepted defeat. 'My children are coming,' he growled, ordering Armitage to leave by the back door.

Rebuffs did not trouble Fayed. Women were dispensable. The trail of girls invited to Park Lane who subsequently complained alarmed no one, least of all Tim Dale, a personnel officer. Many, Dale reasoned, were willing participants in the chairman's antics. Normally, there were no problems. Occasionally, one girl protested fiercely, in particular an innocent Irish Catholic who summoned her parents. It fell to Dale and other personnel officers to defuse those embarrassments, but such chores were obligatory if they were to earn their high salaries. Equally for Fayed, they were setbacks of no importance. Compared to his pre-eminent challenge – to force his acceptance by British society and to discredit the DTI report – the girls were forgettable detritus no different from other casualties of his opportunism.

*

THE SAME OPPORTUNISM, enhancing his reputation, had lured a succession of celebrities to Oxted. Kirk Douglas, Barry Humphries, Angela Rippon, Roger Moore, Tony Curtis and Donald Trump were all given exquisite hospitality to spread the word that Fayed was rich and powerful. Even Douglas Hurd, the foreign secretary, reportedly arrived in his official car with his family to enjoy sandwiches on the summer lawn. Fayed's ultimate quest was to win acceptance from the royal family. Certain that he was edging closer, he savoured attending a solitary dinner in honour of the queen and his annual meeting at the Windsor Horse Show. Under Michael Cole's stewardship, a group of photographers always surrounded Fayed to snap the best angle of his greeting the monarch, and their photographs would be rushed to newspapers and magazines in London. Cole knew that his employer would be irate if no photograph of the encounter appeared in the following day's newspapers. Harrods hampers to the editors, he hoped, guaranteed the space, and thankfully the celluloid never captured the soulless frigidity of the greeting. The monarch always moved on, committing Fayed to sit separately in the spectators' stand, while Cole, still in disgrace for his indiscretion at the BBC and not expected to sit under the same roof as the monarch, crept unseen into the stand's back row.

Fayed could however console himself that thanks to Earl and Countess Spencer, upon whom he showered gifts, Princess Diana was a regular visitor to Harrods. But the vulnerable princess, although always friendly, rejected offers of hospitality. Only Prince Michael of Kent and his Austrian wife, 'Princess Pushy', had eaten Sunday lunch at Oxted and had accepted a week's skiing at Gstaad. Notorious for their acceptance of freebies, they had flown to Switzerland in the Gulfstream to be entertained by Salah. Hilariously, Fayed's dissolute brother had regularly kept them standing outside in the cold for more than an hour while he overslept. 'Good morning!' he called to the shivering couple from his bedroom window, still in his pyjamas. The prince forced a smile. Money always lived by its own rules.

Salah's eccentricities abroad could be ignored, but in London they threatened Fayed's reputation. His brother's excessive misuse of drugs, Fayed feared, could harm his image. Only recently, his younger brother had tethered two miniature horses on the seventh-floor balcony of his flat in Park Lane. 'How they get up there?' demanded Fayed.

'Mr Salah took them up by lift, sir,' replied the po-faced guard.

'What dey do all day?' asked Fayed.

'He took them for a walk in Hyde Park.'

'Fuggin' crazy.'

The following day, commandeering a new Espace used for transporting Ali Fayed's children, Salah ordered the seats to be removed, the floor to be covered with hay, and the horses driven to Oxted. Shortly after, his collection of pornography had been packed with Dodi's in several black plastic binliners, entrusted to Tony Evans, a bodyguard, with orders to transport them to Oxted. 'Burn them,' Evans had been ordered.

Slightly more irksome were the reports of Salah's visit to Egypt with Christoph Bettermann. Swanking around Cairo's Sheraton Hotel, parading a blonde, buxom Swedish prostitute imported on a first-class ticket from Stockholm, his vulgarity in the hotel was only marginally less offensive than his woman's. Unlike his constant visits to night clubs in London and the stream of prostitutes arriving in Park Lane, Salah's antics in Cairo had delighted the gossips, especially the sight of the famous owner of Harrods chewing whole onions in the lobby to cure his dysentery. 'A fuggin' donkey!' screamed Fayed. Salah's wilful lack of self-control, stimulated by his new wealth, betrayed the increasingly dysfunctional relationships among the four Fayeds, just as their financial plight deteriorated.

To care for Salah, their eldest son, Ali and Tracey had

moved to Connecticut near New York, to use a school which reputedly provided the world's best education for dyslexic children. Ali's promise to Mohamed to commute weekly to London by Concorde did not conceal the slight rift in their relationship, influenced by another decision of Mohamed's to please his son.

In mid-1990, Dodi's flight to Bahrain had been delayed at Luton airport after Magic, a GEC subsidiary, had, he claimed, failed to service the Gulfstream. Infuriated that he, a man of such great importance, should be inconvenienced, Dodi persuaded his father to buy an aircraft-handling company. Fayed successfully bid for Metro, based at Heathrow.

'That's a bad deal,' said Webb, bewildered how a storekeeper could hope to profit from the complicated new business.

'When have I ever done a bad deal?' challenged Fayed, insulted that his judgement had been questioned.

'Sears,' Webb shot back.

'Besides that?'

Webb remained silent. To suggest the same about his management of House of Fraser would be dangerous but true. The Fayeds were veering towards bankruptcy.

12

Bankruptcy and Betrayal

'HARRODS BEER,' announced Fayed triumphantly. 'We'll sell our own.' The murmurs of approval from his staff reinforced his belief in himself as the great visionary, a man aching to prove his artistic genius and survive his enemies' sneers. Unrestrained by Ali's despair over his profligacy, his ambitions had become pharaonic. 'Harrods is show business like the Tower of London,' he enthused to his architect Bill Mitchell, who shared his belief that the store should 'offer a surprise around every corner'. One of his big surprises was the Egyptian Room on the ground floor, inspired by a man who had sworn never to return to Egypt. Even after colossal quantities of unsold Harrods beer had been dumped, his iron control over his domain remained undiminished.

On his daily march through the Food Hall, Fayed's striving for perfection certainly reflected his competence but also betrayed a nagging identity crisis steering his business towards expensive chaos. His plan radically to transform Harrods catering by converting the former fur store in the sub-basement into a £4 million kitchen, to centralize the store's food preparation for all its twenty restaurants and the Food Hall was sensible, but his phobias suggested that his business interests were easily compromised by trivia. Staring at the fruit display, he selected a peach. His stare turned to rage. A blemish scarred the skin. Imperfection was intolerable. The explanation was obvious. Disloyalty. Dishonesty. Clearly, the buyer had been bribed to accept defective produce. 'Fire the man!' he snarled to a bodyguard, who rapidly scribbled instructions on his pad. The alternatives, an oversight or an incompetent buyer, were inconceivable.

'Sack that man,' Fayed ordered a personnel director, pointing at an Arab working in the haberdashery department.

'Why?' asked the director.

'He's ugly,' replied the store-owner. Fayed was convinced that Harrods customers resented being served by blacks and browns. Offences against the new 'Harrods Dress Code', imposed as the Egyptian toured the store, included wearing nose studs, even for religious reasons, and unacceptable facial expressions. To avoid prosecution under the race laws, offenders were 'promoted' by troubled personnel officers to the warehouse in Osterley, rarely visited by Fayed. Compared to other London stores, the complaints by black employees against Harrods were five times as high and while one-third of other London stores' employees were black, Fayed had limited the numbers of blacks serving customers to 15 per cent of the staff. 'That man. Out!' he ordered his bodyguards, pointing at a casually dressed customer. Under Fayed's blazing stare, a bewildered man was escorted from the premises. The security guards at the doors were briefed not to allow entry to shoddy boors. On his return to his office, Fayed summoned Jenny Duckham, the store's doctor: 'Check all employees in the Food Hall for Aids.'

Duckham gulped. 'I don't think that would be sensible or even possible,' she replied.

'I want. Do!' commanded Fayed, unimpressed by the repercussions of inevitable publicity.

Fayed's erratic edicts were worsening the disillusion among his employees. The annual turnover of staff in 1988 was approaching 100 per cent, and, although improving, the cost of recruitment remained high. Requests by the personnel directors to increase wages were brusquely rebuffed: 'I own this store. They don't work hard enough so why should I pay more?' Labour relations appeared less important to Fayed than maximizing profits. 'These people work for me and will do as I order,' he told Stephen Taylor, the personnel director, in a crowded meeting, 'or they won't work for me.' The latest omen was the fate of the senior manager, spotted by a security guard walking through the empty store, taking a single cotton bud from a display to clean his ear. The following morning Fayed had telephoned. 'Do that again,' he warned, 'and you're fired.'

Rather than blame Fayed for the climate of fear, Stan Frith and Jeremy Nordberg, the senior personnel directors, condemned Christoph Bettermann's inexperience. 'It's the ultimate stupidity, Mohamed,' Nordberg had said of the appointment of a salvage expert to manage Harrods. 'The final straw.' Despite his best intentions, Bettermann had ignored the personnel directors' advice about the treatment of staff. Fayed backed the German rather than the Englishmen. Frith was the first casualty. 'I don't think things are right between us,' said Fayed, infuriated by a whisper from Michael Cole that Frith had joked at a presentation: 'Whenever Mohamed speaks, you can see Michael Cole pulling the strings.' Frith's mockery was disloyalty. Cole's status was undiminished by his unbenign disclosure. Few tears were shed for the 'Angel of Death's' dismissal but his reward for five years' loyalty was a rumour falsely alleging his dishonesty. Nordberg was the next to be dismissed. Both accepted their fate. Like those many employees whom they had themselves dismissed, the personnel directors understood the rules: they had passed their 'sell-by date'.

Disillusionment among Harrods staff infected the atmosphere inside the store. Previously the staff bowed to cutomers. Now they were expected to bow to Fayed. For the first time, Harrods staff had voted to strike for a pay increase. Traditional British customers, sensing the disgruntlement and repelled by tardy displays, drifted away. Increasingly, foreigners were filling the store, but too many were looking and not spending – the consequence of transforming Harrods from a utility into a spectacle.

The raw statistics confirmed Fayed's predicament. In 1985,

the store had earned £35 million in pre-tax profits. By 1990, profits had fallen to £9 million and the turnover was unaltered. Thanks to earlier innovations, Fayed could read on a computer screen a comparison between each department's current earnings and profits, and their performance on the same day the previous year. The slide had been aggravated since 1989 by a collapse of property prices, a rise in mortgage rates and several transport strikes. Costs since 1985, especially of distribution from the warehouses, had escalated and, despite the increasing number of franchise shops inside the store, the margins had fallen. The crunch in August 1990 was Iraq's invasion of Kuwait. Tourism collapsed and Harrods' income dived. Contrary to Fayed's projection that House of Fraser would earn profits of £181 million in 1991, the pre-tax losses were £25.7 million. 'We must cut costs,' grumped Fayed to a finance director. Complimenting the store-owner on his draconian new accounting routines which had reduced 'shrinkage' to 'an acceptable one per cent', the director was stung by a tirade. 'Have you seen the size of the turnover?' shouted Fayed. 'That one per cent is my money. I won't accept any shrinkage.' The director recoiled. Seeking a cure for his own mistakes, Fayed blamed Paul Taylor, the deputy managing director, for his predicament. 'I'm tired of him,' he complained. 'He must go.'

Fayed's chosen saviour was Peter Bolliger, a fifty-five-year-old Swiss managing a chain of fifty shoe shops in South Africa. Germans, even if born in Switzerland, were Fayed's chosen people. One year earlier, Bolliger had rejected Ali's offer to manage Harrods' shoe department. In September 1990, Ali's offer had improved. 'Do you want to run the whole of Harrods?' There was some desperation in his voice.

'I'll only come as boss,' stipulated Bolliger. Bettermann, it was mutually agreed, still commuting between London and Dubai, would return to the Gulf.

'I know we can make £50 million profit,' Fayed told Bolliger, sipping a glass of whisky. 'I want quick action.' The solution, they agreed, was to reverse Brian Walsh's reorganization, reduce Harrod's staff by 1,000 to 4,000 and cut salaries. Pointing to the photograph of himself and the queen at the Windsor Horse Show, Fayed said seriously, 'I walk next to the queen. One day, perhaps, you can walk behind me.' The Swiss smiled gratefully. 'Live in one of my Park Lane flats,' offered Fayed with apparent generosity.

'Many thanks,' replied Bolliger innocently.

Soon after, the Swiss was told by Bettermann that his flat and his office were certainly bugged. 'That Mohamed's way,' said Bettermann. 'Talk to Bob Loftus.' After listening to Loftus's juicy tapes of a furious argument between two female employees about their affair with the same building contractor, Bolliger accepted that surreptitious eavesdropping was an unalterable method of Fayed's control.

*

BOLLIGER'S APPOINTMENT came too late to cure the financial crisis. Uncertain how to escape from debt, Fayed's business failures were exposed. The £110 million investment in the Ritz could never be recovered, his $20 million investment in a San Antonio bank had crashed to $1.4 million after bad property loans and the value of his Sears shares had fallen by £60 million. Even his bodyguards noticed that 'the bungs got fewer and our suits were cleaned only once a month, not every week'. The Fayeds' bold gamble of vast loans to finance their ambitions, recklessly spending rather than saving, appeared fatal. Lacking any hidden sources of wealth, they had used House of Fraser as security for borrowing over £1 billion without sufficient cash to repay the interest and the capital. In Wall Street's slang, Mohamed was a debt-junkie, unable to resist the temptation of borrowing to spend. The visit in autumn 1990 by Ernest Cole, the unpretentious Samuel Montagu banker responsible for managing the loans to House of Fraser, resembled an undertaker advising the dying man of his fate. 'We're going to pull the plug,' warned Cole, 'unless there are some radical changes.'

281

Bitter that his credibility should be questioned, Fayed unleashed his wrath. 'You're racist,' he screamed at the banker, convinced that any critic impugning his honour and dignity was conspiring to seek his destruction. 'You're anti-Arab! You're fired! Out!' Since Cole was not employed by Fayed, he could not be dismissed; and since he was owed money by Fayed and could, if necessary, plunge his assailant into liquidation, he was less dispensable than the store-owner wished to imagine. To Fayed's good fortune, the banker was a solid, unmercurial type who understood his customer's considerable embarrassment and regarded his contempt for unfavourable contracts with bankers as just another hurdle to overcome.

Ernest Cole had been introduced to Fayed in 1986 to organize the refinancing of the loans of £901 million to House of Fraser Holdings by a consortium of international banks. The loans had been secured against the House of Fraser shares, the Sears shares and the Fayeds' property. The refinancing had been repeated in 1988. On the bankers' insistence, Fayed had sold twenty House of Fraser stores to reduce the group's debts. Three years later, in 1991, as interest rates rose and property prices fell, the Fayeds' debts had risen to £1.1 billion and the value of the banks' security fell. The only solution, to sell more assets, had proved difficult. Bettermann had failed to find a buyer in Germany for Fayed's stake in Freemans, the mail-order company, for between £10 and £12 million; and the plan to sell the Harrodian Club and its sports fields in Barnes for £12 million collapsed after the local council delayed granting building permits. Fayed's failure to produce new cash alarmed the banks, particularly the Deutsche Bank and the Japanese banks. 'Is Fayed trustworthy?' the Deutsche Bank's manager in London asked one of the Egyptian's senior executives.

The doubts intensified just as his enemies on the House of Commons Trade and Industry Committee had summoned Robin Leigh-Pemberton, the governor of the Bank of England, to justify the Fayeds' continued ownership of Harrods Bank.

The governor, the MPs complained, had ignored the DTI report and their own conclusion of 'grave concern' after the secret testimony of Graham Jones describing Fayed's pressure on the bank's managers to 'find a way of avoiding the restrictions and reporting requirements imposed by the regulations'. The Fayeds, the Committee reported, were 'not fit and proper' to manage the bank. After a tense encounter in the Commons, Leigh-Pemberton hastily ordered the Fayeds to transfer control of the bank to trustees, an unusual humiliation. Graham Jones's treachery had damaged Fayed's status in the City just as his financial plight impelled his reliance upon the banks for survival.

In previous years, Fayed had seemed unconcerned about his cool personal relations with certain bankers. Sitting around polished tables with prim City employees nurtured on reason and facts irritated him. At dinners for bankers hosted by House of Fraser, he had preferred not to confide his financial secrets to men who might spread gossip in the City village the following morning; instead he would put in a cameo appearance, distribute teddy bears and then depart. Arriving late for an appointment with John Ingraham of Citibank, he had burst through a door holding a giant plastic phallus which he handed to the stranger, laughing, 'This is for you to handle.' Previously, that performance had been greeted by uncritical laughter. The bankers had allowed their professional assessments to be influenced by the Fayeds' claims to their collection of apparently valuable trophies: Kurt Geiger, Turnbull & Asser, the Park Lane apartments, the Ritz, the Rockfeller Center in New York and all their homes. Despite the warnings of the DTI report, they had succumbed to the same performance as Kleinworts in 1984. Pliantly, they had tolerated Mohamed Fayed's casual attitude towards new perils and his stubborn conviction that black was white, and vice versa.

But in recent months that benevolence had abruptly faded. Even Fayed had noticed his audience's quizzical expressions, reflecting uncertainty about his strategy and finances. With increasing frequency in mid-1991 visiting bankers were asking, 'How do you intend to repay the loans, Mr Al Fayed?'

'I'm the fuggin' boss. I'm in charge of fuggin' everything,' snapped Fayed unappreciatively. Answering in expletive-infested staccato English was proving counterproductive. As protection, Michael Cole was introduced as an interpreter. 'What the chairman means', soothed Cole, 'is that he intends to repay the loans as soon as possible.' Reassured by boasts of a multi-million-pound fortune in safe Liechtenstein trusts, the British bankers comforted themselves that if pressurized the Fayeds could produce sufficient cash from their large, anony-mous deposits. The foreign bankers were less benevolent. Fayed, they complained, was too unstable, not least because he appeared unwilling to read a balance sheet. In late 1991, Fayed was summoned to the City for a reckoning.

'We can't let Mohamed address the banks,' urged Michael Cole. Mindful that, unlike Murdoch, he would antagonize rather than dazzle the bankers, Cole's opinion was even shared by Mohamed.

'You go,' ordered Fayed.

Flattered by his elevation as a director of the group, Cole was chauffeured to Poultry in the City to address the banks' representatives. 'We don't want a messenger boy,' shouted one banker in fury.

'What do you know about banking?' scoffed another. 'You're just a scribbler. Get out.'

Protected by his considerable self-esteem, Cole had not flinched at their acidic sarcasm, but even he acknowledged the unhelpfulness of his presence. 'We'll use Ali,' he suggested, 'and script him carefully.' Quiet-spoken Ali, a considerably accomplished actor, was the acceptable face of the Fayeds, but even he feared addressing the bankers without House of Fra-ser's finance director, and the inexplicable dismissal of succes-sive finance directors had fuelled the bankers' suspicions.

Forging a close relationship with finance directors was not

easy for Mohamed Fayed. In his compartmentalization of information, he found trusting any employee impossible. Since finance directors were handling his money and Fayed employed donkeys to obey not to frustrate him, he found their questions about the probity of his instructions especially difficult: too many questions, and their value to him as employees was ended.

Rosemary Thorne, the Harrods finance director until 1990, had been fired at Heathrow airport by Macnamara – 'Don't return to your office,' he had ordered abruptly. David Simmons, her successor, after uttering a succession of bizarre denials to bankers that there were any problems, had suddenly resigned. Simmons's successor had been dismissed two weeks after his appointment. Jim Walsh, a smart and slightly eccentric American with a pony tail, was House of Fraser's latest finance director. Isolated in their fifth-floor bunker, even the Fayeds recognized that without Walsh, appointed from United Technologies, they could not survive the crisis.

In spring 1992, accompanied by Walsh, Ali arrived in the City to present his proposals for the repayment of the loans and satisfy the bankers' demand for better security. In that moment of truth, Ali was asked whether the £1 billion debt could be repaid by the family's Liechtenstein trusts. Ali prevaricated and then admitted, 'If we had sufficient money we wouldn't be sitting here.' It was convincing evidence that the Fayeds had not used their own millions to finance the original purchase. Tottering on the brink of bankruptcy, Ali admitted to a financial adviser the consequences of their excesses: 'I can't stop Mohamed living beyond his means.' His audience was staggered.

The bankers' jolting discovery that the Fayeds possessed much less money than they had led the world to believe and could not repay their loans soured any cordiality. Ernest Cole's simple rejoinder – 'Either you reveal all your finances or we'll pull the plug' – cast the brothers into perilous quicksand. Ali said little more as Jim Walsh presented their request for help.

As the tense negotiations to reorganize the Fayeds' finances resumed, Mohamed decreed that his original instincts had been right. Commercially, there was no benefit in retaining House of Fraser, whose remaining fifty-nine stores required huge investment for modernization and produced scarcely any profits despite their £750 million turnover. House of Fraser, Ali was told, was to be sold; Harrods would be retained and its brand name used worldwide to generate extra profits; and critically, the brothers would call the bankers' bluff.

John MacArthur, tarnished by his gullibility in 1984 and relegated to a lowly status in the City, was Fayed's emissary to Derek Higgs, a senior partner at Warburgs, to sell House of Fraser. Sheepishly, MacArthur explained Fayed's proposition. 'Of course,' he added to overcome the banker's scepticism, 'you'll make all the checks you need to reassure yourselves. You'll not be representing the Fayeds but House of Fraser.'

'It'll have to be 100 per cent,' said Higgs. 'The City won't buy any partnership with the Fayeds.' MacArthur concurred. 'And it's got to be totally independent of the brothers.'

Suspicious of their clients, the bankers began investigating the accounts. 'Don't ask them where they got their money to buy the shares,' ordered Higgs, who declined Fayed's offer to produce their Liechtenstein and Swiss bank accounts. 'I don't want to hear lies. Just make sure that they do own the shares.' The company structure produced a surprise. The Fayeds had barely amended the traditional accounts used by the Frasers. Despite all Rowland's propaganda, there was no evidence that the Fayeds had either syphoned off any money or charged any of their expenses to the company – not even their cars, their helicopters or their meals. If only due to the constraints of VAT, it was impossible to falsify the stores' accounts. 'They're clean,' Higgs was told. 'They've even lost money by failing to change the accounting methods.' He could only speculate whether the finance directors had been dismissed for preventing Fayed challenging the rules.

Although the atmosphere between the bankers and their

client was sweetened by the delivery of Harrods' hampers – 'At least Mohamed tries to buy people rather than bump them off,' laughed one banker, maliciously recalling Warburgs' past battles with Tiny Rowland – negotiations ground to a halt over the price for the store group.

'I want top price,' said Mohamed Fayed, combining menace, humour and expletives. He had invested approximately £110 million in the stores and wanted some profit.

'I don't think we'll get more than £300 million,' said the bankers, appreciative of Fayed's good food but wearily anticipating unpleasant wrangles.

'Fug, no!' protested Fayed, insensitive to the bankers' politesse. Bankers were to be bullied until they delivered what he demanded. He had already rejected a management buy-out for £300 million negotiated by Jim Walsh.

'It's a good deal,' Walsh had urged unsuccessfully.

Despite pressure for a sale, Fayed also rejected Warburgs' price. 'No. I want £500 million.' His hand pulled a package from a nearby table. 'Open it,' he ordered Higgs. The banker unwrapped a clip-on tie, similar to one worn by Fayed. 'I gave one to Prince Phillip,' beamed the Egyptian. 'Now you're safe. When I want to throttle you, it'll come off.' The roars of laughter soon passed.

'You've got a rosy view of the price, Mohamed,' said Higgs, undaunted. Fayed exploded. The Fayeds had not escaped from the slums of Alexandria to be defeated by a gaggle of self-important City employees. Negotiations for the flotation, inexplicably for Warburgs, slowed down. Unknown to them, the previously hostile bankers owed over £1 billion had been suddenly and miraculously placated by Fayed's promises. The unexplained reason was one banker among the consortium of lenders who was more sympathetic than others. Piet Jochen Edsel, a vice-president of the Dresdner Bank, had been wooed by Mohamed's charm to help in a manner, quipped one eyewitness, which seemed at the time, 'above and beyond the call of duty'. Edsel was the Fayeds' secret reassurance that, regardless of any antagonism, the banks would not force the brothers into liquidation. Encouraged by Edsel's assessment that the 'banks will now wait', especially the friendly bank managers of Credit Lyonnais and Credit Suisse, Fayed had bought time to ride out the recession until he could sell for a better price. 'Don't worry any more,' he sniffed to Walsh, the major casualty of the crisis: as the pioneer of the unsuccessful management buy-out, he was irrationally no longer whole-heartedly trusted by the brothers. Increasingly plagued by paranoia, Fayed found reason to doubt the loyalties of several close advisers.

*

In June 1991, after four years' collaboration, Francesa Pollard had sensationally defected to Tiny Rowland. 'I am conscious', she said in a statement written by Rowland's lawyers, 'of the wrong I have done to R. W. "Tiny" Rowland by the long and vicious campaign against him under my name.' Her betrayal – induced by a generous payment – had been used by Rowland to accuse Fayed falsely in the *Observer* of prompting the execution in Iraq of one of that newspaper's journalists. That defamation had been the precursor to something worse.

Amid contradictory stories relayed to Fayed, Richard New, his trusted investigator, had been secretly negotiating with Rowland in Switzerland. Either the victim of blackmail or desperate for money, New appeared to have negotiated to accept £500,000 from his enemy if he betrayed Fayed and tempted Royston Webb also to switch sides. Webb would be offered £5 million for his betrayal. Although Webb remained loyal and had even humiliated Rowland in a national newspaper's exposé, Fayed was paralysed by the fear of treachery: 'Shows Tiny's a bastard. Shows he's got no courage. He's all talk.' Nervously, he was interpreting mundane conversations gleaned from his telephone intercepts as proof of wider treason.

At the end of April 1991, Macnamara had told Fayed that Christoph Bettermann had been overheard on his telephone talking to a headhunter. Although Bettermann had given no commitment to the offer from a shipping company in the Gulf, Fayed, incapable of self-restraint, challenged his protégé: 'I hear from the Ruler of Sharjah you're thinking of leaving.' Bettermann was stunned. The ruler, he reasoned accurately, would not be aware of trivialities. Fayed had certainly invented the conversation. Suddenly, the truth dawned. Although he had not protested about Fayed's bugging operation, he was outraged that he had become a target.

'I'll pay you $500,000 a year if you stay,' continued Fayed.

'Will you put that in writing?' asked Bettermann.

'What? Don't you trust me?' replied Fayed impervious to the contradiction. 'If you stay with me, I'll make you rich,' continued Fayed, 'but if you leave, I'll destroy you.'

Bettermann shrugged.

Not trusting his former protégé, Fayed dispatched an auditor to Dubai to hunt for evidence of fraud. His search was unsuccessful. Two months later, Bettermann decided that their relationship was permanantly fractured. 'It's no good, Mohamed,' said Bettermann in June 1991, 'I'm resigning.' In Fayed's eyes, a resignation assaulted his divine dignity. No one important could depart painlessly.

'You're obstinate,' snapped Fayed. 'I'll destroy you.'

Surrounded by the royal warrants proving his importance among the world's famous personalities and forever mindful that thousands of faces glowed in servility wherever and whenever he walked through his empire, Mohamed Al Fayed resolved to punish the man who dared to desert. Employees were threatened with dismissal if they dared accept Bettermann's invitation to his wedding to House of Fraser lawyer Francesca Armitage – 'a crook marrying a slut' was his outrageous slur. Macnamara was tasked to warn one female lawyer repeatedly of dismissal if she accepted the invitation, and a surveillance team photographed the Bettermanns' guests to check whether any employees had disobeyed. 'Don't let him into our office or out of his home,' Fayed ordered IMS's employees in Dubai as Bettermann flew home to the Gulf with his new wife. Fearing embarrassment after Bettermann returned and spread the news of his resignation, he contrived to damage his employee by accusing him of fraud.

The invented fraud involved IMS's salvage of the *York Marine*, an oil tanker hit by an Iranian shell in the Gulf War. To increase IMS's profits, Bettermann had negotiated an unusual deal between the salvage companies and the owners of the *York*'s uninsured oil cargo. In a plan to help the owners recover money from the Iranian government for the damage, the cargo's value had been inflated and there had been an unorthodox exchange of cheques. Bettermann had explained the deal to Fayed, emphasizing that the cargo was uninsured. 'The profit to us', he said, 'is $150,000.'

'Good,' replied Fayed. As usual, he wanted nothing in writing. The irregularity – a common occurrence in the salvage trade – was his excuse to allege that IMS had lost $450,000 because of a dishonest 'kick-back' paid to Bettermann. His allegation, that Bettermann had stolen money paid by an insurance company, albeit on an uninsured cargo, was unquestioningly accepted by Royston Webb and John Macnamara.

To entrap Bettermann, Macnamara was dispatched to secure a sworn statement from another German employee of IMS. Macnamara failed. Undeterred, he contacted Bettermann on 7 August 1991 in Malaga, Spain, and suggested a meeting. 'Come round to my suite,' said Macnamara. Before Bettermann's arrival, Macnamara hid a microphone.

'Are you recording this conversation, John?' asked Bettermann, as he sat down.

'No,' lied Macnamara. 'Do you want me to?'

Dismissing the need, Bettermann was presented with a surprise.

'Here's a sworn statement', said Macnamara, 'that you defrauded an insurance company and Mohamed of $450,000.'

Not noticing that the statement was an unsigned draft

written by Macnamara, Bettermann pleaded, 'But there wasn't any insurance, John. How could there be a fraud?'

Macnamara remained impassive.

'I acted on instructions of Mohamed Al Fayed,' said Bettermann.

'Mr Mohamed says he doesn't know anything about this.'

'Then he is not saying the truth.'

Towards the end of their conversation, Macnamara became irritated. Fayed had said that he had been defrauded of $450,000 but the German's explanation was a riddle. 'Mohamed's instructions to me are that if this can be prosecuted criminally, he will prosecute.'

'Yeah, fine,' smiled Bettermann. How could the Egyptian, thought Bettermann, contrive to prosecute himself? But looking at Macnamara he realized that the highly paid former police officer had become so tamed by Fayed that his objectivity had disappeared. Macnamara travelled to St Tropez to report.

The Fayed family journey that summer – first to Helsinki and then to France – had required extraordinary logistics. The advance party to Finland – two cars (a grey Mercedes estate and a Toyota minibus), a Luton van and a Harrods truck carrying eighty-four suitcases and boxes – had departed from Britain three days earlier. A few pieces of antique furniture and lamps collected by Heini were also packed for a new house. As usual, Fayed had spent the day before his own flight to Finland touring the Food Hall, ordering the food and drink to be sent to Finland and a second shipment to the South of France. 'And add twenty boxes of Perrier water,' he ordered the bodyguard, 'fifty boxes of tissues and lots of nuts.' His bodyguards gave off an image of oppressive security, but in reality they were glorified servants and porters relieving his solitude. He was paying for companionship.

Fayed made little effort to conceal his dislike of Finland and his coolness towards Nana, his mother-in-law, who cared for the house. Having flown to Helsinki with Heini and the

four children (Omar had been born in October 1987), he ate
Nana's excellent lunch, satisfied himself that the eight bodyguards were properly briefed, and returned the same day to
London. Heini was expected to care for herself despite her loss
of contact with her Finnish friends. Three weeks later, Fayed
had returned to Helsinki to collect his family for a joint holiday
in the South of France.

His latest Gulfstream was the epitome of vulgar luxury.
Decorated in deep pink, Egyptian motifs and hieroglyphics had
been woven into the fabric covering the walls and floors, which
was surrounded by a trim of brown marble. An extra-wide
seat had been installed for Fayed himself, separated from the
others by a marble and gold table. Regularly before take-off, a
taped prayer, similar to an imam's chant from the minaret of a
mosque, would be played to bless the passengers for a safe
landing.

His arrival in St Tropez, a military-style operation involving
thirteen bodyguards, was executed smoothly. From the Gulfstream at Nice airport he drove to the harbour and sped across
the bay on the *Cujo* to his villa. Fifteen minutes later there was
an explosion of rage: 'Where's the fuggin' fish? Where's my
fuggin' fish?' That morning, Nana had prepared and wrapped
a lobster salad – Fayed's favourite – to be taken on the plane
for his dinner. After packing the cars, the van, the lorry and
the Gulfstream, the solitary package had been forgotten by the
donkeys on Nana's kitchen table. Fayed trembled with anger.
The world had collapsed. Grown men who had stacked bodies
and executed enemies in the most dangerous conditions for
queen and country feared dismissal because Nana's lobster had
failed to arrive in St Tropez. Sending the Gulfstream on a
mercy mission from Nice to Helsinki to retrieve the lobster
was, after reflection, ruled out. It would no longer be fresh the
following day. Since none of the bodyguards could be individually blamed, no one was dismissed.

Security around the Castel Ste Thérèse had been intensified.
Six Racal sensors, used by the British army, had been buried in

the ground around the 700-yard perimeter. Not only could intruders be detected but the children could be constantly monitored. To keep the public from his small beach – a hazard from the coastal path – the guards at daybreak spread towels, boats and sun loungers across the sand to deter those strangers who were undaunted by the two caged rottweilers, Lennie and Leo, prone to outbursts of frenzied barking whenever someone approached. Only Clint Eastwood treated the dogs' deadly chorus with humour. 'Hey,' said the cool actor as he passed their howls at midday, 'I've come for dinner. Not to be your dinner.'

That summer, Heini's attitude had soured. The demure twenty-four-year-old whom Fayed had entranced in Paris had developed into a slightly heavier, occasionally screeching woman, clearly resentful of her suppressed life. 'I'm fed up with that fat old man,' a bodyguard, reported her as cursing. 'She's an ice maiden,' the bodyguards sniggered after witnessing quarrels between the couple. Heini's bitterest complaint was the enforced isolation and the intrusion of the bodyguards. In Oxted, her only activity was shopping for clothes and toys, even at the local Woolworths, and meeting Stephanie Parker, her friend, for coffee. Once a week, she attended an evening course in Sevenoaks, driving her own Mercedes. Surreptitiously, two bodyguards were ordered to trail her car and report on their surveillance. In protest against the strangers' encroachment on her holiday in St Tropez, she reduced the bodyguards' food and openly nagged Fayed to cut their bonuses.

Only the visits by neighbours appeared to improve Heini's mood. To all her callers, Barry Humphries and his wife Lizzie, Major Hanbury, the sultan's representative, and Charles and Carla Powell staying near by with friends, Heini acted as a charming hostess and loyal wife while Fayed was the doting father playing with his four children. Omar, his youngest son, was the star. Karim's meningitis had left him permanently deaf while his two daughters, Jasmine, eleven years old, and

Camilla, five years old, were not, in Fayed's world, considered as successors to the business. None of those leaving the estate at the end of the day would have reconciled the image of happiness with the reality of the marital relationship. Fayed, it seemed, was incapable of forging permanent and stable relations with women. Intolerant of any intellectual or personal challenge, he preferred beauty to brains, yet was impatient with his choice. Only the most perceptive contrasted the marriage with the happy relationship between Heini and Dodi.

Life for the Fayed family should have been bliss. With passion and flair, Fayed had developed the simple villa into a spectacular three-tier residence. Beneath the tennis court, he had constructed a storage and accommodation complex for the security guards. At the beach, he had transformed a fisherman's shack into a dazzling three-level glass and marble house enhanced by a waterfall cascading over boulders and by a patio suitable for helicopters. Amid that stunning setting, Monica Weiss, an employee at the Ritz, occasionally played the piano. Fayed's daily routine, between his weekly commutes to London, was enviable.

After a morning pottering around the villa or lying by the swimming pool – the children were forbidden by their father, who was afraid of pollution, to swim in the sea – a tender was sent from the *Sakara* to the beach. Followed on the CCTV monitors, Fayed, disliking the steep steps, was driven in a Mini Moke from the villa down the winding path to the waterfront. As his wife and children were helped into the tender, he opted 'for exercise' to use the pedallo to cross the seventy yards to the schooner. Naturally, it would be 'Bravo', the accompanying bodyguard, silently cursing that there was 'not much pressure from Fayed's side', who actually performed Fayed's pre-lunch workout. After 'Bravo' had washed his employer's feet to remove any sand, Fayed climbed on board to join his family under the awning. Lunch – always outstanding food prepared by an excitable Italian chef flown from Britain – lasted three hours, much of the time spent by Fayed on the telephone, while his children became bored and fractious. Oblivious to the surrounding beauty, he was focused that summer upon the financial fate of Harrods. He had identified Michael McCrae, a good-looking promotions executive, as a cause of his store's misfortune.

Ranked among the dwindling band of green-blooded Harrods managers, with twenty-two years of outstanding service, McCrae could count among his many successes promoting the Egyptian Room in the British media. A celebration of McCrae's triumph, published in *Drapers Record*, the trade newspaper, irritated Fayed. The article, he complained, omitted any mention of himself. 'Why?' he demanded. Understanding his master's drift, Michael Cole also fumed. The article, he puffed, had not been cleared through his office. Egos were bruised. The lust for blood required satisfaction. 'Get rid of him,' Fayed ordered, blaming McCrae for ineffective and costly promotions. Executions were by then a practised ritual. For six weeks, McCrae was ignored. While no one on the fifth floor spoke to the promotions director, he was tactlessly denigrated in neighbouring offices by ambitious colleagues, and security staff repeated gossip obtained by eavesdropping on McCrae's telephone. The brazenness at the climax was intentionally fearful. Stephen Taylor, the personnel officer, accompanied by Eamon Coyle, the security officer, entered McCrae's office. McCrae was accused of misappropriating funds. The charges were farcical but, with his integrity besmirched in this way, the accused was guaranteed to leave the building swiftly and without a fuss. In a humiliating manner, forbidden to bid farewell to friends, he was escorted to the front door. Standing on the pavement in Knightsbridge, defenceless against the slander, he was a non-person. By successfully denigrating McCrae's reputation, Fayed was reassured that he could also successfully exact vengeance against Christoph Bettermann.

During those summer weeks Fayed had pondered Macnamara's report about the conversation with Bettermann in Spain. The German's honest denials were irrelevant. Vindictiveness was how Fayed demonstrated his power. Just as his use of the British police against Graham Jones had confirmed his influence, Fayed addressed a letter to the Crown Prince of Sharjah. 'I fired Christoph Bettermann from [IMS]', he wrote, 'due to his dishonesty and his abuse of position in running the company, by embezzling millions of dollars from the company and I am in the process of filing legal action against him.' The result proved Fayed's leverage.

On 22 February 1992, Bettermann was prosecuted in Dubai for embezzling $900,000. Sitting in a cage among common criminals for the first of twenty-four court hearings, he was presented with the transcript of his conversation with Macnamara in Spain. 'Idiot,' he cursed. Naively, he had accepted Macnamara's word that he was not being secretly recorded. 'Goddammit,' he cursed again. The transcript was inaccurate, either twisting Bettermann's replies to suggest an admission to the fraud or a gap, described as 'recording inaudible', where the conversation had conflicted with Fayed's version. The contrast between persecuting his former protégé on false charges in Dubai while demanding justice for himself in London never occurred to Fayed. A new ruthlessness had crept into his operation.

13

Revenge

ELECTION DAY, 9 APRIL 1992, was marked by an execution. The casualty was a ginger tom cat. 'Get rid of it,' Fayed ordered his head of security in Oxted. 'Poison.'

'We'll kill all the rest of the animals,' said the bodyguard, thinking of the poison that would be spread across the estate.

'Okay, okay. What do we do?'

'Shoot it.'

'Good,' grunted Fayed, walking past his organic vegetable garden.

The operation was handed to John Evans, a former SAS soldier and the bearer of the Military Medal for covert activities in Ulster. In a careful manoeuvre, Evans shot a ginger cat. Unfortunately it was the wrong ginger, which happened to be the children's favourite. Hearing the news from the house-keeper, Fayed exploded. 'Fuggin' nothing', he yelled, 'is fuggin' done properly.' In punishment, Evans was to be dispatched to Scotland, but only after shooting the proper cat. Camouflaging himself in SAS-style fatigues, he planned a night-time ambush. Under the moonlit sky, the cat appeared and he fired. The cat was only wounded. Blood dripping from its head, he limped towards the house and disappeared. Terrified that Fayed would discover the latest mishap, every bodyguard and dog handler with their labradors was roused for a massive dragnet: finally, Fayed's £4 million security apparatus had a task. The *coup de grâce* was silently executed in the Japanese garden. That misadventure symbolized Fayed's plight over the following months.

One week after the unexpected re-election of the Conservative government, Fayed wrote to Neil Hamilton. Fatefully, his parliamentary champion had been appointed minister for corporate affairs in the DTI, the same position as Michael Howard in 1987. The politician who had accepted his hospitality and cash, and had repeatedly damned the report in the Commons as 'a monstrous injustice', was blessed by an extraordinary opportunity to reverse his predecessor's calumny by manoeuvring an official renunciation of the inspectors' judgement.

In the letter, also drafted by Michael Cole and Royston Webb, Fayed combined joviality and a blatant reminder of favours owed: 'Well, I suppose they can't keep a good man down for ever! Congratulations on your appointment. Long overdue . . . I shall be expecting you to contribute to my Trade and Industry by popping in with your orders . . .' More soberly, the letter reminded the new minister that Fayed was challenging the DTI report in the European Court of Human Rights in Strasbourg on the ground that the inspectors had ignored the principles of natural justice. Hamilton, he hoped, would pre-empt the hearing by conceding his case.

Fayed's optimism that the minister would have 'the courtesy to review the situation' was misplaced. Clearly embarrassed by his conflict of interest – the DTI officials would certainly not allow the new minister to revoke its inspectors' report – Hamilton opted officially for silence. 'He thinks he is already God,' raged Fayed after hearing that Hamilton would not reply. 'He's got what he wants. He's a minister. He thinks that he doesn't need me any more.' By chance Alex Carlile, a Liberal MP sympathetic to his cause, invited Hamilton in a parliamentary question in May 1992 to denounce the DTI report. Instead, Hamilton repeated his departmental brief about the inspectors' 'independent . . . carefully considered and thorough investigation'. Fayed fumed. He had trusted Hamilton as a friend. The politician had slept in his homes, eaten his food and taken thousands of pounds. The reward for his generosity was betrayal. The traitor was marked for retribution, just like Graham Jones and Christoph Bettermann. Fayed's influence seemed limitless. A telephone call on the morning of 3 June 1993 from Bob Loftus tested that predisposition to revenge.

His brother Salah, reported Loftus, was under suspicion by Scottish police for possession of drugs. Fayed became agitated as his security chief revealed his brother's latest folly. Flying to Scotland with Rachel Crowe, his personal assistant, Salah had landed in Aberdeen rather than Inverness and travelled to Balnagown by taxi. Confused, he had forgotten a leather bag in the car, which the taxi driver later delivered to the police. Inside the bag, the police had found Salah's passport, a large amount of cash, some crack cocaine and a 'well-used homemade pipe' – the customary tool of cocaine users.

Salah's antics irritated Fayed. Not only had he acted foolishly in Egypt, but there were complaints about his propositioning of girls at Harvey Nichols' bar and, worst of all, the bodyguards in Park Lane joked about a stream of prostitutes arriving for Salah – sometimes three simultaneously – all demanding to be paid. Few were fooled by his claim that the drugs he took were required to relieve his 'back problem'.

'Tell the police', Fayed ordered Loftus, 'that the bag belonged to the girl.' While Salah remained hidden when the police arived at Balnagown, Crowe confessed that she owned the bag and the drugs. The police departed unconvinced, not least because the girl was baffled about how to ingest cocaine using a pipe. To suppress further investigation, Salah and Crowe were flown to France while Macnamara and Fayed consulted Sir David McNee, the former Scotland Yard chief. Living in St Tropez had limitations for Salah and he ordered Crowe to return briefly to Britain. Spotting the distressed woman at Heathrow, Special Branch searched her bags. Finding about £4,000 in cash and a Harrods staff card, the officers telephoned Loftus. The security officer's assurances halted further inquiries. Shortly afterwards, the Scottish police announced that although Crowe had been investigated for possession of drugs, no further action would be taken. Once again, Fayed could congratulate himself on his ability to control mishaps. Returning to Britain, Salah invited Crowe to stay in his penthouse flat at 55 Park Lane. Reflecting once again upon his invincibility, Fayed rewarded his bodyguards with more cash. Separately, Loftus received a regular two-week summer holiday in St Tropez.

Within his domain, Fayed chortled, he could behave without fear of rebuke. In particular, he had enjoyed ribbing Frances Healey, an attractive interior decorator. Employed to renovate the flats in Park Lane, Healey was often summoned by Fayed to discuss her plans. 'Had a good fug last night?' he regularly asked, passing close enough to her to touch her breasts. On trips to Paris and Scotland, she had also suffered his sexual advances. 'I can teach you things,' he pouted. 'Your boyfriend no good. You sleep with me.' On a flight to Inverness with Healey and two other women, Fayed, talking constantly about sex, had flicked pistachios, attempting to land the nuts inside the woman's shirt. Having failed to woo Healey, Fayed urged her to sleep with Mark Griffiths – 'He's virgin. You show him.'

Fayed felt no shame about his conduct. Indeed it was fun, which over the past years he had grown to enjoy – by assuming that Harrods' young female employees, so vulnerable and financially dependent, belonged to him. Thankfully, his senior directors tolerated his attitude. Many of the girls, they convinced themselves, were eager and grateful for their employer's largesse. 'They're his toys,' murmured the personnel directors, knowing that Katherine McMahon, a personnel officer, specially recruited pretty girls for Fayed's executive offices. With nothing to fear, Fayed had no reason to vary his method: the invitation to work in his office, the cash gifts, the Paris trip, more spending money, a Cartier watch, and finally the proposition – sex for money and goodies.

Asking a pretty secretary, 'How is your pussy?', or a

marketing assistant, 'Did you have a good fug over the week-end?', or a management trainee, 'How many different positions you use for fuggin'?' was more fun than saying, 'Good morning.' Most were accustomed to the routine. 'Call me papa,' smiled Fayed, embracing them after they innocently entered his office. Touching their breasts and their legs, he occasionally attempted to push fifties into their cleavages. 'Come to papa and have a cuddle,' he simpered to a good-looking blonde, trying to hug and kiss her, and thrusting £200 in cash into her hands. It was the preliminary to an examination by Dr Ann Coxon in Harley Street for HIV and sexually transmitted diseases and then a trip to Paris, a late-night entry into her bedroom at the Villa Windsor and a proposition in Park Lane that, in return for money, foreign travel, a car and a flat, she should become his mistress. 'No,' replied Griffiths firmly. By the end of the week, she was no longer working in Fayed's office.

His next target was Louise McLeod, a director of marketing. The method was unsubtle. 'What are you doing tonight?' he asked, pushing the horrified woman's legs apart. Like so many others, McLeod recoiled in fear. 'Why you no have more children?' he scoffed: she had had one child but had lost two during pregnancy. 'Husband has bad sperm,' he quipped. His mirth turned to anger towards Frances Healey after hearing that the designer was seriously involved with Derek 'Del' Healey, his supremo for bugging operations. 'End it or you're fired,' he warned, emphasizing that relationships among his staff were forbidden. His threat was ignored. Both were dismissed as redundant. Shortly afterwards, Detective Inspector Dick South called on Del Healey. There had been, alleged the policeman, threats to a Harrods employee.

'Absolute crap,' said Healey, understanding the source of the false complaint.

The policeman never returned and the Healeys, after filing a complaint at an industrial tribunal, received compensation for unfair dismissal. Fayed was untroubled. Little people could never restrain him. Only governments wielded that power, and few ever tried. On the rare occasions he was mistaken, the consequences were costly.

The arrival in early 1993 in his office at Harrods of Mohamed Alabbar, the twenty-seven-year-old director of Dubai's Department of Economic Development, heralded one of those occasions. Small and slim and presenting an undaunting personality, Alabbar belonged to the new generation of energetic Dubaians whom Fayed only occasionally encountered. Educated in finance at a Jesuit college in Seattle in the United States, Alabbar had trained at the Bank of England and Holland's Central Bank before working for five years in Singapore. Shortly after his return to Dubai in 1992, he had been appointed by the Maktoums as the new economic supremo, tasked with eradicating the legacy of commission payments harvested by wheeler-dealers during the former era. For the old guard Alabbar's enthusiasm was cataclysmic. Among his first casualties was Mahdi Al Tajir, challenged in British courts to repay alleged excessive profits earned from Dubai's aluminium smelter; and another was Fayed, targeted for his twenty-year management contract of the Trade Centre.

Fayed had already heard that Alabbar, on the Maktoums' behalf, had queried his management fees as excessive. Resolved to retain his composure and charm during their first meeting, Fayed told the young man in Arabic, spoken in a Gulf dialect, 'I built Dubai, you know. Dubai's wealth is all due to Mohamed Al Fayed.' The visitor was startled. Unaware of Dubai's history, the son of a poor family had no cause to disbelieve the owner of Harrods. He was less enchanted by Fayed's attitude towards his customers. 'I piss on the British,' Fayed snorted. 'I bought Harrods so I can sit up here and piss on them as they pass down there. I want them to come here every day so I can piss on them. And when I'm dead, I'll be buried in a mausoleum on the roof, and I'll still piss on them. I hate them.' Grunting, he pointed to a photograph of himself with Rashid. His real loyalties, he appeared to suggest, were towards the

Maktoums. Bidding Alabbar farewell, Fayed assessed his predicament.

Indisputably, the original agreement with Sheikh Rashid allowed the Maktoums unilaterally to terminate the agreement. Yet his relations with them, he believed, were good enough to overcome the interference of a young bureaucrat. After all, the owner of Harrods was equal to the ruler of the 'flea pit' in the Gulf. The only cloud was the Maktoums' refusal in early 1993 to renew his passport. Since its expiry, he and Ali had once again travelled on their Eygptian passports with all the irksome requirements of applying for visas to Switzerland, America and every other country. The consequences were unpleasant. At Luton airport, a Customs officer, suspicious about his new, gold-coloured aluminium briefcase, demanded that it be opened for inspection. 'You give 'em fuggin' hell,' Fayed ordered Macnamara that night. Dutifully, Macnamara complained to Scotland Yard, but shortly after, at Gatwick, immigration officers had insisted that Fayed could not step from his Gulfstream into his waiting Mercedes. Instead, he was to present himself in the immigration office for a passport check. Visibly outraged, Fayed had no alternative but to drive in a cold minibus and wait while an officer leafed slowly through his Egyptian passport ostentatiously checking whether he was eligible for an entry visa despite seeing on his white card, 'Occupation, "chairman of Harrods"'. The authorities, he realized, were not prepared to accord him the privileges he expected. That caused humiliation.

Only six months earlier, he had landed at Biggin Hill in his Sikorski from Paris. By chance, Gerald Ronson, the disgraced property developer, was his passenger. Marooned by a French air-traffic controllers' strike at Le Bourget, Ronson had asked for a lift. To Ronson's surprise, British Customs officers had asked Fayed whether he or his security guards were carrying weapons. To avoid those harassments he and Ali had decided to apply in February 1993 for British citizenship. Their application mentioned that House of Fraser Holdings had paid £32 million in corporate tax and that the Fayed family had paid £28 million income tax. Paying taxes, they believed, was a qualification for British nationality.

Ali had applied in January 1993 after obtaining a private assurance from Kenneth Clarke, the home secretary, that there would be no objections (an assurance which Clarke 'cannot recollect'). His application was supported by Sir Gordon Reece and Sir Peter Hordern. Mohamed's application one year later was supported by Lord Bramall, and Lord Archer, the controversial novelist, politician and unsuccessful businessman, whose fabrications about his own past appropriately matched Mohamed Fayed's. Bramall agreed to support Fayed, not least in gratitude for the Egyptian's support for the reunion in early 1993 of Victoria Cross holders in London. After encouraging British Airways to provide free air tickets for the veterans, Fayed had hosted a lunch for them at Harrods. 'He was on the side of the angels. Own troops,' the respected soldier told friends and Fayed had always spoken of his 'great admiration for Britain'. That was not the sentiment Mohamed Alabbar recalled on his return in summer 1993 to Britain from Dubai.

Having failed to persuade the Maktoums in his telephone calls to reverse their termination of his management contract, Fayed had demanded millions of pounds in compensation for loss of earnings. With instructions from Sheikh Maktoum to avoid confrontation, Alabbar waited in Fayed's office with his lawyers and accountants to discuss a settlement. Jovially, Fayed entered the room. Over previous months, his conduct had encouraged an unalterable conviction that his dogmatic demands were always satisfied. 'Have you settled everything?' he asked Royston Webb.

'There's no compensation,' replied Webb.

Disbelief sparked an outburst. 'You fuggin' think you shits can bring your fuggin' fishmarket from Dubai here?' he screamed into Alabbar's face. For eight minutes, without pausing for breath, Fayed raged, and his fury continued after Alabbar rose and departed.

The economic secretary's orders, after reporting to the rulers on his return to Dubai, were explicit: 'That's the man we know. It's time he left Dubai.' All Fayed's investments were to be scrutinized with prejudice. Not for the first or last time, Fayed had turned friends into enemies, and he risked losing assets worth about £100 million. Royston Webb was ordered to sue the Maktoums for compensation for the loss of the management contract.

*

THAT SETBACK WAS NOT evident as Fayed regularly appeared in public during the summer of 1993. He had reason to believe that everything else was moving favourably in his direction. The economy was improving and his latest £50 million investment to rebuild and redecorate Harrods' 130 departments had radically transformed the store. Energetically, he had sold the Harrods brand name to nearly thirty signature stores across the world. Thanks to his stubborn resistance of the bankers' demands, the financial crisis would be resolved by the flotation of House of Fraser. Best of all, Tiny Rowland, devastated by Lonrho's financial collapse, had been forced to sell his shares to Dieter Bock, a hitherto unknown German property developer, casting doubt on whether a huge trial – relating to Fayed's phoney claims to inherited wealth and Rowland's defamations of Fayed – between the two men listed for January 1994 would occur. Remarkably like an Iranian mullah uttering his chants, Fayed's mantra – 'my dignity, my integrity, my honour, my family' – was evoking genuine sympathy. In a performance he gave regularly, with his face crumpling and his eyes glistening, he moved his audiences by his passionate expressions of pain about the DTI's calumny. Only the handful of hardened sceptics, indifferent to his suffering and unimpressed by Michael Cole's claims about his master's hitherto 'secret' donations to charities, were unwilling to forget the inspectors' damnation. With that record, Cole worked diligently to arrange for Fayed to sit next to the queen during the

Windsor Horse Show. The photograph of the Egyptian walking across Windsor's turf beside the monarch to the stand confirmed his successful denigration of the DTI report and the irrelevance of the City Takeover Panel's censure of him for misleading shareholders. The establishment, he had cause to believe, accepted his whitewash. But the hubris remained. Fayed wanted complete vindication and he convinced himself that he wielded sufficient power to achieve his demand in an appeal to the European Court of Human Rights.

Lord Lester, the human rights lawyer representing Fayed, had encouraged his client's belief that, despite the DTI's meticulous records, he had been denied natural justice by the inspectors. But the court's preliminary decisions in the summer dashed Fayed's optimism. His anger towards Hamilton, the DTI minister responsible for the government lawyers in Strasbourg arguing against him, intensified. Just as he raged against Hamilton, Lester telephoned with a request: could Fayed meet Peter Preston, the editor of the *Guardian*?

On 22 June 1993, Preston found himself in difficulty. That day, the *Guardian* had accused Prince Bandar bin Sultan, the Saudi Arabian minister of defence, of secretly contributing £7 million to Conservative funds before the 1992 election. The prince threatened to sue for defamation and the newspaper's editor feared he could not justify the report. Having listened to Preston's predicament, Lester suggested that Fayed, with his Middle East contacts, was worth contacting.

Considering their incompatible backgrounds, the encounter in Fayed's office at the end of the following day was unlikely to herald a soulful relationship. The *Guardian*'s leftish agenda, sharply critical of dishonest tycoons, was not naturally sympathetic towards Fayed. Yet after thirteen years as the *Guardian*'s editor, Preston, aged fifty-five, had little experience of City affairs and, while 'not forgetting' the DTI's condemnation of Fayed as a liar, he could only hazily recollect a headline rather than quote any substantive knowledge about his host. In truth, at that moment, Fayed's misdeeds were irrelevant.

The unprovable accusation about the Saudi prince jeopardized the *Guardian* and the possibility of help from the Egyptian outweighed history.

As Preston soon discovered, Fayed knew nothing about Prince Bandar or about foreign contributions to the Conservative Party. Michael Cole had collected the newspaper cuttings allowing Fayed to repeat what Preston already knew, but that was not the reason for welcoming the editor. Over the previous weeks, Britain's newspapers had published several revelations of sexual indiscretions by Conservative politicians and disreputable contributions to the Conservative Party by mysterious Greek and Hong Kong tycoons and the disgraced fugitive Asil Nadir. Only one year after its election victory, the government was enfeebled by recurring accusations of sleaze and corruption. That was precisely why Fayed had welcomed Preston in his office.

Hamilton's betrayal rankled. Despite giving so much money to the Conservatives, Fayed was angry about receiving only indignities in return. Juxtaposing the fevered media reports and his own relationship with Greer and the politicians, he easily persuaded himself that his commercial relationship, by which he bought loyalty and support, was akin to the corruption revealed daily in newspapers. In the mirrors of Fayed's Alice in Wonderland world, contradictions were produced as logic: since his corruption had failed, the British public ought to know about corrupt politicians prepared to take the money of a victim. Hungering for revenge and certain of his enormous power, Fayed calculated that the *Guardian* was a natural recipient of his bile. Flattered that an editor rather than a reporter was visiting him, he posed not as Father Christmas, a boy scout, a chef, a Harrods doorman or a fly fisherman, but in a Turnbull & Asser shirt and a Savile Row suit as an outraged, upright citizen. Pausing for breath while speaking about Conservative funds, he abandoned his duty of loyalty towards his supporters and uttered the first clue to his secret relationships.

'That Tim Smith. He come here too for money.'

Preston was puzzled. 'What's Tim Smith got to do with this?' he asked.

'I told him to go to his Saudi friends for money,' replied Fayed.

'Well, why were you brassed off about Smith coming?' asked Preston, thinking that here was the first clue of a Conservative relationship with the Saudis.

Disappointingly, Fayed's answer disproved Preston's story. Smith had approached Fayed for introductions to rich Saudis who might contribute to Tory funds. 'I showed him the door,' scoffed Fayed. 'That fugger was taking money off me. Like Hamilton and that fugger Greer. British politicians, they're all corrupt.' Fayed's outburst, mentioning the Hamiltons' greed at the Ritz and their receipt of money, provided him with an enjoyable catharsis, despite his careful concealment of his full relationship with the team. 'They ask questions in parliament because they're paid cash in brown envelopes.' Although his expletives and exaggerations undermined his credibility, Fayed's status and disclosures guaranteed him an audience unaware of his distortion: 'I pay Greer and he pays Hamilton and Smith to ask questions. The money is stuffed in brown envelopes.'

Preston was perplexed. Preoccupied by his Saudi problem, he could not quite understand the outburst. Fayed, after all, was admitting his bribery of politicians, yet he was accusing the same men of corruption. Other editors might have dismissed Fayed's allegations but Preston, disdainful of the individuals whom Fayed named, believed the 'general truth' that having paid cash to politicians the businessman was dissatisfied. On his return to the newspaper's offices, Preston assigned two reporters, David Hencke and John Mullin, to research the activities of Ian Greer, who, Fayed had said, was the paymaster. It was, the editor believed, 'a simple story: politicians were receiving secret payments'.

*

FAYED WAS NOT surprised when, three weeks later, with Tory sleaze still dominating the newspapers, Preston returned. His journalists' research, explained Preston, had revealed that, contrary to the rules of the House of Commons, neither Hamilton nor Smith had registered in the book for members' special interests their invitations to the Ritz (which only Hamilton had accepted) or payments from Ian Greer. Preston wanted more information. This time, Michael Cole was in Fayed's office. The press spokesman had been alarmed by Fayed's unguarded conversation with Preston.

After five years as Fayed's spokesman, Cole still retained his public image as an independent BBC journalist, but in truth he was utterly converted to his employer's cause. Regardless of occasional humiliation and enforced 'gardening leave', his adoring respect for Fayed inspired a desire to recast his employer's unscrupulousness as virtue. Smilingly he handed out glossy books about the Ritz, edited in 1991 by Mark Boxer, describing how the Fayeds' father had owned a hotel in Egypt and explaining that the three brothers had been 'raised by British nannies, educated in British schools' and had paid £800 million for House of Fraser 'without the help of banks'. Cole possessed no evidence that Greer had paid the MPs £2,000 per question, but he accepted Fayed's lie that Greer had been reimbursed for all the thousands of pounds paid to the politicians. Fayed, he reasoned, had committed no wrong in paying the MPs through Greer. The perfidy was the MPs' failure to declare the receipt of that money in the register of members' interests. Accordingly, on hearing that Fayed intended to show Preston a copy of Hamilton's signed bill at the Ritz, Cole suggested that, to avoid the accusation of corrupting politicians, Fayed should present himself as 'Mr Clean', a champion of the people. 'Good,' Fayed grunted.

'I'm on a mission to clean up British politics,' Fayed told Preston, reciting Cole's script. Preston appeared sympathetic, pleased that the businessman shared his objective. 'I was surprised that no one was prepared to take up my case in parliament unpaid.' Allowing Preston to see the Ritz bill and take notes but not keep a copy, Fayed emphasized that he wanted neither publicity nor mention of their meeting.

'He did not strike me', Preston would say four years later with the appearance of naivety, 'as having any particular sinister motive in telling me what he told me and, indeed, he did not seem to think it was much of a story.' Simply wanting facts, the editor believed that he could ignore the character of his source. Dealing with a journalist who 'wasn't interested in motivation' appealed to Fayed and Cole.

Fayed's compelling performance as the honest victim was repeated shortly afterwards, during Preston's third visit. Not only Cole but also Royston Webb were present when the editor returned with Geraldine Proudler, a sparky defamation solicitor, to check the facts. Enjoying the attention and warming to his theme, Fayed's heated invective against Greer, Hamilton and Smith as recipients of his cash to ask questions appalled Webb. 'Mohamed, please be quiet,' urged his lawyer, fearful of any publicity. British society, he knew, would not thank an Egyptian for tearing off its scabs. The impression Fayed made on the visitors was of Mr Big, an amiable unguided missile, barely restrained by his courtiers' warnings not to destroy himself. His emotions as he uttered his old mantra about 'his family's honour and dignity' and his effusive protestations of love for Britain persuaded the *Guardian*'s editor, its lawyer and subsequently its journalists that their informant was 'an Egyptian innocent abroad. He reminded one observer of a lad up from the country in a Ben Jonson comedy, immediately surrounded by the smart operators of Bartholomew Fair seeking to empty his purse.'

Any lingering doubts about the performance were squashed by Cole and Webb when they confirmed the veracity of their master's soliloquy. In reality, Fayed's plan had become precise. As the victim of Rowland's ten-year propaganda campaign in newspapers, he would now also manipulate journalists to wreak revenge. Encouraged by the visible excitement on his visitors' faces, and mindful that Preston had not queried whether he had instigated the payments, Fayed left the room. 'It's all strictly off the record,' urged Cole, before his employer returned with a teddy bear. 'For you,' he laughed, stuffing the toy into Proudler's arms. 'Thank you,' said the lawyer, in that same office where many others had reluctantly accepted bank-notes stuffed into their hands, pockets and cleavage. Seduced by the generous storekeeper's well-rehearsed performance as the victim not the perpetrator, even she was disarmed by the image of the innocent waving a teddy bear. Fayed, the *Guardian* journalists would write, was 'more the naughty schoolboy sent out to fetch a teddy bear while the hard men got weaving'. Just as he calculated, his performance would smother Preston's doubts about collaborating with the corrupter of politicians.

Any notion that Fayed's performance was impulsive rather than contrived was demolished by his deliberate failure to mention his relationship with Sir Michael Grylls, the chairman of the Conservative Trade and Industry Committee. Unlike Greer, Hamilton and Smith, his relations with Grylls had become personally closer thanks to a friendship between Heini and Sally Grylls during the politician's visits to the Fayeds' homes in London, Scotland and St Tropez. Despite his scornful refusals to Hamilton's lunch invitations, Heini had compelled her husband to accept an invitation to dinner at the Gryllses' home in Kennington. 'He's impossible,' Heini confided to Sally Grylls about Mohamed's resistance to food prepared by strangers, 'but I'll get him to your house.'

Obviously irritated by the prospect, Fayed had arrived late, accompanied by bodyguards, clutching a large box of expensive chocolates. 'Oh Mohamed,' sighed Sally Grylls, 'how wonderful to see you.' An awkward shuffle followed. Unexpectedly, Fayed clung on to the chocolates. They were, his hostess belatedly realized, not a present. After more grunts and shuffles, Fayed expected to sit down immediately for dinner. Once seated, he announced, 'No food for me. Just coffee,' and ripped open the box's wrappings. As the other guests, including Sir

Peter Hordern, sipped their soup, Fayed munched the finest chocolates. A pot of coffee in a cafetière was placed at his side. As his hand moved erratically downwards, depressing the plunger in an unaccustomed fashion, the pot seemed to explode, spewing coffee across the table. Thick brown liquid stained and rapidly seeped through the immaculate white linen on to the carpet. Amid chaos and embarrassment, Fayed announced that it was late. He was needed in Park Lane. If the Gryllses were upset, they could be thankful that their ungracious guest had protected them from the *Guardian*'s investigations. 'Michael Grylls did nothing for me,' he would insist, denying any payments to the MP. The *Guardian* would remain unaware of the lucrative relationship between Greer and Grylls for another fifteen months.

Concentrating on Greer's operation, David Hencke and John Mullin met the lobbyist in his elegant office to test Fayed's allegations against Hamilton and Smith. To conceal the source of their information, they did not challenge the lobbyist outright. Instead, Greer was asked to comment on the proposition that, 'in return for a parliamentary question being asked by a friendly MP, a brown envelope stuffed with fivers would be passed to the MP'. Truthfully, Greer rejected the notion. Hencke was disarmed. Untruthfully, Greer also denied inviting Tim Smith to stay at the Ritz.

The following day, Smith and Hamilton were interviewed. Both, the journalists agreed, would be asked whether they had accepted free holidays at the Ritz which they had failed to register in the book for members' special interests. Against Hamilton there was documentary proof. Both would also be asked about cash for questions.

Tim Smith, while truthfully admitting an invitation to the Ritz which had been cancelled, was visibly shaken by the allegation of secret payments of '£2,000 in a brown envelope for asking questions'. The embarrassment in his denials convinced Hencke of his guilt. Interviewing Hamilton soon after on the Commons terrace overlooking the River Thames, the junior minister also became irritated when forced to concede his stay at the Ritz. But he would dispute whether he was also asked if he had received '£2,000 in a brown envelope for asking questions'. The proof of that question was in an unsatisfactory note compiled afterwards on a computer at the *Guardian* by John Mullin, but it seems unlikely that the journalists would ask Greer and Smith about the cash payments and not Hamilton.

Late that afternoon, Hencke telephoned Greer to enquire again about the visits to the Ritz and the cash payments. Greer denied knowledge of both. In one respect, Greer was truthful. The original visits to the Ritz had been cancelled after the DTI investigation was announced. Hamilton's later visit was arranged between the politician and Fayed. Greer was also uninvolved in Fayed's cash payments to the MPs. Yet Greer's credibility was undermined by his denial of paying any MP's election expenses, while admitting 'a donation to their fighting fund' from money provided by Fayed. That unsubtle distinction contradicted Greer's denial in a television interview recorded ten years earlier in 1984 that he had ever paid MPs.

During the summer, the *Guardian* journalists wrestled frustratedly to establish Greer's financial relationships with two MPs using money provided by Mohamed Fayed. The physical reaction of both politicians to Hencke's questions suggested that Fayed's story was not fantasy, but since they denied accepting any money and Fayed's involvement was a secret, the journalists had reached stalemate. Their predicament was partially cured on 1 October 1993 when Preston received a long letter from Hamilton.

After weeks of careful drafting to minimize his relationship with Greer and Fayed, the junior minister admitted to the editor his visit to the Ritz but, he argued, the hotel was 'in effect . . . [Fayed's] private residence' and therefore he was not obliged to list any benefit in the Commons register. Disingenuously, he understated his activities for Fayed, claiming to have asked just two casual questions whereas in truth he had asked nine questions, written eight letters and joined two delegations to ministers. Hamilton's letter omitted any mention of 'cash stuffed in brown envelopes'. The omission, he would later claim, proved that the journalists had not asked the question. Hamilton, it seemed later, had orchestrated a clever manoeuvre, but at the time he was undermined by his admission of undeclared free accommodation at the Ritz.

Grateful that something could be extracted from their research, the *Guardian* published on 6 October 1993 a full-page story under the headline 'The power and prestige of Ian Greer'. In carefully lawyered phrases, the article described the influence of Greer in the Conservative Party, referred to Tim Smith's acceptance of teddy bears and Neil Hamilton's failure to register a stay 'at a European hotel' at the expense of 'a leading British company'. Fayed had no complaints. His stipulation that the Ritz should not be mentioned had been honoured. Neither Hamilton nor Greer, still retained by Fayed at £500 per month to provide parliamentary information, had perceived his treachery. On Fayed's orders, Webb had responded to Greer's anxious enquiries after publication that the newspaper's source was certainly a disgruntled former member of the lobbyist's own staff. Unblushing, Webb concealed from Greer his knowledge of Fayed's relationship with the *Guardian*.

*

READING ARTICLES in a newspaper inspired by himself excited Fayed's sense of power. Like Rowland previously, he reassured himself, he was exercising decisive influence. Discomfiting the Conservatives added extra pleasure and, aided by Michael Cole's gloss, he persuaded himself that his lust for revenge was in reality a crusade to save Britain's morals. Four weeks earlier, Fayed had seen an opportunity to offer the *Guardian* another story.

Glancing through the daily list of guests at the Ritz for 17 September sent by Frank Klein, Fayed had spotted the name Jonathan Aitken. The presence at his hotel of the handsome fifty-one-year-old junior defence minister responsible for weapons procurement was unremarkable, but Fayed, always curious for salacious gossip, wondered why Aitken, who had described himself in the hotel's register as a minister, was staying alone in Paris over the weekend. Since all the telephone conversations in the hotel's rooms could be recorded, he could also discover some of the minister's private activities. Fayed asked Klein to send the politician's bill. The payer, he saw, was Said Ayas, a Lebanese businessman. According to Klein, Wafic Said, a wealthy Saudi commission agent involved in arms deals, had also visited the hotel. Since Aitken was responsible for selling British weapons to the Middle East, Fayed naturally concluded that the three men were discussing business.

By any measure it was an unremarkable meeting between friends, but Fayed had not forgotten that in 1989, after the *Observer*'s publication of the DTI report, Aitken had been among the MPs demanding Fayed's punishment. He also harboured an angry jealousy towards Aitken. He was mixing – for business and pleasure – with powerful Arab commission agents who, by enjoying easy access to Britain's prime minister, earned millions. The combination of smooth Aitken, secretly taking unscrupulous risks to satisfy his ambitions, and apparently respectable Wafic Said, obviously earning hundreds of millions in commissions, inflamed Fayed's inferiority complex. Perhaps, he speculated, the *Guardian* could cause some mischief. 'Everyone's against me,' he told Royston Webb to justify his intended revelation. 'No one treats me properly.'

'You're risking the Ritz's reputation, Mohamed,' warned Webb. Fayed was not listening.

Summoning Preston to his office on 16 October 1993, Fayed launched into his customary vitriolic lament that the British public were victims of corrupt politicians, and he mentioned in passing that, 'Aitken is one of those corrupt bastards.' The omission of any theatrical gesture in the revelation successfully persuaded Preston that Fayed neither had a master plan nor was seeking to manipulate. Preston trusted Fayed's veracity. 'No mention of the Ritz,' insisted the Egyptian, excited by his power to attract a newspaper editor to his office. So different to Max Hastings, the *Daily Telegraph*'s editor, who refused to accept Harrods hampers and encouraged disparaging articles about the Fayeds in his newspaper.

Unfortunately, Preston appeared less excited than Fayed had anticipated. The total Ritz bill was 8,010 francs, a sum so insignificant for a man as rich as Aitken, thought Preston, that there was probably an explanation why the bill was clearly marked as paid by Said Ayas. 'I was walking through the bar,' explained Fayed, 'and I saw Aitken sitting with Ayas and Wafic Said. I asked, "Who is in charge?" and I was told, "He's a guest of Mr Ayas." I knew what was involved.' As Fayed expected, Preston reasoned that, since the Egyptian had proved to be correct about Greer, the minister's visit to Paris was worth investigating. Two journalists were assigned to question Aitken. Fayed had reason to be satisfied. At least four *Guardian* journalists were serving his agenda. His taste for manipulating the media increased after Preston's visit.

A telephone call from his brother Ali offered some astonishing news, and a new opportunity to mould the media. Hassan Yassin, a cousin of Adnan Khashoggi, had signalled the possible end of the terror and a new life. Yassin, a genial senior Saudi government official and oil consultant, had studied in California while Ali Fayed was employed by Khashoggi and stayed in contact ever since. Like the other Khashoggis, Yassin had also cared for Dodi and knew Tiny Rowland. On Wednesday, 20 October 1993, Yassin and Khashoggi had lunched with Rowland in Lonrho's headquarters. Other guests included Palestinians excited by the recent peace agreement with Israel. At the end of the meal, Yassin pulled Rowland aside. 'If the Israelis and Palestinians can make peace,' he said, 'why don't I broker a deal between you and Mohamed?' Rowland sprang at the idea. Yassin contacted Ali Fayed and, during the following day, the Fayed brothers negotiated with Rowland by fax. By nightfall, Mohamed Fayed understood his own strength.

This was not the first time Rowland had considered peace. In November 1991, he had made an unsuccessful approach through a 'Mr Ostrich', but Fayed had spurned the suspicious emissary. This time, the store-owner had everything to gain. Rowland was financially and emotionally exhausted by the conflict he had launched. Lonrho's mammoth trial against Fayed listed for January 1994 was opposed by Dieter Bock, the strange German purchaser of Rowland's Lonrho shares, and, having argued with Bock, Rowland had found a new person to hate. Vendettas were Rowland's oxygen but he could only wage one vendetta at a time. True to his aphorism – 'I never forgive my enemies unless I need them. Then they become my friends' – he had as little taste for appearing in a witness box as Fayed. From Fayed's point of view, as the owner of Harrods, he was the victor and, in seeking allies to wage war against the Conservatives, Rowland was an ideal recruit.

Meeting after lunch on 22 October 1993 in Yassin's elegant Knightsbridge house, Fayed and Rowland hugged and kissed each other, laughing as old friends. The extraordinary enmity of their nine-year war seemed forgotten as Yassin poured tea. The press release, discussed over the previous twenty-four hours and announcing that the two were 'pledged to work together in expanding their mutual interests', was agreed and signed. To Rowland's delight, none of his closest colleagues at Lonrho knew about the negotiations towards reconciliation. The only casualty of the peace would be Rowland's young solicitor, who, having worked exhaustively in his cause, suffered a heart attack after hearing the news and dropped dead. 'We must make up in public,' urged Fayed compellingly. 'Under the shark.' Six years earlier, he had hung a huge preserved shark from the Food Hall's ceiling with 'Tiny' painted in white on its fin. Weakly, Rowland agreed that he would enter Fayed's kingdom and pose as the shark was lowered in a manner which signalled surrender.

Grinning and touching the jaw of the shark at four o'clock that afternoon, Rowland and Fayed were surrounded by over one hundred journalists and photographers to record the end of London's infamous battle. 'We are very old friends and we've become friends again,' gushed Rowland. Tickling him under the chin, Fayed smiled and wrapped his arm around his enemy. Once again, Rowland had been fooled.

As they rose to Fayed's fifth-floor office on the new escalators, the store-owner's face reflected his iron will. Drinks had been prepared in his dining room to celebrate the honeymoon and there were teddy bears, toys and Fayed's normal trinkets for Rowland and Josie, his wife. Yet his agenda was not peace but war. Rowland, he was determined, would provide the evidence that Michael Howard was bribed to approve the DTI investigation and that Margaret Thatcher had masterminded the corrupt conspiracy. 'They enjoy each other's company,' Michael Cole said about that afternoon's celebrations. 'They're swapping old war stories and comparing notes. There have been lots of interesting comments.' For once, Cole was the master of understatement.

'If you'd shown a flicker of interest in my £5 million offer,' Rowland quipped to Royston Webb, referring to his proffered bribe, 'I'd have increased it to £10 million.' Webb laughed.

Fayed showed ill-concealed impatience. 'Can Macnamara speak to Etheridge?' he asked, referring to Rowland's security adviser.

'Yes,' replied Rowland with noticeable sincerity.

'And Jones?' asked Fayed, refering to Graham Jones, his former finance director.

'I'll give you something of interest about that,' promised Rowland.

Fayed gurgled excitedly. By then Simon Greenwood, Modena's former managing director, had been convicted of fraud and sentenced to three years' imprisonment. Fayed would recover £3.5 million from Modena's vendors, justifying his self-righteous suspicions of his employees and enemies. No one, he reasoned, could be trusted, least of all those managing his finances.

One week later, Webb received a call from Rowland: 'I'm sending a package across to you.' Ripping it open, Webb was astonished. Rowland had delivered the evidence of his corruption of Jones. Included were not only internal Lonrho memoranda directing payments of £550,000 to Jones in a Liechtenstein account, but Lonrho's contract with Jones, and Jones's lengthy reports to Lonrho describing his secret activities in the City to undermine House of Fraser's financial status. 'This is very useful,' Webb told Fayed.

His employer grinned. Here was proof of his victimization. 'The City and Westminster should read this,' he thought to himself. That evening, he telephoned a journalist at the *Financial Times*.

'It's terribly embarrassing,' Rowland complained to Webb in an irate morning telephone call after reading Saturday's *Financial Times*. 'First the embarrassment under the shark and now this leak.' Secretly, Webb sympathized. His employer possessed no self-restraint. To score a burst of favourable publicity, Fayed was willing to sour the new relationship. But Webb misunderstood his employer. Fayed was interested not merely in publicity but in vindication and revenge, and encouraging reports from Peter Preston suggested that his leak of Jonathan Aitken's bill was stirring mischief.

Politely, David Pallister of the *Guardian* had asked Aitken to explain how his meeting at the Ritz with prominent Saudis 'relates to your job in government'. In his curt reply, Aitken categorically denied meeting Ayas or Wafic Said in Paris and explained that his visit to Paris was 'to meet up with my wife and daughter – who was going to her new school that weekend'. Like Hamilton, Aitken did not realize that his lie was exposed by the Ritz bill. Fayed's credibility was enhanced as Aitken, during an exchange of letters with Preston, begrudgingly admitted that he had after all met Said Ayas in Paris but minimized the encounter as a 'family matter'. The unanswered question was why the minister, contrary to fixed government rules, had failed to declare Ayas's hospitality. Just as in Hamilton's case, there was no crime in a politician receiving payments. The wrong was the politician's failure to register his receipt of the financial benefit.

Excited by the minister's contradictions, Preston returned to Harrods on 23 November. Seated with Cole, Webb and Mark Griffiths, Fayed heard how Aitken was lying and that the *Guardian*'s investigations were stymied without a copy of the bill. 'OK,' said Fayed, 'I give it.'

Instantly, his approval was opposed by his three employees. 'It'll lead to trouble, Mohamed,' warned Cole. Webb agreed. The hotel, they argued, would be accused of a breach of confidentiality. Consquences were rarely of interest to Fayed but, searching for a ruse to overcome their protests, Preston suggested that he send a fax on Aitken's House of Commons notepaper to the Ritz asking for a copy of the bill. The reply telephone number would be the *Guardian*'s.

'Good,' smiled Fayed. He would tell Klein what to do when the 'cod fax' arrived. In return, Fayed's representatives would be allowed by the *Observer*'s new owners to search that newspaper's old files for evidence of Rowland's misdemeanours and bribes.

In the excitement, Fayed no longer cared that on 25 December 1993, after twenty-four court appearances, Christoph Bettermann had been acquitted in Dubai. Of course, he would not allow the German to enjoy his release. He risked nothing by appealing and pursuing a civil claim to recover damages. To remind his enemies and employees that his persecutions never ceased, a defamatory story about 'Bettermann's fraud' was placed in *Private Eye*. The only casualty, Fayed believed, would be Bettermann.

After Christmas in Balnagown, Fayed returned to London with a crowded agenda. Uppermost in his mind when he met

Andrew Neil, the editor of the *Sunday Times*, for lunch appeared to be the accomplishment of his new year's resolution, to become a media tycoon. 'You need to own a newspaper to be powerful in Britain,' he had complained to his staff. If only he owned a newspaper, he could wage a campaign to rewrite his past. Fayed hoped that Neil might provide wise counsel about realizing his ambitions. Neil, who would write, 'The country needs another one hundred Al Fayeds', was sympathetic to his host's complaints although unaware of his plot to use the media for his own advantage.

*

ONE YEAR HAD PASSED and there was still no reply to Fayed's application for British citizenship. If he was trusted to walk beside the queen at the Royal Windsor Horse Show, he had reasoned, he could be entrusted with a British passport. But he feared the worst. By appalling coincidence, the new home secretary was Michael Howard, who, in Fayed's outlandish conspiracy theory, had been bribed to initiate the DTI investigation; and the junior Home Office minister responsible for immigration was Charles Wardle, a former Lonrho auditor who, again according to Fayed's conspiracy theory, was Rowland's stooge. Wrongly, Fayed believed that Wardle was a paid parliamentary consultant to Peat Marwick, Lonrho's auditors, but he correctly recalled that in March 1990 Wardle had denounced the Fayeds, urging that they be disqualified as directors. As the victim of their plot and, as always, keen to attract the spotlight, Fayed wanted revenge on those to blame for his humiliation. Neil would serve his purpose.

'Those fuggin' MPs', he told Neil, 'ask questions for £1,000. I know because I'm paying MPs.' Having won Neil's complete attention with his tale of a crusade against corruption, he secured the editor's promise not to reveal his source. 'You must not use those MPs who have asked questions about my business,' Fayed warned. Telling Neil that the questions cost £1,000 rather than £2,000, he thought, would disguise the

Sunday Times's source from the *Guardian*. Grateful for the tip, Neil detailed journalists to test Fayed's story. Three teams were now working to the store-owner's agenda.

The latest bravado reflected Fayed's rising self-confidence as his finances, despite horrendous losses, improved. To win the banks' agreement to refinance his loans and avoid bankruptcy, he had been compelled to sell the Barkers building in Kensington High Street for £100 million and the Harrods credit card operation, with access to 250,000 card holders, for £180 million. Painfully, he had also been pressured to sell the Sears shares in March 1993, choking on a £62 million loss. Fayed had cause to suspect the banks after they had ordered him to disclose in advance his lowest sale price. '£1 per share,' he had replied. An unknown banker, mischievously indiscreet, had possibly leaked that information. In the weeks before his sale, the share price had never risen above that level, convincing proof that at least one banker had profited by sabotaging his negotiations. City bankers, he regretted, were no different from stallholders in Alexandria's bazaar. Every secret was used for someone's profit.

With his debts reduced to just over £700 million, Fayed's final salvation would be the sale of House of Fraser. Having rejected £300 million in a management buy-out and sticking for one year to £500 million, Fayed finally agreed with Warburgs to float the fifty-nine stores for £414 million. But there was a caveat. Cautious about unknown liabilities, the bankers insisted that they would retain £100 million for one year. 'No way,' raged Mohamed. 'That's an insult.'

The alternative, said Derek Higgs, was to pursue due diligence right through his finances. Warburgs would not risk their reputation on the Egyptian. Fayed's face blazed and he left the room. 'Ali is our route,' agreed the bankers. 'He doesn't call the shots but he understands. He's our intermediary.' After bitter fighting, the compromise was £40 million.

'That's still an insult,' spat Fayed.

'No other way, Mohamed,' replied Higgs. The cynical

bankers regarded their client as 'a weird genius' whose qualities – vision, weakness and blindness to problems – could easily have led to his bankruptcy. 'I had to show my underpants to get a settlement,' laughed Fayed, referring to the bankers' intrusive investigation before they finally agreed to the terms of the flotation.

After signing the mountain of documents for the flotation in the City, Royston Webb stopped off on his way back to Harrods at the Army & Navy Stores. 'These are for you, Mohamed,' said Webb, offering Fayed a plastic A&N bag. Inside was a jumbo pair of pants. Fayed hugged him. 'It was closer than you realized, Mohamed,' sighed Webb.

'I always knew you'd do it,' said Fayed emotionally. The flotation of House of Fraser by Warburgs, he convinced himself, signalled that he had won the trust of another British institution, the City. Summoning Jim Walsh, he offered £300,000 to the American as a reward for organizing the refinancing. 'You want cash?' asked Fayed, meaning it could be paid into an offshore bank to avoid income tax.

'No,' replied Walsh. 'I'll take it through my regular pay cheque.'

Fayed looked puzzled. Cautious people aroused his suspicions. There had been too many arguments with the American, he believed. It was time for a change.

In April 1994, the Fayeds owned Harrods free of an excessively burdensome debt and liberated from bankers. But only momentarily. Unable to resist the urge, Fayed immediately negotiated a new £100 million loan, using Harrods as security, to buy out Salah's troublesome interest, and then contemplated how to raise even more money to satisfy his yearning for spending more on his lifestyle. Fayed was an incurable debt-junkie.

Ali Fayed, owning one-third of Harrods, shared his elder brother's desire for more cash. Delighted to slide into semi-retirement owning Turnbull & Asser and using his stake in Harrods to buy a yacht and a Gulfstream jet and to build a

luxurious lifestyle in America, he feared that Mohamed, resisting any interference in the management of the store, might risk
the whole business by indulging in expensive litigation and
political agitation. Long term, his share of Harrods was also
jeopardized without a suitable plan for the succession. Dodi
was not a suitable candidate nor were his own children.
Although Mudi, Salah's son, was old and intelligent enough,
neither Mohamed nor Ali trusted that solution. 'All our eggs
are in one basket,' agreed Mohamed. 'Let's sell 20 per cent.'
The answer, they decided, was to float Harrods on the London
Stock Exchange. They would secure a mountain of cash and
win respectability as conventional businessmen. Neither had
any doubt that Omar Bayoumi, the son of an Egyptian and a
Warburgs banker on the House of Fraser flotation, should
mastermind the sale. Bayoumi, aged thirty-nine, would be
employed as Fayed's new group finance director.

Bayoumi's arrival at Harrods coincided with an outbreak
of war in the fifth-floor jungle between Bolliger and a new
Fayed protégé, a German computer expert. Over the previous
three years, Fayed and Bolliger had become close. Tactfully, to
cope with Fayed's infamous five-minute attention span, the
Swiss spared him humiliation by refraining from discussions in
front of other staff. As their relationship developed and Bolliger's management improved Harrods' profits, Fayed provided
the Swiss with a family home in Knightsbridge and invited the
executive for dinner to Oxted; whenever Bolliger appeared
tired, Fayed would encourage him to holiday either at Balnagown or at the Ritz.

Bolliger had not been immune from the vicissitudes of
Fayed's autocracy. Passively, he had watched executives hired
and fired within twenty-four hours; he had remained silent
when girls complained about Fayed's harassment; and he had
not protested when told about telephone taps or after witnessing an executive escorted from the premises on the ground that
he was 'treating Harrods like a whorehouse'. Unemotionally,
he had observed the covert entrapment of David Morris, a

concessionary jeweller in the store, whose long-standing tenure was terminated for breach of contract. Like all Fayed's executives, the Swiss had lived with the fear and insecurity of the store-owner's unusual regime and naturally, as managing director, had initiated some dismissals himself. Yet despite his loyalty, Fayed had unjustifiably decided during March 1994 that Bolliger was untrustworthy. The Swiss, according to the German computer expert, was treacherous. In Fayed's court, the whisperer was not questioned but rewarded. Bolliger, pronounced the king, had passed his sell-by date. But to avoid his expensive contractual obligations Fayed staggered the execution. After signing a succession of letters accusing Bolliger of mistaken decisions, he anticipated that his letter on 7 April 1994 would finally provoke the predictable response.

'I'm going. I've had enough,' exclaimed Bolliger a few hours later in his office.

'Think about it,' suggested Fayed. Bolliger was assuaged with the offer of reorganizing Kurt Geiger.

Days later, their relations soured further. 'You're fired,' snapped Fayed. 'Leave your company house immediately.' There was no surprise within Harrods. The survival of the store's managers was frequently compared with the fate of second lieutenants on the Somme. Reflecting his master's desire, Michael Cole could not resist a dig in his press release announcing Bolliger's departure, 'for family reasons. Harrods is a very big store and no one is bigger than the institution.'

Unlike most of Fayed's victims, who left quietly, Bolliger was too proud of his achievements to tolerate Cole's snide epitaph. A *Mail on Sunday* journalist was given pugnacious quotes. 'You simply cannot have two kings in an organization like Harrods,' said Bolliger, explaining that his efforts had produced 'sensational profits, the best in the store's history'.

Reading the newspaper on Sunday morning, 25 April 1994, Fayed was incensed. The dismissal now reflected badly upon himself. The man, treated as his surrogate son, had betrayed his trust. Bolliger was to be maliciously humiliated. 'The man's a crook,' Fayed breathed at Macnamara. 'Fraud, he's guilty of fraud.' He was to be thrown out of his company house on to the street. His bank accounts were to be frozen. He was to be sued for every penny. Convinced that in Britain 'You can buy anything you like,' Fayed automatically expected Macnamara to call his friends in the Metropolitan Police to report a criminal offence and return the favours bestowed by Harrods.

Fayed's next call was to Cole. His faithful mouthpiece understood long before the tirade was completed what was expected. Contacting trustworthy journalists, Cole dictated the new version of Bolliger's sins. 'He was fired for incompetence, dishonesty and dereliction of duty,' he puffed. A dossier of Bolliger's 'dishonesty' would be handed to Chelsea police. The following morning, the *Daily Mail* and the *Guardian*, under its headline, 'Harrods gives police dossier on former managing director', faithfully repeated Cole's allegations. Neither Cole nor Macnamara scrutinized Fayed's denunciation. His edict was the Gospel. Like all employees within Fayed's empire, Bolliger had ignored the tyranny until touched by the suffering.

Efficiently, Fayed's machine served a brutal indictment against its target. An audit of Kurt Geiger was claimed to have discovered incompetence and dishonesty; Harrods had been defrauded of £2 million; thousands of pounds had been mis-spent in personal telephone calls; Bolliger had grossly mishan-dled a £3.3 million modernization plan; he had paid without authorization a £22,000 severance payment to a dishonest employee; and he had employed his daughter's South African fiancé in contravention of immigration laws. Despite these distortions, a judge issued a *Mareva* injunction freezing all Bolliger's assets in Britain. The bulldozer was irresistible.

Disgracing Bolliger fired Fayed's self-confidence. All employees were reminded of the awesome consequences of antagonizing the chairman. To Fayed, the outcome was irrele-vant, even though it was a defeat. On the eve of the court hearing one month later, Ali, the unprotesting, compliant brother, negotiated a settlement agreeing to the release of all

Bolliger's possessions, the withdrawal of all the charges and the payment of £50,156 in compensation.

By then, Bolliger was, despite his complete exoneration, just another forgotten victim. Walking with his bodyguards across the hills at Balnagown, Fayed lifted his .410 game gun, worth £20,000, swung with the bird and fired. Simultaneously, behind him, his two bodyguards lifted their Remington Wing-masters and pulled the triggers. A cloud of lead pellets filled the sky. In a burst of feathers, the bird spiralled to the ground. Fayed grunted: 'Got it!'

'Yessir,' replied the former soldiers. 'We missed.'

'Bah,' scoffed Fayed. 'You no good.'

14

War

OSTENSIBLY, IN JULY 1994, Mohamed Fayed, aged sixty-five, suffered few ills. Blessed with gross wealth veering towards £1 billion, he could commute between his nine homes in his Gulfstream jet, Sikorski helicopter and a fleet of armoured Mercedes limousines. Despite a back problem treated in Houston, Texas, the hypochondriac's health was excellent. His recent alarm about prostate cancer had passed, after he had consulted several doctors. Befitting an emperor, a penthouse in the style of a Roman villa was being built on the new eighth floor in Park Lane. Solid gold fittings on his double bath and a vast, ornate quilt on his antique four-poster bed were testament of enviable luxury. Expensive Flemish oils hung on the walls, but few believed that Fayed knew their provenance. Accompanied everywhere by Karen McKenzie, his house manageress, his exquisite wardrobe, his food fetishes and even the precise position of air fresheners in any room he cared to enter were supervised by an army of compliant employees. Obedient himself only to the sultan – a small, leather-jacketed man seen occasionally eating in the Georgian Restaurant – he massaged the illusion of deserving a privileged place in Britain.

After Fayed had dismissed Norman Bartholomew as his security chief, and fired six other bodyguards in a characteristic mass purge, General Norman Schwarzkopf, the American hero of the Gulf War, had, over lunch at Harrods, recommended Maurice Tudor as a replacement. 'A great SAS officer in the Gulf,' said Schwarzkopf. 'He's just retired.' Hiring the former

SAS colonel reassured Fayed that his occasional encounters with the royal family, senior politicians, newspaper editors and celebrities confirmed his membership of the club. At the Gulfstream advisory board, Henry Kissinger and Conrad Black had listened respectfully as Fayed boasted how he had sold five Gulfstream jets with solid gold taps in the lavatories. 'Well done, Mohamed,' one tycoon cooed, silently jesting about the Egyptian's childlike yearning for praise. Fayed glowed. Everyone, he believed, sympathized with him as the victim of monstrous injustice, let down by the British.

The delusion soon passed. Dissatisfaction reeked from every pore. Virtually friendless except among those accepting his money, Fayed was an unloved, tormented loner. Classed as an outsider, his persecution of employees contrasted oddly with his craving for acceptance. Incapable of self-criticism, he blamed his ostracism on conspiracies. The perpetrators were not hard to identify. Daily, the media was filled with reports of sleaze in the Conservative government. 'You can buy anything you like,' Fayed mused, thinking about his own relationships with the police, the media, the politicians and his own employees. There seemed no reason for his notoriety when so many, exposed as guilty of much worse, escaped any shame. He had done so much for England. Acceptance by the islanders was his right, but outrageously it was denied.

His latest rage had been innocently sparked by Geoffrey Dickens, a Conservative MP. After a brief conversation with Charles Wardle, the junior Home Office minister responsible for immigration, Dickens reported that the brothers' applications for British nationality were not progressing smoothly. The possibility of rejection incensed Fayed, and the culprit, he assumed, was Michael Howard, the lackey of the conspirators. As usual, his assumption was wrong, but Dickens could not have imagined the consequences of his message.

The Fayeds' applications had in fact been rejected outright six months earlier. On 23 December 1993 a report from Department B4 in Liverpool, responsible for naturalization, had arrived at the Home Office advising that the DTI report disqualfied the Fayeds' from British citizenship. Instinctively, Wardle agreed. The Fayeds, the junior minister believed, were dubious and the inspectors' condemnation was unequivocal. Anticipating controversy, Wardle's private office had listed the issue for discussion with Michael Howard at a regular meeting on 21 January 1994.

To Wardle's surprise, the Fayeds' application was mentioned earlier by Howard. On 6 January 1994, at the end of a departmental meeting in Howard's office, Wardle was asked to remain. 'You know they've turned down the Fayeds' application for citizenship?' asked Howard.

'Yes,' replied Wardle, implying that he saw no reason to contradict the recommendation.

Howard appeared preoccupied. 'This is all somewhat embarrassing for me. Do you remember all those letters that Fayed and Rowland sent MPs and everyone else about their war? My name was mentioned in connection with Landy. It all died down but with this citizenship issue I'm afraid that it will revive. My name will be all over the place. The whole DTI row is going to be raised again. Could you ask them to review their decision?' Noncommittally, Wardle nodded. 'Get some references from the Bank of England,' Howard added. On returning to his private office, Wardle mentioned Howard's request.

Two weeks later, Howard raised the subject again: 'Any news from Liverpool?'

Wardle was rather astonished. Although nothing had been done, he had re-read the DTI's conclusions. 'It's not surprising,' he told Howard. 'The DTI report is the roadblock.'

'Did you make further enquiries at the Bank of England?' asked Howard, clearly searching for any route to grant citizenship. Wardle had not but, on returning to his office, told his private secretary that Howard wanted the decision reconsidered and left his official to refer the request back to the Home Office's Department B4. On 27 April 1994 the file returned to Howard's desk with the decision unaltered.

In July, Wardle moved to the DTI and was replaced by Nicholas Baker. Over lunch in the Commons dining room, Baker and Wardle discussed the Fayeds' application. 'Michael wants references from the Bank of England,' said Wardle, 'but, even if they're favourable, the DTI report remains a roadblock.' By then, not only Dickens but also Sir Peter Hordern, House of Fraser's official parliamentary consultant, had at Fayed's request approached Wardle for information. The news about the probability of rejection coincided with a sensational report about corrupt Conservative MPs in the *Sunday Times*.

On 10 July, the newspaper's headline – 'Revealed: MPs who accept £1,000 to ask a parliamentary question' – provoked a mocking yell. Jabbing his direct-dial telephone console in his tent, Fayed excitedly rang up Cole, Webb and Macnamara. 'This shows they're all fuggin' corrupt. I'm going to get Michael Howard. I'm fuggin' going to get all of them.' The suspension of two Conservative MPs, both parliamentary private secretaries to ministers, named as prepared to take cash for questions, persuaded Fayed that his influence in dictating the agenda extended beyond Harrods and the media into Westminster.

Royston Webb was not enthusiastic about his employer's ambitions to expose Greer. 'I don't think that's a good idea, Mohamed,' he advised. 'It'll end badly.' Cole echoed a similar warning. Irritated, Fayed retreated, grumbling that a victim surely had the right to expose a conspiracy.

Beyond the tent walls was his qualification for respect: horses, a splendid swimming pool, cultivated gardens, a huge house, 2,000 acres and dozens of donkeys waiting to serve his whims. Within the tent was his refuge from disturbance. The estate was blighted by the new eight-lane M25, and a nearby landfill site was emitting methane gas which he feared would explode. While his lawyers fought the local council at £250 per hour to reverse the invasion, his only defence was hundreds of trees planted to absorb the fumes. Domestic life inside the house was also disturbed. Keeping young girls as nannies at Oxted had become a problem. Omar's demanding behaviour and Heini's, interfering commands, especially her fanatic concern for hygiene, unsettled the domestics. Heini's ban on nannies eating in the same kitchen as her children and her constant reprimands of the young women for drinking from the children's cups and other minor offences caused frequent departures. Fayed's own conduct was also unhelpful. In his search for domestics, he had recruited Hermina da Silva, an attractive Portuguese at Harrods, and offered her employment first as a domestic and then as a nanny. Da Silva worked unprotesting until, one night, Fayed had inveigled her into his room to touch and kiss her. Faced with her adamant refusal to co-operate, he had soon after dismissed her. Unlike others, da Silva was unwilling to suffer his harassment silently. She gave notice that she would sue for wrongful dismissal and mention his attempted assault. As usual, John Macnamara had been asked to 'sort out' the threat. Unfortunately, a surreptitious tape recording revealed her obduracy. Delivering an acceptable solution, Macnamara believed, would help his promotion.

Following the flotation of House of Fraser, Macnamara's job as director of security had disappeared. Based in Park Lane, he now worked with Bob Loftus, and together the men listened to the taped conversation of a Harrods manager with da Silva. 'It's no good,' she had said in broken English. 'He's a very bad man and he mustn't get away with this. I'm a Catholic and I don't care. He tried to assault me.' Macnamara favoured a warning. A complaint was made to the police station at West End Central that da Silva had stolen property from Salah's apartment in Park Lane. 'We've done a moody,' Macnamara told Loftus, using police jargon. 'She's going to be nicked.' Arrested on fales charges of theft, da Silva was later released without charge. Unintimidated, she pursued her claim. At the end of the summer, Fayed agreed to pay £12,000 compensation. There was nevertheless a reward for all those who had performed special services.

Every three months, Loftus, like many other employees, presented himself in Fayed's office. By summer 1994, the routine was well established. 'Have you got my expenses?' asked Loftus.

'Yes. How much I pay you?' replied Fayed, relishing the performance.

'£2,000, Mr Al Fayed,' replied Loftus.

'So much?' asked Fayed quizzically. 'Are you worth so much?' Tiring of the game, Fayed either dipped into his case or ordered the security officer to return later: 'I'll leave envelope with Nancy Bush.'

At the end of the day, a white envelope with the cash was waiting on the fifth floor. Another envelope for Eamon Coyle, Loftus's deputy, contained £1,000. Cash payments to all his senior employees was Fayed's method of seduction and entrapment and not always in private. At the wedding celebration of Mark Griffiths, his increasingly powerful but uninspiring assistant, Fayed created a spectacle by walking into the crowded dining room, surrounded by bodyguards, and marching towards the bride and groom seated at the head table. Like the mafia don, he halted silently in front of his trusted employee and presented a thick, white envelope. A brick of fifties, three inches thick, calculated the cognoscenti. It must be £20,000. As Griffiths, red-faced, spluttered his gratitude, Fayed turned and departed. His power and patronage had been registered. More than ever Fayed valued the services of Loftus, Macnamara, Webb, Cole and Griffiths. For money and gifts they were prepared to perform many unusual services to protect their paymaster. Just like Greer and the MPs. His money was power and, in the simple equation, he could no longer distinguish between his power at Harrods and his influence over women, over journalists and over politicians. He was entitled to respect, obedience and acceptance from all. Unfortunately, some did not comply with his wishes.

*

'THEY'RE SHITTING ON ME. They've insulted my honour,' hollered Fayed. Royston Webb squirmed. Fayed had heard on 18 September 1994 that the European Court had unanimously rejected his complaint against the DTI. Nine independent judges, derided by the Conservatives for successive anti-British decisions, had declared that the inspectors had been impeccably fair and that the Fayeds had been given every reasonable opportunity to respond to all the allegations. There was no further appeal.

'We've lost, Mohamed,' sighed Webb. 'Forget about it and let everyone else forget it. Just get on and run Harrods. Enjoy everything you've got.' Equally cautious, Cole urged his idol to draw a line. Fayed appeared to accept the advice. Moments later, the wave of indignation returned. Building his fortune had not been a selfish enterprise but was for the good of humanity, a tireless sacrifice for Britain and for his family. Like an automaton, blind to his own faults and oblivious to his own corruption of the politicians, he chanted a refrain which would become familiar to a wide audience over the following months: 'I have a conscience. I have my dignity. My honour. Britain is my country. I have paid my taxes. And all that for bunch of crooks in power.' Temporarily, Webb, the *consigliere*, again silenced the urge for revenge.

'Disillusioned' was the phrase Cole put into his master's mouth. 'Mohamed can't understand what has happened to him,' Cole would repeat to enquiring journalists. 'We believe it was a victory in that the court heard the case.'

The spokesman's conversations were interrupted by Fayed. The obsession to rewrite his past had suffocated reason. 'Get Preston. Tell him to come.'

Cole was hesitant: 'I don't think that's a good idea, Mohamed.'

'Do,' ordered Fayed. Perpetually dazzled by the unquestioned power he wielded within his store, he had decided to challenge the British government. Obediently, Cole summoned the editor.

Peter Preston found Fayed emotional and slightly unsteady when he arrived on the fifth floor on the evening of 19 September 1994. Drinking whisky, his trouser flies undone, his braces askew over a rumpled, sweaty shirt, Fayed was suffering. 'I don't owe these fuggin' corrupt politicians anything,' he bayed. 'I'm going to ruin them. Now we show the bastards. Now I right behind you.' Fayed promised to provide Hamilton's bill from the Ritz and files of correspondence between himself and Greer. 'The government must cancel the DTI report,' he spluttered. Nothing other than an official revocation would satisfy him. The notion was so ridiculous that Preston remained silent. All he wanted, as he watched Fayed the Egyptian move restlessly around his office, was a copy of Hamilton's bill at the Ritz. The image of confusion reassured Preston. Fayed had not sinisterly, as in a bad James Bond film, presented a master file. The chaos of a rambling Arab, he reasoned, confirmed the absence of a conspiracy. 'I'm baffled by Fayed's motivation,' he would later say. But the store-owner's invitation to Preston had been germinating for over one year. 'You get the bill,' Fayed promised, leaving the editor uncertain if he could rely on the promise.

Fayed's next visitor, responding to a warning of imminent damnation if his invitation was ignored, was Ian Greer. Although his contract with the lobbyist had ended three weeks earlier, the Egyptian had decided that Greer would be thrown to the jackals. The shirt-lifter had done nothing for his money. Now he would serve his purpose in an unexpected way for which he did not list a charge. Sitting with Mark Griffiths, there was no hint of shame as Fayed offered tea and disguised his betrayal over the past year. 'He was meant to be a friend,' he began as he launched into a fifty-minute denunciation of Hamilton, 'but he has ignored me ever since he was made a minister. Even my letter of congratulation he ignored.'

'Well, Mohamed,' began Greer, 'as a minister he cannot allow his personal sympathies to enter into the matter. He's duty bound to—'

But Fayed was not listening. His eyes were glistening, even bulging: 'That Thatcher. She's taken millions from Wafic Said for arms deals. How else could she live in that house? And Michael Howard, he's taken £1 million from that crook. All are crooks. All are taking money. I'm going to see Brian Hitchen. I'll tell him to go to Major and warn him that unless he pulls back the report I'll expose the corruption of ministers. The government will fall. You see if I care. I'll sell my business and move to France. They appreciate me there. You give my message to Major. Tell him he can't fug Mohamed Al Fayed.'

Confused, Greer departed and telephoned Royston Webb. 'What evidence does Mohamed have about corruption in the government?' asked the lobbyist.

'None that I've ever seen,' replied Webb. Greer had no reason to doubt the lawyer's assurance.

Fayed's next call was to Tiny Rowland. He wanted the conspirator's confession. Rowland was delighted to accept the invitation to lunch at Harrods on 26 September. In the dining room, just inside the security doors on the fifth floor, he appeared quite relaxed as 'Tootsie', his pet name for his enemy, squeezed prodigious quantities of lemon on to a plate of smoked salmon. To lighten the atmosphere, Fayed reverted to his favourite topic, sex. Mentioning the possibility of a penis transplant and complaining about jet-lag, he pointed down to his groin. 'It too is jet-lagged and doesn't know what to do.'

Rowland laughed, 'There's an old saying, "Life doesn't agree with me" – I've got to do something to agitate me. I've got to look at Marilyn Monroe, haven't I, and all sorts of pictures to get any sort of life down there.'

Both pensioners roared, Fayed somewhat exaggeratedly. Past antagonisms seemed to have disappeared as they reminisced about their twenty-five-year relationship and their good fortune in enjoying good health. 'You got some winners,' laughed Fayed, 'I got some winners.' Since Fayed owned Harrods and Rowland had lost Lonrho, the winner of the financial battle was obvious.

CASH FOR QUESTIONS
Wrongly convinced that Michael
Howard (*right*) had been bribed to
order a DTI investigation of himself,
Fayed secretly paid Tim Smith (*bottom,
left*) and Neil Hamilton (*below, right*)
to promote his case in parliament. Ian
Greer (*below, left*), his hired lobbyist,
introduced the MPs. Sir Michael Grylls,
(*bottom, right*) the senior government
backbencher, who failed to declare
payments from Greer, was also
close to Fayed.

Bob Loftus   Michael Cole and John Macnamara

OBSESSIVE SECURITY

Fearing that too many Harrods staff were dishonest, Fayed ordered Bob Loftus
to monitor his employees' conversations and movements secretly. Loftus reported to
John Macnamara, a former senior police officer at Scotland Yard. Together with
Michael Cole, Fayed's spokesman, Macnamara repeatedly sought to influence the
media's reports. No other storekeeper in the world is surrounded by as many
bodyguards as Fayed, pictured arriving in Paris in June 1998 for a hearing
about the death of Princess Diana.

PEACE AND WAR
After 1984, Tiny
Rowland waged an
unprecedented vendetta
against Fayed. Among
his allies was Adnan
Khashoggi, Fayed's
former brother-in-law,
who introduced the
Swamiji, an Indian guru,
to Rowland. Exhausted
by the battle, Rowland
agreed to public
reconciliation in 1993
under a stuffed shark in
Harrods' Food Hall. The
smiling image belied
Fayed's secret intention
to use Rowland to
expose the Conservative
government's 'conspiracy'
against himself.

THE MEDIA EMPIRE

Celebrating the re-launch of *Punch* in 1996, a £7 million flop within one year. This was Fayed's last hope to realize his dream of a media empire. Peter McKay (*centre*), his first editor, soon departed; while Stewart Steven (*right*), a senior adviser, resisted Fayed's publicity gimmick to push a cream cake into his face.

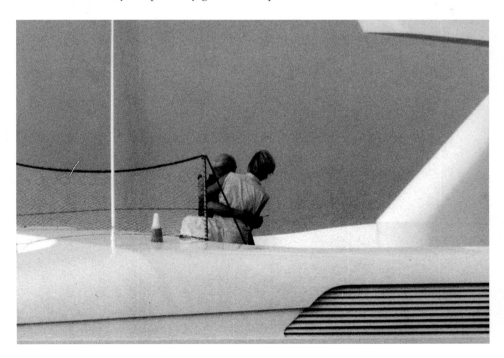

GOING FOR BROKE
Princess Diana's visit to St Tropez in
summer 1997 was Fayed's astonishing
publicity coup in his bid to win
acceptance. Fayed, photographed with
his arm around Diana (*opposite*), caused
a storm of protest in Britain, as did
the first photographic proof
of her affair with Dodi.

FATEFUL DAY

Above, left: Henri Paul, the Ritz driver at Le Bourget airport speaking to Dodi on 30 August 1997. *Above, right:* Paul's drinking problem was not noticed by Kes Wingfield (*back to camera*) and Trevor Rees-Jones, the two bodyguards, at the bar of the Ritz that night.

FATEFUL NIGHT

René Delorm (*opposite, bottom*), Dodi's valet, waited in
his employer's Paris apartment while in the streets Dodi was fretting
about the paparazzi, later contriving a scheme for Henri Paul (*above*)
to outwit the paparazzi as they left the Ritz (*below*).

TRAGEDY
Fayed and Heini at Westminster Abbey for Diana's funeral.

'You know,' replied Rowland in his smooth, slightly hesitant voice, 'we needed each other.' Buying people and accusing adversaries of stupidity and dishonesty were common in their peculiar world.

Rowland would choose his moment to reveal a secret approach, and possibly as a sting, from another disgruntled Fayed employee, this time Josef Goedde, the former security director of the Ritz. In June 1993, Goedde had offered Rowland details of a bugging operation inside the hotel. At a meeting at Frankfurt airport, Goedde had told Rowland's lawyer that a telephone recording system had been installed and that 'on Fayed's instructions ... for years the telephone calls were taped of important guests'. Goedde himself had taped the calls, he told Rowland's lawyer. Among the targets was Prince Khaled bin Sultan, the Saudi chief of the defence staff, Wafic Said, the arms dealer, and Victor Dananza, well known for introducing attractive girls to celebrities. The party had stayed in the hotel between 22 and 25 July 1989. Goedde had allowed Rowland's emissary to listen to tape-recorded conversations between Dananza and the prince about 'sex, and other activities'. On the lawyer's advice to his client that he should not become involved with Goedde, 'because you would not wish to engage in sleaze and dirty tricks', the suspicious offer was rejected. But Rowland could imagine Fayed's irritation if he was given the lawyer's report.

Solicitously, as their frugal lunch ended, Fayed guided Rowland to sit in an armchair. Unknown to the guest, Macnamara had, on Fayed's instructions, inserted a miniature camera in the wood panelling to record the conversation.

As an incentive to coax Rowland into admitting that he had paid Michael Howard a bribe, Fayed dangled a lie. Terry Robinson, he claimed, Lonrho's former finance director, had been prepared to accept £1 million for documents. Rowland was shocked. Since he had dismissed the loyal Robinson, Fayed's invention, based on an invitation to Robinson to a meeting which had been ignored, could not be verified. With

Rowland discomfited by the thought that there might be traitors in his camp, Fayed asked him to confirm that Howard had been bribed.

Hesitantly, Rowland admitted extricating Harry Landy from jail. The fraudster 'gave Michael Howard encouragement . . . and he was friendly with Michael Howard because he is Michael Howard's uncle'. He continued, 'I worked on Harry Landy very hard in order to persuade Harry Landy to help and what Harry Landy gave Michael Howard, I don't know how much.' To Fayed's ears it sounded as though Rowland was uttering an unconditional admission that he had given a bribe, while self-protectedly surrounding his own knowledge with obfuscation.

'He gave him £1 million?' said Fayed.

'That's possible,' replied Rowland with an expression of sincerity and acceptance.

'£1 million?' repeated Fayed.

'Well, that's half a million or £1 million. I don't know what it was,' agreed Rowland.

The following day, on 27 September, Rowland returned to the dining room for tea and sat in the same winged armchair opposite the hidden camera. 'Michael Howard's got a million?' asked Fayed.

'A million and a half or whatever it is,' replied Rowland.

'Million and a half!' exclaimed Fayed. 'Now he's got another half million.'

'Whatever the bugger's got, I'll find out from Harry Landy,' said Rowland, with seeming commitment, but again suggesting his own ignorance and innocence.

In Fayed's opinion, he had extracted a confession of a bribe. To Rowland, the interpretation of the conversation on the raw transcript would be starkly different to Fayed's. His inflections, he would say, demonstrated his simple teasing of Tootsie; answering Fayed's questions with his own questions or with meaningless promises to discover the 'truth' was an enjoyable dangle. Fayed however persuaded himself, with Macnamara's agreement as a former police officer, that Rowland had confessed. Excitedly, he abandoned his earlier attempts to win the support of opposition MPs and aimed for a direct threat to the prime minister. 'Tell Brian come,' he ordered Michael Cole.

Brian Hitchen, a short, pugnacious-looking tabloid journalist, was the genial editor of the *Sunday Express*. Like so many newspaper editors, Hitchen had been entertained by Fayed and was often prepared to publish stories offered by Cole. On this occasion, Fayed was offering not drinks or hampers, but his well-honed mantra and allegations of corruption. Tim Smith and Neil Hamilton, he told Hitchen, were paid to ask questions. 'Whenever you talk to Major again,' said Fayed, 'say that this guy has been sat on.'

'I will talk to Major,' replied Hitchen. 'I'll tell him that he needs to listen to something of national importance because things are happening here that shouldn't be happening.'

'I'm ready to sit with him and show him the same documents.'

'Suppose he refuses to withdraw the report . . .?' asked Hitchen.

'Then I will go to the courts or I'll go to the Labour Party,' replied Fayed.

Within two days, Hitchen was sitting with John Major in Downing Street recounting a more sensational, confused version of Fayed's demand that unless the DTI report was withdrawn the Egyptian would reveal his information about four ministers to 'other people'. Alex Allan, Major's private secretary, took notes as Hitchen explained, 'Fayed claims that he has a file on Jonathan Aitken with proof that he was whoring for the Saudis.' Aitken, he continued, owned two model agencies, one in London and one in Paris, which provided prostitutes for visiting Arab businessmen.

To the prime minister, besieged by sleaze accusations, Fayed's allegations were incredible. 'Fayed's attempting to blackmail you,' warned Allan. Sir Robin Butler, the Cabinet secretary, was summoned and asked by Major to check discreetly with Hamilton and Smith about the allegations that they had been paid thousands of pounds by Fayed via Greer. Although Butler's rise through Whitehall had bestowed limited experience in understanding the machinations of types like Fayed, Aitken, Greer or Hamilton, the prime minister, an uneducated former press officer, naively trusted the articulate Oxbridge mandarin to discover the truth.

Some of the allegations were not entirely new to Butler. Ever since January 1994 he had been aware of the irreconcilable exchange of correspondence between Peter Preston and Jonathan Aitken. 'The hotel bill', Aitken wrote to Preston, 'was paid by my wife with money given to her by me for this purpose, some hours after I had left Paris.' Unaware that the editor had seen the Ritz bill, Aitken had bluntly denied that the signature of Said Ayas, his Arab friend and the godfather of his daughter, had been firmly written on the invoice. The junior minister's dishonesty was compounded by his suicidal assertion to Preston that the Ritz management had confirmed his own version. On 30 January, Preston had sent the collected correspondence to Sir Robin Butler. Foolishly, Aitken welcomed that development with flourishing defiance about the editor's 'enthusiasm for barking up the wrong trees'. By May 1994, Aitken's revised versions of the minor saga had persuaded Preston to publish an article in the *Guardian* reflecting the puzzling inconsistencies. The prime minister was unimpressed by the newspaper's denunciation. Accepting Aitken's new assurances to Butler without further inquiry, the junior minister was promoted in July 1994 to chief secretary of the Treasury, appointed a privy councillor and welcomed into the Cabinet. Aitken's career remained untroubled until Hitchen's visit to Downing Street ten weeks later.

Once again John Major asked Sir Robin Butler to question Aitken. Once again, the mandarin's approach was superficial. At 3.30 p.m. on 5 October 1994 the Cabinet secretary asked Aitken about Fayed's 'wild allegations' which he was threatening to pass to the Labour Party. Coolly assured by the minister that he was 'entirely relaxed about this', Butler told the prime minister that Fayed was lying. Four days later, Butler spoke to Neil Hamilton. The junior minister, emboldened by the House of Commons Select Committee's refusal to investigate the first allegations about his free hotel accommodation published by the *Guardian* in 1993, waved the mandarin aside. 'I've only asked two parliamentary questions related to Fayed,' Hamilton told Butler, 'and I've certainly never received any cash from him.' Any evidence Fayed proferred, Hamilton blustered, would be 'fabricated'. To complete his inquiries, Butler sanguinely approached Tim Smith. To his astonishment, Smith confessed that he had accepted up to £25,000 in cash in envelopes from Fayed. The weak, friendless and petulant accountant explained that he had deposited Fayed's cash in bank accounts and declared the income in his tax returns. He had not, however, entered them in the House of Commons register of members' interests. Smith's confession staggered John Major. Not only would the government face another substantiated accusation of sleaze, but Fayed's credibility was confirmed.

Unaware of the imminent maelstrom, Fayed had by 17 October lost patience. Three weeks earlier, at the end of Rowland's visit to Harrods, Fayed had persuaded his guest that John Macnamara and Ken Etheridge, their two security chiefs, should meet to discuss Landy's payments to the minister. 'OK, Tootsie,' smiled Rowland. Considering the ex-policemen's hatred for each other at Scotland Yard, there had been little chance of reconciliation or co-operation over lunch at Harrods. Frustrated, Fayed urged Macnamara to write a file note that Rowland's man had nevertheless confirmed payments to Howard by Landy. The file note was 'confirmed', according to Macnamara, seven days later in a noisy Italian restaurant chosen by Etheridge to sabotage Macnamara's attempt to record their conversation. Etheridge did promise to provide the proof of the payments if Rowland agreed. Silence followed.

Despite Rowland's promise to provide proof of the bribe to Michael Howard, he had delivered nothing. In desperation, Fayed wrote to Rowland urging that he sign a statement confirming Landy's bribes to Howard. Rowland's silence compounded the store-owner's anger. Propelled by his inconsolable thirst for revenge, Fayed ordered on Monday, 17 October 1994, that Mark Griffiths deliver a file of correspondence between himself, Greer and Hamilton to the *Guardian*.

Realizing that after fifteen months Fayed was on the verge of committing himself publicly to admitting bribing the politicians, Preston visited him the following day. Few tycoons, the editor knew, courted publicity and none, in living memory, had ever directly challenged the government on this scale. Publicizing payments to politicians was a sensational scoop. The newspaper's vulnerability to criticism that the whistleblower was himself corrupt and motivated by dissatisfaction with Ian Greer's services was irrelevant. Reporting the simple facts was the priority. 'Do you absolutely realize', asked Preston, 'how much shit is about to hit the fan?' Fayed's posture – truculent, daring and brave – washed the editor's doubts aside. Clearly, the Egyptian was prepared to raise his head above the parapet and launch the crusade against corruption. Standing like a hero, he relished the moment. Preston, impressed, hurried from Harrods confessing thereafter his incomprehension of Fayed's motives. The precise timing, the editor did not realize, was dictated by Fayed's humiliation that morning in Dubai as a cheat and a liar. He was seeking a diversion.

In October 1994, the trial of Fayed's claim for compensation – variously estimated between £30 million and £90 million – for the termination of the Dubai Trade Centre management contract had reached a critical stage. Sitting in Dubai, the arbitrators, three retired British judges, had heard allegations of Fayed's corruption and bribery and awaited his personal testimony. Among the critical witnesses about his management presented by Mohamed Alabbar, the economic secretary, was Ahmed Lutve, a Dubaian. To Fayed's despair, Lutve had dubiously testified that in return for signing the accounts he had been paid over £500,000 by Fayed into a bank account in London and had been introduced to women during his annual visits to London. 'That's a lie,' Fayed had cursed, accusing the Maktoums of constructing a false scenario to terminate his management contract and take the profits in a blatant act of nationalization. To settle without submitting himself to cross-examination, he had been searching for an escape. Several times he had telephoned the two Maktoum brothers. 'You're losing the case,' he laughed. 'Why don't you give in and we'll settle?'

He had spoken so persuasively that the sheikhs summoned Alabbar. 'Why are we losing?' they asked.

The contrary was true, Alabbar reassured the Maktoums.

In early October, Royston Webb prepared to fly to Dubai for the hearing.

'You're sure you are coming, Mohamed?' asked the lawyer.

'Yes, yes,' snapped Fayed. Even Webb, so close to him for nine years, was convinced, despite the Foreign Office's refusal to protect his employer in Dubai, by the Egyptian's sincerity. Fayed's testimony was due on Monday, 17 October. Just after 10 a.m. that morning, four hours ahead of London time, it fell to Peter Leaver QC, Fayed's lawyer, to rise and tell the judges, 'Unfortunately, Mr Al Fayed has been taken sick with serious neck and back complications. According to the best medical advice, he has been told not to fly.' Fayed, the court was told, due to his injuries could only walk with crutches and a brace. Leaver had been told the news during the night. 'If you're genuinely sick, Mr Al Fayed,' he had said, 'that's fine. But I don't want to see pictures of you presented to the court showing you up and running.'

'Peter,' replied Fayed solemnly, 'believe me. I am sick.' In truth, he was sick with terror.

In the court room, Mohamed Alabbar glanced at the judges. 'I was expecting something like this,' one judge murmured. Hurrying from the room, Alabbar called on his mobile

telephone his solicitor's home in London. Normally the partners of Simmons & Simmons did not welcome early calls but
this message was particularly welcome.

The events in Dubai had been far from Mohamed Fayed's
mind when he rose that morning. From his tent, he jabbed the
normal digits to speak to his managers at Harrods and the
Ritz, and he confirmed the dispatch of the Greer file to the
Guardian. At 12.30, after lunch, he was driven 400 yards in
an electric car to the helicopter pad and, covering his face as
usual in a full-face respirator to avoid the fumes, climbed into
the helicopter. After checking that his two leather briefcases
and the newspapers were positioned properly, he nodded his
approval for take-off. Nine minutes later, the Sikorski rotated
over the River Thames and landed at Battersea. Donning his
respirator mask, he walked smartly down the steps, exchanged
a few words with a bodyguard, slid into the front seat of his
bullet-proof Mercedes and sped through south London's narrow streets to Knightsbridge. At 1.30 p.m. precisely, he walked
through number-ten door of Harrods in Hans Road and, as
the security video recorded, surrounded by four bodyguards,
stepped confidently on to the shiny escalators heading for the
fifth floor.

The following morning, 18 October, Fayed was roused by
an early telephone call from Royston Webb in Dubai. Sounding
unusually agitated, the lawyer spoke of 'disaster'. Webb
recounted that in the courtroom that morning, as Mohamed
Alabbar smiled, a video had been shown of Fayed's journey
the previous day from Battersea to Harrods. Unseen by all his
bodyguards, three security teams hired by Simmons & Simmons had filmed the allegedly crippled Fayed jumping out of
his helicopter into the limousine and striding into the store.
The evidence of Fayed's good health was irrefutable. Exposed
as a liar and a cheat, Fayed was trumped. The Dubai government's allegations of Fayed's questionable accounts had, by
default, been proved. His fortune in Dubai, he knew, was lost
– outwitted, he yelled, by that young, corrupt, lying wretch

Alabbar. But he had been terrified of arrest and perpetual incarceration by the Maktoums. Immediately, Fayed made two calls, the first to John Macnamara. The security chief was ordered to retrieve the security video of his arrival the previous day and re-record the tape with the same date but the time altered from 1.30 p.m. to 4 p.m. to suggest that Alabbar's evidence was falsified. Macnamara was also ordered to send crutches and a neck brace to Oxted. Had he also demanded an inquiry into his own security, he would have discovered the flaws in his organization. Air-traffic controllers had been bribed to reveal his flight plans and his staff had been bribed to reveal his health. The money, in £20 notes, had been delivered in Oxfam envelopes.

Fayed's second call was to Michael Cole. His revenge against his humiliation in Dubai would be against the Conservative government in London. 'Get Preston.'

If the same surveillance team had bothered to film Fayed's arrival at Battersea that morning, 18 October, they would have seen an apparently pained figure, wearing a neck brace, helped down the aircraft's steps and hobbling on crutches towards the Mercedes. The performance was convincing, but by the time he reached Harrods Fayed had lost interest in his pointless ruse. Abandoning his crutches in the car, he walked into the building.

In Downing Street that same morning, John Major was meeting Sir Robin Butler and Richard Ryder, his chief whip. The previous day, Butler had reported that Hamilton 'emphatically denied throughout my inquiries that he received any payments from Mr Al Fayed'. Butler continued, 'I have found no evidence that controverts Mr Hamilton's assurances . . . I have found nothing which would cause me to throw any doubts on the validity of those denials . . . I am confident that the allegations are demonstrably false or . . . entirely unsubstantiated.' Only partially reassured, John Major had decided to obtain a signed statement from Hamilton, and, anticipating new demands from Peter Preston, Jonathan Aitken was asked for a statement. 'I can confidently assure you', wrote the chief secretary to the prime minister, 'that I know absolutely nothing arising out of Fayed's ludicrous claims that would discredit me or the government.' In the Commons that afternoon, Major pledged to root out corruption. Three hours later, Fayed took an irrevocable step.

*

APPARENTLY PREOCCUPIED by a welter of business problems, Fayed greeted David Hencke with some haste in his office that evening. His arrival had been delayed by Michael Cole still arguing against disclosure of the bribes. Fayed's response was to meet Hencke but to invent a false scenario. By lying, he would put the blame for corruption entirely on Ian Greer.

Seated with the young journalist, Fayed explained that his original motivation had been to counter the influence of Edward du Cann, Lonrho's highly paid chairman and parliamentary organizer. Greer's suggestion was acceptable, he admitted: 'He said questions in the Commons could be bought at £2,000 each.'

'They've asked seventeen questions,' said Hencke, 'so I suppose you've paid them £34,000?'

'That's right,' said Fayed. 'And I paid £8,000, £10,000 a month to IGA [Greer's company]. I gave tens of thousands of pounds to Greer.' Not understanding the mathematics, Hencke assumed that Fayed's payments to Greer had been converted into cash and handed over by the lobbyist to the MPs. Fayed's mention of also giving Hamilton vouchers to spend in Harrods was noted but forgotten. 'I didn't understand what he meant,' Hencke would say later. 'I was concentrating on the Ritz and the cash for questions.'

Hencke steered the conversation to the Hamiltons' stay at the Ritz. 'I get charged,' scolded Fayed, as if the whole enterprise had been a huge, unexpected burden. 'They even wanted to come back but we told them the hotel is full. He even ordered a bottle of wine for 10,000 francs. The most expensive.' Unrestrained, Fayed now poured out his motives for betraying the MP. 'When he became a minister at DTI I sent my congratulations. I didn't hear one word.' Sensing his audience's rapt attention, the actor knew that journalists savour colourful quotations to enrich their reports. Fantasies flowed easily from Fayed, especially against those he had discarded. The appropriate metaphor had been supplied by an obliging adviser. 'Greer told me,' Fayed recounted to Hencke with theatrical panache, ' "You are not properly represented." I realized the truth. He told me, "These people are able to rule the country – you can buy them like you rent a taxi, a London taxi, you rent an MP." ' Unequivocally, Fayed stated that Greer had offered two MPs for sale: 'I was shocked. All my illusions about Britain were shattered.' His voice rose to be heard in the upper circle as he questioned Britain's 'standards'. The MPs were not only corrupt but greedy. They kept returning.

To Hencke's excitement, Fayed finally handed over Hamilton's Ritz bill. Fayed understood the journalist's emotions. Hamilton's lies in his letter to Preston in July 1993 were exposed. After twelve minutes, the interview was over. To Hencke's embarrassment, Fayed gave the journalist a teddy bear. Preoccupied by his task, Hencke felt it impolite to decline the gesture.

Monitoring Hencke's departure, Cole returned to Fayed's office. Knowing that Fayed had lied about payments to the MPs through Greer and fearing dire repercussions once the truth emerged, he repeated his warning about the store-owner's self-incrimination. Fayed waved the warning aside. Quite coldly, he had also ignored the consequences to Hamilton, Smith and Greer. Ruining the lives of loyal supporters was irrelevant if it served his purpose. The man who repeatedly preached about injustice and martyrdom did not reflect upon the irony. The victim of Rowland and the DTI, posing as the champion of purity on a crusade to salve the conscience of Britain, could effortlessly create victims in his own cause. The notion of hypocrisy never occurred to him as he justified his betrayal because he had 'no respect' for Hamilton.

In writing their article about cash for questions during Wednesday, 19 October, Hencke and Preston specifically stated that £2,000 in cash was paid to Hamilton and Smith by Ian Greer. The source of the money, the report explained, was Fayed's two special payments to Greer of £18,000 in 1987 for election expenses and £13,333 in 1990; and regular monthly sums of £8,000 to £10,000 to IGA, Greer's company. By repeating Fayed's lie, the *Guardian* had mistakenly identified the money given by Fayed to Greer for election expenses as the Egyptian's indirect payments to the two MPs. That inaccuracy was compounded by repeating that Fayed was paying IGA regular monthly sums of £8,000 to £10,000, whereas the only provable sum was £25,000 per year. Fayed's own cash payments to Hamilton and Smith, stuffed into white envelopes, were still unknown. Geraldine Proudler, the *Guardian*'s lawyer, had been unconcerned by the absence of documentary proof of the payments. The correspondence between Greer, Hamilton and Fayed proved, in her opinion, the corrupt relationships.

To ensure Fayed's total support for the inevitable court battle following publication, the *Guardian* faxed a copy of their article to Harrods in the afternoon. Thrilled by the sight of the story – he rarely read much of any text before his attention wavered – Fayed ordered that the pages be faxed to Royston Webb in Dubai.

'I think it's an absolute fucking disaster, Mohamed,' said Webb thirty minutes later, uncharacteristically fuming.

'Why?' asked Fayed, puzzled.

'Because the British mentality will not understand the transaction. You are admitting taking part in one-half of a questionable transaction. It'll cause you damage.'

There was an unusual pause. 'It's my decision,' snapped Fayed. 'You're always arguing with me.'

Fearful that Fayed was heading towards catastrophe, Webb

sought out Anthony Lester, the lawyer who had originally introduced Preston to the store-owner. 'You must get Preston to stop this article,' pleaded Webb. 'It'll show Mohamed in a bad light.'

'It's too late,' replied Lester.

Webb was distressed. Only the previous day, Fayed had been exposed as a liar in Dubai and the allegations of his corruption appeared proven. Now, his admission of bribing British politicians would confirm his dishonesty.

Thursday, 20 October was Fayed's moment of glory. Staring lovingly at the *Guardian*'s huge headline, 'Tory MPs were paid to plant questions says Harrods chief', he congratulated himself on hoodwinking the journalists. Wagging his finger at Michael Cole – 'I told you so' – he boasted how, rather than being destroyed by the exposé, he had become a hero.

Dressed in a garish blue shirt and a particularly sharply cut grey suit, Fayed strutted through the fifth-floor suite, excited to be at the centre of a sensational show. The news broadcasts on every radio and TV station spoke only about that morning's *Guardian*. The Harrods telephone switchboard was jammed by enquiring journalists. Mohamed Fayed was the Man of the Moment and Michael Cole, equally excited, had prepared the juicy quotations for Fayed to utter with relish. 'I could not believe that in Britain, where parliament has such a big reputation, you had to pay MPs,' he recited to callers. 'I was shattered by it.' To other callers, he recited, 'I now regret giving money to such a broken-backed bunch of discredited politicians, but there was nothing dirty about the money, which I gave in good faith with no strings attached and which was eagerly accepted.'

To those who spoke to Michael Cole, there was a lengthy denunciation of Britain, the glorification of Fayed's performance as a public duty and a solemn denial that the rejection of British nationality had motivated Fayed's revelations: 'He wishes to expose the sham of men in high office who are quite content to see his family's reputation attacked in a travesty of an official report but whose own conduct is dubious to say the least.' Cole did not blush as he distorted history. 'Mr Al Fayed is prepared to demonstrate the rottenness within an establishment which was prepared to see him vilified even though there were no grounds for any action against him whatsoever. Mr Al Fayed followed every legal course open to him, but his appeal for fair play and British justice was denied. Mr Al Fayed was advised that no one in the Commons would take an interest in his case or raise a finger in his defence unless he was prepared to pay for their services. He now knows this advice to be worthless and bitterly regrets any contacts with those who purport to peddle influence but are simply parasites in pinstripe suits.'

Fayed was enjoying every second and, to celebrate, he invited Tiny Rowland again for lunch. Once again, their conversation was secretly recorded. Sex, never far from Fayed's mind, was his ruse to relax his guest. 'Get me one of those nigger cocks,' he told the bemused Rowland, 'because I want a bigger one. I want a transplant. Now they can transplant everything, what about a fuggin' penis?' His ramble climaxed with a demand for 'four wives but they have to be virgins'. The progression from penises and virgins to Michael Howard was seamless. 'Did you pay £0.5 million or £1.5 million? Or £2 million? How much you pay?' He was pushing, pushing so hard. The smile hid his burning irritation that Rowland remained silent. 'Honestly, how much you pay? I'd just like to know,' he pushed again for an answer. Over-excited and lacking the self-control to query why Rowland again refused to answer, Fayed repeated his question about Harry Landy. 'He gave him £1 million?'

'That's possible.'

'£1 million?' interrupted Fayed, cutting Rowland off in mid-sentence, just as he appeared to be on the verge of mentioning a crucial fact. All Fayed heard was an admission that the payments to Landy were through a Swiss bank and that he would question Landy by inviting him 'for supper. I'll sit quietly with him.' That was not what Fayed had in mind. Rowland, he was sure, knew the truth but was yet again feigning ignorance. But his disappointment was partly assuaged by his boasting about his past discovery of Rowland's secrets. 'I know because I also have my secret service. You have your secret service. I have my secret service.' Rowland seemed impressed. 'You know we should combine and then we will find out anything about anyone.' He had reached an impasse. Rowland was unwilling to give any more. As they emerged from the dining room, Fayed presented a box of mangoes to his guest. Rowland's parting pat on his head aggravated Fayed's feeling of impotence.

Padding along the corridor to his office, he could hear a television news reader reporting Labour attacks against the government. Facing uproar in the House of Commons, John Major was limply acknowledging Tim Smith's resignation and unconvincingly accusing Fayed of blackmailing the government. Watching the writhing politician, Fayed was content: 'I got the fuggin' bastards.' Stunned Conservative MPs and baying Labour MPs waving £5 and £10 notes heard Major declare that, 'regardless of the cost to the government's reputation', he had rejected any 'deal' with Fayed. Instead, Fayed's threat, said Major, would be referred to the director of public prosecutions, an admission of his desperation. Lamely, the British government was allowing a condemned liar to dictate a crucifying agenda and simultaneously rewrite history. 'No one has the authority to speak on my behalf,' Fayed told enquiring journalists, denying that Brian Hitchen had passed a message on his behalf to Major. 'In my life I have never authorized anyone to issue an ultimatum on my behalf. That is simply not my style.' This was little short of war, and Fayed sensed that the government was retreating. 'The prime minister stands in the House of Commons and says I am a blackmailer. I am a sonofabitch because I have thrown a bomb in his court. Right? To uncover all of the corruption and all the malpractices he has. I'm not worried. He says public prosecution, Scotland Yard, OK, take your time. I've done nothing wrong.' Paralysed Conservative politicians, reeling from the sheer audacity of the briber claiming to act in the public interest in a moral crusade, sought protection in greater deceit.

Unseen within the Palace of Westminster, David Willetts, an arrogant junior whip, was discussing with Geoffrey Johnson-Smith, the amenable chairman of the Commons Committee of Members' Interests, how its meetings could be manipulated to save the government from criticism. Simultaneously, in a telephone conversation, Neil Hamilton was lying to Michael Heseltine, the deputy prime minister, by denying any financial relationship with Ian Greer. 'I am', pleaded Hamilton, 'a victim of Fayed.'

In the deluge of telephone calls, self-restraint was abandoned. Fayed, the victim of the Conservatives, gleefully ranted to journalists telephoning for a comment: 'We are ruled by crooks and bastards who infiltrated the political life. They are in power to enrich themselves. They don't give a shit about the country.' Asked about Hamilton's virulent denials and his refusal to resign, Fayed's emotions rose: 'Those politicians are beggars on the street. Those who can be bought are not worth buying.' Neil Hamilton, he raged, 'is a liar, a bastard and a shit'. Wallowing in the spotlight, Fayed sprayed more allegations. 'I'll name the Tory minister who took £500,000,' he announced, claiming that Margaret Thatcher's house, worth £4 million, had been bought by Saudis; and he disclosed a donation of £250,000 to the Conservative Party. Asked about a rumour that one minister had been paid in jewels which he later resold for cash, he smiled. The herd was charging in his direction.

The following morning, a new mantra was born in the *Guardian*, reported in uncorrected Fayed-speak: 'I am a taxpayer in this country. I have devoted thirty years of my life, employing people, bringing in business, paying hundreds of millions in taxes. This is my country. You don't want to end after your sacrifice for all this, to be humiliated in a report commissioned by a corrupt Tory government. I am fighting a crusade for the masses, for the ordinary people.' Peter Preston endorsed the latest mantra. Fayed, wrote the editor, was a victim of 'a monstrous ingratitude and the long nightmare of the Lonrho war for Harrods'. Amid the fuming, there was one moment of pure honesty to the *Sunday Times*: 'I am a merchant. People come to me selling ice cream, selling sausages. Greer came selling MPs. For a monthly retainer he promised to mount a lobbying campaign.' Less accurately, he implied that Greer had been given £130,000 for the MPs. Fayed felt not a scintilla of shame for corrupting politicians.

Ian Greer, watching his business collapse, evoked no pity, especially after Michael Cole, ballooning with self-importance, announced, 'One month ago, Ian Greer had urged Mr Al Fayed not to publicize the corruption.'

Even as he tumbled into the abyss, Greer was stung by Cole's inaccurate claim. Three weeks earlier, after the heated meeting with Fayed, as Greer was thereafter keen to remind people, he had asked Royston Webb, 'What evidence does Mohamed have about corruption in the government?'

Webb had replied, 'None that I've ever seen.'

Furious about Cole's behaviour, Greer telephoned Webb in Dubai and asked what he knew about the cash payments. 'I have no knowledge of payments whatsoever,' the lawyer replied, unaware that he was being taped. By the time Webb admitted that Fayed had told him about the payments in 1988, no one cared. Greer was dead meat.

Euphoria lingered in Fayed's office that night. Watching every television news broadcast, Fayed listened to Michael Cole's voice tirelessly fostering the image of the victim's moral crusade to innumerable callers. Glancing up, Fayed might have glimpsed Paula Leeson passing down the office corridor. The twentysomething tall, slim, blonde American recruitment supervisor was not only talented but also attractive. Her breasts aroused his fantasies. In the past, he had stuffed fifties into her cleavage despite her protests. 'He's outrageous,' she had occasionally complained to Bob Loftus. 'What a groper!' Loftus smiled sympathetically. 'Leeson is big enough to cope,' he thought.

*

BAD NEWS BROKE over the weekend. A technician hired to edit the videos of Fayed's conversations with Rowland had leaked the secret. Four QCs and a raft of other senior lawyers were urgently summoned on Monday, 24 October to view the edited tapes at Harrods. Fayed wanted their agreement that he possessed a weapon to cut the government's jugular. The £40,000 session produced the wrong advice. 'You haven't got the evidence of a bribe,' he was told. Ignoring the rebuff, he announced his fantasy as a fact. 'I have a recording from Tiny Rowland,' he confided to the *Financial Times*, 'who told me how a government minister was paid £1 million or maybe £1.5 million. I have a transcript and I have a video.' Unable to resist embellishing his story, Fayed added, 'We had a BBC cameraman. I interviewed him like David Frost.'

Asked for his comment, Rowland replied that he was 'staggered'. Lonrho, he insisted, had 'never paid bankbench MPs or ministers'. He had forgotten his employment of Edward du Cann.

Reflecting on Rowland's inevitable anger, Fayed telephoned his scorned ally, his best source for proving the bribe to Howard, with a remarkable jest. 'Your Majesty,' he began without introduction. 'What you say? I'm talking about my cock, not your cock. I'm going to make the transplant, not you. I'm going to give you the best in the world. Right? You betray my confidence.'

Amid Fayed's laughter, Rowland struggled to protest.

'Betraying confidences! Are you recording this?' he asked.

'I'm not recording this,' lied Fayed. 'I'm not.'

'How could you do that?' asked Rowland, referring to the secret videos.

But his protest was drowned by Fayed's raucous laughter and his counter-accusation. 'Why you betray me?' asked Fayed shamelessly. 'On personal things. Now everyone knows my cock is not big. Is small. You talk about my sacred piece of my body. Right? Now all the girls will keep away from me.' Amid more laughter, he launched into breathless banter, presenting himself as the victim: the victim of Rowland's refusal to provide the incriminating evidence against Michael Howard. 'You know I was recording you.'

'I did not,' protested Rowland.

Ignoring that truth, Fayed invited his adversary for lunch. The agenda was simple. 'What the heck you give a shit about Michael Howard? All the crooks; we agreed to flush them out.'

Struggling to make himself heard, Rowland challenged Fayed to deliver on the deal of an 'exchange of information'. He had delivered on Graham Jones, now he wanted Fayed to deliver on one of his enemies.

Knowing that the conversation was being recorded, Fayed repeatedly smothered Rowland's attempts to express the name of the man Fayed had offered to betray. Contriving louder and louder laughter, Fayed invited Rowland to join him in exposing the crooked politicians to the British public. The notion of two dishonest businessmen preaching virtue did not strike either man as other than eminently reasonable. 'You have a lot of shit from the establishment,' continued Fayed. 'Time to show what sort of people they are. And don't get frightened. Because my balls is big. My cock is little.' More laughter. 'I have children. You have children. I have about two hundred unofficial kids. All right? All have British passports. But they don't know that. Don't go publishing that. All going to be called Fayed, because Fayed has to be everywhere.' Laughingly, he corrected his myth: 'Al Fayed. Al Fayed.' Too intrigued to resist, Rowland agreed to meet again.

Not only crude pugnacity but savvy instincts had lifted Fayed from obscurity to become a destabilizing influence on the British government and the following day his instincts about Hamilton were proved to be more accurate than he had realized. The reproduction in the *Guardian* of Hamilton's original denial to Peter Preston about the Ritz bill alongside a copy of the bill with Hamilton's signature had galvanized government inquiries about the junior minister's other financial activities. The still unrevealed picture was of a greedy and dishonest politician. Hamilton had failed to declare payments for asking questions for Mobil Oil; he had remained associated with Plateau Mining, a dubious company, after appointment as a minister; he had not declared payments from Skoal Bandits, a US tobacco company; nor had he declared the £4,000 paid by Greer as an introduction commission for National Nuclear Corporation; and he had not declared his lobbyist contract for a South African company. Although Hamilton's postulating eloquence denied all the allegations, his extravagant conduct, intensively monitored by the media, had become too damaging for the beleaguered prime minister. That afternoon, 25 October 1994, after John Major announced the creation of a Committee on Standards in Public Life to be chaired by Lord Nolan, Hamilton was abruptly summoned to Downing Street and dismissed.

Reading the morning's newspapers on 26 October, Fayed could be forgiven for gloating. Thanks to him, two ministers had been forced to resign and the government was in turmoil. Looking out across Hyde Park from his penthouse, he reassured himself that he was not a shopkeeper but a powerbroker, a man of enormous influence in London. At last, the victim of a conspiracy was wreaking his revenge. Even the home secretary was under pressure, although not as he had intended.

Accusing innocent people of wrongs had become so normal for Fayed's machine that Michael Cole had not anticipated that his briefing to the *Daily Express* on 21 October, jointly accusing Charles Wardle and Michael Howard of blocking Fayed's application for British nationality, might produce an unexpected answer.

To rebut the accusation, Howard had issued a press release

describing his personal intervention to ensure fairness. Charles Wardle, explained Howard, had initially raised the issue and he, as home secertary, had mediated. Rushing home from Washington, Wardle telephoned journalists to contradict Howard's version. 'This is a gross distortion,' protested Wardle. 'I refused to obey Howard. On three occasions Howard asked me to re-examine the Fayeds' application to find a way to grant them nationality, and three times I told him that the DTI report was a block.' Howard, it appeared, was concealing his benign attitude towards the Fayeds. That scenario was too complicated for the conspiracy theorist. Pursuing Howard was temporarily postponed for easier targets.

Telephoning Peter Preston, Fayed told the editor that he would be given the necessary documents to expose Jonathan Aitken the following day. The *Guardian*'s report, illustrated with the Ritz bill, set the agenda for a beleaguered prime minister, battling to protect his government by vilifying a disgraced foreign businessman for unashamedly manipulating a witch-hunt. Immune to any accusation and again watching his agenda performed on television, Fayed chortled at Jonathan Aitken's cool declaration that Sir Robin Butler had exonerated him and that his wife had paid the bill. To the viewer who knew the truth, the Egyptian's complaint of corrupt politicians was proved. His betrayal of Greer, Hamilton and Smith had been hugely profitable. Authorizing Cole to add Aitken's scalp was pure heaven. 'Lolicia Aitken', announced Michael Cole, controlling his excitement, 'was not a guest [at the Ritz] and the whole of his bill was put on the account of a Saudi businessman.'

Six weeks later, the process of reckoning began. Greer and Hamilton had issued writs for defamation and Fayed was required to produce a statement substantiating his allegations. Telling the precise truth had always posed difficulties for Fayed. In giving evidence to the Select Committee on Members' Interests, investigating Hamilton on 5 December, he had sought refuge in broad gestures, glossing over detail and excusing any inconsistencies by referring to 'my age', 'distance of time', 'my thirty thousand employees' (forgetting that since the flotation he had employed only 5,000) and 'constant problems running my business'. Mistakenly, he had adopted the same attitude when David Solomon, his solicitor, had arrived earlier to draft an affidavit. 'When did you pay Hamilton?' asked the lawyer.

'Every time Hamilton came, I paid him,' replied Fayed curtly.

With that brief, the solicitor scoured his client's diary, listing all Hamilton's visits. Finding twelve visits between June 1987 and November 1989, he prepared Fayed's statement that Hamilton had received in total £24,000 in cash and £4,000 in Harrods gift vouchers. 'On every occasion when I met Mr Hamilton alone,' Fayed swore on 29 November 1994, 'I made payments to him.' The payments to the MPs, continued Fayed, were made in two ways: either through Greer or at personal meetings with the MPs. Unfortunately for the *Guardian*, Fayed's version contradicted the report published by the newspaper. Consistently, Fayed had told Peter Preston that the cash payments to the MPs were paid by Greer. Now, according to the sworn statement, not only had Greer paid the MPs cash for questions, but Fayed was admitting personal payments. Later, he would add that cash in envelopes was also left for the MPs to collect in Park Lane. He had little choice but to tell the truth. Since Smith had confessed, Fayed was compelled to do likewise.

On 14 December 1994, the *Guardian* completed its defence to the libel writs. Faced with Fayed's contradictions and the new evidence from the plaintiffs, the defence argued a substantially different case from what had been stated in the original article, but there was no suggestion that Fayed had paid cash to Greer. Since the newspaper's sole witness to the undocumented transactions was a proven liar, the outcome of the defamation trial might have seemed uncertain, but Fayed was living for the present, oblivious to the consequences.

15

Frustrations

THE EXCITEMENT WAS inevitably followed by disappointment. Sitting at the centre of his own universe, Fayed perceived
his image as an individual of unique interest, vast wealth and
mighty importance. Beyond the limits of his natural influence –
the fate of 5,000 people and the store's suppliers depended
upon his whims – money had bought influence; but the acceptance and admiration which he desired remained elusive.
Instead of basking in praise for his courageous exposure of
corruption, he felt snubbed.

'I should be given at least a knighthood,' he had told Peter
Bolliger with obvious anguish two years earlier. 'Harrods was
a heap of shit when I bought it. I've done so much. I should be
recognized.' There was some truth in that claim. Fayed's
achievement in improving and modernizing the store deserved
applause, but the DTI report and his vendetta against the
Conservatives sabotaged any chance of appreciation.

In silent protest, Britain's great and good had begun to
boycott Harrods, endorsing the opinion of Boris Johnson, a
siren of bathos in the *Daily Telegraph*, that Hamilton had been
dismissed 'most unfairly since no evidence of [his] wrong-doing
ever emerged'. Conservatives who loathed the combination of
a dishonest foreign businessman and the *Guardian* damaging
trusted friends agreed with Paul Johnson, the veteran commen-
tator, that Jonathan Aitken was the victim of 'a forgery'. The
culprit was not the politician but Fayed, whose 'ruthless' and
'immoral' decision was 'to leak details of the Ritz hotel bill to

the *Guardian*'. 'One wonders', speculated Johnson, 'whether Fayed feels ashamed of seeking to corrupt the politicians and the British system he claims to revere.' Fayed, the outsider, was even boycotted by the NSPCC, which cancelled a charity fashion show in Harrods after its committee members, including Mrs Douglas Hurd, refused to enter the store. The hypocrisy enraged Fayed.

Compared to the politicians' dishonesty, Fayed's misdeed was to have lied about his past and exaggerated his wealth to buy a company. But, whereas he had been brutally castigated, the Conservative ministers (who had evinced no shame for all their misconduct) were content to judge him for daring to expose dishonesty. He could have built bridges to win sympathy for himself but eschewed that opportunity after receiving a formal rebuke for his old lies.

The curt letter on 23 February 1995 from Nicholas Baker, the immigration minister at the Home Office, rejected without reason the brothers' application for British nationality. 'We're being treated as pariahs,' moaned Fayed, posing in Harrods as Father Christmas with a giant passport. 'I played by the rules and played it their way. But now I've been dumped.' Since the government had recently announced that any applicant, including non-residents, worth £1 million would qualify for British nationality, his grievance had some merit. 'They could not accept that an Egyptian could own Harrods so they threw mud at me. Much as I love Harrods, I would give it away to a passing beggar if the choice was it or the good name of my family.' The sixty-six-year-old Egyptian suffered no doublethink in attacking the government for 'the slur on our reputation which denies me the opportunity to share the nationality of my children. There is residual racism here and snobbism.' His riposte was typical of men thwarted despite their wealth.

Summoning Bill Mitchell, his seventy-year-old loyal architect, to Park Lane, Fayed explained in a sentence notable for its unusual omission of an expletive a new desire. 'I want something to show my success.' His millions, he continued, could not buy eternity. 'When I go, my money stays. I want something here when I go.'

Ten years after buying the House of Fraser, Fayed had pondered the fate of the Frasers. Both father and son were dead and forgotten. Like so many tycoons of recent years – the Clores, Cottons and Cohens – no visible legacy reminded the world of their individual distinction. A similar fate might befall his achievements and perhaps worse. If he suddenly perished, his name, thanks to the DTI report and the *Guardian*'s revelations, would rank among the notorious with Robert Maxwell's. Desperate for eternal life and a secure mention among the ranks of the great, he contemplated a permanent memorial. Like so many self-made autocrats, he often explained his life's ambition to 'leave the world a better place'. Unsophisticated about the traditional methods – bequests to theatres, libraries, galleries and educational foundations – he alighted upon a permanent memorial to his glory. 'I want this!' he exclaimed to Mitchell. 'An escalator.'

For years he had planned a new escalator in the centre of the store, rising from his Egyptian Room. But this was to be a special escalator. Along the sides of the moving aluminium staircase, Mitchell was to build and erect thirty-six huge, identical pharaoh faces. 'Plain face?' asked Mitchell anticipating the answer. 'I suppose you want your own mug on the statues?'

'Yes,' replied Fayed.

'Wot? On all thirty-six of them?'

Fayed nodded. The four-foot-high faces built of sand and cement towering over the new £22 million escalator would remind his enemies about the genius of the King of Knightsbridge.

The vulgarity of commissioning an escalator as the shrine for the eternal glory of Mohamed Fayed did not occur to either man. Nor did either man grasp the paradox of Fayed's association with Egypt, a country which he refused to visit to avoid the truth of his origins and whose nationality he desperately sought to shed although his ownership of Harrods had transformed him into an Egyptian hero. Mohamed's Kingdom, a one-dimensional world consisting of his fame, fortune and influence, lacked rational interpretation since it fed on the aura pervading his fifth-floor offices.

Beyond the security doors, men who in previous careers were noted for their independence and honesty had become sycophants, hailing their employer as a Man of Vision for commissioning an escalator or dreaming of owning a newspaper. In return for feeling important and avoiding 'Mohamed's shit list', they curried favour by eagerly supplying the chairman with juicy gossip and tirelessly enduring humiliation, cancellation of meetings and postponement of decisions. As a compliant chorus, all clapped, laughed and frowned as an appropriate response to their employer's performance, carefully deflecting any suspicions of harbouring unfriendly sentiments. Only the most vain employees deluded themselves that they exerted meaningful influence. Unusually for a huge business, they obeyed paperless commands, often communicated through Mark Griffiths, the chairman's ultra-loyal courtier, as acceptable management across his strictly compartmentalized world, constructed to protect his secrets and prevent any employee acquiring knowledge and power. Delegation and initiative were anathema to a man suspicious of his staff, and in early 1995 he was particularly irked by Omar Bayoumi, the banker recruited to organize the flotation of Harrods. Fayed's anger was born, as always, from frustration.

Harrods, he believed, was worth £2 billion. He and Ali wanted to sell about 30 per cent of the shares and divide over £600 million between them to fund their lifestyle and finance expansion. There was every reason for Fayed to regard his business optimistically. Harrods' pre-tax profits in 1995 – an excellent 11 per cent profit on sales – were £70.9 million. The brothers had taken a £50 million dividend, paid to AITSA, their holding company transferred from Liechtenstein to Bermuda. Those results, the Fayeds believed, would enhance the value of their shares for the flotation. The new wealth would finance Mohamed's ambitious development plan of the furniture depository in Trevor Square; the development of 250 houses and flats on the eleven-acre sports field in Barnes; and the construction of a Harrods hotel and luxury flats on the Crown Court site behind Harrods and on Knightsbridge. All of that prospective 'new wealth', hyped by Fayed's self-salesmanship, would be financed by loans using the Harrods shares and the property as security.

Dazzling his entourage with his vigilance to the smallest details, Mohamed Fayed had transformed Harrods by innovation. Every department – toys, glassware, bathrooms, electrical, food and fashion – outclassed grand stores in other cities. His latest idea was a pizza bar in the Food Hall. Built despite his executives ridiculing the notion, its popularity enhanced Fayed's image as a theatrical retailer with flair. He was indifferent that traditonal old money was closing its accounts, complaining that the soul of a British institution had been replaced by a cosmopolitan, glitter bazaar of boutiques and franchises. The disparity that 70 per cent of Harvey Nichols customers lived locally and the majority of Harrods customers were tourists, Fayed believed, proved his success, even if too many tourists only bought a packet of biscuits just to possess the distinctive green plastic bag. Harrods had been transformed from a single store into a franchise operation in European airports, on the *QE2* and throughout Japan. There were plans to open more franchises in Thailand and Malaysia. The winning strategy was only undermined by Fayed's management style.

To develop the Harrods brand name, Fayed had recruited through head-hunters Trevor Bell, a thirty-seven-year-old marketing director formerly employed by Rémy Cointreau, the French multinational. At noon on Bell's second day, Fayed issued a precise instruction: 'Go organize Harrods crisps.

Franchise. Worldwide.' Bell understood: the world was to be offered a Harrods brand of crisps. At the end of that same day, Fayed walked into Bell's office. 'What ye doing?'

'Working on the proposal to sell a brand of Harrods crisps, Mr Al Fayed.'

'What a fuggin' stupid idea,' screamed Fayed. 'Drop it at once. Idiot.'

Bell looked perplexed. Only later did he learn that Fayed had mentioned the idea to another executive, who had clearly opposed it. In the Harrods jungle, Fayed followed the advice of the last person.

Bell's introduction to fifth-floor politics was caustic. Asked by Fayed to negotiate the franchise of a new store, Bell discovered after one week that the parameters of his brief had been totally altered. 'You've changed everything. What are the rules?' cried Bell, frustrated that their discussion was being conducted while Fayed fed pizza to his children.

'Don't matter,' snapped Fayed. 'Now. I want ideas for the Christmas displays in the store's windows. All the fuggin' merchandising people have come up with the same fuggin' ideas: Santa Claus and reindeers. You give me something special.' Over lunch, two hours later, Bell discovered that eight other executives were obeying the identical command. For the volatile owner, causing distrust by disparagement was a normal management technique.

Among the casualties were twelve graduates – 'they gotta have brains the size of a fuggin' planet,' Fayed had commanded – all recently qualified with masters degrees in business admin-istration recruited on his orders by Steve Mercer, a personnel director. Those selected, Fayed decreed, would be pushed to the 'forefront of the business'. Six weeks after their appoint-ment with promises of a fabulous future, Mercer was dismissed by Fayed on the ground that he smiled excessively. Soon after, the twelve MBA graduates arrived and sat unemployed in the executive offices, including Trevor Bell's. Walking into Bell's office, Fayed glared at one of the bewildered graduates. 'I didn't give you that person to hang your fuggin' coat on in the morning,' he shouted at Bell. 'Fuggin' nothings.' Creating misery was his palliative for changing his strategy. The graduates' fate was identical to the dozens of potential executives, hired from Germany and relocated to London. All were dismissed as redundant.

Four months after Bell's arrival, his execution began. 'He's wrong,' growled Fayed. 'Temperament no good.' Fayed's entourage understood. Another star had fallen from grace. An iron curtain fell around the hapless executive. Overnight, his telephone calls and handwritten notes asking for meetings with Fayed remained unanswered. Two weeks later, Mark Griffiths and Clive de Boer, a passive, invisible man who survived by never raising his head, entered Bell's office. 'The chairman says it's not working out. Your terms have been agreed.' No further explanation was offered. Bell joined the long queue of talented executives hired and fired at the caprice of the owner.

The consistent pattern of Fayed's method of management – whims confusing the strategy – unsettled Omar Bayoumi, the former Warburgs banker arranging the Harrods flotation. For the Fayeds, the flotation was to signal their acceptance by the City, but by April 1995, the prospect had become a nightmare. 'How much control are you willing to cede?' asked Bayoumi, mindful that – despite Fayed's properly audited accounts – memories of Robert Maxwell's antics were seared in the City's consciousness.

'None,' screeched Mohamed.

'You want to have your cake and eat it,' retorted the banker. 'You can't take the public's money and expect no control. No one will buy the stock.'

His eyes blazing, Fayed stared silently.

'You're not very good at board meetings,' continued the banker, who had noticed Fayed's habit of arriving one hour after the meetings began, only to ask, 'What you are doing here?' After a five-minute monologue, often not even bothering to sit down, he would terminate his rant: 'Well, I'm off to do some real work.' Committees bored the chairman. Corporate governance in Knightsbridge, Bayoumi understood, meant Mohamed Fayed making all the decisions.

Intolerant of the banker's criticism, Fayed snapped, 'I've got to see someone in the Food Hall.' Appointments in the Food Hall were his excuse to escape from embarrassing plain talking.

A placatory call to Bayoumi from Ali broke the deadlock. 'Let's have breakfast.'

Fearing that Mohamed would not gladly hear negative news, Bayoumi told Ali the unvarnished truth. 'Mohamed will never accept any restrictions on his management. No responsible merchant bank could back a flotation of Harrods without guaranteed controls.'

Ali was displeased. All their money was locked up in one business, unusable millions permanently fixed in Knightsbridge.

Ali's displeasure was compounded by his slightly estranged relationship with Mohamed. For years, Ali had served as the reality check on his elder brother. Outsiders, suspicious of Mohamed's business morality and aghast at the sycophantic employees, were reassured by Ali's calm presence tempering Mohamed's emotional outbursts. But the younger brother was irked by the routine of perpetual subservience, tension and argument. Mohamed's crusade against the Conservatives offended Ali's lust for the shadows and an easier life in Connecticut. His elder brother's lifestyle cost millions and their business was not producing sufficient profits to sustain that expenditure. Bayoumi's news that flotation on the Fayeds' terms without City control was impossible restricted Ali's chance for escape. Yet he was not surprised by Mohamed's reaction to the banker's obduracy. Waving his hands, eyes inflamed and expletives gushing from his curled mouth, Mohamed snarled at Bayoumi, 'If that's what they want, we'll tell them it's off. You insult me. Get out.' Bayoumi was assigned a new office, out of Fayed's sight. The gentle, respectable banker had committed a cardinal sin. He had spoken the truth.

'Let's float in New York,' suggested Ali. His brother agreed.

'The man's got to go,' Mohamed Fayed had ordered John Macnamara in mid-June 1995. Omar Bayoumi's dismissal was particularly brutal. Without a knock or advance notice, his office doors burst open. The finance director was confronted not only by the former police officer but also by Michael Cole. Bayoumi was startled. Macnamara had become renowned as vicious, but Cole, regardless of his irritating idiosyncrasies and slight pomposity, had seemed a decent man. Often, especially during the cataclysm since the *Guardian*'s report, Cole had cautiously steered Fayed away from impetuous self-destruction. But evidently the mouthpiece of the moral crusade had been transformed over the past months into another henchman. With Cole glowering and Macnamara looking sour, Bayoumi had minutes to clear his desk before his escort marched him down the escalators into Knightbridge. As so often, Fayed's haste was damaging. Ali had negotiated with Salomon Brothers in New York to mastermind Harrods' flotation. Since the business was so good, the unprejudiced Americans, he calculated, would certainly be keen. Foolishly, he did not anticipate the obvious: that the bankers' first call would be to Bayoumi.

*

SELF-INFLICTED WOUNDS caused Fayed no fear. His unrestrained anger selected victims regardless of their deeds. Among the casualties in the midst of his challenge to the government were three honest, hard-working and loyal women managing Hyde Park Residence, the company letting 170 luxury flats at 55 and 60 Park Lane. Sandra Lewis-Glass, the twenty-nine-year-old letting agent, had been employed by Fayed for ten years, organizing short-term leases for many celebrities paying up to £4,500 per week. Among Lewis-Glass's less pleasant duties was to prevent blacks and Arabs occuying flats in 60 Park Lane where Fayed lived. Her employer, she knew, disliked seeing black faces in his own block – landing an unpleasant chore on Lewis-Glass, who was herself the black daughter of a Home Office clerk.

By the mid-1990s, Hyde Park Residence was earning annually over £4 million gross profits. Most of that money was transferred as 'administrative expenses' to Prestige Properties, Fayed's holding company in Liechtenstein, formerly called Balnagown Estate SA. Hardly any tax was paid in Britain.

Fayed's problems had started when Westminster Council, alerted by a disgruntled tenant, suspected that the company was wrongly reporting the flats as let on long leases to avoid paying the higher business rates imposed on short tenancies. Unexpectedly, the council levied a demand for an additional £1.1 million. To avoid the extra tax while negotiating with the council, special leases were drafted and Lewis-Glass was instructed how to conceal the continuing ruse in the records. Council officers were unpersuaded, and Fayed wrongly suspected that Lewis-Glass and two other female employees were betraying his ploy. Lewis-Glass's superior was dismissed. 'She's been taking bribes and stealing the profits,' Fayed told Lewis-Glass, restorting to his familiar invention. 'And you wear long dresses now. No friendly talks with guests. Or you're sacked too.'

Fayed also suspected Lewis-Glass. 'Watch her,' he ordered Macnamara. After listening to the woman's telephone calls, Macnamara's survelliance team followed Lewis-Glass from the Park Lane building to a meeting with her former superior. 'Fire her,' ordered Fayed. On 29 September 1995, Lewis-Glass was escorted from the building.

'Follow her,' directed Macnamara.

That night, Lewis-Glass and her former colleagues ate dinner at a Mexican restaurant in Whiteleys in Bayswater. At a neighbouring table, Macnamara's team secretly recorded the women's statements of regret at having left behind vital computer disks and their angry discussion whether to reveal the truth about the phoney leases to Westminster Council.

On 3 October 1995, Macnamara lodged a complaint at

West End Central police station in Vine Street. Fayed's security officer alleged that Lewis-Glass had stolen two floppy disks worth eighty pence. At 8.30 p.m., four CID officers arrived from London at Lewis-Glass's home in Croydon to arrest her. Driven fifteen miles back to London, she was locked in a police cell. 'You were fired', the arresting police officer told the terrified woman in a late-night interview, 'because you took bribes and stole money from Mohamed Al Fayed.' Consistently denying the false accusation, Lewis-Glass was eventually released uncharged at three o'clock in the morning.

Over the following days, police officers toured Mayfair's letting agencies 'investigating' Lewis-Glass's superior in response to Fayed's bogus complaint of fraud. 'You can buy anything you like,' the Egyptian had bragged about MPs for sale. Through Macnamara, it appeared, he could also initiate police investigations. Lewis-Glass's proceedings for wrongful dismissal, an irrelevant administrative chore to Fayed, coincided with an interview connected to his war with the government. The irony did not cause him to hesitate. 'They are playing with fire,' he told the journalist. 'If they take away my dignity, my honour, they take away my life. I am not going to leave them thinking they can get away with murder.' Sensitive only to his own humiliation, he was pulling every lever to secure an official investigation into the 'Howard conspiracy'. His only vulnerability was the absence of proof.

Tantalizingly, Rowland had again offered a glimmer of hope. At his meeting with Fayed on 11 January 1995, he had admitted that Harry Landy might know how 'any money might have been paid', but he added, 'If I can help you I will, but at the same time I can't shoot myself in the foot or commit suicide.' Ten weeks later, Rowland reassured Fayed that he had appealed to Landy 'to do everything possible to help', but silence followed. Refining his technique, Fayed presented a draft statement to Rowland on 27 March for signature: 'Landy did not inform me of all the details of his negotiations with Howard but I am not in a position to deny that money did change hands. To this day I remain convinced that Inspectors would not have been appointed to look into the affairs of House of Fraser but for the dealings between Landy and Howard.' In Fayed's opinion, Rowland had admitted that much in their recorded conversations. 'Sign it for me,' the store-owner beseeched Rowland, 'and I shall go to any lengths for you, as far as Australia even. Afterwards, I shall not run away. It will be Tiny and Tootsie for ever. Together we must stand. Together we shall prevail. Never again could anyone be in doubt that there was a man.' This last allusion was a tribute to Rowland's courage in joining the battle.

Two days later, Rowland had refused Fayed's entreaty: 'While I would like to oblige you in anything, I cannot fabricate the world to be the way that you would like it.' Ignoring that setback, Fayed was determined to utter his charges to the House of Commons Select Committee on Privileges.

Anticipating embarrassment, the Conservatives had originally restricted the committee's investigation to the *Guardian*'s 'cod fax' to the Ritz on Jonathan Aitken's official House of Commons notepaper. Aitken's deception of the prime minister and Sir Robin Butler was to be ignored, as was Fayed's own role. That stealth had been undermined by the publication in May 1995 of Lord Nolan's report on standards in public life and by Aitken's resignation in July embarrassed by the reports of his long affair with a prostitute and his knowledge of illegal arms shipments from Britain to Iraq. As the Tories floundered, Fayed had, among some Labour supporters, become a semi-hero. His exclusion from giving evidence to the Committee had become untenable. The invitation for his appearance on 1 November 1995 nevertheless contained an instruction to limit his submission to the 'cod fax'.

Fayed faced Conservative MPs whose hatred for him equalled their incomprehension of the public's antagonism towards their government's dishonesty. Successive scandals had tainted ministers as liars. The worst, the investigation of the secret supply of weapons to Iraq, had exposed Alan Clark, William Waldegrave and Sir Nicholas Lyell as uncritically permitting the prosecution of innocent men and their misleading of parliament. Their double standards, cursed Fayed, were intolerable. Lord Howe had even vociferously bullied Lord Justice Scott with the claim that his inquiry into the arms-for-Iraq saga was a 'double-barrelled inquisition' because reputations should not be vulnerable to those 'unjust procedures', but the DTI's procedures were no different except that, unlike a politician who only had to fear 'a sharp exit to the House of Lords', Fayed had suffered a permanent stigma. And what about David Willetts, the government junior whip who had 'dissembled' the truth to a select committee? Shamelessly, he had nevertheless accused the Labour party of 'misleading' the country. Even Tim Smith had resigned without questioning or censure and had been appointed deputy chairman of the Public Accounts Committee. Fayed felt justified in ignoring the limitations imposed on his submission and delivered a twelve-page polemical rebuke written by his advisers. Inevitably, it could not be characterized as completely accurate.

As a 'model citizen', Fayed told the MPs, 'I was instrumental in securing for this country literally billions of dollars' worth of Middle Eastern construction contracts over a period of years, as recognized by David Douglas-Home of Morgan Grenfell.' His patriotism, he argued, had been besmirched by Michael Howard's acceptance of Rowland's bribe.

> I have been the victim of a massive and protracted campaign of victimization perpetrated by elements of the government . . . The whole sorry exercise has been orchestrated to denigrate my good name . . . The issues that I have raised betray a complex and extensive web of dishonour, petty resentment, revenge and abuse of power, all of which have been perpetrated in the name of the British people . . . It is nothing short of a monstrous scandal, an

enormity, and what have I done to deserve this vicious and vindictive treatment? My crime has been to speak out the truth, to condemn corruption.

The Conservatives did not want to hear Fayed's melodramatic attack against 'arrogance' and 'human rights abuses' or his homily that 'this country is teetering at the edge of an abyss, in mortal danger of degenerating into the sort of endemic corruption seen in southern Europe'. Egyptians condemned as liars were unconvincing propagandists for 'truth and honour [against] arrogant Tory grandees in Whitehall and Westminster', especially after Lord Lester, his lawyer, had never produced evidence to support his own allegation in the House of Lords that his 'client' had also paid four peers.

'Mr Al Fayed, I really cannot allow you to go over all this ground again at this stage,' interrupted Tony Newton, the Conservative chairman.

'I am wondering,' replied Fayed, irritated that the questions were limited to the 'misuse' of House of Commons notepaper, 'are you defending Mr Aitken or are you defending the country?'

'Humbug,' murmured a disgruntled Conservative, as the hearing ended in disarray. Even he did not realize the complete accuracy of his instincts.

*

FIVE WEEKS LATER, Fayed temporarily sidelined his moral crusade. On 6 December 1995, a Harrods security guard noticed on the video monitors covering access to customers' safe deposit boxes in the basement of the store a strikingly familiar face. Grabbing the cassette, he ordered a Polaroid photograph to be delivered to the chairman's office. 'Fuggin' hell!' screeched Fayed, looking at Tiny Rowland innocently pass under the camera. 'Why you not bloody say he has box?' he spluttered to Bob Loftus. Right under his nose, under his own control, was the repository of his enemy's secrets. Within that box, Rowland might have stored the secrets which he so desperately desired. There was no hesitation in Fayed's thoughts. Oblivious to the charge of hypocrisy and worse, the self-professed victim of the criminals in Westminster ordered Macnamara to open the box. The trespass was justified to win the war.

'If the chairman wants it done,' quipped Macnamara, 'we do it.' Five days later, after the store closed, the security system was demobilized while Macnamara with Loftus and Griffiths supervised a locksmith breaking into the box. Wearing rubber gloves, they carried the metal container to Fayed's office. Closing the door, they nervously shuffled through Rowland's documents, photocopied some, and replaced the box with an identical lock.

During the night, Fayed fretted that his quick search might have missed crucial evidence. 'Do again,' he ordered Macnamara the following day. The box was again brought upstairs. In a jovial atmosphere, Fayed's door was closed, a chair placed underneath the handle, and all the contents systematically photocopied. Two sound tapes were also copied.

His possession of new, embarrassing information about Rowland's early life revived an old complaint. Like other rich and distrusted businessmen eager to influence politicians and secure public endorsement of their opinions, Fayed believed that if he owned newspapers and radio stations he could humiliate Rowland and the government by unfettered publication of his discoveries and his opinions. 'You're no one in Britain unless you own a newspaper,' he frequently lamented. Naturally he ignored the failure of other rejected tycoons like Jimmy Goldsmith and Robert Maxwell to impose their prejudices. The mere sight of his name in print would reinforce his sense of selfhood. A Fayed newspaper, part of his media empire, could be the mouthpiece of his own political party and propagate his opinions as scripted by his own, independent think-tank. Every day, millions would read his exposure of politicians' corruption, crafted into elegant prose on page after page by his journalists. Unfortunately, his ambitions had so far been thwarted.

His bid for *Today* from Rupert Murdoch had been trounced by Rowland in 1986 and then again in 1995, after eight weeks' negotiations and on the eve of completion, by Murdoch himself. Fayed rightly suspected that the government had urged Murdoch not to allow their enemy to buy the loss-making newspaper. 'They are like the Mafia,' he complained about the government. 'Like organized crime. They can fug anybody. They can appoint every fuggin' body. I am not going to live with this.'

Buying into the media, Fayed realized, required the employ-ment of an expert. His first recruit was Andrew Neil, who had resigned from the Murdoch empire. Neil agreed with Michael Cole to target London News Radio, a badly managed station owned by Reuters. With Neil nominated as the executive chairman, the £4 million takeover was agreed, subject only to the approval of Sir Peter Gibbings, the regulator at the Radio Authority. Gibbings had written to Neil that he would be 'pleased to consider the request' to transfer the licence to Fayed. But at the last moment there was silence. Fayed's faxes to Reuters were ignored and the deal collapsed. Like Murdoch, Gibbings had bowed to a government request to deprive Fayed of an opportunity to broadcast propaganda.

Fayed's next step was an approach to Stewart Steven, the successful and ebullient former editor of the *Mail on Sunday* and *Evening Standard*. Fayed's greeting to a sympathizer embodied his unique notion of friendship: 'How's your cock? If everything else is dead, you got no troubles as long as it works. Man's got to have girlfriends. You have trouble, I'll give you girl.' Prompted by Fayed's giggle, Michael Cole and Mark Griffiths laughed uproariously in support, expertly con-cealing their weariness at hearing the identical greeting on previous occasions.

'Thank you, Mohamed,' replied Steven. 'I think I'm OK.'

Fayed's pitch to Steven was attractive, and was identical to his inducements sixteen years earlier when he had boasted to film producers that, flush with million, he wanted to build a film empire. 'We're floating Harrods for £2.2 billion in New York. Ali and I are keeping half. That means there's £1 billion to build a media empire.' Even though Steven was unaware that Fayed intended to sell only 30 per cent for perhaps £600 million, he believed that his journalistic and political expertise could, with Fayed's war chest, realize the ambitions of 'Fayed the radical'. He accepted a part-time post.

Steven joined John Dux, a rough Australian who had recently resigned from News International and been appointed as chief executive of Liberty Publishing, Fayed's media company. 'I want newspaper,' the Egyptian had announced. Dux controlled neither a budget nor a guarantee of money. 'Come to me when you need,' ordered Fayed. Regularly, Dux scurried across Knightsbridge to extract cash from his employer. By March 1996, Fayed's media ambitions were stymied. Negotiations under the codename 'Project Image' for the ailing newspaper the *People* owned by the Mirror Group and the Midlands Independent Group, which runs regional newspapers, were mired, not least by the 'Al Fayed factor'. To override the obstacle, Dux retained the Communications Group, a public relations company, to spin the fable that Liberty Publishing was independent of its owner, a difficult challenge for the hypists. Only one other newspaper option remained.

Stewart Steven was asked to realize Fayed's last hope of a major coup, to buy the *Observer*, owned since 1993 by the *Guardian* and losing about £8 million a year. The chance of using Britain's oldest Sunday newspaper to attack Rowland, Michael Howard and the Conservatives titillated Fayed. 'It'll cost a lot of money,' warned Steven, before agreeing to deliver an offer. 'The *Observer* was destroyed by Rowland. Its only chance of restoration is to appoint an independent editorial team and for you to stand back.' The notion of independence under the Egyptian's ownership was risible, but

Steven interpreted his nods and grunts and a three-page letter written by Cole explaining Fayed's promise to re-establish the *Observer*'s former glory as assurances of autonomy.

The offer was to be made in the Garrick to Hugo Young, one of the *Guardian*'s renowned columnists and chairman of the Scott Trust, owners of the newspaper. At the last moment, before driving to Leicester Square, Steven feared that Young might query Fayed's finances. 'How can I be sure you've got the money?' asked Steven, rushing into the store-owner's office.

'No problem,' replied Fayed. Minutes later, Steven was carrying a signed cheque, with no name entered as payee, for £17 million.

Young, a serious political writer, had been unimpressed by Steven's approach but, since some *Guardian* trustees wanted to sell, he had a duty to listen. 'I'm really a radical at heart,' explained Steven, 'and Mohamed would be the ideal proprietor because he would not interfere. I would run the show.'

'How can we be sure you've got the money?' asked Young. To his surprise, the tabloid journalist pulled out the cheque.

'He's said no,' Steven told Fayed soon after.

'Offer him more,' replied Fayed, oblivious to nuances behind the rejection. '£25 million.'

'That's mad,' said Steven.

'Do,' insisted Fayed. But Young's contemptuous refusal to allow the *Observer* to fall into the hands of 'a man with Fayed's track record' at any price ended the Egyptian's dream.

John Dux produced the consolation prize, Viva Radio, a disastrous women-only station. Crippled by poor reception on medium wave and attracting a maximum audience of 500, the shareholders would have been grateful to receive £500,000 for their albatross. To their amazement, the desperate tycoon offered £3 million. The new manager of the station, Mike Hollingsworth, a well-regarded broadcast executive, accepted Michael Cole's invitation to work for Fayed in the same belief as the other recruits: his huge war chest was buying a media empire including a television station. At the end of their first discussion on Viva's relaunch, Fayed effectively told his latest recruit, 'I own you now.' Hollingsworth laughed. He thought his new employer was joking. But Fayed, having retained or employed four serious executives – Steven, Neil, Hollingsworth and Dux – was confronted by a dilemma. Despite offering huge sums of money, he still did not possess a newspaper. His only solution was to relaunch *Punch*, a humorous magazine closed in 1992 after 150 years' publication suffering annual losses of £1 million. He bought the title for £0.5 million and Steven agreed to mastermind the operation.

Before buying *Punch*, Fayed had only glanced at the original magazine's jokes, hesitating to read the articles. They were too long, too sophisticated and never mentioned sex. However, it had been a British institution and therefore, alongside the Windsor Horse Show, the Villa Windsor, the charities and Harrods, its revival suggested Fayed's commitment to Britain. Explaining what he expected in the relaunched magazine was difficult. Unlike other aspiring media tycoons, Fayed was not only unread but inexperienced. If asked why anyone would pay £2 every week for a glossy magazine lacking nude women, he mentioned *Private Eye* and *Scallywag*, an outrageously defamatory newsletter published by impecunious anti-socials. The defamation of the establishment appealed to Fayed, especially *Scallywag*'s wholly untrue assertion that two senior Cabinet ministers were homosexual lovers. 'I love *Scallywag*,' he told Steven, inadvertently revealing that in 1994 he had secretly contributed money to *Scallywag*'s fast-declining fortunes. One year later, concerned about the use of his money, he had sent John Dux to scrutinize the accounts. Soon after, the magazine collapsed and the publishers fled pursued by victims.

Fayed's dream publication was a vulgar weekly magazine, similar to *Loaded*, splattered with defamatory articles about his enemies, creating glorious havoc. Instead, Stewart Steven recruited a team of tabloid journalists to produce a London version of the *New Yorker* for readers who did not like the

New Yorker. The new editor, paid £180,000 per annum, was Peter McKay, a witty, tubby Scotsman with a talent, between long, entertaining lunches, for producing a pithy comment column. Fayed paid little attention to McKay's qualities and weaknesses. Ever since he had financed, with spending money, Donald Trelford's weekend at the Ritz, only to be later attacked by the same man in the *Observer*, he realized the fickleness of the so-called profession. In his bitter experience, most journalists were easily persuaded to perform as required by their paymasters. The dearth of questions by either Mckay or Steven about their employer's personal and professional conduct, or his attitude towards newspapers' investigations about himself, caused Fayed no surprise. He ignored the irony that, just as his journalists were launching a magazine budgeted to cost £1 million in the first year, two cases in London's High Court exposed some distasteful traits in his character. Like so many other cases in the courts and industrial tribunals, he expected these two would also pass unnoticed.

*

IN 1994, AFTER HIS acquittal in Dubai, Christoph Bettermann had sued Fayed for libel in London. His claim for damages and for the costs of his three-year fight to prove his innocence was also a crusade to prove that Fayed possessed 'an infinite capacity to invent wild allegations calculated to do the utmost damage to the reputation of professional people and to pursue them ruthlessly regardless of expense'. Fayed had no fear of the action. His deep financial resources and his own threats of litigation usually deterred the majority of complainants. Most of the stubborn few who refused to withdraw were placated just before the trial by a settlement. Ocasionally, a handful refused and he lost. The award of damages against him by industrial tribunals was a tolerable overhead to deter others from embarking on the exhausting process.

To sabotage Bettermann's claim, Fayed had used many

ruses, including a contested affidavit that the former managing director had confessed to the court in Dubai to his involvement in the insurance fraud; and inaccurate statements by Macnamara. When those tactics failed, Royston Webb was ordered to seek a settlement.

'We'll pay £1 million,' offered Webb one week before the trial.

'I want a public apology,' replied Bettermann.

'We weren't thinking in those terms,' said Webb.

'No deal,' replied Bettermann.

In February 1996, Fayed's lawyers conceded defeat. 'Mr Al Fayed', announced the Egyptian's barrister in open court, 'now accepts that Mr Bettermann was not guilty of any embezzlement or fraud.' Fayed's apology and payment of nearly £1 million in costs and damages passed practically unnoticed in London. He could expect his employees to regard the Bettermann case – an alleged fraud by a foreigner in the Middle East – with some scepticism. But the consequences of a profile published in August 1995 by *Vanity Fair*, the monthly American magazine, were leading Fayed towards the unforeseen.

Michael Cole had welcomed the opportunity offered by *Vanity Fair* to profile Mohamed. Unlike the prejudiced British media, the Americans were generous to him, and Graydon Carter, *Vanity Fair*'s editor, had commissioned the article in the belief that he was a foreigner victimized by the xenophobic British. Dismissing warnings by Henry Porter, his London editor, that Fayed was not a saint, Carter had expected an amusing profile of a colourful character. Instead, Maureen Orth, the American writer, had gradually discovered the resolutely untold saga of Fayed's racism, sexual harassment of women, ill-treatment of staff and regular bugging of telephones. The publication of her critical report under the headline 'Holy War at Harrods' might have aroused a storm of anguish. Instead, although bought by 34,000 in Britain, the article generated little comment. Despite the irony of Fayed, a self-proclaimed victim, persecuting others, the inertia of the summer holidays and the fear of his writs for defamation discouraged Britain's newspapers from repeating the American's allegations.

Michael Cole and Fayed were oblivious to the public's lack of interest. Cursing his misjudgement about the *Vanity Fair* writer, Cole raged that the magazine should be instantly sued for defamation. Sustain the terror of writs, he urged his employer. 'Unless you sue, it will be impossible for me to rebut journalists' questions based on the article.'

Fearing the truth, Royston Webb cautioned that Fayed should ignore the article. 'It'll be forgotten,' he soothed. Uppermost in his thoughts was that the magazine was owned by S. I. Newhouse, an American richer than Fayed with ample resources to unearth sufficient evidence to cause damage and embarrassment.

'Bah,' smirked Fayed, unimpressed. His rollercoaster against the government had gathered new momentum. 'Sue,' he ordered. Any mortal daring to criticize or challenge would be mercilessly squashed, and *Vanity Fair*, he expected, would fall like the rest. The proof of his power in summer 1996 was the delivery to Sir Gordon Downey, the new parliamentary commissioner for standards, of Fayed's indictment against Michael Howard. In the climate of sensationalized sleaze, and given the vindication of some of Fayed's charges against MPs, his dossier on Howard could not be ignored.

After an eleven-year campaign, Fayed had been finally rewarded with an official inquiry into his allegation that Rowland's bribe of Howard through Landy was the reason for the DTI's appointment of inspectors and the publication of the report. Appointed on 26 January 1996, Downey was an undistinguished government auditor inexperienced in the forensic investigation of political corruption. Yet, pressured by the store-owner, he had finally agreed to investigate 'the political conspiracy against me [Fayed] since 1985'. Persistence, money and betrayals had compelled Britain's political system to satisfy his demand. There was every reason for Fayed to celebrate.

'We get those fuggin' bastards now,' he told his entourage – Webb, Cole, Macnamara, Griffiths and Stuart Benson, a solicitor recruited into the orbit. All that was missing, Fayed regretted, was concrete evidence to prove his conviction.

Few morals or principles had ever inhibited Mohamed Fayed's ambitions. One result was his ownership of Harrods. Naturally, he adopted similar fervour to unearth proof of the Howard conspiracy. His first target was Carla Powell, the colourful wife of Charles Powell, Margaret Thatcher's trusted Foreign Office adviser whom Fayed had first met in 1985 in Downing Street as the representative of the Sultan of Brunei. Over the following decade, Carla Powell had emerged as a sparkling socialite spotlighted in newspaper gossip columns. Attracted by his hospitality and equal passion for celebrity, she had gradually counted the Fayeds among her many friends. The Powells had lunched at Oxted and returned the invitation at a dinner party in their home. Carla had occasionally spoken with Heini in fluent Finnish and there were visits to Fayed's house for tea during their August holidays in St Tropez.

At the time, Carla Powell's telephone call to Fayed on 26 September 1995 was an innocuously amiable gesture. The bubbly Italian explained that visiting friends, anxious to sell their jewellery to Harrods, would like to meet Fayed. 'Come immediately,' said the store-owner. Powell's fortuitous visit presented an opportunity to confirm the scenario conjured by his fantasy. After looking at the merchandise, he invited Powell into a room 'for a private conversation'. Initially, the two chatted about life. Indiscreetly, Powell complained that her husband had not received a peerage from Thatcher. Fayed's eyes twinkled. His appetite for gossip about Britain's political personalities was insatiable. But unknown to Powell, his curiosity disguised a frenzy to prove his conspiracy theory. Secretly videoing business contacts and enemies had been extended to his friends. With the video secretly activated, he challenged the unsuspecting woman to recall 'the truth'.

Nine years earlier, in January 1987, Fayed suggested, Carla

Powell had telephoned twice, leaving messages that he should call back on a 'quite urgent' matter. Days later, he continued, they met and Powell had warned, 'Mohamed, watch out.' Her husband had overheard Michael Howard discussing with Thatcher in Downing Street a plot whereby the *Observer* would in the weeks before the general election cease its anti-Thatcher campaign and its attacks against her son Mark if the DTI appointed inspectors. Their appointment three months later proved the accuracy of Powell's prophecy. 'You remember?' asked Fayed vigorously. With equal vigour, Carla Powell rejected Fayed's proposition. 'No, Mohamed, I said nothing about that.' Disappointed but not surprised, Fayed was unconcerned. After all, it was a fabrication, but skilful editing of their conversation could turn her denials into agreement. Innocently, Powell departed. (Curiously, Royston Webb would recall a different version: namely, that Ali Fayed had received the same warning from Carla Powell in 1987 during a chance encounter in Harry's Bar.) At the time, Fayed was unaware of the flaw in his fantasy: in January 1987, the DTI's civil servants had not yet proposed appointing inspectors.

Eight weeks later, in November 1995, Fayed resumed his entreaties to the one man who knew the truth, Tiny Rowland. In a long letter, Michael Cole appealed to his uncertain ally to 'set the record straight'. Recalling Fayed's success in forcing the resignation of three ministers, he warned Rowland that with 'right on his side ... Mohamed will not rest while the dishonour heaped upon him as a result of perjured evidence provided by paid witnesses remains on the public record'. Four days later, Fayed sent Rowland a birthday cake – Rowland was seventy-eight years old – with an invitation for lunch. 'As you have always been a big boy with big balls, have the courage to join my crusade; and to show you the size I had in mind, I have enclosed some samples.' A package contained the usual sex toys. Persuading Rowland to meet, especially after Fayed's distribution to journalists of their edited videoed conversations, was difficult, but the Egyptian's persistence was rewarded.

'Josie is very much against it,' Rowland told him.

'Tell her not to worry,' laughed Fayed. 'You're a big boy and there's no tricks. I promise.' To avoid secret taping, Rowland insisted that the venue would be his normal table at the Berkeley Hotel in Wilton Place. As the two sat in the sombre dining room on 6 February 1996, Rowland did not check for any tiny microphones on Fayed's lapel. But outside Josie Rowland, after leaving the hairdresser, walked around the hotel. Just as she feared, a Range Rover with darkened windows was parked adjacent to the building. It sprouted six aerials and, as she reported to her husband when she handed over the car's registration number, she certainly saw men inside operating tape recorders.

The following day, unaware of Josie's discovery, Fayed received a polite but uncompromising letter from Rowland denying that Landy's relationship with Howard gave 'any foundation' for the DTI inquiry. 'Both of us have caused each other quite a lot of public embarrassment and I am sorry that you are still dealing with the consequences. It is understandable that you do not accept the DTI report. These things rankle for a long time.' Ignoring that letter, Fayed ordered Webb to draft a succession of statements for Rowland to sign, admitting Landy's relationship with Howard and the conspiracy. 'It's entirely untrue,' Rowland retorted. 'At the time I had no idea that he had a relative in a senior position in the Department of Trade. It is odd that Harry never mentioned it to me.'

Fayed's desperation, his astonishing unwillingness to accept defeat, aroused Rowland's excitement. Mischievously, he again accepted the store-owner's invitation to lunch at Harrods on 20 March 1996. Fayed had resolved to stage a final showdown to justify Downey's inquiry. At last, he believed, he possessed a weapon to intimidate his foe. In the course of lunch, he disclosed that he had 'information' about the conspiracy. Carla

Powell had provided 'a statement' that Howard, with Thatcher's clearance, had appointed the inspectors.

Rowland was puzzled. Why, he asked, would Thatcher be so ungrateful? 'After all, you brought the sultan.'

Those facts could not interfere with the conspiracy, countered Fayed. Her overriding interest was to stop the *Observer*'s attack on her son. 'Politicians, they don't give a shit,' he exclaimed. 'She took from me as much as she can.' Rowland's silent amusement turned to bewilderment as, unexpectedly, Fayed flourished his anticipated ace. Holding up a brown envelope, he suggested that unless Rowland admitted bribing Howard, he would release embarrassing documents about the Basle bank fraud in the 1950s involving Rowland posing as 'Raven'. The unmentioned source of that information was Rowland's safety deposit box in Harrods. One document showed that Dusko Popov, the wartime double agent, having identified 'Raven', the fraudster, had successfully blackmailed Rowland in 1973 for thousands of pounds in compensation for his ordeal in jail. Fayed's revelation flabbergasted Rowland. Although he had bowed to Popov's blackmail, he had no intention of pleasing the corpulent, immoral Arab. 'I'll never bury the hatchet with Mohamed as long as I live,' he told Royston Webb soon after. In retaliation, in his evidence to Downey, he would claim that during the lunch Fayed offered a £10 million bribe if he would confess.

Stymied by Rowland's obduracy, Fayed turned in desperation to Adnan Khashoggi, his estranged brother-in-law. Telephoning Hassan Yassin, Khashoggi's cousin, Fayed suggested reconciliation with the man whom he had last met ten years earlier at the Ritz. Since then, Khashoggi's fortunes had plummeted. In his roulette lifestyle, he had lost billions of dollars and was worth barely $1 million. Beguilingly, he admired Fayed's achievement. The two cousins arrived in Fayed's fifth-floor office in mid-April.

Fayed's laughter and jokes were, as always, disarming. As

always, he trusted that preconceived suspicions would disappear if he played the generous fool. 'Have some of this,' he prattled to Khashoggi.

'What is it?' asked the Saudi, holding a bottle.

'Cod-liver oil. To lubricate the heart. You'll live for ever,' roared Fayed, suggesting concern for Khashoggi's health. 'These are for your children,' he added, pointing at the huge teddy bears and boxes of toys.

'What can I do for you?' asked Khashoggi, staring into Fayed's unreliable eyes. There was always an agenda.

'I want you to sign that the evidence you gave to the inspectors was untrue. Admit you took money from Rowland.'

Khashoggi smiled: 'I'll sign whatever is true.'

Fayed returned the smile. Khashoggi, he believed, was willing to co-operate. 'I'll give you £2 million if you help,' he offered.

Plunging his hand into Fayed's jacket pocket, Khashoggi laughed. 'I'll sign whatever is true,' he repeated, 'and have this to start.' Six fifties – £300 – were in his hand. 'Talk to Evans,' laughed Khashoggi. 'We'll spend this downstairs.'

The draft affidavit Royston Webb presented to Sam Evans, Khashoggi's lawyer, stated that Khashoggi had provided false information and forged documents for the inspectors: 'I gave inaccurate information to the Inspectors . . . I did this at the request of Mr R. W. Rowland because he agreed to pay me a substantial sum of money . . . I have been ashamed of the part I played in damaging the Fayeds' reputation.'

Evans laughed: 'He's not signing this.'

Webb, still a true believer in Fayed, seemed surprised. 'But Mohamed said you'd agreed.' Returning without a signature, Webb was perplexed.

'It's all rubbish,' raged Fayed, instinctively searching for an excuse for the failure. 'They won't give me what I want. He says he'll only sign if I pay millions. I'm not paying.' Webb's bewilderment grew.

Accordingly, the file presented to Downey to prove the

conspiracy was weak. There were two unsigned affidavits (from Rowland and Khashoggi), two sharply edited videoed conversations (with Rowland and Powell) and notes of fruitless attempts by Macnamara and Fayed's solicitor to extract incriminating information from Rowland's personal accountant, from Ken Etheridge and from Lonrho's new managers.

*

FAYED WAS NOT DEPRESSED. His certainty that their lies would be exposed was encouraged by Charles Wardle, the former junior Home Office minister. Annoyed about Michael Howard's denial of any interference in the Fayeds' application for British nationality, and believing that Howard's relationship with Landy was suspicious, Wardle had become sympathetic to the Fayeds, a conversion he was intent on publicizing. Ignoring his party's hatred of the Egyptian, he told the House of Commons that the Fayeds were victims of an 'injustice' proven by the 'numerous inconsistencies' in the inspectors' report. 'For the duration of the inquiry', he declared, the inspectors had been led by the nose by Rowland and his stooges and no one at the DTI shouted 'stop' or told Rowland 'unequivocally to get lost'. Fayed was delighted. An unbribed MP was an ally. He even accepted Wardle's invitation to lunch in the Commons. Unfortunately, while carefully eating nothing, he realized that the MP's reservations about Howard's conduct provided no evidence to include in his submission to Downey alleging Howard's corruption. The coincidence that during the same week of August 1996 he was ordered by an industrial tribunal to pay £13,500 to Sandra Lewis-Glass for wrongful dismissal from Hyde Park Residence had passed unnoticed among his supporters. His victims, even those wrongfully imprisoned, attracted no sympathy in London. Fayed had little reason to think that would ever change. Two years after the *Guardian*'s exposé of the two Conservative MPs he was still regarded as semi-respectable rather than an accomplice to corruption. With utmost care, he had suffocated and concealed his murky lifestyle. As Sandra Lewis-Glass moved permanently to the United States to rebuild her life, over one thousand of Britain's top journalists accepted Fayed's invitation to a champagne party on 4 September to launch *Punch*, the new weekly magazine.

The first issue, promoting an article by Joe Haines, the discredited hagiographer of Robert Maxwell, had displeased Fayed. 'Put Howard hanging on the gallows on the cover,' he told Stewart Steven. Only the front cover interested the proprietor and the vulgarity of Howard's execution, every week if possible, would have provided the instant gratification he demanded. Hammering the establishment was his single desire. Gloomily, Steven realized that a demon-eyed Mr Punch on the cover, Fayed's unwillingness to read the magazine and its lacklustre reception in the media foretold failure. The appointment of McKay was equally doomed. The columnist refused to write a column for his own magazine. Irritated by his expensive folly, Fayed stood to make a speech of welcome at the launch party, itching to push a cream cake into Steven's face. In retrospect, Steven regretted a missed opportunity for great publicity. Equally, Fayed regretted failing to vent his anger. Owning a magazine which missed humiliating his enemies served no purpose. He did not discuss his displeasure. Conversations to disentangle problems were unknown under his management. *Punch*, it was silently concluded at the end of the first week, was pointless.

Frustrated by his inability to influence politics through his fledgling media empire, Fayed's next thought was to enter politics. Wealth had made him wise and his opinions deserved dissemination. Guided by Michael Cole, he announced that he would either, like Jimmy Goldsmith, establish a political party, or alternatively fund a think-tank to propagate his opinions. 'I want a Civic Forum', he announced, 'to clean up the country.' Rich men offering cash-starved academics the finance to research their beloved passions always manages to dull the objectivity of reputable individuals. Through his force of personality and the image of huge wealth he managed to persuade his two closest political advisers, David Alton and Alex Carlile, the Liberal MPs, and Lord Lester of his genuine interest in objective studies of constitutional issues such as asylum and nationality. Uncritically, they accepted his pitch that despite his lack of education and his intolerance he would spend millions for no personal gain. Eagerly, they proposed an approach to David Selbourne, a respected academic living in Italy. Selbourne was naturally cautious about moving and about the terms.

'I'll provide a free home in London and pay £80,000 a year,' offered Fayed.

'I must have complete independence,' stipulated the academic.

'Yes, yes,' agreed Fayed dismissively.

'I must have absolute independence,' repeated Selbourne over one week.

'Yes, yes,' replied Fayed with increasing irritation. At the end of two weeks, he finally understood that Selbourne's insistence on independence was serious. The Civic Forum was dead. 'We'll have a Liberty Trust,' he announced.

After ordering Cole to invite the faithful – David Puttnam, David Alton, Andrew Neil, Lord Lester, Frances Lawrence, the widow of a murdered London headmaster, and Alex Carlile – Fayed summoned Mike Hollingsworth, racing frantically to relaunch Viva in November. 'Build your programmes around Liberty Trust,' ordered Fayed.

Hollingsworth was stunned. 'You can't do that in Britain. It's like standing on top of the mosque and broadcasting a tirade against the government.'

Fayed's eyes blazed. 'You do it. If you don't, you fug me and I fug you!'

Breaking the tense silence, Mark Griffiths coughed: 'What the chairman is trying to say is that he would hope you might include some items using Liberty's ideas.' Hollingsworth said nothing.

Shortly afterwards, Fayed cornered Simon Bates, a Viva broadcaster. 'I want you to tell the people how corrupt the government is.'

The chairman had not realized the truth about Viva. The radio in his office, directly linked to the studio, broadcast Viva's programmes crystal clear. But the 3,000 listeners, receiving programmes transmitted on medium wave from two shabby rooms in Marylebone, suffered a crackly signal. 'You listen to my radio station,' Fayed ordered every visitor to his store, handing out radios tuned to Viva. Few obeyed. Hollingsworth was given another order: 'You employ Dodi. Time he did something for a living.' A new office, including casting couch, was provided in Marylebone. 'Don't disturb me until after two o'clock,' ordered Dodi. The vanity of Viva had already cost his father £5.5 million.

Vanity and frustration about his life also aroused Fayed's interest in Pip Dumbill, a twenty-four-year-old attractive blonde New Zealand nanny employed at Oxted. At sixty-seven, the Egyptian needed affection as much as he wanted sex. Propositioning girls had become an ingrained habit, as had the production-line procedure that led towards his bids. After a medical examination, including a search for sexually transmitted diseases, arranged by Katie Manning had proved her to be healthy, Dumbill had entered a disinfected, guarded, volatile, gilded cage where Heini slept one floor above her husband and children. Exhausted and perhaps bored when he returned home, Fayed encountered the young woman in the living room. 'If you do well here, you can work at Harrods,' Fayed promised.

'Thank you, Mr Al Fayed,' replied Dumbill.

Three days later, Fayed invited Dumbill into the living room. Summoning her close, he hugged her 'a little too long and too squashy' and gave her £100 in cash. 'Buy nice clothes,' he laughed. At eleven o'clock that night, the telephone rang in Dumbill's bedroom. 'Come and have a drink,' suggested Fayed. 'I'll come and get you. Security otherwise sees.' Arriving in his dressing gown, he led the unsuspecting girl through the maze of corridors to avoid the security cameras. As they approached his bedroom door, he signalled for extra silence. A female bodyguard, formerly serving in the Royal Navy, was on duty in the opposite room. Inside his bedroom, pouring a glass of wine, Fayed offered to explain his paintings. The nudes hanging twenty years earlier had been replaced by traditional oils and watercolours. Impatiently, clasping Dumbill's hand, he walked towards his bed, lay down and pulled the girl next to him. 'Come with me to Paris,' urged the unloved man. 'I'll give you money. You can live in Park Lane. I give you great time.' As he spoke, he hugged the bewildered nanny. 'Oh, you don't like hugs?' he asked with apparent surprise.

'I gotta go, Mr Al Fayed,' said Dumbill, appalled.

'I'll take you back,' sighed the old man.

At breakfast for the children the following morning, Heini screamed at the nanny for an apparent error. 'I resign,' replied the girl.

Before she left, Fayed thrust another £100 in her hand: 'Come and work for me at Harrods.' The faithful Katie Manning organized the interview. At 8.45 p.m. in Park Lane, Dumbill was led into Fayed's flat. Lured by a fascination for millionaires and the need for employment, she waited patiently.

Fayed entered. 'How about we have sex?' he asked with the subtlety of a sledgehammer.

'No way,' she replied.

Without a flicker of emotion, Fayed terminated the interview: 'Go to Harrods tomorrow. They sort you out.'

Rejected, Fayed had long made himself immune to ridicule. His hatred of those whom he could not buy was little different from his hatred of those he had bought. His victims, he knew, were too embarrassed to reveal his misconduct. Driven by his compulsive urge to escape a loveless life and win acceptance, the greater the rejection, the more he strove to trample the wretches. Any wretches. Chewing up the mudslingers was occasionally an alternative to sex, and fate had delivered a unique opportunity. After a seven-year struggle, his battle to restore his credibility was approaching an astonishing climax in parliament and in the courts.

16

A Year of Judgement

IN SEPTEMBER 1996, Mohamed Fayed was standing in the eye of a storm which he had manufactured. In parliament, Sir Gordon Downey was conducting two investigations, one against Michael Howard and a second against twenty-five MPs with alleged links to Ian Greer; in the High Court, Jonathan Aitken, Neil Hamilton and Ian. Greer had instituted libel actions against the *Guardian*, and Fayed's libel action against *Vanity Fair* was set to become a major investigation into his life; in the Court of Appeal, three judges were considering Fayed's action against the government for failing to give reasons for the denial of British nationality; and, among the many cases for wrongful dismissal against Fayed to be heard by industrial tribunals, was one by Bob Loftus, Harrods' former security chief.

The link between all that extraordinary investigation and litigation was Fayed's wealth, his vengeance and his rejection of any judgement other than his own. According to his scriptures, the possessors of wealth dictated the rules. The callow tycoon, the author of his own truth and reality, objected to other mortals unless they bowed to his will and, over the previous two years, sheer perseverance had enshrined his cause as Holy Writ. While, in the shadows, David Hooper, *Vanity Fair*'s lawyer, after two years' exhaustive research had accumulated unprecedented statements describing Fayed's racism, intimidation, telephone bugging and sexual harassment, he presented himself to the public as the victim of political corruption. The moment of judgement beckoned, or – in the vernacular favoured by Fayed to a German journalist – 'The government has been shitting on me and my honour too long ... [and] it's going to pay a price.'

In early September, the *Guardian*'s lawyers and journalists were frantic. Unexpectedly, two weeks earlier, the trial of Hamilton's and Greer's complaint had been advanced by one year and was set to start on 1 October. The newspaper risked losing £2 million and £8 million if special damages were awarded. Its reputation relied upon the veracity of Fayed, an Achilles' heel by any measure since he had blatantly contradicted his version published in the newspaper's original report.

'I was specifically asked by Ian Greer', he had declared in his witness statement in June 1995, two years after first meeting Preston, 'for money (two cheques for £12,000 and £6,000) to pay Messrs Hamilton and Smith and I paid it to him for that reason. These two cheques were not paid to Ian Greer to pay to Conservative candidates in the 1987 General Election ... Secondly, I made a payment of £13,333 to Ian Greer in February 1990. Mr Greer told me that this was, again, for services rendered by MPs including Mr Hamilton and for which I had to pay.' The documentary evidence proved the contrary. Greer's audited accounts indisputably recorded that Fayed's contribution for election expenses had been used for that purpose and none had been paid to Hamilton or Smith; while the third cheque for £13,333 had been paid by Royston Webb and the lawyer, disingenuously, had denied to Greer any knowledge of payments to MPs. More importantly, Fayed had subsequently revealed his own cash payments to the MPs, exposing his arithmetic of all the payments as a cascade of contradictions. His vulnerability in the witness box could be revealed by the plaintiff's first question: 'What is your date of birth, Mr Al Fayed?' Any answer would have established his dishonesty.

In the newspaper's favour was the confession of Tim Smith; Neil Hamilton's lies about his week at the Ritz and his false denial to Michael Heseltine of a financial relationship with

Greer; and the voluminous correspondence between Fayed, Hamilton and Greer showing an orchestrated campaign in parliament. The case against Greer however was weak. Although his testimony in 1990 to a parliamentary committee about his financial relationship with Sir Michael Grylls had been false, Fayed had never suggested giving cash to Greer, and Greer's accounts revealed no secret payments on Fayed's behalf to the MPs.

In the hectic race to complete her preparations, Geraldine Proudler, the newspaper's solicitor, recovered from storage the boxes of documents handed over by Fayed one year earlier, after the writs had been served. Among those documents, logged among hundreds of other items for further investigation, were telephone message pads from Fayed's Park Lane office containing two messages from Ian Greer mentioning a quarterly payment of £5,000. One year earlier and again just before the trial, Proudler considered those two items less important than pinpointing and extracting under 'discovery' all the plaintiff's documentary records – accounts, income tax returns, itemized telephone lists, correspondence and diaries – and the files of the Cabinet Office and the government. The inevitable obstacles thrown up by the reluctant plaintiffs and civil servants were compounded by the apparent powerlessness of Stuart Benson, Fayed's in-house solicitor after Royston Webb's retirement, to deliver anything Proudler requested. 'Benson's impossible,' screamed a *Guardian* lawyer in frustration, fearful that Fayed was disinclined to break his habit of secrecy. 'He seems to tell Fayed what he wants to hear.' The logjam began to break on 16 September, two weeks before the trial.

In the three weeks since he had been retained by the *Guardian*, Geoffrey Robertson QC had become agitated that access to Fayed and his staff had been barred. Only vaguely aware that the trial was imminent, Fayed was travelling abroad unconcerned by the momentum in London. Unable to win Benson's sympathy, Robertson appealed to Michael Cole. 'It's vital', Robertson insisted, 'that I talk with Mr Al Fayed about

his witness statement and that he gives us access to his staff.'
Suddenly and mysteriously, Douglas Marvin, a tall, austere
Washington attorney, casually arrived to offer his help. In
Fayed's compartmentalized world, his most sensitive tasks in
the previous eighteen years had rarely been allocated to British
lawyers, including Royston Webb, but to the American. Boasting aggressive qualities which British lawyers lacked, Marvin
would surprisingly deny consulting Fayed about his close
involvement in the Hamilton case, but he was, Robertson
judged, critical to winning Fayed's co-operation. During the
course of an afternoon, Robertson convinced Marvin that
among his many requirements was access to Fayed's secretaries. Although Proudler was less interested in the secretaries
as witnesses because the testimony of his employees would be
discounted by a jury, Robertson was intrigued by the two
handwritten telephone messages. One, written on 19 September 1988 by Iris Bond, Ali's secretary, was from Ian Greer:
'July/August/September payment due'. A second message on 4
November in the same book read, 'From Ian Greer to MF:
You owe July, Aug, Sept £5,000. Iris tell AF.' That message
had been written by Alison Bozek, Mohamed Fayed's secretary.

'Who is Iris?' asked Robertson.

'One of Mohamed's secretaries,' replied Marvin.

'Could you ask her about this?'

Marvin nodded: 'Let me see if I can track the secretaries
down and see if they remember anything.' Until then, there
had been no suggestion that Fayed's secretaries might have
witnessed any cash transactions, nor that Greer had received
any cash.

On 26 September 1996, Robertson and Proudler arrived
on the fifth floor for a two-hour conference with Fayed,
Marvin, Cole and Macnamara. Six days before the trial, the
lawyers listed their urgent requrements. As they pressed for
better co-operation, Fayed, in between one of his flits in and
out of the conference room, told Marvin, 'Do everything they
want.' Fayed's new eagerness was understandable. As a key

witness in the trial, he would be ruthlessly cross-examined. Everything should be done to tilt the case in the defendant's favour.

Two days later, Marvin surfaced. Laid back and seemingly operating on the sidelines, he told Proudler that Iris Bond's immediate reaction to his question whether she knew anything about cash for questions was, 'Neil Hamilton's a liar.' Alison Bozek, he added, also knew 'a lot' about the cash payments. 'I'll get some draft statements,' offered Marvin obligingly. He would subsequently deny having consulted his client, Mohamed Fayed, in any respect about his employees' statements.

Alison Bozek, a former air stewardess with Genavco Air, Fayed's company, had been appointed Fayed's assistant in Park Lane in March 1981. After thirteen years' loyal service, she had resigned in September 1994 and, with Fayed's help, had been accepted despite her lack of the usual high standard of academic qualifications as an articled clerk at Allen & Overy, a prestigious firm of solicitors which normally required trainees to possess first-class degrees. Without the knowledge of the *Guardian*'s lawyers, Marvin compiled a formal statement for Bozek, dated Friday 27 September 1996, incriminating Hamilton and Greer.

In devastating detail, Bozek admitted sealing several envelopes containing between £2,000 and £5,000 in cash for Hamilton to collect. More dramatically, she also told Marvin that every three months Ian Greer had received £5,000 cash payments from Fayed: 'Greer would often telephone and ask me whether Mr Al Fayed had left an envelope for him. Sometimes he would ask bluntly whether Mr Al Fayed had his money ready.' Bozek described how bundles of £50 notes were stuffed by Fayed, often irritated by Greer's demands for money, into brown envelopes – watched by Bozek and Bond. Regularly, his irritation was made worse by Greer being 'very persistent', because he 'would sometimes phone four or five times asking for the envelope'. 'Let him wait for his money!' Fayed exclaimed. Iris Bond confirmed the scenario by stating that

Greer's secretary also telephoned demanding the cash. At the rate of £5,000 every quarter, Fayed had allegedly given Greer £200,000 in cash. Yet, according to Bozek, 'There was no curiosity in the office as to what was happening' in relation to the cash payments.

Fayed had clearly hoped that the womens' astonishing revelations would damage Hamilton's and Greer's prospects. Yet there were inconsistencies for Hamilton and Greer to exploit. Neither secretary had ever seen the envelopes handed over to either the MPs or Greer; Bozek could 'not remember' any cash payments to Tim Smith or Francesca Pollard, although both came several times into her office to receive cash from Fayed; and critically Fayed had never mentioned paying cash to Greer. 'I cannot remember everything,' he would explain later.

The receipt of those two statements by the *Guardian*'s lawyers five days before the trial was greeted with modest euphoria. By then, the lawyers had received through discovery a mass of the plaintiffs' personal letters, telephone records and bank accounts, and also some records from the Cabinet Office which fatally undermined the plaintiffs' case.

Scrutiny of Greer's accounts revealed the lobbyist's undeclared payments and 'gifts' to Hamilton, and showed how Hamilton, as the DTI minister, had helped Greer win a contract representing the Big Eight accountancy firms by permiting the lobbyist to write that the junior minister was 'sympathetic' to the accountants' case. The formal Cabinet Office memorandum recording Hamilton's denial to Heseltine of any financial relationship with Greer was damning. Greer's accounts also showed secret commissions to other MPs for introducing business and that some MPs had not declared his contributions to their 1987 election expenses. All that incriminating information, proving the deceit of the plaintiffs, would compensate for the *Guardian*'s inability to prove the entirety of Fayed's original allegations.

During that final week, relations between Greer and Hamilton had deteriorated. By Friday morning, 27 September 1996, still unaware about the statements signed by Bozek and Bond, both blamed each other for the damaging revelations seeping from their records. Faced with the chance of defeat which neither could financially afford, they argued bitterly. Amid tears and screams, their lawyers ruled out the possibility of jointly representing both men. Early that afternoon, Geoffrey Robertson was asked about the possibility of a settlement. By the end of the day, after the affidavits of the two secretaries were faxed to the defendants, the plaintiffs were discussing surrender. On Monday afternoon, 30 September, just eighteen hours before the trial was due to open, both men discounted the possibility of requesting a postponement of the trial and preferred to capitulate. On the eve of their pre-election conference, the Conservatives were devastated. Ecstatic, the *Guardian*'s journalists composed a memorable edition for the following day, placing a photograph of Hamilton looking shifty under the banner headline, 'A liar and a cheat', precisely the headline the newspaper could have placed over a report about Fayed's phoney submissions of illness to the arbitration court in Dubai two years earlier.

Inevitably Fayed did not notice the paradox. In the latest cataclysm engulfing John Major's government, he basked beneath a halo of righteousness as a champion of truth and justice. Thanks to the *Guardian*'s lawyers and Douglas Marvin, he had avoided the risk of cross-examination in the trial. Regardless of the nuances, those who had disparaged the corrupt foreigner and supported Hamilton were crippled. 'Why Hamilton run from the court if he's innocent?' Fayed chortled. 'You go to court to clear your name. Hamilton ran away.' Three days later, 3 October 1996, John Major announced that Sir Gordon Downey would investigate the cash-for-questions allegations. The British distaste for vendettas, which were seen as insulting fair play, had tilted in Fayed's favour.

*

THE VINDICATION OF Fayed and the extraordinary atmosphere in the capital might well have influenced the judges of the Court of Appeal considering Fayed's case against the government's denial of British nationality. In February 1996, the High Court had declared that the home secretary could not deny, without explanation, the Fayeds' citizenship despite the explicit provision in the 1981 British Nationality Act exempting the home secretary from giving a reason and barring any appeal to the courts. On 10 November 1996, the Court of Appeal upheld that radical judgement, stating that the home secretary was obliged to be fair and, in some circumstances, to explain why an application was rejected. The government's announcement of an appeal to the House of Lords looked spiteful. Even some of their enemies conceded that the Fayeds, after thirty years' residence, were entitled to British nationality. Emotionally and personally, Fayed believed himself to be unassailable.

The unseen flicker of Mohamed Fayed's flame, caused by the unreliability of his case against Michael Howard, did not weaken his boasts of vindication. The mere announcement of Downey's investigation of Michael Howard had been paraded as a milestone on Fayed's quest for exoneration. 'Look at the videos,' Fayed told Downey in his first interview. Aggressive certainty, he reasoned, was his surest tactic for overcoming the paucity of his evidence. 'Rowland admits corruption of Howary.' Unfortunately, Downey was unconvinced. The parliamenary commissioner had demanded the original video tapes of Rowland and Carla Powell. Both sets, he was told, had been 'lost' by Macnamara in the course of 'good housekeeping'. 'Find them,' the commissioner ordered, noticeably unimpressed when, after persistent prodding, Fayed admitted that his original source of information about Howard's corruption was Francesca Pollard, the unstable housewife. An awkward silence followed Macnamara's admission that his own source about Howard's corruption was Fayed himself. Although similar evidence – edited tapes, unsigned affidavits and unverified notes of conversations – had incriminated Christoph Bettermann and had been sufficient for Macnamara to mobilize Metropolitan Police officers to arrest his ex-employees, they were insufficient to smother Downey's doubts.

Nor could Fayed's bluster compensate for the catalogue of denials submitted to the investigator. There were rebuttals from Carla Powell and Ken Etheridge about Fayed's versions of their conversations, a denial from Margaret Thatcher about the alleged conversation with Howard, and complaints from Harry Landy and Lionel Kaufman, Rowland's accountant, about Macnamara's aggressive door-stepping for statements. Both had resisted talking. On Downey's desk was a letter from Tiny Rowland's lawyers insisting 'there is no truth whatsoever in the allegation made by Mr Fayed that Mr Michael Howard accepted payments from Lonrho'. Solemnly, Rowland explained in his oral evidence that his retort to Fayed in the secretly videoed conversation, 'I worked on Harry Landy very hard,' was a tease. 'That is what Tootsie wanted to hear,' said Rowland, 'and I knew that would please him.' Adnan Khashoggi had also sent an affidavit that Fayed had offered £2 million for his signature on an affidavit prepared by the Egyptian himself.

'He's lying,' Fayed told Downey. 'I was unprepared to pay for Khashoggi's evidence.' The evidence presented to Downey, Fayed knew, was unconvincing since, on its own, it failed to convict Howard.

Fayed's indictment relied upon Downey's powers to demand sight of private documents and bank statements shielded from Macnamara's operation, but to his disappointment the commissioner restricted his enquiries. Although he perused in Rowland's home some private bank statements, Downey failed to follow up Rowland's admission of private payments to Landy through Swiss banks and merely relied upon Lonrho's assurances that the accounts of their subsidiaries revealed no payment to Howard. Downey's attitude – his gullibility, according to Fayed – could be judged from his eventual statement: 'it should be noted that Mr Rowland expressly denied to me that either he or Lonrho had been involved in any bribery or corruption'. Fending off investigators, fumed the Egyptian, was an art perfected by Rowland over the previous sixty years. Insensitive to the impression he created upon the blandly polite civil servant, Fayed feared that Rowland's evidence, cunningly disguising his deceit in his impeccable English style, would ring true. His fear was justified.

In choosing whether to believe Fayed or Rowland, Downey wrote, 'in some ways they were alike'. Both were 'powerful and predatory commercial figures combining a ruthless approach to business with considerable personal charm . . . Both seem to believe that with sufficient expenditure of time, money and effort, that grievance could be remedied.' But the balance had tilted against Fayed, owing to a fatal flaw in his argument. For thirteen years he had denounced Rowland as dishonest. Now, relying upon his taped conversations, he claimed that Rowland was telling the truth.

Everything therefore depended upon Downey's investigation of Michael Howard. The crux of Fayed's case was that Howard and Landy had profited from Rowland's bribe. According to Fayed, Rowland had given Landy a house in return for fixing Howard and, according to Fayed, Howard's lifestyle and homes, based upon Macnamara's valuation, could only have been financed by Rowland's bribe.

Howard admitted that he had met Landy at most six times at family occasions over the previous thirty years; and 'so far as he could recall' he had had no contact with Landy in the twelve months before the inspectors' appointment. Landy had however telephoned once after September 1985. 'I think,' recalled Howard, 'shortly after I was appointed a minister at the DTI, I was telephoned by Mr Landy. He told me in his opinion Mr Al Fayed was not fit to be a company director by virtue of the anti-semitic views he held . . . I took no action as a result of this conversation . . . I had no further conversation with Mr Landy on the subject of Mr Al Fayed.' Howard had made no note of the call. Strangely, Landy would deny ever telephoning Howard at the DTI.

Having examined the bank accounts and the house purchases of the two men, Downey found no evidence to support any of Fayed's allegations about Rowland's bribes.

Downey's conclusions did not please Fayed. 'Investigating Mr Al Fayed's complaint', wrote the commissioner, 'has entailed sifting through a tangled web of evidence – much of it contradictory, some of it coloured by the motives of those involved.' Mr Al Fayed, he continued, 'discovered fragments of evidence which, when pieced together, seem to support the explanation of a bribe [which] appears to have been distorted by emotion'. Blaming his 'burning obsession', the commissioner condemned the store-owner for 'believing what he wants to believe'. In other words, Fayed was a fantasist – precisely the conclusion reached by the DTI inspectors.

The conclusion that Macnamara and Fayed were unreliable witnesses destabilized the Egyptian and his team. All were mortified, yet, cushioned by the public's antagonism towards a 'sleazy' government, there was no sudden recrimination against Fayed. Instead, after modest newspaper coverage, the issue was forgotten. Nor was there any comment about Michael Cole's retreat from one of Fayed's more outstanding fantasies. In an interview with the *International Herald Tribune*, Cole admitted that Fayed's statements about his past had been 'somewhat exuberant', and he volunteered his employer's 'pride' that his father was 'a language teacher in Alexandria'. He blamed Fayed's distortions on an insistent adviser, who had warned that 'he would otherwise be disqualified as a purchaser of something as precious to the Establishment as Harrods'. That admission of past lies was minor compared to the inconsistencies exposed during Fayed's second examination by Downey concerning the charges against Hamilton and Greer.

Suffering from flu, Fayed appeared before Downey on 23

January 1997. His motives were indisputable. He had been, he told the commissioner, 'insulted by a bunch of crooks and corrupt bastards who are in power for no reason, just to enrich themselves'. His memory, however, proved particularly unreliable. Across a whole range of critical subjects – his invitations to Hamilton, the circumstances and amounts of cash he had paid and the gifts he received from Hamilton – his answers were contradictory.

Fayed had no records of the payments, but he alleged, 'Each time Hamilton comes, he wants to sell himself, says what he's done and that Greer is not paying enough so I gave him £2,500 and he was happy.' Hamilton, however, had produced an eyewitness who had sat throughout one of his meetings with Fayed and swore that he had never seen any payment. Asked how much Hamilton had received, Fayed replied, '£40,000, £50,000 or £60,000.' Yet he had previously stated that Hamilton had been given £20,000 in cash and £8,000 in vouchers. He was also imprecise about the vouchers he had given Hamilton. '£3,000,' he testified on that occasion and was unsure whether each voucher's value was £1,000, £500 or £100. Fayed was also inconsistent about when the payments started, alternating between November 1985 and June 1987. 'I am sixty-four,' he simpered, unable to explain the contradictions. 'Things start dehydrating. You do not remember things.' In fact, Fayed was sixty-eight.

Trusting Fayed's memory was equally complicated when he was asked about bugged telephones at 60 Park Lane: 'All this is bullshit. People talk rubbish. Why do I need to bug people with recordings? I would like to know who mentioned this.' That outright lie evoked no response from Downey. Possibly, he was becalmed by the *Guardian*'s endorsement of Fayed's credibility: 'Mr Al-Fayed . . . does not have a head for detail, but nor, it appears, does he habitually exaggerate the truth.'

Inextricably, Fayed's and the *Guardian*'s reputation depended upon the testimony of Bozek and Bond, the secretaries. Both women were damned by Hamilton and Greer as liars suborned by Fayed to give false testimony. Ian Greer, especially outraged, had sworn on the lives of his beloved parents that he had neither taken cash from Fayed nor given cash to MPs on Fayed's behalf.

As Fayed knew that Hamilton and Greer had condemned the secretaries as liars, he felt it prudent to dispatch Benson and Christopher Carr QC, his lawyers, to sit on either side of the women during their appearance before the commissioner. Their performance was immaculate. Nevertheless, while voicing outrage as stalwart Conservative voters that a Conservative MP should accept cash, Bozek, the trainee solicitor, pleaded amnesia when asked whether she knew of other cash payments. Downey and Nigel Pleming QC, his lacklustre counsel, feebly accepted the witness's reply, which decisively influenced their conclusions.

In his second report, Downey explained, unconvincingly to some, that, while he had 'erred on the side of caution' towards Mohamed Fayed's evidence, the corroboration of Iris Bond, Alison Bozek and Royston Webb was too powerful to ignore, especially after comparing the pattern of Hamilton's unaccompanied visits to Fayed's office with his parliamentary activities on Fayed's behalf. Downey concluded, despite the evidential flaws, that Fayed's allegations were true. The 'compelling evidence' against Hamilton, and against his colleagues, he wrote, showed that they 'fell well below the standards expected of MPs'. Hamilton, he judged, had accepted between £18,000 and £25,000 in cash from Fayed, but he ruled that there was no evidence he was given vouchers. Once again, it appeared, Fayed was vindicated.

*

ALTHOUGH DOWNEY'S REPORT was published on 2 July 1997, two months after the general election, its findings had been anticipated by widespread leaks during an election campaign dominated by sleaze. Watching the Labour Party's landslide in the general election on 1 May 1997, Fayed expected a call from Downing Street to thank him, one of the nation's powerbrokers, for his contribution. The electorate, he gloated, had responded to his campaign. All those Conservatives embraced by Fayed had been decimated. Tim Smith had been compelled to withdraw his candidacy for the new parliament, while Neil Hamilton and Jonathan Aitken had been massively defeated. He had exposed the moral degeneracy of the Conservatives: until his initiative discredited politicians had not been punished by shame, ostracism or universal public disgrace. Yet there was no word of thanks from Downing Street. Fayed was puzzled. Surely Tony Blair recognized his importance and enormous popularity? He was nothing less than a public hero. To remind the new incumbent not to trifle with his influence, Cole issued a press release:

> I was proud because I showed the masses and I showed voters that they were ruled by a bunch of crooks and my message got through. The win by the Labour Party and its majority – I have caused maybe 70 per cent or 80 per cent of it – because the voters have woken up. I have the support of the ordinary people – that is why I am still here. It's still my country. I'm not leaving. I am going to fight the bastards to clear this system and I am trying to have decent politicians again.

None of Fayed's advisers disabused their employer of his fantasy of heroism. On the contrary, the rollercoaster confirmed his influence, if not his propaganda.

On 20 June 1997, Jonathan Aitken's libel trial against the *Guardian* and Granada Television dramatically collapsed amid allegations of perjury. The discovery of Aitken's payment for two British Airways return tickets from London to Geneva for Lolicia Aitken and Victoria, her daughter, and a car-hire agreement at Geneva airport debited to Mrs Aitken's American Express card, proved that neither Aitken's wife nor his daughter had stayed at the Ritz in Paris or paid the bill. The costly self-immolation of another senior Conservative again supported Fayed's contention that a corrupt political system lacked any moral authority to judge his own excesses. To his delight, those who had revelled in his humiliation since 1989 squealed in anger about the injustice meted out to his targets. 'No unifying thread of principle', wrote Paul Johnson, 'runs through the efforts to destroy the characters of men like Hamilton and Aitken ... Whenever you lift the lid on the *Guardian*'s doings the stench of humbug enters.' Simon Jenkins, the columnist, voiced the minority's irritation against Downey's 'hypocritical' report. 'All we know is that Mohamed Al Fayed ratted on Mr Hamilton whom he had paid as a lobbyist when the latter became a junior minister and refused to reopen an Industry Department inquiry into Mr Al Fayed's business dealings.' Criticizing Downey's investigation, Jenkins continued, 'The effort is wholly disproportionate to the public evil.' Nothing had been learnt, he wrote, 'about the governance of Britain but only about the self-importance of the media and the vanity of politicians because what MPs always do – on behalf of farmers, trade unionists, insurance brokers, lawyers, teachers and doctors – is speak in Parliament about their own interests. No one is fooled.' There was, he concluded, 'nothing wrong' with an MP if he 'takes money to push a cause'.

Inside Fayed's sanctum, the cries of the minority were ridiculed. Visitors to his office and homes were greeted by a man delighting in his fame and success. 'I got those corrupt bastards,' he scoffed as Michael Cole beamed in admiration. Despite the DTI report, he crowed, his veracity had been endorsed in the courts and by Downey. The collapse of his campaign against Michael Howard was ignored. Any suspicion that his victims might retaliate or that his business was vulnerable was suffocated by his grandiosity. His performance was disguising a crumbling position.

Secretly, the Fayed brothers, due to Mohamed's excesses, were confronted by spiralling debts. By 1996, Harrods Holdings had borrowed £206 million and, after negotiations, the brothers had raised their loan facility that same year to £370 million. The company's profits, despite an increase in turnover, had fallen from £58.7 million to £37.6 million. The company's dividend paid to the brothers in Bermuda had been reduced to £20 million. There were other signs of financial mismanagement and of Mohamed's profligacy. The Ritz in Paris had accumulated debts of £138 million. Containerization had destroyed Genavco. Fayed's investment – a 30 per stake – in Mallett, the Bond Street antique dealers, had failed to provide a business for his wife. Worst of all, investigations by Mohamed Alabbar, the Dubaian official, were unravelling his lucrative Gulf businesses. IMS, Alabbar had discovered, had been secretly registered in Bermuda and was therefore unlawfully trading in Dubai. Fayed had no alternative but to sell the salvage company and his property. His loss on the forced sale would be nearly $50 million. Their salvation, the flotation of Harrods, was also doomed. Salomon Brothers, their New York advisers, had found not a single major bank or broker willing to subscribe to the shares. An executive of Salomon Brothers told Ali an unpleasant truth: 'You're not wired up for a joint venture with the market. You can't operate with structured boards, public controls, non-executive directors and accountability. It's off.' Some £4.8 million had been wasted. Naturally Michael Cole's spin sounded anodyne. 'We've abandoned it', he announced at the beginning of an unprecedented bull market, 'because market conditions were not right.'

The first casualty was Fayed's lust to be a media mogul. On Ali's insistence, Liberty Publishing, having lost £6.5 million, was deemed an expensive folly for massaging Mohamed's vanity. The projected losses for *Punch*, deemed by the market an unsalvageable flop, would add, after one year, additional debts of £7.21 million. Viva Radio was judged by Andrew Neil to be worthless. 'Cut it all out,' ordered Ali. 'I can't hear Viva and I can't read *Punch*.' His elder brother agreed. Stewart Steven, just another rueful casualty of Fayed's self-salesmanship, blamed his own vanity for believing that he could influence or even alter Fayed's thoughts. He, John Dux,

Hollingsworth and the management team recruited to build an empire were jettisoned. Only Andrew Neil remained as a consultant. 'I need him,' Fayed explained. 'He says he can bring me the newspaper I want.' The collapse of his media dream coincided with the entanglement of two seemingly unimportant pieces of litigation: his libel action against *Vanity Fair* and Bob Loftus's suit for wrongful dismissal. Money, Fayed had believed, would as usual smother both, but his expectations remained stubbornly unfulfilled.

The dismissal of Loftus in February 1996 had been in Fayed's opinion unfortunate but necessary. After the sale of House of Fraser, Macnamara had moved to Harrods and gradually impressed Fayed that Loftus was redundant. Although Loftus's loyalty and dedication had been appreciated, Macnamara's network of contacts with the police and private investigators was too valuable to lose. After offering Loftus the directorship of security at Metro Aviation, his new aircraft-handling business at Heathrow, Fayed agreed that it was, compared to Harrods, too menial. As usual, he sought to minimize the cost of a redundancy. Gossip, sparked by an injudicious letter from Loftus, stirred Fayed to renege on his agreed financial settlement. The inevitable claim by Loftus in the industrial tribunal would, he expected, be settled as usual. His familiar strategy was interupted by *Vanity Fair*.

Backed by unlimited funds, Henry Porter, *Vanity Fair*'s London editor, and David Hooper, the magazine's hired solicitor, had skilfully found witnesses to substantiate the original article's allegation that Fayed's employment policies were racist and that he sexually harassed young female employees. In the process of the litigation, those statements had been delivered to Fayed. For the first time he was confronted with an unpalatable scenario. Witnesses were prepared to testify in court about his character and misdeeds. Even worse, he heard that Loftus was prepared to help *Vanity Fair*. Money, intimidation and entrapment would he hoped sabotage the magazine's operation. As an insurance, he also launched the People's

Trust, a new £1 million think-tank to 'promote honest and ethical behaviour in public life'.

Fayed offered Loftus £90,000 on condition that the former security director sign a draconian confidentiality clause preventing any co-operation with *Vanity Fair*. Loftus refused. As soon as the industrial tribunal awarded him £39,000 compensation, he revealed to David Hooper that not only had he witnessed many instances of Fayed's racism and sexual harassment, but he had access to over 300 tape cassettes of the secret bugging operation which he had conducted on Fayed's orders. Over the years, the tapes had been smuggled out of Harrods. *Vanity Fair*'s case was considerably enhanced.

In a desperate attempt to destroy Loftus's credibility and persuade *Vanity Fair*'s witnesses to renounce their testimony, Fayed relied upon Macnamara. Firstly, the former Scotland Yard detective had attempted to collect evidence to destroy Loftus's credibility. Secondly, pressure was exerted on witnesses not to testify.

To destroy David Hooper's credibility, Fayed mounted an entrapment operation. Paul Handley-Greaves, a former captain in the Military Police who had replaced Loftus, telephoned Hooper and lied that, having been dismissed by Fayed, he wanted to sell a video showing his former employer involved in compromising activities with female staff. The attempted entrapment backfired, with serious consequences for Fayed. Outraged by his behaviour, *Vanity Fair*'s lawyer and Henry Porter steeled themselves to defeat their adversary completely. Fayed was undaunted.

In May 1997, while celebrating his victory over the Conservative politicians, Fayed agreed with the senior managers of *Vanity Fair* in New York and London to terminate the litigation quietly. The settlement would have entombed the incriminating evidence, preserving Fayed's new, pristine image. Outraged by Fayed's attempted entrapments and intimidation, Henry Porter argued against any settlement. Persuaded not to back down, S. I. Newhouse agreed to finance further investigations. Instead of permanently burying the distasteful evidence, Fayed's conduct was again destined to be tried in open court in October. But just as Fayed's reputation seemed irredeemably endangered, he appeared in St Tropez hosting the world's most glamorous woman. Judgement was no longer suspended. Worldwide, Fayed was hailed as the King.

17

The Last Blonde

PERSISTENCE HAD BEEN REWARDED. Ignoring her earlier refusals to holiday in his homes in Gstaad, Balnagown and St Tropez, Mohamed Fayed rarely missed an opportunity during Princess Diana's shopping trips to Harrods to proffer invitations. Playing host to the world's most famous woman, especially a beautiful blonde, was a prize worthy of great effort. Although Heini had been heard to decry his energetic wooing of Diana – he would beckon her to his office whenever she was spotted in the store or would approach her when he attended parties associated with her charities – Fayed felt genuine sympathy for the isolated woman, who he could see was made almost frantic by her predicament. She was a natural target for the generosity which a tycoon could offer.

'Come to the South of France,' he suggested in late May 1997 after a formal dinner at the Churchill Hotel in Portman Square. 'Bring the boys. I fly you down. You have your own house by the sea with swimming pool. Very private. You need a holiday.' As a father, and as a friend of the late Earl Spencer and his wife Raine, Diana's stepmother, Fayed had an unquestioned interest in caring for a woman ostracized by the royal family. But his concern was not purely altruistic. As a celebrity hunter, he relished the prospect of being photographed standing alongside Diana on his own territory, not least to destabilize his critics. The news in early June from Michael Cole that the princess had, in a telephone call to his home, expressed interest in his latest invitation aroused extraordinary excitement and effort. Urging Cole to encourage Diana to commit herself, Fayed contacted Yachting Partners International, a small company, and described his immediate requirement: a ship fit for a princess. Nothing less than a floating palace would suffice.

Michael Cole, the loyal spokesman, was as excited by the prospect of Diana holidaying in St Tropez as his master. Over the previous nine years, he had become convinced of Fayed's victimization by Britain's politicians and establishment. Regardless of Sir Gordon Downey's conclusions, he remained a passionate believer in the existence of a conspiracy between Michael Howard and Margaret Thatcher to launch the DTI investigation that ruined his employer's reputation. Diana's presence in France, he knew, would sensationally deflect and hopefully even undermine the insidious doubters of his employer's innocence. Energetically, Cole reassured Diana, 'If we handle this thing properly, nobody will ever even know that you've gone. The idea is that you have a quiet, private, family holiday.' Whether Diana believed that is questionable. Her daily movements were perpetually scrutinized by a small army of journalists and photographers whose income depended upon recording her life. Among that group, it was common knowledge that she would be taking her sons on holiday during July. Only the destination was unknown.

Certainly, Fayed could not guarantee privacy without imprisoning his guests inside the estate, and even then, as Cole well knew, his employer was renowned for indiscretion. Nevertheless, the assurances were sufficient to persuade Diana to ignore the warnings of her friends and accept the invitation. 'I know he's naughty but that's all,' she replied to those who relayed the news of *Vanity Fair*'s discovery of alarming flaws in Fayed's character. By 11 July, when the Egyptian's car collected her luggage and his helicopter landed on Kensington Palace's lawn to transport her and her two sons to Stansted airport for the flight to Nice and a Dom Pérignon welcome at the Castelle Ste Thérèse, she was looking forward to the sun and sea, unaware that her host had committed himself to something more than mere hospitality.

For less than the £15 million asking price, Fayed had bought from a Milanese textile tycoon the *Jonikal*, a 195-foot yacht built in 1991 and requiring a crew of sixteen. Soon after the rapidly completed purchase, Fayed had conceived the eight-berth yacht as a love boat.

Playing Cupid had never been one of Mohamed Fayed's noticeable talents, but his considerable experience with women, his sensitivity for spotting weakness and his talent of diving for opportunities all coalesced in the days after Diana's arrival. The practised host, offering an exciting variety of excellent food, swimming off the *Jonikal* and laughter by the swimming pool, glimpsed Diana's current happiness and profound loneliness. Encouraging the vulnerable woman to confide her fears, he perceived the vacancy which he could fill. Diana needed companionship, love and a man. To pamper the princess, he could provide the ideal candidate: his son Dodi. On the matter of women, the understanding between father and son, both of them victims of a motherless childhood, was unusual, but it had certainly been productive. It was thanks to Dodi that Fayed had met several women, including Heini, and now he could return the favours.

Fayed's relationship with his son had stabilized but hardly improved in recent months. As ever lazy, disorganized and reluctant even to read newspapers, Dodi was the target of several new writs in California for large unpaid debts and for selling film rights which he did not own. The fantasist's redeeming feature was his scrupulous politesse. Unvindictive and generous with his father's money, he tirelessly maintained friendships with celebrities to avoid isolation and shine in the reflection of their fame. No one had any illusions about Dodi, least of all Ali Fayed. Sitting with Ali at the bar of the Ritz shortly before Diana arrived in St Tropez, a relation had enquired after Mohamed's eldest son. 'He's missed the boat,' replied Ali dismissively. 'We offered him Harrods, Turnbull and Asser, and lots more. He's screwed it.' Regretfully, Mohamed could only agree. But, in matters of pleasure, Dodi was a player.

Normally, Mohamed Fayed's summons to his son, even at 2 a.m., to leave a London night club and present himself in Paris by daybreak would be obeyed instantly, but even Dodi must have paused when ordered on 15 July to fly to St Tropez.

After three days, the secrecy of Diana's holiday had long been forgotten. Less than twenty-four hours after she had left London, the journalists and photographers pursuing her had scurried to the Côte d'Azur. The source of their tip was unknown, and Cole credibly denied responsibility for that particular leak. Finding Diana had posed little difficulty. After the first sensational reports about Diana's host appeared in Britain's national newspapers, the stream of photographs of the princess and her sons enjoying themselves boosted Fayed's confidence. Britain, he was pleased to read, was divided. Despite the contrived storm of vilification, many championed Diana's desire for fun after the pain of her divorce. To them, Fayed was at worst a harmless rogue.

Excited by the controversy, Fayed could effortlessly ignore the carping about the princess's judgement, since he now controlled the agenda and the initiative. Diana, he was certain, could not have taken her children out of Britain without the permission of their father and possibly the queen. That alone was sufficient to stoke the indignation of his two old rivals, Rowland and Tajir, both holidaying near by. Rowland, on board the *Hanse* moored in Monte Carlo, had indeed telephoned Tajir at his villa in Roquebrune to muse about their foe's extraordinary achievement. Both, Fayed imagined, were scanning the Mediterranean with powerful binoculars in an effort to spot the *Jonikal*.

Revelling as the focus of worldwide attention, the storeowner did not hesitate to issue his edict that Dodi hasten to St Tropez – although he could well imagine what one consequence would be. Dodi, he knew, had been engaged for eight months and was due to be married three weeks later in Los Angeles, where Fayed had just paid $7.3 million for Paradise Cove, a six-bedroom seaside house in Malibu which was being expensively refitted for the newly weds. But in his telephone call to Dodi in Paris he ordered that Kelly Fisher, his thirty-one-year-old fiancée, was to be abandoned. Endangering that relationship was irrelevant. The American model, who had accompanied the Fayeds to inspect the *Jonikal* before its purchase, was to remain in Paris comforted by some mindless excuse while his son raced southwards on the Gulfstream.

Mentioned only rarely in gossip columns, Dodi's presence in St Tropez was unnoticed by the Diana-watchers. Even Diana, despite an introduction eleven years earlier at a polo match, was unaware of Dodi's taste for fantasy and cocaine. Surrounded by ostentatious luxury and the glorious sun-kissed blue sea, she was susceptible to his kindness, to his interest in films and to his romanticism. Watching the couple, Fayed appreciated how well his forty-two-year-old son, the polite, passive listener, was weaving the familiar spell of a summer romance, hidden not only from hundreds of prying journalists' eyes but even from Kelly Fisher, by then marooned alternately on the nearby *Sakara* and *Cujo*. Coldhearted, Dodi flitted between the boats and the villa, persuading his fiancée that his father required his presence either in London or discreetly with Diana.

*

NATURALLY, THE WORLD beyond Britain was interested in the background of the hitherto unknown host. Michael Cole obliged by circulating a new biography. 'Mr Mohamed Al Fayed', it began, 'was born on 27 January 1933 in Alexandria, Egypt, where his family was well established and had extensive interests. He graduated from King Farouk University with a Master's degree in Management and Business Administration.' The addition of a master's degree risked embarrassment since Fayed would have had to have completed the five-year university course at the age of twenty, before he began employment as a shipping forwarder with the Khashoggis. But at that moment, engrossed by Fayed's guest, no one was paying attention to inconsistencies, not even to the Egyptian's announcement of the sale of the contents of the Villa Windsor.

Forty thousand items were to be auctioned by Sotheby's in New York. He needed space, Fayed explained, to live in the house with his family. Although that decision was censured by Jean Lisbonne, a past president of the International Law Association, who complained that Fayed had promised that any sale of the contents would be discreet, and by Paris councillors, who attacked the sale by a 'mysterious foundation . . . based in Bermuda' and demanded that the house should be transferred to 'someone who respects his agreements', Fayed was past caring. The French were powerless, and, as for the British, their criticism provoked his contempt. 'Not one single letter', he complained, referring to the British establishment's silent ingratitude, 'from one single official.' His expensive commitment to collecting and cataloguing the Windsors' possessions had been unappreciated. He damned the consequences of breaking his agreement.

Similarly, he was unbothered about the furore aroused by the hazy photograph published across the world on 18 July of Fayed himself with his arm around Diana while she positioned her hand on his shoulder. On the contrary, he was delighted. Having encouraged her to pose for the cameras in her Tarzan swimming costume, he was content that the newspapers were publishing the images and the good news which he desired.

That Friday, he took a telephone call from Brian Vine, a trusted journalist. Keen to share his excitement and unrestrained by Cole, Fayed exuberantly revealed his true feelings. 'I'm like a father to Diana,' he said, 'and Diana's attitude to all the criticism is that these people can go to hell if they don't like it. She was vaccinated against poisonous criticism a long time ago.' Fatefully, he justified her indifference to the paparazzi: 'She has superb security, both Scotland Yard and my own twenty-four-hour bodyguards, who are ex-British army, either SAS or Marines. There were always four security men wherever she and the children go.' Boasting of how much Diana's children were enjoying themselves and of how they had spoken to their father and the queen on his telephone to confirm their happiness, he emphasized that both had given Diana permission to go on the holiday. 'My relations with the royal family are good,' he declared with wild exaggeration. Finally, unable to restrain himself, he spoke on Diana's behalf about Prince Charles's friend: 'She doesn't think or care about Camilla Parker-Bowles. She is something out of a Dracula film.'

Fayed's flimsy repute among the royal family nose-dived on Sunday morning, 20 July. The *Mail on Sunday*'s headline that Diana regarded Camilla as Dracula hurt Prince Charles, whose patronage he had tirelessly cultivated, especially at polo matches. Even Diana's whoops of laughter failed to alleviate Fayed's misery as Cole spelled out the consequences on the telephone that morning. Instinctively, the store-owner blamed Brian Vine, the journalist, for failing to exercise self-censorship. The remedy was easy. Distributing 'exclusives' to chosen journalists was Fayed's way of obtaining leverage to secure positive coverage. Standing in the sun on the *Jonikal*'s stern, he telephoned Nigel Dempster, the *Daily Mail*'s columnist, at home and chortled, 'I have a friend who wants to talk to you, dear Nigel.' He handed the mobile to Diana.

'Nigel, what does everyone expect?' asked Diana. 'That I spend the whole summer cooped up in KP?'

By evening the Dracula blip was forgotten. Fayed was bidding farewell to his guests. The generous host sensed success but even he had not anticipated Diana's report on her return: 'It was the best holiday of my life.' 'I merely honoured my duty', Fayed would later tell trusted journalists, 'to Earl Spencer, my old friend, whose deathbed request was to keep an eye on his family.' There were no living eyewitnesses to that exchange.

Six days later, on 26 July, Dodi Fayed was waiting at the heliport near the Eiffel Tower for Diana's arrival. Amid secrecy and with the continuing need to deceive his fiancée, Dodi had invited the princess to visit Paris overnight. His art of seduction had been perfected over the previous twenty years: 'I'll send you my helicopter'; 'You can stay at the Ritz'; 'I'll pay for this'; and 'I'll take care of that.' On this occasion, there was no danger that his promises would be unfulfilled: his paymaster guaranteed the provision of everything required. Fayed, forgetting his recent reluctance to pay his son's £500,000 debts in California and Dodi's dishonouring of a $200,000 cheque to Kelly Fisher, had encouraged his son to offer the moon to entice the beautiful princess. Once Diana had accepted the invitation, Dodi scrupulously planned the programme while his father, through his network of chauffeurs and bodyguards and with the help of Frank Klein, could monitor the couple's movements during her twenty-four-hour trip.

From the heliport, they would visit the Windsor villa; then the princess would be driven to the Ritz. After she had been taken to the Imperial Suite to change, they would dine at Lucas Carton, one of Paris's finest restaurants. 'Everything has to be perfect,' Dodi had told René Delorm, his fifty-four-year-old Moroccan-born valet. Indeed, everything chimed magnificently. From the restaurant, the couple drove to Dodi's flat in the apartment block owned by his father off the Champs-Elysées, where Diana sat drinking water. By the end of forty minutes the atmosphere was charged. Dodi, so unlike her previous consorts, had enraptured the princess.

After midnight, he escorted Diana out of the building, and the couple stood on the corner of the busy avenue, close to the Arc de Triomphe. Intoxicated by Paris's warm air and the stream of strolling lovers, Dodi murmured to Philippe Dourneau, his chauffeur, 'Find a place where we can walk in peace.' Dourneau drove across the River Seine to the Boulevard St Germain on the Left Bank. Stopping at the Café de Flore, he watched as the two walked from the car. Within minutes, like thousands of others in Paris that night, Diana and Dodi, hand in hand, had disappeared along the river embankment. Astonished Parisians stared in disbelief. A telephone call on the driver's mobile arranged the couple's pick-up at 1.30 a.m. After sleeping alone in the Ritz, Diana was joined for breakfast by Dodi before they returned to the heliport. At 11 a.m., Fayed's helicopter rose through the sunlight. 'It's very romantic,' quipped Dourneau, thinking of all the women he had chauffeured for Dodi over the previous three years.

'What's romance?' chuckled Dodi.

Over the following days, Dodi set a deliberate course. Encouraged by his father to ignore his fiancée and pursue the princess, he discovered that Diana was an eager conquest. Alone in August and attracted to a sympathetic, unthreatening listener, she accepted the invitation for a second trip alone with Dodi to the *Jonikal* on 31 July. The consequences were perfectly understood by father and son. Once on the boat, Diana would become Dodi's lover.

Amid complete secrecy, the couple arrived in Nice and boarded the yacht. Over the next six days, as the *Jonikal* cruised around Corsica and Sardinia, the two frolicked on the sundecks, inside the sumptuous craft and in the sea. Ceaselessly they whispered, talked and laughed. 'How can people have so much to say to each other?' thought René Delorm, watching as they held hands and kissed lightly. 'The flower has opened.' By the end of the trip, as he regularly served her coffee and carrot juice in the morning, cherries and fruit at lunchtime, fish in the evening, endless bottles of Evian water and two bananas a day, Diana's habits had become second nature to the valet. Even the repeated playing of the princess's favourite music – the theme of the film *The English Patient* – as the yacht glided through the blue sea had won over the crew. 'Such a marvellous film,' she told René. 'And you miss the music when you're watching.' René was happy to agree. During her first solo trip with Dodi in early August, he had seen how 'they had clicked'.

No one on the *Jonikal*, however, had heard the clicks of an

Italian photographer's camera as the couple enjoyed the sea in Sardinia on 4 August. Mario Brenna had arrived from Monaco after receiving a tip-off. The suspected source would be a Fayed employee, not least because no one else could have pinpointed the *Jonikal*'s exact location, moored one mile off the coast. The result delighted Fayed. On 10 August, the *Sunday Mirror* published proof of the romance: a fuzzy photograph of Dodi and Diana in an embrace, assumed to be a kiss. Other photographs confirmed the intimate relationship. In the *Daily Mail*, Richard Kay, Diana's friend and her authentic voice, confirmed that Diana was involved in her 'first serious romance' since the divorce.

*

MONITORING THE AFFAIR hourly, Fayed was ecstatic, although the stakes, he concluded, were too big to allow Dodi their sole management. Decisively, he took control of his son's destiny, continuing to brief chosen journalists and photographers as he had ever since his conversation with Brian Vine on 18 July. On the advice of Max Clifford, the publicist, he told callers that the romance was genuine and not fleeting: 'I give them my blessing. They are both adults. We must see what happens.' The studied casualness disguised Fayed's determination not to allow fate to progress without his guidance.

A few days earlier, on 7 August, as scores of photographers recorded Diana's leaked arrival in Park Lane for dinner with Dodi, Kelly Fisher was telephoning to discuss her wedding, still notionally fixed for two days later. Fayed's response was telephone terrorism. 'Don't ever call again,' he snapped.

'This is my fiancé,' cried Fisher. 'What are you talking about?'

There was no reply. Fayed had cut the line. Fisher redialled, to be turned away by an uncaring secretary. 'Don't ever call here again,' threatened the anonymous female. Anticipating that the forlorn woman would cause trouble, Clifford advised

Cole that, while Dodi's romance should be publicized as genuine, Fisher should be labelled a bimbo.

'Kelly, if you need a psychiatrist,' the discarded woman heard from her suitor in their last conversation, 'I'll pay for one.' Anxious to control the publicity which would inevitably arise, Fayed retained Bertram 'The Pitbull' Fields, a tough news manipulator, to minimize any flak.

That Saturday, 9 August, while Diana toured Bosnia to promote her campaign against landmines amid the frenzy of the romance, Fayed paraded himself at Fulham football club, which he had bought five months earlier. The unusually secret purchase for £7.5 million was the result of an introduction by Brian Basham. Hailed as a hero – an increasingly frequent epithet – for promising to invest £30 million to transform the second-division club's fortunes, Fayed had so far installed new seats, painted the walls and appointed Kevin Keegan as manager. Conscious of his new fame as he sat in the directors' box, visible to 8,000 loyal supporters, Fayed had been unable to resist the temptation of exploiting it. Effortlessly, he had enticed the *Observer* to run a new allegation that an MP, dubbed 'Mr K', had taken £30,000 bribes from the Saudis; and other newspapers had publicized his boast of the queen's invitation to sit near her during the last Windsor Horse show.

Gloating over his ability to influence the media, especially given his proximity to the Palace, he urged his son to intensify the affair. After Diana's return from Bosnia on Saturday, he suggested, they should fly the following day to Oxted by helicopter and enjoy his country house. Her agreement cemented his attitude towards the affair: like every other person who had accepted his largesse, Diana was now under his control and owed him loyalty. One week later, on 15 August, at the end of the second week of the affair, Diana's flight to Greece for a holiday with Rosa Monckton, a close friend, was transferred on to Fayed's Gulfstream. While he was feigning a desire to help, the Egyptian's possessiveness was taking hold. The palliative for his ambitions was Diana's repeated appearance in newspapers, invariably in the context of fiery references to the affair with his son.

His press machine moved up to full throttle. Michael Cole's telephone call to Nigel Dempster on 21 August was one of many the spokesman made during that month. Exclusively for the *Daily Mail*, Cole tipped off the columnist that Diana was landing that morning on Fayed's jet at Stansted airport from Greece. Dempster's gratitude disappeared the following morning when he saw that the *Sun*, by extraordinary coincidence, had exclusively photographed Diana arriving at Battersea on the Harrods helicopter from Stansted. Whether Cole continued leaking Diana's movements during the day was uncertain, but that same evening, after Diana flew from Stansted to Nice for her second holiday with Dodi, Jason Fraser, the salesman of Mario Brenna's 'The Kiss' photograph, was waiting in St Laurent du Var, in the South of France, certain that the couple would walk down the pier to board the *Jonikal*. The photographer had been tipped off about the arrival and would remain well briefed about the yacht's erratic movements around the Mediterranean over the following ten days.

The daily reports in all the newspapers and from Dodi personally had excited Fayed enormously. Nothing, he resolved, as the *Jonikal* sailed between the Riviera and Sardinia, would interfere with his dream. Naturally, he affected innocence. 'Nothing is organized,' he burbled to the *New York Times*, parading the relationship as between the children of old friends. 'It's just normal. It's nothing really very special. She's a free woman. My son is free. Normal people fall in love. That's it. Princess Diana is one of the greatest customers here. It's just life. Destiny.'

On board the *Jonikal*, René Delorm would not have agreed unequivocally. Dodi, he realized, had scored an extraordinary hit thanks to meticulous planning. 'Things are going beautifully,' he thought. 'They're going pretty far.' In the sunshine,

Diana either paced the deck talking on her mobile, or lay on a recliner reading *On Being Jewish*, a 280-page book by Rabbi Julia Neuberger. 'Unusual,' thought René, impressed by the princess's reading. 'The book is so thick.' After light lunches – their favourite was soon established as a wide selection of vegetables followed by sorbet – the two slept. Only once did they watch a video, *Murder at 1600*. After changing for dinner, Cristiano, the Italian chef, produced fish dishes, always served with the same white Loire – chilled Baron L 1992, Dodi's favourite. Diana drank just half a glass. 'There's never any champagne,' laughed René. 'Just a lot of water.' The evenings' background music, as the two chatted ceaselessly, was Frank Sinatra or jazz. Occasionally, Dodi smoked a Havana.

'You are not demanding at all,' René told Diana.

'If I ask you for a bottle of water,' giggled Diana, 'will that make you happy?' Never before, Diana confessed, had she enjoyed such freedom, despite the flotilla of paparazzi boats which had followed from Nice. On board the *Jonikal*, Alex 'Kes' Wingfield and Trevor Rees-Jones, the new bodyguards assigned by Fayed to protect Diana, watched the pursuers helplessly through binoculars. Over the ten days, wherever the *Jonikal* sailed – even at night – the bodyguards would, the following morning, spot the paparazzi sticking like leeches. Their request for reinforcements had been refused by Fayed. 'It's a low-key trip,' he said. 'No need.' Accustomed to the intrusion of the powerful lenses, Diana sought to calm Dodi. 'Don't worry,' she repeated, unable nevertheless to disguise her own irritation. Compared to the suffering which she had recently seen in Bosnia – 'She had been so sad about Bosnia,' René recalled – the paparazzi were a minor burden. Dodi's patience by the end of the holiday, however, was evaporating.

On board the *Hanse* in Monte Carlo, Tiny Rowland, fuming about his enemy's success, could not resist telephoning Nigel Dempster. 'I've got a friend of yours who wants a word.' Adnan Khashoggi took the receiver. 'It's the wrong Fayed with

Diana,' he laughed. 'It's Mohamed who wants her.' The jest underestimated Fayed's achievement. The Egyptian's successes were greater than Khashoggi imagined.

In London, on 29 August, Fayed was also celebrating a business coup. Two years earlier he had successfully bid £25 million for a site in Basil Street, directly behind Harrods, including the old Knightsbridge Crown Court, and he had just obtained planning permission for Harrodsopolis – a complex of garages in a seven-storey basement, luxury apartments to be sold for over £2 million each, offices and a 140-room hotel. One obstacle to the redevelopment had been the owner of Wolfes, a restaurant behind the store successfully owned for twenty-two years by Wolf Gelderblom. Stubbornly, Gelderblom had refused Fayed's low offers to buy his lease to allow the redevelopment. 'A foolish man,' thought Fayed and retaliated. Overnight, obtrusive scaffolding surrounded the restaurant, cutting its trade by 30 per cent. Compelled to negotiate, Gelderblom had, on the last day of Diana's holiday, accepted a derisory settlement to abandon the premises. On signing the agreement and closing his beloved restaurant, he looked at his lawyer and said, 'I put a curse on Fayed.' Even Gelderblom could not have imagined the events over the following twenty-four hours.

*

FAYED HAD APPROVED Dodi's plan to return from Sardinia to London via Paris on 30 August. His son wanted to collect a ring selected by himself and Diana at Repossi, the jewellers in Monte Carlo. At the jeweller's insistence, instead of selling a ring from his 'Tell Me Yes' series, he would produce a special design for Diana to be collected in Paris. Only a handful of Fayed's employees knew about the revised travel plan, yet a large group of paparazzi awaited the Gulfstream's arrival at Le Bourget. Once again, some assumed that a Fayed employee had leaked the couple's intentions to secure more newspaper coverage.

Holding hands, Dodi and Diana had talked ceaselessly until the jet landed at Le Bourget at 3.20 p.m. Waiting in the heat were two cars: a Mercedes 600, driven by the reliable Dourneau, and Dodi's own black Range Rover driven by Henri Paul, the acting head of security at the Ritz. While Diana's three suitcases were squeezed into the Mercedes' boot, Dodi, Diana and Rees-Jones jumped into the air-conditioned limousine. Despite the paparazzi's pursuit, the Mercedes escaped on the Périphérique motorway and arrived unnoticed at the Villa Windsor. The couple remained, Kes Wingfield recalled four days later, 'around ten minutes'. On their drive into the city, the chauffeur glanced in his mirror. Gently, Diana was kissing Dodi on his cheek and whispering in his ear.

Thirty minutes later, at 4.35 p.m., that brief, unobserved freedom was crushed. Gasping as they stopped in front of the Ritz, Dodi watched about twenty photographers surge towards the vehicle. 'We can't get out here,' he snapped. 'Let's go round to the back.' After five minutes, the Mercedes arrived at the hotel's rear entrance in the Rue Cambon. Accompanied by security guards, the two dashed out and walked the flight of stairs to the hotel's Imperial Suite on the first floor. Leading the way was Claude Roulet, the deputy manager.

'I've never spoken to a princess before,' stammered Roulet excitedly. 'How would you like to be addressed?'

Outside door 102 of the Imperial Suite, Diana stopped, put her hand on Roulet's arm and replied, 'Just call me Diana.'

While Diana's hair was washed by the hotel's hairdresser and she spoke on the telephone to friends, including Richard Kay, Dodi, Wingfield and Roulet drove sixty yards across the Place Vendôme to Repossi's. Having approved the jeweller's work, Dodi returned. At 6.30 p.m., Roulet knocked on the door of the suite and, while standing in the corridor, produced two rings. 'This one's the "Tell Me Yes" ring,' he smiled, proffering a large diamond surrounded with a cluster of smaller glittering stones in a square of gold, 'and this is the special.' Dodi put the second, considerably smaller ring in his pocket.

Within minutes Roulet had negotiated a special price of 115,000 francs, about £12,000.

At 7 p.m., Dodi and Diana were hesitating about their journey to Dodi's apartment. The hotel's two exits were marked by paparazzi. 'I'm sorry for all the trouble I'm causing you,' Diana sighed to Roulet. The manager smiled and led the way towards the front door. Thereafter her protection depended upon the security provided by Fayed.

In Oxted, Fayed was informed about the couple's movements. He knew about their intention to return to the apartment, eat dinner at Chez Benoît and then return to the flat near the Champs-Elysées for the night. It was an unexceptional plan.

At 9.40 p.m., Diana stood in the dimly lit stairwell of the apartment block. Her face shone. Tilting her head to one side, her eyes flashing with warmth and humour, she smiled: 'Thank you, René. Thank you for everything.'

'It's a pleasure, madame,' replied the valet. 'Have a pleasant evening.'

'See you later,' said Dodi.

Outside, Dodi and Diana encountered the paparazzi, swarming and somewhat aggressive. After struggling into the Mercedes, Dodi made a fateful decision. Glancing at the grizzly faces and squinting at the flashing lights, he ordered Dourneau to cancel the reservation at the Benoît. 'We'll go to the Ritz,' he ordered, exasperated that increasing constraints ruled out his plan for a romantic dinner. Driving southwards at speed, Dourneau glanced in his mirror. Diana was placing her hand on Dodi's knee. 'Don't worry,' she said soothingly. 'Don't worry.'

Dodi *was* worried. Unaccustomed to such intensive intrusion, his agitation was magnified by his fantasies. Irritated by the stares of other diners, he insisted that they move from the Ritz's dining room to the Imperial Suite for dinner. Forty minutes later he had recovered to speak to his father and receive a telephone call from Hassan Yassin, his uncle and the cousin of Adnan Khashoggi. Outwardly, despite the excitement of his romance, Dodi appeared calm, but he was already planning how to outwit the waiting photographers.

Downstairs, François Tendil, the acting deputy head of security, was urgently briefing his superior, Henri Paul. Forty-one-year-old Paul, employed at the Ritz for eleven years, had left for the evening at 7 p.m. after Dodi and Diana had driven from the hotel to their apartment, intending not to return. Alarmed by the hordes of paparazzi after their unexpected arrival at the hotel, Tendil had summoned his superior at 9.50 p.m. on a mobile phone. 'They're back,' he cried, 'the paparazzi are swarming around the hotel. We're having trouble keeping them out. You'd better come back.' Ten minutes after the call, Henry Paul was making heavy weather of manoeuvring his Mini Cooper into a huge parking space in front of the Ritz.

Born in Brittany and moderately educated, Paul had been appointed to the Ritz by Josef Goedde, the German head of security, who had resigned in 1992. Before his departure, Goedde had written a long memorandum for Frank Klein. Concerning Henri Paul, Goedde had noted that the amateur pilot was suitable for administrative work but was untrained and unfit to be the hotel's security chief, not least because he was liable to drink excessively. Nevertheless, over the intervening five years, Paul had contrived to become the acting head of the hotel's security by sabotaging other appointments and by zealously obliging Fayed and Klein. The last security chief had resigned after just three weeks. Ambition, pressure of work and broken relationships had taken a toll on Paul and, unknown to his employers, his doctor had prescribed Prozac and other drugs to calm his emotions and cure his excessive drinking. When Tendil, an unperceptive man, saw his boss walk into the hotel at 10 p.m., still dressed in his grey suit, he did not notice any change from his demeanour three hours earlier. 'Paul was certainly not drunk,' he would tell the police.

Told that Diana was upstairs, Paul sat for twenty minutes in the bar with Wingfield and Rees-Jones while the bodyguards ate dinner. Drinking two Ricard pastis, Paul, a calm, secretive man, spoke in English about Fayed's security organization. When he rose at 10.35, smoking a cigarillo, neither Briton had seen any sign that Paul was intoxicated from the alcoholic pastis. However, Alain Willaumex, a barman, would claim that Paul was so drunk that he bumped into a customer.

Upstairs, Dodi was discussing his plans with Fayed in Oxted. Unable to tolerate the chase, he contrived a ruse which had featured in so many Hollywood cowboy and thriller films. Acting as a decoy, his own car would leave the front of the hotel while he and Diana slipped out through the back and escaped in a getaway car driven by Henri Paul. His idea was approved by his father. As he went to sleep, Mohamed Fayed was content. The prize was within his grasp.

At 11.25 p.m. in Paris, opening the door of the Imperial Suite, Dodi announced, 'We're leaving in five minutes. We're going to use another Mercedes. Paul's driving.' Both British bodyguards, sitting in the corridor, began questioning the order. Unusually, Rees-Jones had on arrival at the hotel exchanged sharp words with Dodi, rejecting his employer's criticism that the bodyguards had provided insufficient protection against the paparazzi. 'I asked for more men,' Rees-Jones had snapped. But the bodyguards' protest about Dodi's stunt was stifled by Henri Paul's arrival. 'It's been okayed with Mr Mohamed,' insisted Paul, who had rushed up after attempting to dupe the paparazzi in Place Vendôme that the couple would shortly be leaving from the front exit. Under Fayed's terms of employment, the bodyguards had no alternative but to obey Dodi's orders or face dismissal.

At 12.10 a.m., Diana, Dodi, Rees-Jones and Henri Paul stood for nearly ten minutes at the hotel's rear exit in the full gaze of Patrick Rocha, a twenty-year-old guard, waiting for a telephone call announcing that the hired Mercedes driven by Frédéric Lucard of Etoile Limousines had arrived outside. As Paul emerged in the Rue Cambon, Lucard heard him warn a group of waiting paparazzi, 'Don't bother following – you won't catch us.' Paul was right. At 12.25 a.m. on 31 August he drove off at high speed, as dictated by Dodi's plan.

*

ABOUT ONE HOUR LATER, Fayed was roused from his sleep to be told about the crash in Place de l'Alma tunnel. The announcement of his son's death, the worst news that any parent can hear, was a crushing blow. After the extraordinary excitement of the previous six weeks, witnessing the development of a relationship based upon undoubted love, fate was doubly cruel.

In the first streaks of dawn, Fayed crossed the Channel by helicopter to be met at Le Bourget by Philippe Dourneau and Kes Wingfield. After some confusion, he arrived at 5.30 a.m. at the Pitié-Salpetrière hospital to be greeted by Sir Michael Jay, the British ambassador, and a host of senior French officials. Despite earlier hopes, Diana had been declared dead. After receiving condolences, Fayed drove on to the mortuary near the Pont d'Austerlitz to suffer every parent's nightmare. In the grim, chemical-infested atmosphere, he witnessed the consequence of irresponsibility. Whatever his weaknesses, his son had never sought more than honestly to bestow pleasure. 'I could see that Dodi was at peace,' Fayed would say later. 'He looked like a little boy again. For a moment I thought that his soul had come back in his body and he would live again but the injuries to the back of his head were too severe.'

While the formalities were rushed to allow Dodi's body to be brought back to Britain in time for burial before sunset, as required by Muslim law, Fayed sat grief-stricken in the Ritz. Meanwhile, in Dodi's flat, Diana's possessions were collected and the mementoes of their brief relationship discovered by René Delorm and a maid: the Repossi ring in a cupboard, a silver cigar cutter bought by Diana at Asprey's inscribed 'With love from Diana', silver cufflinks which had belonged to Earl Spencer, and a silver-framed poem presented by Dodi to the princess.

By late afternoon, Dodi's coffin was on the floor of the Harrods Sikorsky helicopter *en route* to Battersea. Sitting close by was his weeping father. The monotone, high-pitched whine of the engine cast an eerie paralysis over the silent passengers. After a perfunctory autopsy in Fulham, his son's body was released for burial at 8 p.m. By then, in Paris, Madrid and New York members of the Khashoggi family were puzzled that their repeated requests for information about the funeral of their beloved Dodi had been ignored. Jets, hired for the dash to London, were cancelled as the Khashoggis realized that Fayed was taking his forty-year vendetta to a hurtful, bitter conclusion.

Exhausted and tearful, at 10 p.m. Fayed stood in the front row of the gold-domed mosque in Regent's Park. Five hundred mourners, including the Egyptian ambassador, had gathered for the funeral service. More than one dozen carried the coffin to the hearse. Accompanied by a police escort, the father met the deadline and, just before midnight, arrived at the Brookwood cemetery near Woking. Even autocrats are occasionally humbled by the irresistible laws of nature and, as Dodi's corpse was lowered into its grave, Fayed's emotions were a jumble of sorrow, remorse and anger. Unwilling to accept any responsibility for the tragedy, he had already identified the culprits and imagined the scenario. During that night, talking from his home in Oxted to Frank Klein and Michael Cole, he concluded that his son and Diana had been hounded to their deaths by ruthless paparazzi. Briefed further by Klein, Cole was well versed to speak as the world awoke on Sunday morning to the horrifying news.

As the anguish spread across Britain during those first hours, Diana's death demanded an immediate, authoritative explanation. The only English-speaking voice available to fill the void was Michael Cole's, still associated with the familiar and trusted tones of the BBC. Understandably emotional, Cole emphatically reassured the dozens of journalists who called that the crash was caused by 'a Gallic kamikaze faction' of paparazzi, 'a load of disgusting creeps', who had harassed the couple to their deaths. Since nine photographers had been arrested in the tunnel and eyewitnesses had described their callous behaviour after the tragedy, no one questioned his explanation. Nor was his description of Henri Paul, also killed in the crash, doubted. 'A sober, model employee,' said Cole, 'who, after receiving a special course by Mercedes in Stuttgart, was qualified to chauffeur the limousine. After a recent medical check to requalify for his pilot's licence, Paul was clearly fit to drive the car.' Trevor Rees-Jones, wearing a seat belt, had survived but his head injuries were described as too severe for him to recall the last moments before the Mercedes crashed into the tunnel's thirteenth pillar. The cause of the accident was, it appeared, indisputable. Throughout Sunday and in the extraordinary newspaper coverage on Monday morning, Fayed and Diana were regarded as the victims of the media's criminal irresponsibility. But, just after lunch on Monday, the first fissure in Cole's storyline spread across the world. As if in a slow-motion earthquake, the grieving father was suddenly, even awfully, perceived as a possible culprit.

Word had leaked from the paparazzi of Paul's challenge: 'Don't bother following – you won't catch us.' Cole immediately derided the notion. 'They're lying,' he assured questioners. 'There were no photographers in the Rue Cambon who saw Diana's departure.' The evidence, he added, was the hotel's videoed recording of the scene. Monday morning's newspapers across the world, partially influenced by Cole's briefings, unequivocally accused the paparazzi of causing the deaths.

An announcement on Monday afternoon sent the second fissure snaking across Cole's and Fayed's credibility. On the release of the first autopsy report by French pathologists, Henri Paul's blood was revealed to contain nearly three times more alcohol than legally permitted for drivers. He had apparently consumed the equivalent of eleven shots of whisky. Both Cole and Fayed were stunned. The announcement threatened a mortal blow to the store-owner's reputation. Regardless of his grief, Fayed roared for retaliation in his defence. Any facts undermining his credibility, Cole and Macnamara assumed, were the products of a conspiracy. The two men knew exactly what their employer needed.

Moving into overdrive, Fayed's press machine ridiculed the pathologists. Given Britain's instinctive distrust of the French, it was not difficult for Cole to dispute the pathologists' conclusions and to emphasize the paparazzi's exclusive culpability. 'They were like Red Indians surrounding a Wells Fargo coach,' he told American television in the first of dozens of satellite interviews, 'firing their flashguns.' Cole went further and claimed that paparazzi had fired flashguns through the windscreen. 'Henri Paul was dazzled by the flash, while Trevor Rees-Jones was lowering the sun-visor to protect himself from the photographers and Princess Diana was hiding her face in her arms.' No photograph like that had so far been found, but François Lévi, a convicted criminal who would later rename himself Levistre, had presented himself to the Ritz as an eyewitness of the accident. He reported seeing through his rear mirror, while driving through the tunnel, a flashlight fired from a motorcycle swerving in front of the Mercedes. Although his story was swiftly discounted as the invention of a fantasist by police investigators and by *Sunday Times* journalists, it was the birth of the first of many myths.

By Wednesday, the newspaper headlines, 'Diana's drunk driver' (the *Mirror*) and 'Di driver drunk as a pig' (the *Star*), were causing Fayed serious concern. Unable to believe that an employee would breach a cardinal rule, he dispatched Professor Peter Vanezis, a pathologist employed at Glasgow University, to Paris. Vanezis, he hoped, could disprove the French reports. Late on Thursday night, he heard from John Macnamara, accompanying Vanezis, 'good news'. Although the hired pathologist had been forbidden to inspect Paul's corpse or test any of the samples stored by the French, he had, working in the Ritz Hotel, studied the pathologists' report. To Fayed's satisfaction, Vanezis was prepared to say that the French autopsy had been 'unreliable' on the grounds that the French had failed to take a blood sample from Henri Paul's eye and that the alcohol content of the blood could have fermented and increased after the complete rupture of all Paul's organs. Neither criticism, it later transpired, was correct. But at that moment Vanezis served Fayed's precise needs as, during the forty-eight hours before Diana's funeral, the Egyptian played for stakes higher than ever previously in his lifetime.

On Thursday, Lady Sarah McCorquodale, Diana's sister, arrived at Harrods. Urged by Fayed to meet him, she had succumbed reluctantly to his entreaty, 'I have something of extreme importance to tell you.' Having refused to allow Fayed into her home, she had considered meeting in a hotel before agreeing to call at his office. Unknown to the store-owner, on the flight to Paris to recover Diana's body Prince Charles had been asked by his sister-in-law, 'What will happen to the coffin when we return to Britain?' Lifting his head and screwing up his tear-filled eyes, the future king replied, 'One thing's for sure. She's not going into London in a green carriage drawn by horses.' The dislike was already profound when Fayed welcomed McCorquodale mistakenly assuming that he would be embraced in shared grief by the Spencer family. Insensitive to the antagonism, not least because of his friendship with Raine Spencer, Sarah's disliked stepmother, he had contrived a fantasy to bond himself to the Spencer family. He would deliver the silver-framed poem given by Dodi to Diana for inclusion in the princess's coffin, and he would also deliver a message – a top-secret message – to forge a relationship. Lady Sarah would hear from himself Diana's dying words, surely the most poignant epitaph of that glorious woman. Adopting what he assumed was the appropriate, dignified pose, he told her, 'I know her last words.' In her last gasp before losing consciousness for ever, Diana had uttered a wish, he said: 'Please make sure that all my possessions get to my sister Sarah in Lincolnshire.'

'Preposterous' and 'unbelievable' was McCorquodale's

reaction after bidding Fayed politely farewell. By then, the Spencers had been briefed about the nature of Diana's injuries. Despite immediate medical assistance from Dr Frédéric Mailliez, a doctor driving through the tunnel, Diana, they had heard, may have briefly mumbled some words about the pain before passing from semi-consciousness into a permanent coma induced by internal bleeding from a severed artery. But only Fayed, uneducated, materialist and oblivious to the habits and observances of British society despite thirty-three years' residence in London, could have believed the plausibility of his invention. Insensitive to British manners, he assumed that Sarah's composure signalled acceptance of his concoction.

Bad news awaited Fayed on his return to Park Lane. Until that day, Wingfield's insistence that Henri Paul had drunk two fruit juices and the supporting testimony by Roulet, Rocha and Tendil, the Ritz employees, that Paul had not appeared to be drunk, had remained credible. But Klein now revealed that the Ritz barman had reported seeing Paul drink two pastis. Although the barman was told to tell a different story in public 'to protect the royal family', French journalists were quoting the eyewitness. Control of the news was slipping, and Fayed feared that other journalists might discover that Paul had been unlicensed by the police to drive as a chauffeur. Niels Siegel, the director of Etoile Limousines, hoping that the car's defects would remain concealed, told the police that he, rather than Frédéric Lucard, had delivered the Mercedes. That delayed Lucard's confirmation of Paul's defiant challenge to the waiting paparazzi. But, as Cole, Klein, Macnamara and Fayed understood as they ceaselessly consulted each other during Thursday night, the lengthening fissures undermined their credibility. Their solution was a radical plot for the following day.

*

ON FRIDAY, 5 SEPTEMBER, Britain was preparing for Diana's funeral the next day. The trauma across the nation, as reflected by the media, had intensified. Unprecedented and previously

unimagined displays of grief by tens of thousands were performed in front of Kensington Palace. Bouquets of flowers
were piled for one hundred yards across the lawn, and similar
shrines built up elsewhere around the capital and other towns.
Thousands were queuing for hours to sign books of condolence. More than one million mourners were expected to line
the streets of central London and half the country's population
were planning to watch the unique ceremony on television.
Literally billions across the world would watch the live coverage. In those sensitive moments, Fayed was thinking about his
own reputation. Not only were the allegations about Paul's
drunkenness gaining credibility, but there were new and correct
reports that Paul had after all not been licensed to drive the
Mercedes. Feeding off French newspapers, there was also a
flood of other sensational and unproven stories: that the car's
speedometer was stuck at 200 kph (125 mph) on a road where
the speed limit was 50 kph; that the Mercedes had been filmed
on a police video at the tunnel entrance speeding at 200 kph;
that Diana had spoken before relapsing into a coma; that
cocaine had been found in the car; and that cars and motor-
bikes, present in the tunnel during the crash, had mysteriously
disappeared. Most sensationally, foreign newspapers, especially
in the Arab world, were reporting that Diana had been pregnant and that she had been murdered by British intelligence
officers to prevent both her marriage to Dodi and the birth of
a Muslim half-brother to the future King of England. Naturally
Fayed, who had hoped for a marriage, had reason to accept
the credibility of those particular reports, especially since they
had started in London.

On the day of Diana's death, in the emotion of frenzied
reporting, no one had coolly and objectively assessed the
romance. Few journalists were personally more affected than
Richard Kay, a friend and confidant of the princess. In the
hours after the death, Kay wrote an article in the *Daily Mail*
describing his last telephone conversation with Diana in the
Ritz as she revealed her intention to withdraw from formal

public life. In Monday's newspaper, Kay had speculated, 'I cannot say for certain that they would have married but in my view it was likely.' With Kay's authority, that was an explosive suggestion and one which, based on other information, he would later retract. Yet although he added that Diana had 'feared too much would be read into the affair', he had unwittingly given credibility to the most extreme speculation prompted by an interview between Hassan Yassin, Dodi's uncle, and a journalist employed by *Asharq al-Awsat*, a Saudi newspaper based in London, about his conversation with Dodi shortly before the fatal drive.

Yassin, also staying in the Ritz, had telephoned Dodi in the Imperial Suite for a gossip. 'She's a nice girl. You should propose and get married,' Yassin told his relative exuberantly. Speaking in Arabic, Dodi replied, 'We will.' They agreed to meet for a drink later that Saturday evening in the hotel's English Bar. Hassan returned late to the hotel to discover that the couple had left. On reflection during Sunday, he assumed that Dodi had intended to propose to Diana, not least to comply with his mother's advice to 'marry into a good family'. But Yassin had certainly not been told that Dodi had already proposed to Diana, or that the two had actually discussed marriage at the end of their four-week affair.

However, on Monday, *Asharq al-Awsat* quoted Dodi as saying to Yassin, 'It's serious. We're going to get married.' Yassin had replied, 'The sooner the better.' Dodi agreed: 'You'll hear it very soon.' The newspaper, suggesting that their rendezvous at the English Bar was intended 'to toast their marriage with champagne', added a final quotation from Yassin: 'Diana was ready and wanted another baby.' In another story, Soheir Khashoggi, Dodi's aunt, was reported to have confirmed that on the Saturday night Dodi had called Adnan Khashoggi, her brother, to suggest they meet and 'celebrate' the impending announcement. The report was a fabrication.

The publication of those translated 'facts' in British newspapers on Wednesday, 3 September was juxtaposed alongside a long interview with Cindy Crawford describing Diana's and Dodi's involvement in a secret affair since November 1996 and the model's eyewitness account as the princess, a close friend, arrived for a secret meeting with Dodi at Harrods. In her defence, Crawford would claim that the interview was fabricated by Italian journalists. Yet that fable, combined with *Asharq al-Awsat*'s reports, could be used by Anis Mansour, an Egyptian journalist, to state with total conviction in *Al Ahram*, Egypt's leading newspaper, that on the queen's orders Diana 'was murdered by British intelligence to save the monarchy'. The article, written without a shred of evidence, was accepted as the Gospel truth throughout the Arab world. Mansour chose to ignore a genuine eyewitness account by Rosa Monckton published on the same Monday reminiscing about their six-day cruise and stating that Diana had never mentioned marriage.

The gathering army of conspiracy theorists also chose to overlook that the affair had only been consummated four weeks earlier. It was barely enough time for anyone, including Diana, to know about a pregnancy, especially since she had menstruated during her holiday in Greece. Instead, the conspiracy theorists preferred to recall Diana's slightly round tummy in her bathing suit in mid-July and her simultaneous revelation to British journalists, positioned on a nearby boat, to await a 'big surprise'. Whatever the 'surprise', it could not have been Dodi's baby or their marriage since Dodi had only just arrived in St Tropez and their affair had not started. Regardless of those facts, the two mid-July reports were juxtaposed into the August romance and cited as explanations for Diana's murder to prevent the birth of a Muslim child.

To the inhabitant of 60 Park Lane, the conspiracy made perfect sense, and fortunately he possessed information to support the scenario of an imminent engagement. The existence of the Repossi ring, exaggeratedly reported to have cost £130,000, had already been leaked by one of his employees. Fayed could add to the evidential list of intimacy a diamond bracelet given by Dodi on *Jonikal* and Diana's presents to Dodi

– the cigar cutter and the pair of cufflinks belonging to Earl Spencer. 'They would have got married,' Fayed told his aides. 'Now they're together in heaven.' The pictures in the Harrods window of Dodi and Diana – lovers united for ever – represented the truth he wanted the world to accept, not least in order to suppress the suggestion of Henri Paul's drunkenness. Unwilling to accept responsibility, he would bully the nation into accepting his version. His messenger was Michael Cole.

Cole had agreed to summon a press conference on Friday to rebut the distasteful allegations and raise the curtain on the scenario now gathering credence across the Arab world. Given his experience, Cole might have objected that Fayed's strategy was insensitive to the nation's mood. But this was the Egyptian's fiefdom, after all, one managed by fear, finger-pointing, screaming and dismissals, and the press spokesman was mindful of the sign in Fayed's office, 'The boss is not always right, but he is the boss.' Unquestioningly, Cole agreed to stake his own reputation in Fayed's cause. Since he had already denounced the true statement that Paul was not authorized by the Paris Préfecture to chauffeur the Mercedes as 'entirely false', he hoped that his authority would undermine other unpleasantries.

At 3 p.m., in front of about twenty television cameras and sixty journalists, Cole, clearly under pressure, launched Fayed's counter-attack. 'There must be no rush to judgement,' he said in his introduction to a series of surprises, forgetting that throughout that week he had damned the paparazzi as 'murderers'. His first surprise was a twenty-six-minute video recorded by the hotel's CCTV system on the fateful night. The jerky images of Henri Paul would confirm, Cole and Fayed hoped, his appearance of sobriety. Guided by a live commentary spoken by Paul Handley-Greaves, the security officer who had lied to David Hooper, *Vanity Fair*'s solicitor, the video was said to have been edited down from two hours in the interests of the journalists. However, since the video failed to show Paul's exits from the hotel to talk to the paparazzi and since Cole had denied the acting security manager's departing taunt to the paparazzi, the tape did little to reassure the critics.

Cole's second surprise was Professor Vanezis. Looking rushed and uncomfortable, the pathologist suggested that the blood samples and the French tests were 'unreliable'. But, rather than submit himself to detailed questions, Fayed's star witness rose and departed for Heathrow. Cynics suspected that Vanezis had already assumed that new tests would confirm the original conclusions, but at that moment his expressions of doubt had served the Egyptian's interests.

Michael Cole's third surprise was pitched to influence the public's perception of Fayed. Fervently accepting the store-owner's version of events in Paris, Cole opened up dangerous territory in a bid to strengthen the image of his employer's close relationship to Diana. After listing the exchange of presents as evidence of Dodi's and the princess's 'friendship', Cole added authoritatively, 'You will know that they never spoke publicly about their life together.' As an introduction to stories about Fayed's visit to the Pitié-Salpetrière hospital, the grief-stricken father was cited as the first Briton to arrive at the hospital, although he arrived three hours after Sir Michael Jay. He was also said to have viewed Diana's corpse. 'She looked peaceful and serene in death,' Fayed had apparently said of a scene which he had never witnessed. The third aspect of the hospital visit related by Cole publicized Fayed's fantasy of Diana's last words: 'While he was in Paris on Sunday, Mr Al Fayed was approached by someone whom I may not name but who helped the princess during her final hours. That person vouchsafed to Mr Al Fayed the princess's final words and requests. Yesterday those words were conveyed to the appropriate person.' Fayed hoped that these claims, combined with the revelation that he had received a letter of condolence from the queen delivered by a messenger from Balmoral, would persuade the public that, despite the crash, he had been embraced by the royal family. Preoccupied by other matters over that weekend, his critics remained silent, encouraging his belief that all of his stories had been accepted.

That night, Fayed kept a vigil and said prayers at Dodi's grave. Skilfully, Bill Mitchell had transformed the small mud plot into a beautiful garden surrounding a three-foot grey headstone inscribed simply 'Dodi'. Mourners personally expressed their sympathy to Fayed, who earlier, walking outside Harrods, had melodramatically traced with his fingers the path of tears down his cheeks. But the image of grief concealed his unceasing attempts to influence the media. The thousands of letters of condolence had encouraged his subordinates to contact the *Sunday Times* with an authoritative leak incriminating the paparazzi who had been formally charged with manslaughter and failing to help the injured. The journalists were told that, as the couple lay in the wrecked Mercedes, a sapphire and diamond necklace had been ripped from Diana and that cash had been taken from Dodi's pocket. Although the story was denied by the French police and was certainly untrue, the fantasy would be published by the newspaper. Only six days after Dodi's death, Fayed was restlessly, and with some success, manipulating the media to divert attention from any accusation pointing to his own responsibility.

*

ON SATURDAY, 6 SEPTEMBER, most of Britain, gripped by trembles of emotion, came to a halt. Fayed's forlorn arrival at Westminster Abbey provoked sympathy. Clutching his ticket for seat B8 beside Raine Spencer and some distance from the royal family, his face crumpled by pain, he appeared as a distraught father rather than a man obsessed with conspiracy theories. Greeted inside the Abbey by a galaxy of celebrities, he was comforted by their acknowledgement and more importantly by the address. In his 'Blood on their hands' speech, Earl Spencer echoed his own condemnation of the media, even though the pulpiteer had once accepted a retainer by American television to pontificate about his sister and would soon be exposed as a cruel husband and serial adulterer. Fayed had every reason to ignore the messenger's hypocrisy after Spencer told the world, 'There is no doubt that she was looking for a new direction in life at this time. She talked endlessly about getting away from England.' Precisely. Here was the proof of the imminent announcement of marriage thwarted by murder. All that was required, Fayed reasoned, was for Judge Hervé Stéphan, the examining magistrate in Paris, to accept the 'truth'.

Unfortunately, during the second week of Stéphan's investigation, the conclusive evidence of Paul's fast driving and the results of the third blood test complicated Fayed's endeavours. The tests released on 8 September also revealed Paul's dependence on drugs, which had been dangerously mixed with alcohol. To the Egyptian's fury, Bernard Darteville and Georges Kiejman, his lawyers in Paris, and Professor Vanezis accepted that their previous doubts had become invalid. Cole had no alternative but to admit the driver's sin and his own growing desperation: 'If any person is culpable I will personally spit on their grave.' Fayed, he added, was similarly 'outraged, shocked and appalled' that Paul 'would drink and drive and take this cocktail of drugs'.

Had normality prevailed, Fayed would have accepted the consequences of his own admission and retreated, albeit reluctantly, into dignified silence. But, as the object of worldwide interest and sympathy, any sense of reason had been lost. Unwilling to remain in the shadows lest it suggest his culpability, he chose three days later to appear at a football match at Fulham rather than attend a memorial service for Dodi. As a gesture, some would regard his choice as unusual. Others would judge the father's priorities as tasteless, but the theatre at the stadium imbued Fayed with self-importance and the certainty of popular support for his opinions. As he walked across the pitch, a solitary figure marching to the lament of a Scottish piper towards his executive box, the crowd stood in silence. Later, after Cole explained over the tannoy that Fayed had chosen Craven Cottage instead of his son's memorial service, the crowd rose again and clapped. As melodrama, the performance of the self-styled people's champion was perfect. Few understood that Fayed's fertile imagination was fired by those scenes of popular support.

Over the previous decade, Fayed had created a publicity and security machine which no other store-keeper would even contemplate. Well funded, efficient and dedicated to the pursuit of an unusual agenda, his agents had wreaked havoc on Harrods employees, his business enemies and Conservative politicians. In autumn 1997, isolated in his homes and offices, Fayed controlled an exceptional network able to respond to the reports from across the Arab world and on the worldwide Internet ridiculing the clear-cut conclusion that there had been an accident caused by a recklessly fast, drunken driver as a deliberate cover-up. As the imagined victim of several conspiracies orchestrated in Westminster and Whitehall, Fayed reasoned, he was once again the target of sinister, secret agencies. A visit to him by Mrs Mubarak, the wife of the Egyptian president, reinforced the paranoid belief he so often voiced to Macnamara and others that he had been targeted by MI5, the domestic intelligence service. Galvanized by his heroic status in Egypt, by his obsession with security and by his own predilection for shaping events to suit his own interpretation, he ordered Macnamara to follow up anything which might cloud his personal responsibility. During September, one particular report seemed to promise much.

French investigators had announced their search for a white Fiat Uno which had possibly been involved in the crash. The evidence was white paint scratches on the Mercedes and the discovery in the tunnel of broken plastic from a Fiat's left indicator panel intermingled with the Mercedes' wreckage. Two eyewitnesses had claimed to have swerved hard to avoid a white Fiat, giving off plumes of smoke as it zigzagged out of the tunnel after the crash. Since Trevor Rees-Jones, in his first police interview, would recall a three-door white car following the Mercedes from the Ritz, the French investigators revised their earlier '98 per cent certainty' that no other car was involved. But, since other eyewitnesses uttered contradictory versions, the police were unsure whether the Mercedes had hit the Fiat and spun out of control, or whether the Fiat had deliberately crashed into the Mercedes. Immediately certain of the truth, Fayed dispatched Macnamara and Pierre Ottavioli, a retired director of the elite Criminal Brigade whom he had retained as a private investigator, to prove a Fiat's involvement in the conspiracy directed by British intelligence officers.

Simultaneously, information was fed to the media to enhance the image of Dodi, the princess's putative husband-to-be. Few newspaper articles were more important than Barbara Broccoli's in *The Times*. Describing her friend Dodi as a 'brilliant sportsman' who 'hated fast cars' (something of a delusion since Dodi was unfit and possessed four of the world's fastest sports cars), Broccoli denounced those who 'label him as a playboy' as 'completely inaccurate' since Dodi was 'deeply involved in his father's empire'. Once sown in the public conscience, the hyperbolic profile would be repeated in later newspaper articles as Fayed developed the authenticity of the romance. Besides Hassan Yassin's 'eyewitness' account, he was helped by a quotation in *Time* magazine from Albert Repossi, the supplier of the ring. 'He told me', Repossi had allegedly said, 'how much he was in love with the princess. He wanted to spend the rest of his life with her.' Repossi had never met Dodi in Monte Carlo and met him for a only fleeting moment in his busy shop in Paris. The 'quotation' was unreliable, yet helpful for Fayed to substantiate his reply to the letters of condolence. 'I take some comfort', he wrote, 'from my absolute belief that God has taken their souls to live together in Paradise . . . If this planet lasts for another thousand years, people will still be talking about the terrible event we are living through. But what they will remember most is the love that existed between two wonderful people.'

The irritation caused to some by the letter's presumption might have been ignored if Fayed's statements, especially about his visit to the Pitié-Salpetrière hospital, had by mid-September not become the subject of unprecedented scrutiny and doubt. To the Egyptian's anger, his assertion that he had heard Diana's last words from a nurse had been denied by the hospital's management. The nurse – her name, 'Michelle Bollet', was disclosed by a Fayed spokesman – 'did not exist', insisted the hospital's manager, adding that there were no last words because Diana arrived unconscious on the verge of a heart attack.

Accusations that Fayed was a liar were not new. Nor was his response. Under pressure, he simply exaggerated his previous fabrication and hugged, ever closer, his conspiracy theories. But, as Cole perceived three weeks after the crash, his employer had reached a new, defining moment. The outright contradictions, Cole fretted, were reawakening antagonism, not least from those whom Fayed had hitherto counted as friends. In particular, the Egyptian and his press spokesman were upset that Dominic Lawson, the editor of the *Sunday Telegraph*, who had been entertained to private lunches at Harrods, had joined the critics – no doubt, they agreed, under the influence of Rosa Monckton, his wife. Sensitive to the tide, Cole negotiated the publication of a long letter in the *Sunday Telegraph* to rebut the critics and publish Fayed's truth. By any measure, Cole's reaction was reckless. 'Mohamed', he wrote, 'has never said a word about the private life of his son and Diana.' That was untrue because he had suggested that they were to be married. Secondly, Cole denied that the edited Ritz security video had been released to prove that Paul had been sober; rather, he wrote, it had been to allow the public to judge whether Paul *appeared* sober or drunk. Since it had been shown to substantiate Vanezis's assertion that the French pathology tests were 'unreliable', Cole was stretching credulity.

His credibility was further damaged concerning Diana's alleged 'final words'. 'History will show', Cole wrote, 'that I was right to let it be known that the Princess had a final request and that it was conveyed appropriately.' The evidence proved the contrary. Subsequently Cole wrote that Fayed had 'no reason to invent' the last words and denied that Fayed had 'personally made any public statement regarding the issue'. Six weeks after the crash, Cole's reputation was in shreds.

Unconcerned by Cole's personal plight, Fayed interpreted the gathering disbelief as certain proof of the conspiracy. Why else, he reasoned, would the establishment attack? At the empty offices of de Castro, one of his original shipbroking businesses in Alexandria, he ordered that a photo-montage of Diana and Dodi, dressed for their wedding, should fill the window. The slogan was unsubtle: 'Who murdered Diana and Dodi?' In London, he was pleased that the *Sunday Mirror* featured an interview with him in which he declared, 'I won't rest till I know if Diana and my Dodi were murdered.' The latest outburst was not the impulsive cry of a bewildered father. Fayed was using the tragedy and the suggestion of a murder conspiracy to divert the media's attention from a succession of revelations threatening his image as a genuine, grieving mourner. A new danger was posed by an unexpected concordat among those whom he had sought to destroy – Neil Hamilton, Bob Loftus and Tiny Rowland – capitalizing on a growing revulsion among some Britons towards Fayed and his antics. Simplistic and crude, Fayed had never anticipated retaliation by his victims.

*

'WHY HAMILTON RUN from the court if he's innocent?' Fayed had chortled months earlier after the *Guardian*'s victory against the MP. 'You go to court to clear your name. Hamilton ran away.' But to his astonishment, on 14 October 1997, Hamilton reappeared with a vengeance. At the end of his unsuccessful plea of innocence to a committee of MPs, the former junior minister melodramatically revealed that Fayed had broken into Rowland's safe-deposit box at Harrods. His source was Rowland and his latest informant, Bob Loftus. Fayed was shocked, not only by his exposure but by the alliance of former enemies: Rowland, Loftus and Hamilton. Although Cole denied the break-in, denouncing Loftus as 'a disgruntled former employee' who had made 'a number of false allegations', Fayed's credibility was damaged. Two weeks later, glorying in revenge, Hamilton returned to the Commons and played a tape, also procured from Loftus, of Fayed's telephone conversation in October 1994 with Rowland in which the Egyptian repeatedly mentioned the size of his genitals.

Fayed recognized that thanks to the unholy alliance his predicament could only worsen, and it did. With Rowland's encouragement, Loftus had allowed the *Observer* to listen to other tapes of Harrods executives' private conversations. Although the revelations of Fayed's bugging evoked hypocritical comments – 'I had no idea I was being bugged,' said Stephen Taylor, the former personnel officer. 'It is completely disgusting and distasteful. I would never have condoned such a thing' – Fayed's culpability and vulgarity was for the first time revealed to the public as an indisputable fact. 'There is no truth in these allegations,' piped Cole, as a major crack appeared in Fayed's image. 'I know nothing at all about these so-called tapes.' By then, Cole and Fayed had acknowledged that Loftus's 300 tapes, smuggled from Harrods during his employment, were undermining their case against *Vanity Fair*.

Although the defamation trial was due to be heard in one year, the continued accumulation of evidence after the collapse of the settlement negotiations was embarrassing Fayed. On 3 November 1997, his defence against the magazine's charge of racism collapsed after Ian Lamb, the chairman of an industrial tribunal, condemned Harrods' defence in a discrimination case as 'malicious and dishonest'. The complainant, Gillian Elmi, had been rejected for employment as a florist because she was black. 'There was an act of blatant racial discrimination', declared Lamb, 'by a very senior personnel officer working in a very large organization . . . There was lying and deceit on the part of Harrods personnel to conceal the act of discrimination. There was dishonest testimony by Harrods personnel.' Combining that condemnation with Loftus's tapes and several new affidavits by girls alleging harassment, Fayed's lawyers persuasively argued that his complaint against *Vanity Fair* was crumbling. If he pursued his case, he would be threatened by catastrophe.

Three weeks later in New York, he bid for a truce. Fortunately, Fayed's American lawyer secured the attention and sympathy of S. I. Newhouse, *Vanity Fair*'s proprietor, and agreed a blame-free settlement. Although the magazine was not required to apologize or retract its allegations, and both sides would bear their own costs, Fayed thought he had permanently buried the incriminating evidence. Superficially, it seemed that neither side could claim victory. Fayed hoped that his public explanation, that he was too grief-stricken to continue and that he had been touched by the message of condolence from S. I. Newhouse, would divert attention from the truth. The opposite occurred. Released from the threat of litigation, several newspapers immediately published long accounts of his bugging, racism and sexual harassment of employees. Fayed's reputation had passed a watershed. His efforts since the publication of the DTI report to salvage his reputation were at last dissolving. Incensed by his enemies' retaliation, he sat slumped in his chair. One enemy in particular, travelling between the *Hanse* and his home in Chester Square, did not disguise the delight he took in the new vulnerability.

Aged eighty and impatient with Scotland Yard's ponderous investigation of the break-in to his deposit box, Rowland was famous for his quip that he never bore a grudge privately but shared it with as many people as possible. Capitalizing on the wave of unfavourable publicity about Fayed, he leaked to journalists that on 27 November he had issued writs against Fayed, Macnamara, Handley-Greaves and Mark Griffiths alleging a conspiracy to break into his safe-deposit box and steal emeralds, rubies, a gold cigarette case and documents relating to 'my activities on behalf of the British government in India at the time of partition in 1947 and also in Africa'. Although a Fayed spokesman condemned the writ as 'false and malicious', everyone knew that Bob Loftus, an ally of Rowland, was an eyewitness to the break-in. A decade of effort to win sympathy, Cole could see, was evaporating as the scale of deception was grasped. Loftus, Fayed snarled, was proving to be a dangerous missile whose unnecessary dismissal was causing mayhem, not least in his assistance to the producers of *The Big Story*, a television programme billed to be transmitted on 18 December featuring victims of Fayed's sexual harassment. In adversity, Fayed's manner was never to surrender but to attack viciously, screaming total denial, and to invent a ruse to deflect attention.

By extraordinary coincidence, *Paris Match*, the French magazine, obtained the material for an article advertised as 'Diana's last interview', to be published on the same day as the television programme's transmission. Although Cole had correctly said at his press conference on 5 September, 'You will know that they never spoke publicly about their life together,' the magazine reported Diana's words about her affection for Dodi, their marriage and her children. The publication, providing no details about the interviewer's identity or proof of the interview's authenticity, served Fayed's purpose superbly. On the morning of the television programme, London's newspapers were dominated by the 'interview'. Their disbelief was irrelevant, since throughout the rest of the world the article's authenticity was undisputed. To Fayed's satisfaction, the programme passed relatively unnoticed, and he did not anticipate any repercussions, least of all in relation to his application for British nationality. The likelihood of success there, he believed, had been strengthened by the crash.

Before the May election, David Puttnam had organized a personal introduction to Peter Mandelson, the Labour Party's spin-doctor. Fayed had hoped that Mandelson would show Labour's gratitude for his exposé of 'cash for questions'.

Although he had subsequently ruined his relationship with the new Minister without Portfolio by publicly deriding him, Fayed appeared to have won favour when, on 22 December 1997, the Home Office abandoned its appeal to the House of Lords against the Court of Appeal's decision that a government should give its reasons for denying nationality to an applicant. The Labour government, Fayed rightly concluded, was tilting in his favour. 'Having lived here for more than thirty years,' he said magnanimously, 'and done my best to play a positive part in the life of this country, I should like to share the nationality of my four British children.' Soon after Christmas, his illusion of immunity from the establishment's censure was disturbed.

An unexpected letter from Michael Bullen, the chairman of the Windsor Horse Show, informed Fayed that his sponsorship was no longer desired. Fayed was flabbergasted. How could the loyalty he had paid for be summarily withdrawn? A 'hot button' sparked the absolute monarch's rage against ingratitude.

Telephone calls by Michael Cole established some unpleasant facts. The show organizers had long been dissatisfied by Fayed's refusal to commit himself to more than a one-year contract, and in the previous six years John Major had been urging Bullen, after a visit to Balmoral, to find a new sponsor to save the queen and Prince Phillip from association with Fayed. Since no alternative sponsor could be found, the royal family had been compelled to continue suffering the disagreeable association. But after Fayed's failure to disprove the allegations published in *Vanity Fair* and his crude jokes with Rowland about his genitals, the queen frowned upon encountering him again. Her decision was finalized by his behaviour after the crash. Asprey's was persuaded to provide a four-year contract, a guarantee which Fayed had never offered. Although Fayed's three-page protest to Bullen, written by Cole, emphasized how much the Horse Show meant to a man who had personally assured the queen at a reception that he would sponsor the event for ever, he was denied the true explanation.

To Fayed, the snub was final proof of a conspiracy against him. Craving attention, he effortlessly convinced himself that the royal family, particularly Prince Phillip and Prince Charles, and the Spencers had deliberately ignored his grief since the funeral. The reason, he fantasized, was the imminence of the marriage and Diana's pregnancy. He was, he told callers, another victim of a Palace-inspired murder plot to prevent the future king suffering 'a half-brother who is a nigger'. By constantly repeating his opinion, it became the Gospel.

*

RETALIATION BY REPEATING his propaganda was his considered response. His vehicle was the public fascination for Diana, whose name guaranteed newspaper sales and attracted huge television audiences. Singlehandedly, the Knightsbridge retailer planned to monopolize the tragedy by offering exclusive merchandise: namely, his own participation. An Egyptian, desperate for British nationality, would use the uncritical foreign press to wage war against Britain. If skilfully packaged, Fayed knew, whatever a foreign journalist wrote would be republished in Britain, provided the ingredients he supplied appeared to be new and sensational. Poignantly, few in Britain yet perceived how much Fayed was exploiting the brief romance, and even fewer anticipated the consequences.

In the second week of February 1998, deflecting attention from the spurious claims of Diane Holliday, a thirty-six-year-old blonde, that she was not only the mother of Dodi's child but had been involved in a bizarre entrapment of Rowland, Fayed's latest media blitz was poised to hurt his British critics. His tool was *Death of a Princess*, a book written with his help by two American journalists employed by *Time* magazine. Understandably, as foreigners neither Thomas Sancton nor Scott MacLeod was aware of the reasons for the antagonism towards Fayed in Britain when they approached Michael Cole for assistance. Astutely, Cole judged that, by coddling the journalists with friendly 'exclusive' access to himself and Fayed, they would repay his favours. Since the authors were barred by French law from speaking to eyewitnesses among the Ritz personnel, they would also rely upon Frank Klein, Fayed's most loyal employee (and not an eyewitness since he was absent in the South of France on the fateful night), about the crucial events inside the hotel.

The result, to Fayed's glee, was the authors' acceptance or uncritical repetition of most of his opinions, distortions and conspiracy theories without casting any doubts on his motives. The book's publication, on the eve of Sotheby's auction in New York of the contents of the Windsor villa, guaranteed Fayed a huge audience in America for Sancton and MacLeod's confirmation: 'That they intended to marry now seems beyond question.' Among the evidence which had persuaded the authors of the impending marriage was Diana's and Dodi's visit to the Villa Windsor. The 'evidence' had been carefully presented by Cole and Fayed.

Three days after the crash, Kes Wingfield had estimated that Diana and Dodi had remained at the villa for 'no longer than ten minutes'. During September, Cole described a stay of precisely thirty-three minutes. But, in early winter 1997, Fayed and Cole spoke to Sancton about a visit lasting two hours. Just as the book was about to be printed, Cole telephoned Sancton and introduced the existence of an anonymous Italian designer who had accompanied Diana around the villa on 30 August as she inspected every room and cupboard from the basement to the cellar. Grateful, Sancton included that detail in his book.

Just before the book's publication in the first week of February 1998, to reinforce the impression of the inevitable marriage Cole gave the same tip about the Italian designer to Robert Lacey, who was writing an article for the *Sunday Times* about the Sotheby's sale. The result gratified Fayed. Under the headline, 'Diana planned future in Windsors' villa', Lacey reported that, during their two hours with the still unnamed Italian designer, Diana and Dodi 'discussed everything from the future colour of the walls to the effectiveness of the boiler'.

Lacey came to the conclusion that their tour of the villa with the Italian confirmed that the Repossi ring was an 'engagement rather than a friendship ring'. That was precisely the conclusion published by Sancton. Three months later, the American would admit that his unquestioning inclusion of the still undiscovered Italian designer 'troubles me'. The designer, it seemed, was a myth. But by then Fayed had used Diana's visit to the villa to endorse a conversation with Dodi. Even before leaving the *Jonikal*, Fayed told Sancton, he had given permission for Diana and Dodi to move into Villa Windsor after their wedding. 'Don't rush into anything,' Fayed had allegedly cautioned Dodi. Dodi had supposedly replied that both were 'sure'. Fiction had become fact.

Consistency in detail was not one of Fayed's virtues but, to his glee, the *Time* book referred to the speculation about Diana's pregnancy, to Fayed's visit to Diana's corpse in the hospital – 'I saw her and I prayed. She looked beautiful, powerful and serene' – and to his receipt of Diana's last words. In his second, revised version of the dying gasp, Fayed described his introduction to 'a medical worker who had treated Diana in the tunnel'. On this occasion Diana allegedly said, 'Tell my sister Sarah to look after my children.' Fortunately for Fayed, Sancton had failed to establish from the hospital authorities that the Egyptian had not seen Diana's body and that the emergency team had left the hospital by the time he had arrived. Similarly, he was fortunate that Rosa Monckton revealed Diana's menstruation during their Greek holiday only after the book's publication.

Those flaws did not detract from the sensational publicity, helped by daily serialization in *The Times*. To help promote the book, Cole and Fayed starred on several American television programmes, in which, to confirm the romance, the store-keeper showed millions of viewers Earl Spencer's cufflinks given by Diana to Dodi. The massive public response and the controversy delighted Fayed. As a fame-junkie, nothing gave him a greater thrill than to occupy the centre of public attention. Nevertheless, when on Tuesday, 10 February he took a telephone call from Piers Morgan, the editor of the *Mirror*, his dissatisfaction was patent.

To preserve Fayed's credibility, Sancton had sanitized and moderated some of the Egyptian's more extreme opinions. The censorship, hardly reflected in *The Times* serialization, irritated Fayed. The Americans, he cursed, had failed to blazon his certainty of a murder plot. Accordingly, he welcomed Morgan's suggestion that the *Mirror* should publish his real story in his own words. With Cole absent in America, Fayed immediately poured his raw fantasies, anger and hatred on to Morgan's tape recorder, excited that he would be featuring simultaneously in two national newspapers. 'There was a conspiracy,' he told Morgan, 'and I will not rest until I have established what happened. I will find the person who caused this accident. I believe there were people who did not want Dodi and Diana to be together. I believe in my heart 99.9 per cent that it was not an accident.'

Naturally, Morgan wanted to hear for himself Diana's last words. Aware that the manager of the Pitié-Salpetrière had the previous day denied that the emergency crew from the tunnel were still in the hospital when Fayed arrived, the Egyptian sourced his third version again to a nurse, this time present in the operating theatre. To avoid the embarrassment of citing a non-existent woman, the third source had 'covered her name badge'. Diana's last words, Fayed excitedly told Morgan, combining his previous two versions, were: 'I would like all my possessions in Dodi's apartment to be given to my sister Sarah, including my jewellery and my personal clothes, and please tell her to take care of my boys.' Mindful of another denial from the Pitié-Salpetrière, he did not pause to reflect before altering one key claim just published by Sancton. 'It was too shocking', he told Piers Morgan, 'for me to go and see her body'. Within the same week, two newspapers had published contradictory versions.

Fayed's serious purpose, as his long conversation with

Morgan continued, was to establish a version of the 'truth' that acquitted him of any blame for the crash. Since Wingfield, the bodyguard, had quoted Henri Paul relaying Fayed's approval of the escape plan, the store-keeper sought to change the impression. 'I told Dodi,' he continued, ' "Now don't do any tricks when you leave the hotel. Be normal, be nice to the photographers and be nice to everybody. Go out of the front door and say hello." ' Morgan was less concerned about the truth than merely reporting Fayed's words. Hence, he did not query the Egyptian's untrue assertion that, since Dodi had been 'alive for five or ten minutes' after the crash, and Diana had been alive for much longer, 'both of them could have been alive today'. Fayed's criticism of the doctors would sell more newspapers.

The *Mirror*'s headline on Thursday, 12 February, 'It was no accident', and the subtitle, 'He says someone killed Diana and Dodi', increased the newspaper's circulation by half a million. The vast majority of readers believed Fayed's recollection that Diana and Dodi were engaged to be married: 'Diana had said yes to Dodi . . . Dodi rang me personally to tell me they were engaged.' To reinforce his version, Fayed added that Diana had told her sons about the marriage and the boys had told Prince Charles. With the promise of 'more astonishing revelations' the following day, Morgan and Fayed shared a mutual interest in escalating the sensation. Among the casualties was Michael Cole.

Returning from America on Thursday morning, Cole did not conceal his unhappiness. The interview with Morgan had occurred without his knowledge. It was not the first time that he had complained of Fayed's hazardous lust for publicity. Ever since the *Vanity Fair* settlement, his employer's campaign had caused him unease and even ill-health. Vulnerable to the pressure and the criticism, he had for some months considered resigning. After reading Friday's *Mirror*, he offered his immediate resignation. 'Betrayed' screamed the headline that day, reporting Fayed's crude venom against the royal family and the Spencers, who 'shunned me in my grief'. Fayed had crossed the Rubicon, and Cole, the master of many subtleties over the previous ten years, declared himself unable to face the universal condemnation from the Palace, Downing Street and across the country.

Fayed was not particularly saddened by Cole's departure. Increasingly drawn once more to Brian Basham, he recalled how his original spokesman had told Cole to his face, 'You're a prat and sometimes a dangerous prat.' No longer would Fayed tolerate restraint. The coverage that week proved his mastery of public relations. Not only had *The Times* and the *Mirror* uncritically paraded his opinions, but the *Sunday Times* had agreed to report Macnamara's 'discovery' of a Fiat Uno belonging to a French photographer. The French investigators would be condemned by the newspaper for failing to find the car involved in the accident. The real truth, that the car had been discovered long before by the French police and discounted as unsuspicious, was unreported.

*

DESPITE THE CONTRADICTIONS and distortions, Fayed was for many, especially *Mirror* readers, a suffering hero. Others took a contrary view. Although Harrods was judged to be the third most popular tourist attraction, after St Paul's and Big Ben, some Britons appeared to be silently boycotting the store. Long-standing accounts were being cancelled. In 1997, despite a boom in high-street spending, Harrods Holdings had suffered a 36 per cent collapse in profits to £37.6 million on £625.7 million turnover. The brothers had paid themselves a £20 million dividend, half the previous year's. Although the fashion houses and other concessions in Harrods were paying annually up to £250,000 and 27 per cent of their profits for the location, the store's glamour could not mitigate the negative publicity about its owner, who, it was suspected, was burdened by increasing personal debts, aggravated in 1998 by *Punch*'s losses of £4.65 million, by then an invisible publication. In 1998, Harrods' accounts had deteriorated. The brothers' dividend had fallen to £14 million and the net profits were set to decline, reflecting the turbulence in Britain's economy. Critics, who previously would have remained silent, emerged to denigrate Fayed as 'ageist, racist and sexist'. 'At Harrods,' alleged John Monks, the general secretary of the Trades Union Congress, 'there is a regime of fear and terror.' As Fayed planned to celebrate Harrods' 150th birthday in 1999, his dwindling band of allies – including Andrew Neil, Stewart Steven and Brian Basham – urged that he adopt a posture of dignified silence. All deluded themselves that because they had accepted Fayed's money, they commanded his respect. But Fayed was not listening to anyone. Under pressure, his self-control was deteriorating. Enemies, he deemed, were everywhere. Worst of all, Rowland had resurrected his campaign and successfully pushed Scotland Yard into action.

For Fayed, 2 March 1998 promised humiliation. Under irresistible pressure, he agreed to present himself to Detective Chief Superintendent Jeff Rees at Kennington police station for questioning about the alleged theft from Rowland's safe-deposit box. Fayed no longer denied knowing that the box had been broken open, but he denied any prior knowledge or involvement. In turn, Mark Griffiths, Paul Handley-Greaves and John Macnamara, the former Scotland Yard officer, also offered themselves for questioning. All denied any knowledge of the alleged theft of Rowland's jewels. To deflect the embarrassment that day, Fayed adopted a tested tactic. Trevor Rees-Jones had been persuaded to meet Piers Morgan of the *Mirror* – although the former bodyguard would subsequently deny knowing that he was giving his first newspaper interview. Although in December Rees-Jones had told Hervé Stéphan, the investigating magistrate 'My mind is a total blank,' Fayed's doctors had been 'working on Trevor's memory . . . assisting him in every way to help him to remember'. The resulting *Mirror* front-page headline – 'I heard Diana call out for Dodi after the crash' – was guaranteed to dominate the morning's agenda. Rees-Jones's recollection that Diana was crying 'Where is Dodi? Where is Dodi?' would, Fayed hoped, elicit sympathy for himself when the news of his surrender to the police for questioning and arrest emerged.

Mirror readers certainly remained sympathetic to his cause. Others, members of what Fayed condemned as the British establishment, were unconvinced by his desire to 'bring this matter to a speedy conclusion'. Fayed was scornful of those convinced of his guilt. Unshamed by all the revelations, he had by summer 1998 ceased trying to win friends. Scornful of rejection and of those urging his silence, he wilfully converted sympathizers into ardent critics. Fighting once again for his old mantra, 'my dignity and my honour', he had renewed his declaration of war. Previously, he had fought against Rowland and the Conservative government. His latest battle was against every critic. Naturally, his tool was the media, and in particular a friendly television producer who had secured a slot on ITV to promote his latest conspiracy theories based upon deception.

Over the previous ten months, Fayed had initially denied that Henri Paul had been drunk, and then he had affected to believe that François Levistre's fantasy of a laser beam fired from a pursuing motorcycle and a Fiat Uno were the instruments of the British conspirators in causing the crash to prevent the marriage. In May 1998 he picked up the bland statement by French pathologists that Paul's blood contained 20 per cent of carbon monoxide. Although the pathologists had mentioned the gas's existence without comment because it is commonly present in car-crash fatalities (the Mercedes engine had briefly continued running after the crash, pumping carbon monoxide directly into the wreck which Paul inhaled in his last gasps), Fayed persuaded the ITV producer that government agents, having masterminded the crash using a laser beam, might have entered the laboratories and substituted the phials of Paul's blood with those contaminated not only by carbon monoxide but also by alcohol. By any reckoning, combined with the deceptive 'visit' to Villa Windsor, it was an extraordinary proposition, but ITV's record twelve million viewers and the network's self-congratulation were the final proof of Fayed's media victory. He had hijacked not only several newspapers and a major television network, but history itself. A majority of Britons certainly accepted his conclusions.

Buoyed by that support, Fayed arrived at the Palais de Justice in Paris on 5 June to witness the testimony of nine photographers and ten eyewitnesses of the accident under the chairmanship of Hervé Stéphan. Three months earlier, the magistrate had extracted from the Egyptian a signed statement that he 'trusts the crash inquiry'. Since then, Fayed had re-affirmed his 'great confidence in the investigators'. Having precluded himself from criticizing Stéphan, he discovered by the end of the uninformative hearing a new target, Frances Shand Kydd, Diana's mother. Her crime was to have ignored him, the author of fantasies and embarrassments, throughout the six-hour hearing. The snub was intolerable. After all, as he had told ITV's viewers two days earlier, Diana had actually confided to him from the Imperial Suite in the Ritz that she planned to marry Dodi. How could he be ignored by the mother of the woman who so nearly became his daughter-in-law? Sick of vilification, his sense of victimization surged. Storming out of the building, he summoned journalists to hear him savage the woman. 'She thinks she's the Queen of Sheba,' he raged, standing on the pavement. 'I don't give a damn about her. People like her are on another planet. She's a snob. If she thinks she belongs to the royal family and doesn't want to talk to ordinary people like me that's up to her. I'm just a working-class guy.' Thirteen years after proclaiming himself to the DTI inspectors as the son of a pasha, Fayed now presented himself as working class. To some it beggared belief. By Fayed, a master of inconsistencies, it went unnoticed. His millions and his minions had secured his isolation from criticism.

In hindsight, Fayed's pavement tirade would be seen as another milestone on his road towards personal catastrophe. Like an automaton, he could no longer control either his emotions or his behaviour. Possessed by a demon and driven by animal-like passion, his petulance was a symptom of his bitterness against Britain's refusal to accept his lies as the truth.

But since his dream of becoming the father-in-law of Princess Diana had vanished in the crash, the tycoon's ambition of winning acceptance had been shattered by his own crass stupidity, negligence and arrogance. For those educated entirely on James Bond and other thriller movies, conspiracies are an easy explanation for their troubles. For a man who constantly talks about loyalty and dignity, facing the finger of blame was intolerable. And being ignored by Diana's family in the Paris courthouse was too galling.

Fayed had always suffered an inferiority complex. Rising from obscurity as an unexceptional Arab middleman and shipping agent, his capture of Harrods catapulted him from the shadows into the spotlight. Unaccustomed to public scrutiny, he believed that displays of wealth and generosity would secure friendship and respect. The disappearance of those halcyon days with Diana outraged him. The master of fantasy demanded the resurrection of the dream. In the summer of 1998, it seemed there might at least be some compensation.

Unexpectedly, during the night of Saturday 25 July, the news emerged that Tiny Rowland had died the previous day in the London Clinic. Considering that only six weeks earlier he had been jovially lunching with Adnan Khashoggi in the London Ritz, the stated cause of death – skin cancer – sounded unconvincing. The tycoon's friends mentioned that Rowland had simply 'given up' after hearing six days earlier that, on lawyers' advice, Fayed and his staff would not be prosecuted for breaking into his safe-deposit box. Rowland had died in a coma and, following his strict instructions, was cremated without a funeral service. His legacy, as extolled in a raft of sympathetic obituaries, was to be classified as one of Britain's last, great tycoons.

One surviving tycoon concealed his double relief. Saved the intense embarrassment of a criminal prosecution, Fayed was also, after fourteen years, liberated from his nemesis. At the age of sixty-nine, Mohamed Fayed could enjoy, without threat of embarrasment and worse, the profits produced by his skills. Concealing his emotions, he issued a benign statement: 'Tiny Rowland and I were business rivals for many years but I take no joy in his death. I am sending my condolences to his family.' Inevitably, it was an unsatisfactory epitaph on the most bitter feud in Britain's corporate history. Both men deserved each other, and neither deserved to win. Yet Rowland's perennial fear, that biologically Fayed was destined to have the last word, had materialized. History would be written not so much by the victor as by the survivor. As he rested in St Tropez, Fayed enjoyed one victory and anticipated another. On the anniversary of the crash, he would unveil at Harrods not only two memorials to Diana and Dodi designed by Bill Mitchell, but a new campaign to reassert his version of the truth, blind to the inevitable consequence.

Like so many autocrats under siege, a prisoner of his own creation, Fayed denies anything which does not suit him. Like so many self-made tycoons, he explains his life's ambition as wanting to leave the world a better place, but both his definition of a better place and his methods have aroused suspicion rather than praise. As he hurtles towards inevitable self-destruction, Fayed might reflect where it all went wrong. He might have simply ignored the DTI's colourfully expressed judgement that he was dishonest. Other businessmen like Robert Maxwell and Tiny Rowland, similarly damned, shrugged off the opprobrium and continued as normal, earning hundreds of millions. But, crudely, Fayed demands that his opinion be unequivocally accepted. Uneducated about the country he professes to love, he seeks to change its foibles to suit his prejudices. Unable to understand why the same tyranny which rules in Harrods does not extend to Westminster and Whitehall, he has become the victim of his weaknesses. Like so many autocrats, Fayed has become his own worst enemy. The inevitable consequence will be the collapse of his empire.

Sources

The sources for this book were government reports, interviews, newspaper reports, television programmes, books and published and unpublished documents. There were three DTI reports, Sir Gordon Downey's two reports, a large number of private documents provided to me since 1990 by Mohamed Fayed's lawyers, the anti-Fayed brochures published by Tiny Rowland, government archives in France and the United States, and a substantial amount of private papers owned by interviewees. I also drew on my research for a previous biography of Tiny Rowland. Most written sources are cited in the following pages.

Over one hundred people were interviewed in the research for this book. Approximately another eighty refused to be interviewed. The common sentiment in both camps was fear of Mohamed Fayed's reaction if their assistance became known. Most of those who, despite the risks, did help preferred to speak on an off-the-record basis.

In an unusual move, based upon the advice of the lawyers who vetted this book, it has been decided that no interview sources will be provided. That decision may tend to persuade some readers glancing through the preceding pages that the sources for this book were solely DTI and other reports. Nothing could be further from the truth. Every fact stated in this book, the reader should be assured, has been sourced and for obvious reasons has been verified to the satisfaction of the lawyers who have vetted the book. Indeed, the major source for the biography is the recollections of the many eyewitnesses.

Among those, it should nevertheless be mentioned, were Mohamed Fayed himself and some of his closest advisers. Between 1991 and spring 1998 I enjoyed long conversations on a wide range of issues covered in this book with several of Fayed's key advisers and long-serving employees, especially Michael Cole, John Macnamara and Royston Webb. All of those conversations were carefully noted. Three days after Princess Diana's death, I flew on Mohamed Fayed's helicopter to Paris and interviewed those personnel at the Ritz Hotel who were eyewitnesses on the fatal night. Since they have been quoted in an article I wrote for the *Daily Mail*, they can be named as Claude Rowlet, Kes Wingfield, François Tendil, Patrick Rocha, Philippe Dourneau and René Delorm. I was given by Mr Fayed's lawyers many documents, indeed volumes of documents, regarding their fight with Tiny Rowland and their submissions to the DTI inspectors. Some are identified in the Sources using Fayed's own references, for example MF B2/22.

Of the television programmes, the most important have been John Plender's *The Harrods Sale* on Channel 4 in March 1985 and Martyn Gregory's *Dispatches* documentary also on Channel 4 transmitted in June 1998. Gregory kindly provided the transcripts of his interviews for that film, which are marked 'MG'. Mohamed Fayed gave me in summer 1997 the unedited tape of a three-hour interview filmed with him earlier that year for a Fulcrum Productions documentary about sleaze.

The three reports by inspectors appointed by the Department of Trade and Industry are the report about Lonrho published in 1976, the report published in 1984 about the suspected concert party to buy the House of Fraser and the 1988 report about Mohamed Fayed's takeover of the House of Fraser. Several other reports published by the DTI and the Monopolies and Mergers Commission are relevant. Instead of quoting them all directly, I have referred the interested reader to my previous book, *Tiny Rowland: The Rebel Tycoon*.

It was that biography, published in 1993, which introduced me to Mohamed Fayed and his advisers. Until 1997, I had never imagined that I would write his biography. Events changed everything.

2. Fantasies and Fortune

7 By then, Aly. DTI 1988, p. 182.
8 In 1948 he. Channel 4, *The Harrods Sale*, March 1985.
17 Carasso would allege. DTI 1988, p. 615.
18 Fayed's bid for. Ibid., p. 616.
22 Over meals, he. Daniel Sanger and Julien Feldman, *Saturday Night*, June 1998.
23 'saw the light'. Ibid., quoting confidential airgram from US ambassador.
32 In return for. DTI 1988, p. 651.
33 Although his agreement. Ibid., p. 681.
36 After Rashid's departure. Ibid., p. 215.
36 On the advice. Ibid., p. 251.

3. Fantasies and Reality: A Man of Property

40 'And', added Tajir. DTI 1988, pp. 607, 619.
43 In fact, the. Ibid., p. 618.
56 He was, Fayed. Tom Bower, *Tiny Rowland: The Rebel Tycoon* (Heinemann, 1993), pp. 288–9.
56 Even Lonrho's accountants. Ibid., p. 290.
56 'Tyranny and madness'. Ibid., p. 281.
57 'I always assumed'. Ibid., p. 282.
57 'I've entered a'. Ibid., p. 297.
58 Local gossip about. *Sunday Times*, 20 August 1995.
59 Delighted to be. DTI 1988, pp. 671–2.
60 Assuming a roughly. Ibid., p. 680.
61 'Between the potted'. Rowland, *The Hero from Zero*, (private publication, September 1988).

61 'just a practicality'. Transcript, Minutes of Evidence taken before Sir Gordon Downey, 23 January 1997 (hereafter Downey/Fayed Transcript), p. 24.
62 Serious profits could. DTI 1988, p. 213.
63 a banking relationship. Ibid., p. 272.
63 he bought the. Ibid., p. 205.
64 Shepheard's, the world-famous. Ibid., p. 616.
64 'most famous hotel'. *Le Monde*, 1 April 1979.
64 'for a few'. AFP, 30 March 1979.
74 Although its vessels. DTI 1988, p. 201.
76 a 'single payment'. *Observer*, 26 June 1983.

4. *A Game of Chess*

79 'Whatever way we'. Bower, *Tiny Rowland*, p. 358.
79 Lonrho's profits were. *Standard*, 7 July 1982.
79 Ignoring his 'bombshell'. Ibid., p. 386.
80 'disgracefully raw deal'. *Guardian*, 10 December 1981.
81 To disguise their. DTI 1984, pp. 134ff.
82 'In terms of'. Ibid., p. 152.
82 Nine days later. Ibid., p. 136.
82 'Rowland cast that'. Ibid., p. 176.
82 Four cards belonging. Ibid., p. 111.
82 To Roland Smith. Ibid., pp. 181, 246.
83 During those early. DTI 1988, p. 282.
83 Fayair and Bermair. Ibid., p. 248.
83 he had earned. Ibid., p. 204.
83 Allied Stars, his. Ibid., p. 215.
83 and Genavco, the. Ibid., p. 244.
83 and from a. Ibid., p. 241.
87 'Of course, based'. Ibid., p. 281.
88 Having advised the. Ibid., p. 284.
88 The power of. Ibid., p. 576.
88 The £50.5 million. Ibid., pp. 80ff.

89 To the guests'. Peter Koenig, *Institutional Investor*, December 1985.

89 'A 100 per'. DTI 1984, pp. 169–70.

89 'I'm not interested'. DTI 1988, pp. 72, 75.

89 'The Al Fayeds'. Ivan Fallon, *Takeovers* (Viking, 1987), p. 63.

90 'His wishes', he. DTI 1984, pp. 87–9.

90 There was, concluded. Ibid., pp. 169–70, 172, 176.

90 'I'll give you'. DTI 1988, p. 73.

92 Not only would. Ibid., p. 463.

93 'He never goes'. Ibid., p. 76.

93 The bank had. Ibid., p. p. 74.

93 The ill-restrained glee. Ibid., p. 75.

93 Having won the. Ibid., p. 282.

94 Seven days later. Ibid., p. 272.

94 On 23 August. Ibid., p. 575.

94 Instead of acting. Ibid., pp. 283, 78, 285.

95 'a complete betrayal'. Letter from Fayed to Ian Fraser, 16 August 1984.

96 'There's the sultan's'. DTI 1988, p. 83.

96 Told with great. Ibid., p. 108.

96 'Another of Tiny's'. Ibid., p. 85.

97 Impatiently, Fayed telephoned. Ibid., p. 87.

98 He would sell. Ibid., p. 88.

98 Long after the. Ibid.

101 Their own wealth. Ibid., pp. 447–8.

102 'I can't stop'. Ibid., p. 92–3.

102 'It was a'. Ibid., pp. 92–5; Bower, *Tiny Rowland*, p. 476.

103 'Ashraf, they must'. DTI 1988, p. 84.

103 'You are lying'. Ibid., p. 96.

104 Instead, he would. Ibid., p. 91.

104 'members of an'. Ibid., p. 175.

104 'Ethics and morals'. *Daily Mail*, 10 November 1984.

105 Two days later. DTI 1988, p. 102.

105 Fayed watched incredulously. Ibid., p. 103.

106 His frantic calls. Ibid., p. 99.

106 Smith agreed to. Ibid., p. 137.

106 'The money Fayed'. Ibid., p. 578.

106 his source was. Ibid., p. 278, Zurich, 14 November 1984.

107 Angrily, Fayed accused. DTI 1988, p. 591.

108 'Private and Personal'. Ibid., p. 287.

109 As Rowland, unbeknown. MF B2/22; DTI 1988, pp. 115, 591.

110 Although without any. DTI 1988, p. 119.

110 'I am delighted'. *Daily Telegraph*, 6 January 1985.

110 'The directors', said. DTI 1988, p. 118.

111 Whatever Fayed was. Ibid., p. 110.

111 'leading shipowners in'. Letter from MacArthur to Llewellyn Smith, 16 November 1984.

111 In his formal. DTI 1988, p. 108.

5. *The Bid*

115 Secrecy still protected. 55 Park Lane bought on 14 February 1985, through Makart Ltd, incorporated on 6 February, as an option which was exercised on 3 June 1985. DTI 1988, p. 275.

119 'weren't a pretty'. Bower, *Tiny Rowland*, p. 421.

120 Assiduously, Fayed had. DTI 1988, p. 126.

120 Accurate rumours suggested. Ibid., p. 122.

121 Five months earlier. DTI 1984, p. 152.

121 'We are satisfied'. DTI 1988, pp. 136, 453.

121 Described as a. MF 6/2; DTI 1988, p. 303. On 31 October 1984, £50.5 million plus $330 million had been deposited at the Royal Bank of Scotland, and $230 million had been deposited at the Banque Gonet.

122 The magic sound. DTI 1988, p. 487.

122 'The Fayeds have'. Ibid., p. 136.

123 'Our fathers met'. Ibid., pp. 447–8.

123 'Mr Al Fayed'. Ibid., p. 280.

123 'My ships carrying'. Ibid., p. 174.

123 'Kleinwort Benson', the. *Sunday Telegraph*, 10 March 1985.
124 'their own resources'. DTI 1988, p. 140.
124 He had successfully. Ibid., p. 457.
124 Having tried to. Ibid., p. 707.
125 To satisfy the. Ibid., p. 145.
125 The builders undertook. Bower, *Tiny Rowland*, pp. 546–7.
126 'Herbert Smith do'. DTI 1988, p. 144.
126 'We are . . . entirely'. Ibid., pp. 148, 462.
127 'I didn't care'. Fallon, *Takeovers*, p. 71.
127 by MacArthur's confident. DTI 1988, p. 457.
127 by the bankers'. Ibid., p. 148.
127 Even that shrewd. Ibid., p. 201.
127 'I've been more'. Ibid., p. 149.
128 'My reasoned judgement'. Ibid., p. 150.
129 'I know people'. *Standard*, 12 March 1985.
130 'The British government'. *Hero from Zero*.

6. Harrods

134 Uninhibited and unaware. *Sinking in Corruption*, published by Tiny Rowland; DTI 1988, pp. 66, 288.
140 Hollywood stars, European. Ronald Kessler, *The Richest Man in the World* (Warner, 1986), p. 2.

7. Bribes and Lies

142 Based on original. DTI 1988, p. 159; *Financial Times*, 31 May 1985.
143 'A sort of'. DTI 1988, pp. 276, 176.
143 'What about your'. Ibid., p. 178.
146 'to prove I'. *International Herald Tribune*, 26 September 1985.
147 'You gotta fight'. Channel 4, *The Harrods Sale*.
149 His contract with. Hamilton heard from Greer on 29 October 1985. Downey, vol. 2, p. 316.

149 'I am anxious'. Letter from Greer to Fayed, 8 November 1985.

150 Well groomed and. David Leigh and Ed Vulliamy, *Sleaze: The Corruption of Parliament* (Fourth Estate, 1997), pp. 64–7.

150 Struck by the. Downey, vol. 2, pp. 335, 121, for Smith history.

160 Turnbull & Asser. Bought December 1985.

165 More than ever. Downey, vol. 2, p. 120.

165 In anticipation, Fayed. Leigh and Vulliamy, *Sleaze*, pp. 65–7.

165 Grylls, the chairman. Downey, vol. 2, pp. 158, 346ff.; Leigh and Vulliamy, *Sleaze*, pp. 29–31.

165 Neil Hamilton had. Downey, vol. 2, pp. 102, 141.

167 In Fayed's mind. Ibid., vol. 3, p. 78.

167 The target, Fayed. Ibid., vol. 2, p. 17.

167 'I want processions'. Ian Greer, *One Man's World* (André Deutsch, 1997), p. 7.

173 Instead she would. Lacey, *Sunday Times*, 8 February 1998.

174 'I want processions'. Downey, vol. 2, p. 426.

175 New information, wrote. June 1986.

176 How, he was. SBC had received repayment of £402.2 million, while £22.8 million was transferred to AITSA, Fayed's Liechtenstein trust, the source of regular funds to House of Fraser to repay interest. MF 11/3.

176 As evidence, he. DTI 1988, p. 416; MF 6/2.

176 'No one has'. MF 11/6.

177 The document purported. DTI 1988, p. 161.

183 The DTI's curt. Downey, vol. 2, p. 408; DTI 1988, p. 162.

184 But McAlpine, like. *Daily Telegraph*, 22 October 1994.

185 '£50,000 a year'. Downey, vol. 2, p. 121.

185 Land would be. Ibid., p. 528.

185 'In considering whether'. DTI 1988, p. 152.

186 'It appears', said. Ibid., p. 162.

187 It seemed to him. Downey, vol. 2, p. 120.

187 In his accompanying. DTI 1988, p. 163.

187 'cannot let the'. Committee on Standards and Privileges,

Fourth Report, *Complaint against Mr Michael Howard*, 5
March 1997 (hereafter Downey, Howard report), p. 7.
188 'I just wanted'. *Sunday Times*, 8 February 1998.
189 He had paid. Ibid.
190 'cast a shadow'. Bower, *Tiny Rowland*, p. 517.
191 'I spoke to'. Downey, vol. 2, p. 238.

8. Storekeeper

195 Cast in the. *Daily Telegraph*, 13 February 1987.
196 Unceremoniously, on 12. DTI 1988, p. 363.
200 a bugged conversation. *The Times*, 19 July 1989.
204 'Sometimes people let'. *Standard*, 2 October 1987.

9. The Reckoning

207 Following the disappointing. Leigh and Vulliamy, *Sleaze*,
p. 73.
207 The next day. Downey, vol. 2, p. 120.
208 'I have now'. Ibid., p. 12, 23 July 1987.
210 'We come from'. DTI 1988, p. 179.
210 'I have no'. Ibid., p. 175.
210 'The Fayeds' case'. Ibid., p. 193.
210 As his self-confidence. *The Times*, 15 April 1988.
210 His fortune, he. DTI 1988, p. 195.
210 He hoped that. Ibid., p. 305.
211 In a subsequent. Ibid., p. 168, 14 August 1987.
211 They wanted nothing. Ibid., p. 192.
211 They could demand. Ibid., p. 279.
212 'There can be.' Ibid., p. 303.
212 The lawyers added. Ibid., p. 252.
212 Their great wealth. Ibid., p. 257.
212 They claimed to. Ibid.
213 a 'quite enormous'. Ibid., pp. 215, 257.

213 If that was. Ibid., pp. 273–4.

214 'manner in which'. Ibid., p. 301.

214 'His Majesty', said. Channel 4, *The Harrods Sale*.

214 On 8 March. DTI 1988, p. 276; *Financial Times*, 25 July 1988.

214 Although the dismissals. DTI 1988, pp. 360, 365.

215 Convinced that the. Ibid., p. 525.

215 The original documents. Ibid., p. 607.

215 'He can have'. Ibid., p. 594.

216 Impressed by the. Ibid., p. 573.

217 Indeed, the inspectors. Ibid., p. 209.

217 In his early. Ibid., p. 467.

218 Like Fayed's other. Ibid., p. 469.

218 Not only had. Downey, vol. 2, p. 21.

219 They should rely. DTI 1988, p. 541.

219 'not blamed for'. Ibid., p. 637.

219 the inspectors preferred. Ibid., p. 326.

219 the sultan's latest. Peregrine Worsthorne, *Sunday Telegraph* 4 August 1985.

219 The inspectors, the. DTI 1988, p. 612.

220 Unimpressed by the. Ibid., p. 375.

220 Detailed answers were. Ibid., p. 311.

220 otherwise the inspectors. Ibid., p. 277.

220 Firstly, they had. Ibid., pp. 207, 255.

221 Similarly, his valuation. Ibid., p. 225.

221 His valuation of. Ibid., pp. 246, 253. The Fayeds' valuation of their other personal possessions was accepted at $318 million: ibid., p. 241.

221 'The first figure'. Ibid., pp. 254, 256.

221 The lawyer had. Ibid., pp. 598, 617, 621.

221 Exhaustively, Carrateau had. Ibid., p. 599.

222 Convinced that the. Ibid., p. 533.

222 'either quite untrue'. Ibid., p. 205.

222 'regardless of any'. Ibid., p. 203.

222 Fayed, they guessed. Ibid., pp. 203–4.

222 Although exaggeration was. Ibid., p. 256.

222 In 1985, he. Ibid., p. 216.

222 On 26 February. Ibid., p. 313.

222 'have made no'. MF B1/2.

222 'immaterial [since] nobody'. DTI 1988, p. 176.

223 'a regrettable fact'. MF B1/2.

223 The tapes, said. DTI 1988, p. 588.

223 Challenging the authenticity. Ibid., p. 579.

223 But Fayed's attempts. Ibid., pp. 208–9.

224 When the consortium. Ibid., p. 311.

224 No further information. Ibid., pp. 262–3.

224 In their enthusiasm. Ibid., p. 266.

224 'Just say we're'. Ibid., p. 261.

225 'could not even'. Ibid., p. 264.

225 'were given to'. *Daily Telegraph*, 19 May 1993.

225 If they had. DTI 1988, pp. 322, 195, 217–18, 260–1, 270.

225 'I didn't care'. *Daily Telegraph*, 20 August 1988.

226 'not normally associated'. MF B4/1.

226 Their draft repeated. MF B2/24.

226 Yet the inspectors. MF B6/14.

226 Both told the. DTI 1988, p. 278.

227 Hence they were. MF 8/19.

227 'The sultan has'. *Financial Times*, 10 March 1990.

227 Not only had. DTI 1988, p. 281.

228 'twentieth-century Spanish Inquisition'. Leigh and Vulliamy, *Sleaze*, p. 87.

228 'unable to meet'. MF 11/10.

228 Individually, Hamilton and. Downey, vol. 2, p. 13, para. 40.

229 whose wife, just. Ibid., vol. 1, pp. 56ff.

229 'no conceivable direct'. Leigh and Vulliamy, *Sleaze*, p. 89.

229 'Borrowing does not'. MF 7/7.

229 Those arguments were. MF 4/2.

229 'looks not only'. DTI 1988, pp. 277, 283.

229 'The evidence', the. Ibid., p. 179.

229 'lies were the'. Ibid., p. 752.

230 On 24 July. Ibid., p. 337.

230 'add insult to'. Downey, vol. 2, p. 66.

230 'injustice and oppression'. Ibid., p. 21.
230 'We started our'. DTI 1988, pp. 7–8.
231 'treated Rowland very'. Ibid., p. 309.
231 'motivated by a'. Ibid., p. 544.
231 The protests of. Bower, *Tiny Rowland*, p. 535.
231 'I never bear'. Ibid., p. 542.
232 Everyone of any. DTI 1988, pp. 66, 288.
233 Not only did. Downey, vol. 3, p. 142.
234 'Forget it, Mohamed'. Ibid., vol. 2, pp. 95, 497, 169.

10. *The Dark Side*

238 After a *Daily*. *Daily Mirror*, 18 June 1988.
244 Those millions, vital. His image as an international tycoon had also suffered after the agency for the Barber Line, a shipping company carrying steel, was withdrawn. That Fayed should be interested in minuscule agency commissions suggested financial weakness.

11. *Conspiracies and Concubines*

250 In parliament, Dale. Downey, vol. 2, pp. 23–6.
250 'The dogs bark'. *Daily Express*, 14 March 1990.
251 To his colleagues. Downey/Fayed Transcript, p. 26; Downey, vol. 2, p. 336.
251 In retaliation for. Bower, *Tiny Rowland*, p. 542.
251 His only public. Downey, vol. 2, p. 21.
252 'I am inspired'. *Daily Mail*, 21 November 1989.
252 $75 million in. *Signature*, no. 190.
252 $30 million in. *Paris Match*, 1 December 1989.
252 $150 million in. *Le Monde*, 16 June 1992.
258 Through skilful detection. Downey, vol. 2, p. 104.
258 Never had Fayed. *Private Eye*, 29 March 1991; *Observer*, 29 July 1990.

259 In anticipation, Fayed/Downey Transcript, pp. 23, 29, 31.
259 showed his personal. Ibid., p. 168.
260 'It is especially'. Chairman Kenneth Warren, 23 May 1990.
260 After twenty-one meetings. Downey, vol. 2, p. 316.
263 'dirty tricks department'. Ibid., pp. 300–1.
264 Therefore, it was. Ibid., p. 138.
266 Unpublished, because it. Ibid., p. 32.
267 After his luggage. Ibid., p. 259.
267 While Jones was. Ibid., p. 265.

12. Bankruptcy and Betrayal

280 Contrary to Fayed's. DTI 1988, p. 383.
281 his $20 million. Ibid., p. 214.
282 The refinancing had. Ibid., p. 374.
283 After a tense. Downey, vol. 2, p. 31, 3 June 1991.
283 'This is for'. *Mail on Sunday*, 16 January 1994.

13. Revenge

298 'Well, I suppose'. Leigh and Vulliamy, *Sleaze*, p. 147; Downey/Fayed Transcript, p. 44.
298 'independent . . . carefully considered'. Leigh and Vulliamy, *Sleaze*, p. 148, 13 May 1992.
306 'not forgetting' the. Downey, vol. 2, p. 63.
308 'They ask questions'. Greer, *One Man's World*, p. 122; Downey, vol. 2, p. 428.
308 'I pay Greer'. Greer, *One Man's World*, p. 122; Downey, vol. 2, p. 428.
309 'raised by British'. *The Paris Ritz* (Fayed private publication, 1991), pp. 114–17.
310 'He did not'. Downey, vol. 2, p. 63.
310 'an Egyptian innocent'. Leigh and Vulliamy, *Sleaze*, p. 164.

312 'Michael Grylls did'. Channel 4, *The Question of Sleaze*, *Dispatches*, 1997.

313 '£2,000 in a'. Downey, vol. 2, p. 139; vol. 3, pp. 54–5; Greer, *One Man's World*, p. 122; Downey, vol. 2, p. 88. See Hamilton's argument on Hencke's rough draft: 'Nothing in the paper work shows that Hamilton was doing any of this for money.' Downey, vol. 2, p. 248.

313 Greer denied knowledge. Downey, vol. 2, p. 72.

313 Yet Greer's credibility. Leigh and Vulliamy, *Sleaze*, p. 158; Greer, *One Man's World*, p. 122.

313 That unsubtle distinction. Downey, vol. 2, p. 104. His credibility would later be undermined by his false denial of receiving any payments from the Serbian government for lobbying.

313 Disingenuously, he understated. Downey, vol. 1, p. 56; Leigh and Vulliamy, *Sleaze*, pp. 159ff.

314 'at a European'. Leigh and Vulliamy, *Sleaze* p. 162; Greer, *One Man's World*, pp. 125–8.

314 On Fayed's orders. Greer, *One Man's World*, pp. 125–8.

315 Since Aitken was. Transcript, House of Commons, Minutes of Evidence, Privileges Committee, 1 November 1995, p. 23.

316 The total Ritz. Luke Harding, David Leigh and David Pallister, *The Liar* (Penguin, 1997), p. 68.

316 'I was walking'. Transcript, Privileges Committee, 1 November 1995, p. 34.

319 To score a. In an eventual court settlement, Graham Jones made a 'full and unreserved apology' to the Fayeds and paid the £500,000 he had received from Rowland to Fayed.

320 about 'Bettermann's faud'. *Private Eye*, 7 May 1993.

324 'treating Harrods like'. *Sunday Telegraph*, 30 November 1997.

325 'You simply cannot'. *Mail on Sunday*, 25 April 1994.

326 An audit of. Downey, vol. 2, p. 30.

14. War

332 Faced with her. 10 August 1994.

335 'I don't owe'. Leigh and Vulliamy, *Sleaze*, p. 173.

335 Fayed's next visitor. Greer, *One Man's World*, p. 149; Downey, vol. 2, p. 216.

335 'He was meant'. Downey, vol. 2, p. 431.

336 'That Thatcher. She's'. Ibid., p. 432.

336 'What evidence does'. Ibid.; Greer, *One Man's World*, pp. 152, 164ff.

337 Terry Robinson, he. Downey, vol. 2, p. 432.

339 'Whenever you talk'. Transcript from *Standard*, 5 January 1995; Leigh and Vulliamy, *Sleaze*, p. 175.

339 Aitken, he continued. David Leigh, *Observer*, 6 July 1997.

340 'The hotel bill'. Harding, Leigh and Pallister, *The Liar*, p. 73.

340 'enthusiasm for barking'. Ibid., p. 76.

342 Despite Rowland's promise. Downey, Howard report, pp. 13–14.

342 Realizing that after. Downey, vol. 2, p. 63.

345 The security chief. Ibid., p. 432.

346 Not understanding the. Ibid., p. 74.

346 'I didn't understand'. Ibid., p. 13, para. 40/4.

347 The notion of. Downey/Fayed Transcript, p. 44.

348 The source of. Downey, vol. 2, p. 74.

348 By repeating Fayed's. Ibid., p. 232.

348 That inaccuracy was. Ibid., p. 1.

348 Fayed's own cash. Ibid., p. 75.

348 'I think it's'. Ibid., p. 264.

349 'I could not'. Ibid., p. 236.

351 Rowland's parting pat. Downey/Fayed Transcript, p. 16.

351 'No one has'. *The Times*, 26 October 1994; Downey, vol. 2, p. 221.

351 'The prime minister'. *Night and Day*, 26 February 1995.

353 'a monstrous ingratitude'. *Guardian*, 21 October 1994.

353 Less accurately, he. *Sunday Times*, 23 October 1994.

353 Webb had replied. Downey, vol. 2, p. 432.

353 Greer was dead. Ibid., p. 186.

354 'I have a'. *Financial Times*, 25 October 1994.

356 Hamilton had failed. Leigh and Vulliamy, *Sleaze*, p. 180.

358 'On every occasion'. Downey, vol. 2, p. 177.

358 Consistently, Fayed had. Ibid., p. 231.

358 Now, according to. Ibid., p. 1.

358 Since the newspaper's. Ibid., p. 96. Instead of referring to the £2,000 per question paid by Fayed via Greer and a £50,000 fee as described in the original article, the newspaper claimed that the £18,000 which Fayed had paid to Greer in May 1987 was for payments to the MPs; and that Fayed had paid £28,000 in cash direct to Hamilton.

15. *Frustrations*

359 'most unfairly since'. *Daily Telegraph*, 18 November 1995.

370 'Sign it for'. Downey, Howard report, p. 99.

370 'While I would'. Ibid., p. 21.

371 'a sharp exit'. *Spectator*, 3 February 1996.

371 'misleading' the country. Downey, vol. 2, p. 105.

371 Fayed felt justified. Ibid., p. 8.

371 'I was instrumental'. Briefing document provided by Fayed to Committee of Privileges, 1 November 1995.

372 'truth and honour'. House of Lords, Sub-Committee on Declaration and Registration of Interests, 15 February 1995.

372 'I am wondering'. Downey, vol. 2, pp. 15–16.

374 'They are like'. *Daily Telegraph*, 18 November 1995.

378 'an infinite capacity'. Downey, vol. 2, p. 475.

382 'right on his'. Downey, Howard report, p. 101, 23 November 1995.

383 'It's entirely untrue'. Ibid., p. 23, 9 February 1996; and pp. 103–4.

385 'I gave inaccurate'. Downey, vol. 2, p. 303.

16. A Year of Judgement

393 'The government has'. Fayed to *Der Spiegel*, 5 October 1996.

393 'I was specifically'. Downey, vol. 2, pp. 190, 205.

393 Greer's audited accounts. Ibid., p. 318.

393 'What is your'. Geoffrey Robertson, *The Justice Game* (Chatto & Windus, 1998), p. 363.

394 Although his testimony. Leigh and Vulliamy, *Sleaze*, p. 131.

395 Boasting aggressive qualities. Downey, vol. 2, p. 492.

395 'July/August/September'. Ibid., p. 492.

396 He would subsequently. Ibid., p. 492.

396 'Let him wait'. Downey/Fayed Transcript, p. 32.

397 'There was no'. Downey, vol. 2, pp. 251, 254.

397 'I cannot remember'. Downey/Fayed Transcript, p. 35.

397 By then, the. Downey, vol. 2, p. 140.

397 Scrutiny of Greer's. Ibid., p. 141.

397 and showed how. Leigh and Vulliamy, *Sleaze*, p. 146.

397 Greer's accounts also. Ibid., p. 213.

398 'Why Hamilton run'. Channel 4, *The Question of Sleaze*.

399 'Rowland admits corruption'. Downey, Howard report, p. 14.

399 An awkward silence. Ibid., p. 17.

400 from Margaret Thatcher. Ibid., p. 33.

400 Adnan Khashoggi had. Downey, vol. 2, p. 303, 8 November 1996.

400 'He's lying,' Fayed. Downey, Howard report, p. 16.

400 Although he perused. Ibid., p. 35.

401 'it should be'. Ibid., p. 23.

402 Howard had made. Ibid., pp. 18–19.

402 Having examined the. Ibid., p. 24.

402 his 'burning obsession'. Ibid., p. 38.

402 'he would otherwise'. *International Herald Tribune*, 21 April 1997.

402 That admission of. List of allegations against Hamilton and Smith, cf. Downey, vol. 2, pp. 124ff., 129ff.

403 Across a whole. Ibid., p. 266.

403 'Each time Hamilton'. Downey/Fayed Transcript, p. 25.

403 Yet he had. Downey, vol. 2, p. 271.

403 '£3,000,' he testified. Ibid., vol. 3, p. 50.

403 In fact, Fayed. Ibid., pp. 36–7.

403 'All this is'. Ibid., p. 42.

403 'Mr Al-Fayed . . . does'. Ibid., vol. 2, p. 134.

404 Ian Greer, especially. Ibid., vol. 1, pp. 45–6.

404 Nevertheless, while voicing. Ibid., vol. 3, pp. 6–7.

404 In his second. Ibid., vol. 1, pp. 56ff.

405 'I was proud'. *New York Times*, 28 August 1997.

406 'No unifying thread'. Paul Johnson, *Spectator*, 5 July 1997.

406 'All we know'. *The Times*, 5 July 1997.

408 As an insurance. March 1997.

17. *The Last Blonde*

412 'If we handle'. Thomas Sancton and Scott MacLeod, *Death of a Princess* (Weidenfeld & Nicolson, 1998), p. 96.

416 a 'mysterious foundation'. Conseil de Paris, Laure Schneiter, 8 June 1998.

416 'I'm like a'. *Mail on Sunday*, 20 July 1997.

420 'I give them'. MG Clifford IV.

422 'Nothing is organized'. *New York Times*, 28 August 1997.

423 'It's a low-key'. MG Wingfield IV.

425 'around ten minutes'. *Mail on Sunday*, 14 September 1997.

428 'I asked for'. MG Wingfield IV.

428 'Don't bother following'. MG Lucard IV.

429 'I could see'. Sancton and MacLeod, *Death of a Princess*, p. 43.

432 'Henri Paul was'. *Sunday Times*, 14 September 1997.

434 'to protect the'. *Mirror*, 8 January 1998.

436 In another story. *Mirror*, 3 September 1997.

436 The publication of. Ibid.

437 Mansour chose to. *Daily Telegraph*, 1 September 1997.

SOURCES

437 It was barely. Rosa Monckton, *Sunday Telegraph*, 15 February 1998.

443 But, since other. *Newsweek*, 20 October 1997.

443 a 'brilliant sportsman'. *The Times*, 11 September 1997.

443 'He told me'. *Time*, 15 September 1997.

443 Repossi had never. MG Repossi IV.

444 'Mohamed', he wrote. *Sunday Telegraph*, 21 September 1997.

445 'no reason to'. *The Times*, 7 October 1997.

445 'personally made any'. *Daily Telegraph*, 9 October 1997.

446 With Rowland's encouragement. *Observer*, 30 November 1997.

446 'There is no'. *Daily Telegraph*, 1 December 1997.

447 Fayed hoped that. 29 November, reported ibid.

449 'Having lived here'. *Daily Telegraph*, 23 December 1997.

450 'a half-brother who'. Sancton and MacLeod, *Death of a Princess*, pp. 92–3.

450 Understandably, as foreigners. MG Sancton IV, p. 6.

451 Since the authors. Ibid., pp. 23–4.

451 Grateful, Sancton included. Ibid., p. 29.

452 Three months later. Ibid., p. 30.

452 Dodi had supposedly. Sancton and MacLeod, *Death of a Princess*, p. 123.

452 'I saw her'. Ibid., p. 32.

452 'Tell my sister'. Ibid.

452 Fortunately for Fayed. MG Sancton IV, pp. 26–7.

453 To preserve Fayed's. Ibid., p. 25.

455 The French investigators. *Sunday Times*, 15 February 1998.

456 'At Harrods,' alleged. *Sunday Times*, 11 January 1998.

456 'working on Trevor's'. Michael Cole cited in *News of the World*, 16 November 1997.

Index

INDEX

INDEX

INDEX

INDEX

obsession with sex 44–5, 46–7, 54, 62, 91, 235, 271, 300–301, 332, 336, 350, 353–4, 379, 389–91, 449
meets Tiny Rowland 50
buys Lonrho shares 55–7
buys property in Paris and New York 57
cash gifts and payments 61, 179, 197, 239–40, 242–3, 333
investments in banking and shipping 62–3
buys Paris Ritz 63–4, 83
affair with Heini Wathen 65–6
and film business 65–70
claims to diplomatic privileges 71
relationship with Tiny Rowland 80–81, 105–6
exaggerated claims to wealth 75, 83–4, 87–8, 89–90, 111, 122, 123, 142–3
visits Brunei 86, 93–4, 108
and sultan of Brunei 86–9, 108–10, 113–15, 121, 127, 141, 143, 214
acquires interest in House of Fraser 90–103
and bankers 98–9, 121, 281–8
first press release 100–101
and House of Fraser shares purchase 103–11, 119–30
refurbishments to Ritz 102, 172, 178, 252
surveillance of staff and security measures 108, 115–18, 139–40, 151–5, 157, 162–3, 201, 236–7, 243–7, 261, 281, 289, 292–3, 337, 379, 403, 409, 416–17, 446, 447
as 'adviser' to Downing Street on Brunei 112–15, 124, 126, 148
visits to Downing Street 113–14, 129–30, 148
successful bid for House of Fraser 130
as owner of Harrods 131–4, 193–206, 235–43, 277–81
and Swami 134
marriage to Heini 135–6
love of his children 136
at St Tropez 139–40
alleged antisemitism 144, 202, 401
feud with Rowland see Rowland, Roland 'Tiny'
homophobia 147, 181
and cash for questions 147–51, 164–7, 184, 229, 308, 309, 313, 346–53, 392–8, 402–4
relationships with and treatment of women 156–9, 269–30, 270–3, 300–301, 378–9, 389–90, 409, 446

and Windsor villa see Paris, Villa Windsor
arbitrary dismissal of employees 23–8, 181, 201–3, 205, 328
and DTI investigations 189–200, 207–34, 263–4
charitable donations 135, 203
statements on own assets 211–14, 220–25
policies on and treatment of staff 237–8, 268, 277–9, 363–7, 379, 409
visit to Dubai (1989) 245–7
income tax problems 250
and Modena deal 255–7, 265
conspiracy theories of 262–5, 318, 321, 329, 335–8, 341, 350, 354–5, 357, 371, 380–81, 386, 412, 437, 440, 442, 444–5, 450, 453–4, 456–7
agreement with Sheikh Rashid 303
allegations against Aitken 339
anger at betrayal by Hamilton 306, 307
application for British citizenship 303–4, 321, 329–31, 356–7, 360, 399, 449
reconciliation with Rowland 316–19
and 'cod fax' to Ritz 320, 370
plans to buy newspaper 321, 373–8
obtains new loan for Harrods 323
flotation of Harrods 324, 362–7, 375, 408
health 328
claims injuries to avoid Dubai hearing 343–5, 349
taped conversations with Rowland 350–51, 354–5, 445–6, 449
evidence to Privileges Committee 370–72
and Rowland's safe deposit box 372–3, 384, 445, 447, 456
purchase of Punch 377
sued by Bettermann 378–9
seeks support from Rowland 382–4
seeks support from Khashoggi 384–5
relaunch of Punch 387
political ambitions 387
sues Vanity Fair 392, 408–10, 446–7
sues government over citizenship denial 392, 399–400
actions for wrongful dismissal against 392, 408
and Diana 411–17
plans for Harrodsopolis 424
and death of Dodi and Diana 429–34
meeting with Lady Sarah McCorquodale 433

485

INDEX

INDEX

INDEX

INDEX

INDEX

transferred to Park Lane 332
valued by Fayed 333, 408–9
McNee, Sir David 182, 192, 299
McShane, Ian 66
Mafia 74
Magic (company) 276
Mail on Sunday 262, 325, 374, 417
Mailliez, Dr Frédéric 434
Major, John 336, 339–41, 345–6, 351,
    356, 370, 449
Maktoum brothers 98, 107, 244–7, 302–5,
    343
Al Maktoum, Sheikh Maktoum 247
Malaga 290
Malaysia 363
Mallett (dealers) 407
Malloy, Mark xi–xii
Malone, Gerry 149
Mandelson, Peter 448
Manning, Katie 137, 154, 178, 245, 272,
    389–90
Mansour, Anis 437
Marbella 120, 140
Marckus, Melvyn 124–5
Marcus, Stanley 195
Margaret, Princess 47
Martinson, Gunilla 135
Marvin, Douglas xiii, 395–6
Marwan, Dr Ashraf 82, 89–90, 92–3, 94,
    97–8, 103, 105–7, 109, 115, 120,
    129, 145, 151, 169, 216, 219, 223,
    230
Mason, Nick 255
'Masseuse' 157
Maxwell, Robert xiii, 92, 97, 361, 365,
    373, 387, 460
Mayers, Dan 169
Mayhew, Sir Patrick 259
Melanie (Harrods employee) 157
Mercer, Steve 364
Mereworth Castle 48
Metro Aviation 276, 408
Metropolitan Police 182, 326
MGM 83
MI5 113
MI6 113
Michaels (Dyrbusz), Louise 3–4
Middle East Navigation Company 17, 19
Midland Bank 176, 179, 266
Midlands Independent Group 375
Military Police 115, 153, 236, 268
Mirror Group 375
Mitchell, Bill 26, 39, 45, 46, 64, 232,
    360–61, 440
Mitsokochi 242

Mobil Oil 356
Modena garage, Horley 255–6, 262, 265,
    318–19
Monckton, Rosa 421, 437, 444, 452
Monks, John 456
Monopolies and Mergers Commission
    78–80, 82, 97, 110, 119, 150, 163,
    174, 178, 185, 228, 231, 232, 264
Montagu, Samuel 175, 177, 186, 266
Monte Carlo 414, 423
    Repossi (jewellers) 424, 443
Moore, Roger 48, 274
Morgan Grenfell 35, 49, 59, 82, 83, 222,
    371
Morgan, Piers 453–4
Morris, David 324–5
Mower, Martin 203, 268
Mubarak, Mrs 442
Mubarak, President Hosni 129
Mudi Star 43, 63
Müller, Martin 36, 87, 134
Mullin, John 308, 313
Murder at 1600 423
Murdoch, Rupert 80, 92, 97, 169, 284, 374
Myerscough-Walker, Trudie 270–71

Nabila (yacht) 2, 72, 136, 137, 140–41
Nabisco 102, 146, 221
Nadir, Asil 307
Al Nasr Trading and Industrial Corporation
    10, 15, 18
Nasser, General Gamal Abdel 14, 16, 19,
    23, 27, 29, 40, 46, 82, 101, 129,
    143, 210
National Nuclear Corporation 356
Nazism 50–51
Neil, Andrew 322–3, 374, 377, 388, 407,
    456
Nelson, Anthony 144
Network Security 258
Neuberger, Rabbi Julia, *On Being Jewish*
    423
News International 375
New, Richard 145–6, 151, 168–70, 186,
    260, 261, 262, 265, 267, 288
    *Fair Cop Fuhrhop: The True Story of
    Tiny Rowland* (with Royston Webb)
    227–8
New York
    Bloomingdales 205
    Pierre Hotel 154, 254
    Rockefeller Center 120–21, 283
    Rockefeller Plaza 111
New York Times 422
New Yorker 377

INDEX

INDEX

INDEX

INDEX

INDEX